An Atlas of

ANGLO-SAXON ENGLAND

For Thomas Hardin of Withycombe
in the county of Somerset

An Atlas of
ANGLO-SAXON ENGLAND

David Hill

University of Toronto Press
Toronto and Buffalo

First published in Canada and the United States
by University of Toronto Press
Toronto and Buffalo
1981
ISBN 0-8020-2387-8 cloth
0-8020-6446-9 paper

Maps 1, 3 and 18 are reproduced by kind
permission of the British Library.

Printed in Great Britain

Contents

Preface and Acknowledgements *xii*
Caveat and General Note *xii*

Introduction 1

1 The British Isles from the world map, Cotton Tiberius, B.V. f. 56v
2 The British Isles from the St Sever world map (1028–72)
3 The Cotton Tiberius world map
4 Diagram

The Background

Geology, Relief and Soil *5*
5 Simplified solid geology
6 Drift-covered areas
7 Highland and lowland zones
8 Relief
9 Land quality

Climate *9*
10 Temperatures in January
11 July
12 Mornings with snow lying
13 Average annual rainfall
14 Oxygen isotope variations

Coastline Changes and Navigable Rivers *11*
15 Coastline changes and navigable rivers
16 Sea level changes in the North Sea area

The Fens and the Wash *11*
17 The Wash
18 Whittlesea Mere and the rivers of the southern Fens according to Saxton (1576)

The Wantsum Channel *14*
19 The Wantsum Channel
20 A reconstruction of the Hastings coastline in 1066
21 Early Dungeness
22 The Somerset Levels

Forest *17*
23 Alternative views of forest cover in Anglo-Saxon times
24 Proportion of shires wooded in 1947

Settlements and Population shown in Domesday Book *17*
25 Settlements in Domesday Book
26 Population estimated from Domesday Book

Regional Bias in the Anglo-Saxon Chronicle *21*
27 Places mentioned in the Anglo-Saxon Chronicle 410–749

28 750–849
29 850–949
30 950–1066

Charters as a Source of Evidence *23*
31 Distribution of estates mentioned in charters
32 Distribution of beneficiaries and lands mentioned in writs
33 Proportion of charters issued by and to the Church
34 Worcestershire estates with detailed charter bounds
35 Distribution of charter bounds

Chronological Bias: Charters and Anglo-Saxon Chronicle *25*
36 Anglo-Saxon charters: distribution by decades
37 Comparative lengths of annals in the Anglo-Saxon Chronicle by decades

Archaeology *25*
38 Archaeology of the Anglo-Saxon period

Kings and Princes *25*
39 Kings and princes: chronology 700–880
40 880–1066

The Events

From Bede to the Rise of Wessex *31*
41 The England of Bede c.731
42 The supremacy of Mercia
43 The rise of Wessex

The Vikings: Introduction *32*
44 Ethnic divisions in Europe in the ninth century
45 Zones of Norse and Danish influence according to coin finds
46 The Vikings in the West: chronology 780–869
47 870–959

The Vikings in the West c.789–c.850 *36*
48 Hoards of coins deposited c.795–c.865
49 The Vikings in the West c.789–833
50 834–839
51 840–844
52 845–850
53 The Vikings in Spain

The Vikings in the West 851–878 *38*
54 The Vikings in the West 851–855
55 856–861
56 862–866
57 867–878

The Vikings in England 866–895 *41*
58 The Vikings in England 866–871
59 872–878
60 892–893
61 894–895

The Vikings in the West 879–896 *41*
62 The Vikings in the West 879–882
63 883–888
64 889–896

Scandinavian Coins and Graves *43*
65 Hoards of coins deposited c.865–c.895
66 Viking graves in western Europe
67 Scandinavian graves of the Viking age

Scandinavian Place Names *46*
68 Scandinavian place names of eastern England
69 Scandinavian place names in the north and west

Mercia 880–906 *46*
70 Mercia 880–906 and the itinerary of Æthelred and Æthelflaed

Scandinavia *49*
71 Scandinavia
72 Snow cover in Norway

Ireland *49*
73 Ireland

Iceland *51*
74 Iceland
75 Early settlements in Iceland as recorded in **Landnámabók**
76 Ice-free days on Iceland's coasts 860 to the present
77 Snow-free days in Iceland
78 The Norse Atlantic

Viking Trade *54*
79 Hoards containing coins of the Vikings of East Anglia and Northumbria
80 Finds of Arabic coins of the Viking Age

The Reconquest 902–921 *54*
81 Hoards of coins deposited c.895–c.965
82 The Peace of Tiddingford 906
83 The Reconquest 902–906
84 907–909
85 910–911
86 912
87 913
88 914
89 915
90 916
91 Campaigns of 917: summer
92 Late summer
93 Autumn
94 Late autumn
95 The Reconquest 918
96 919
97 920
98 921

From Athelstan to Eric Bloodaxe 924–954 *61*
99 Athelstan's campaigns
100 The Brunanburh campaign
101 Athelstan's foreign alliances
102 Edmund and the Kingdom of York

The Submission to Edgar, Chester 973 *61*
103 The submission to Edgar, Chester 973
104 Anglian place names in Scotland
105 Hoards of coins deposited c.965–c.995

The Wars of the Reign of Ethelred the Second *63*
106 Hoards of coins deposited c.995–c.1060
107 The Battle of Maldon 991
108 Ethelred II: the earliest attacks 980–986
109 987–991
110 992
111 993
112 Raids and campaigns 994
113 995–997
114 998
115 999–1000
116 1001–1002
117 1003
118 1004–1005
119 1006
120 Campaigns 1009
121 1010
122 1011–1012
123 1013
124 1014
125 1015
126 Campaigns of 1016: spring
127 Summer
128 Autumn
129 The Peace of Alney

Wales *73*
130 1039–1048
131 1049–1055
132 Wye Valley 1055
133 1056–1063
134 Domesday waste in 1066 as an indicator of previous Welsh raids

Administration

The Administrative Implications of Offa's Dyke *75*
135 Offa's dyke

The Tribal Hidage *76*
136 The Tribal Hidage: place names
137 Comparative assessments
138 Listing

Early Kingdoms *78*
139 Early Lindsey
140 The Kingdom of the East Saxons
141 Charters of the Kings of Hwicce
142 The Tomsætan and Wrocensetnan
143 The Kingdoms of the Magonsætan and Hwicce

The Itineraries of the Early Kings *82*
144 The itinerary of Charlemagne
145 Itineraries of the Kings of Mercia
146 Kings of Wessex to 871
147 The itinerary of Alfred the Great
148 The will of Alfred the Great 873–888

The Burghal Hidage *85*
149 The Burghal Hidage: correlation of wall lengths
150 Place names

151 Order of citation
152 Listing
153 Comparative assessments

The Itineraries of the Kings of England from Edward the Elder to Cnut *85*
154 Itinerary of Edward the Elder
155 Athelstan
156 Edmund
157 Eadwig
158 Itinerary of Eadred
159 Will of Eadred
160 Itinerary of Edgar the Peaceable
161 Edward the Martyr
162 Ethelred
163 Cnut

The Fleet *92*
164 Hampshire beacons
165 Manning a ship from St Paul's Estates 995 × 998
166 Ship-scot for the Bishop of Sherborne 1001 × 1012

Itineraries of Harold I Harefoot, Harthacnut and Edward the Confessor *95*
167 Itinerary of Harold I Harefoot
168 Harthacnut
169 Edward the Confessor
170 Mints for the 1035–1040 issue

The County Hidage *97*
171 The County Hidage: place names
172 Comparative assessments
173 Listing

Law and Land *97*
174 Law
175 Shire sub-divisions
176 Land units
177 Groups
178 North-east Gloucestershire showing changes in shire boundaries

Landholding in 1066 *100*
179 Lands of King Edward
180 Queen Edith
181 Earl Harold
182 The Leofric family
183 Value of lands held by the king and leading families in 1066
184 Earldoms in 1045
185 Earldoms in 1065
186 The proportional holdings of demesne lands in the shires of Staffordshire and Surrey in 1066
187 Landowners and markets in Somerset and Wiltshire in 1066

The Economy

Minerals, Salt and Lime *107*
188 Iron
189 Salt
190 Lime
191 Lead
192 Other metals

Agriculture *112*
193 Medieval open fields in England
194 Open fields in France
195 Germanic place names in France
196 Vineyards

Mills *115*
197 Mills

Roads *115*
198 Estates owing work on Rochester Bridge ?973 × 988
199 Major roads in Anglo-Saxon times

Building Stone *117*
200 Fine building stone eighth to eleventh century
201 Honestones
202 Niedermendig lava

Coins *121*
203 Distribution of finds of sceattas in England and on the Continent
204 Merovingian mints
205 Sceattas: insular findspots
206 Offa's coinage: findspots
207 Stycas: distribution of hoards

The Mints of Carolingian Europe *123*
208 Mints of Charlemagne 768–814
209 Louis the Pious 814–840
210 Charles the Bald 840–875
211 Northern area in the time of Charles the Bald

Mints in England *126*
212 Mints of origin of coins in the Pemberton's Parlour hoard, Chester
213 Mints of Alfred the Great
214 Edward the Elder
215 Athelstan
216 939–959
217 957–1016
218 Cnut
219 Harold I and Harthacnut
220 Edward the Confessor
221 Harold II
222 The ranking of mints: map
223 Diagram
224 Mints striking 871–1066: part I
225 Part II

Towns and their Distribution *133*
226 Towns in the south-west
227 Somerset and Dorset
228 The south
229 The south-east
230 The west Midlands
231 The east Midlands
232 East Anglia
233 The north-west
234 The north Midlands and Yorkshire

The Size of Towns and Forts *143*
235 Areas of burhs
236 An abstraction

The Church

Introduction *144*
237 Western Christendom c.597

Dioceses *147*
238 Dioceses 850
239 940
240 950
241 1035

Missionary Efforts *150*
242 The Church in East Francia

The Monastic Revival *150*
243 The Monastic Revival in late Anglo-Saxon England
244 The interrelation of monastic rules in the tenth century
245 The resting-places of the saints
246 Benedictine houses c.1060
247 Colleges of secular canons c.1060
248 The Domesday valuation of monasteries and nunneries: map
249 Diagram

The Church and its Bishops *155*
250 The Church in the south-west
251 Somerset and Dorset
252 The south
253 The south-east
254 The west Midlands
255 The east Midlands
256 East Anglia
257 The north-west
258 The north Midlands and Yorkshire
259 Bishops: chronology 700–880
260 880–1066

Bibliography *167*
Index *168*

Preface and Acknowledgements

This work is an attempt to display all the evidence on Anglo-Saxon England that can be placed in a topographic or chronological framework. It attempts to cut across many of the narrow specialisms and draw on the fields of history, archaeology, charter studies and all other disciplines which throw light on the period. As such, it tends to be a personal view which reflects the way that I see the evidence and so, unfortunately, also contains my prejudices and shortcomings. What it cannot convey is the great pleasure I have known over many years in the study of the period. That pleasure has been enhanced by the many kindnesses I have received from others in the field.

My principal thanks are due to John Bosanko who introduced me to the subject, to Martin Biddle who fired my enthusiasm for research and to Peter Addyman whose help was unstinting in the years when I first attempted serious work, and whose understanding saw me through university.

Great assistance has been rendered by many people, either in advice or in allowing me to use work in advance of publication: F. Aldsworth, D. Austin, M. Dolley, V. Fearn, A. Goodier, J. Hassall, G. Harling, D. Hooke, H. R. Loyn, D. M. Metcalf, J. Parkhouse, D. Powlesland, and F. Shepherd and many others.

Patrick Wormald has been particularly generous in the time he has spent weaning me away from prejudice and error; faults that remain bear witness to my stubborness.

Caveat and General Note

These maps are an illustration and a starting point. Interest in Anglo-Saxon England is growing apace and serious students will need to validate for themselves the particular items that make up the maps. This is especially true of anything arising out of charter evidence.

A continuous narrative is provided by Stenton (1971) who is an indispensable companion; an introduction to the documents is provided by Whitelock (1955). Current bibliographies are provided by **Anglo-Saxon England** on a yearly basis whilst archaeological work is reported in advance of publication in **Medieval Archaeology**.

Except where otherwise indicated, the maps show present day shorelines and courses of rivers.

For those who work on a basis of measurement which rests on a sub-division of an inaccurate estimate of the girth of the world it may be as well to know that one mile, the unit used on these maps, equals 1.6093 kilometres. The furlong is the eighth part of a mile.

Introduction

Bede began his *Ecclesiastical History of the English Nation* (completed in AD 731) with a chapter entitled 'Of the Situation of Britain and Ireland, and of their Ancient Inhabitants', in which he attempted to sketch the physical background to his historical and ecclesiastical account. Unfortunately, the chapter is brief, and draws heavily on Classical authorities. Other descriptions exist from the period, the latest, largest and most helpful being the massive record of Domesday Book, which attempts to record the state of England in January 1066. All the major recent historians of pre-Conquest England have appended a few maps to their works, as an aid to the student.

This volume is an attempt to illustrate those historians' work. It is not a continuous record but an aid, in which those things which can be looked at spatially have been recorded. It has been said elsewhere that our surest record is the landscape itself and this is an attempt to set various strands against that landscape. It may not be possible for a modern historian to spend a lifetime roaming the face of England, but it is possible to recognize the geographic framework in which our predecessors lived and the constraints it laid upon them. These maps are an attempt to assist towards those insights.

An Anglo-Saxon atlas should begin with an Anglo-Saxon map. The Cotton Tiberius map is a multicolour map of the world, based, like so much Anglo-Saxon learning, on late Antique exemplars. Ker dates the manuscript from which it comes to the first half of the eleventh century (Ker 1957, 255). It was probably produced at Winchester.

The shape of the British Isles on the Cotton Tiberius map (**1**) is reasonably good when compared with other maps of the time, most of which were influenced by the Frankish 'Saint Sever' map (**2**), and made no attempt to describe the shape of Britain. The Cotton Tiberius map, however, is quite unlike the formalized maps that were beginning to appear. England is seen as a country with important towns, sharing the island with other races and surrounded by other, smaller islands, including Ireland, with its monastery at Armagh, and the Orkney Islands. Although the divisions of England appear arbitrary and anachronistic — **Cantiae, Brittaniae** and **Marin Pergis** — the map as a whole provides an interesting comparison with the earlier account in Bede:

Britain, an island in the Ocean, formerly called Albion, is situated between the north and the west, facing, though at a considerable distance, the coasts of Germany, France and Spain, which form the greatest part of Europe. It extends 800 miles in length towards the north, and is 200 miles in breadth, except where several promontories extend further in breadth, by which its compass is made 3675 miles. To the south, as you pass along the nearest shore of the Belgic Gaul, the first place in Britain which opens to the eye is the city of **Rutubi Portus**, *by the English corrupted into* **Reptacestir**. *The distance from hence across the sea to* **Gessoriacum**, *the nearest shore of* **the Morini**, *is fifty miles, or as some writers say, 450 furlongs. On the back of the island, where it opens upon the boundless ocean it has the islands called the* **Orcades**. *Britain excels for grain and trees, and is well adapted for feeding cattle and beasts of burden. It also produces vines in some places, and has plenty of*

1 The British Isles from the world map, Cotton Tiberius B.V. f. 56v.

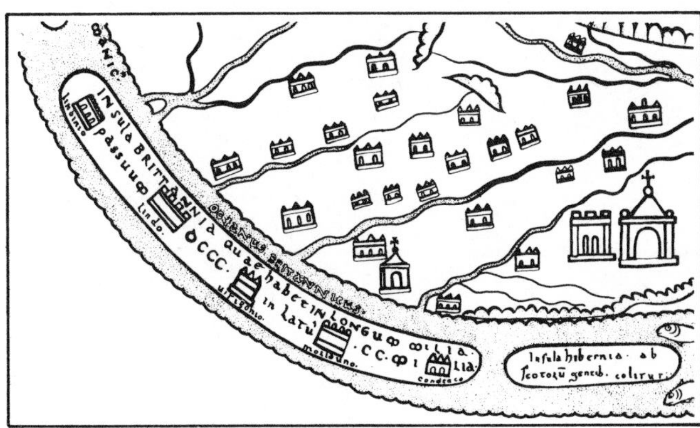

2 The British Isles from the St Sever world map (1028–72)

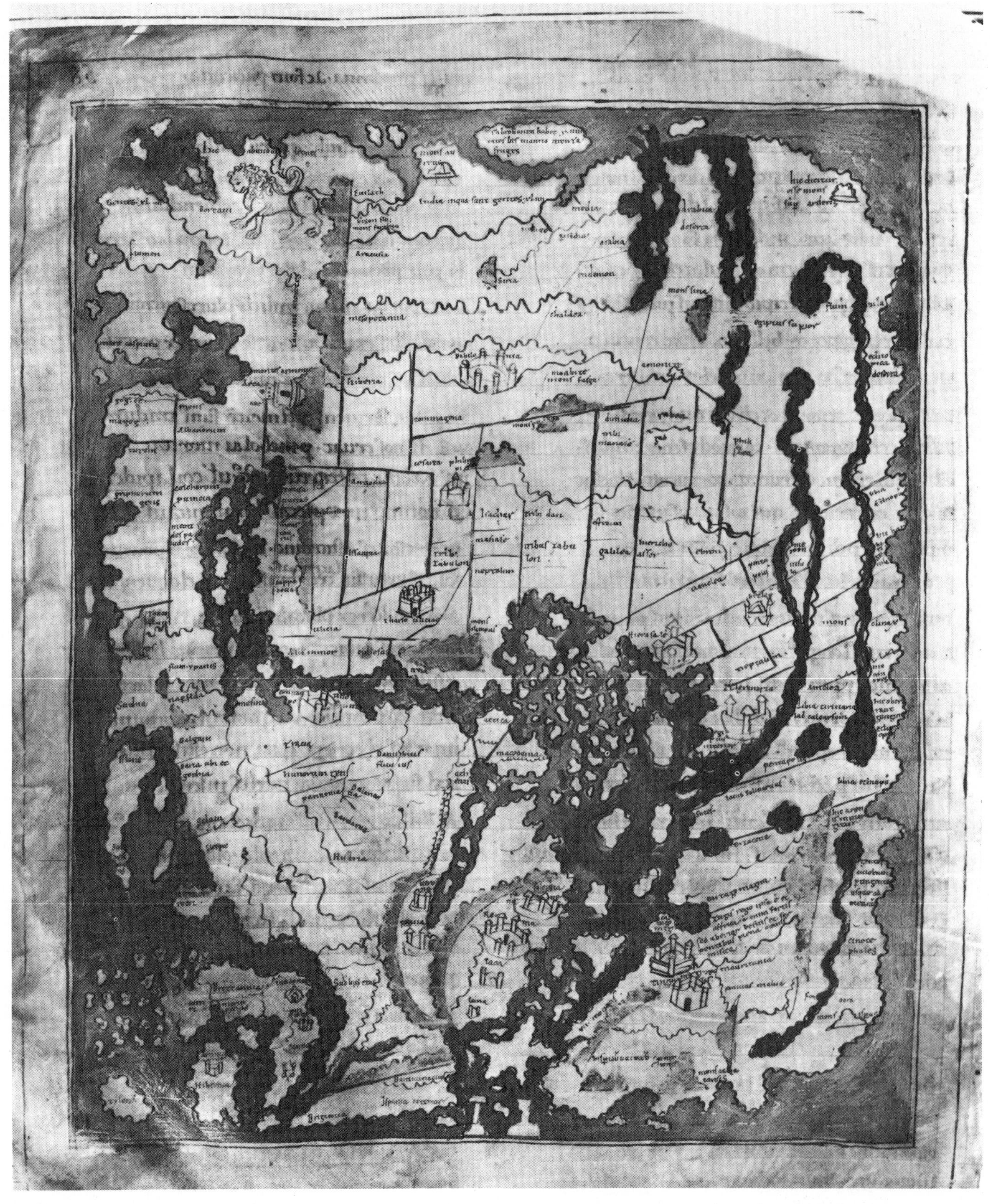

3 The Cotton Tiberius world map

land and water-fowls of several sorts; it is remarkable also for rivers abounding in fish, and plentiful springs. It has the greatest plenty of salmon and eels, seals are frequently taken, and dolphins, as also whales; besides many sorts of shell-fish, such as mussels, in which are often found excellent pearls of all colours, red, purple, violet and green, but mostly white. There is also a great abundance of cockles, of which the scarlet dye is made; a most beautiful colour, which never fades with the heat of the sun or the washing of the rain; but the older it is, the more beautiful it becomes. It has both salt and hot springs, and from them flow rivers which furnish hot baths, proper for all ages and sexes and arranged accordingly. . . Britain has also many veins of metals, as copper, iron, lead and silver; it has much and excellent jet. . . The island was formerly embellished with twenty-eight noble cities, besides innumerable castles, which were strongly secured with walls, towers, gates and locks. And, from its lying almost under the North Pole, the nights are light in summer, so that at midnight the beholders are often in doubt whether the evening twilight still continues or that the morning is coming on; . . . This island at present, following the number of the books in which the Divine law was written, contains five nations, the English, Britons, Scots, Picts and Latins. . . (Knowles 1965, 4–5)

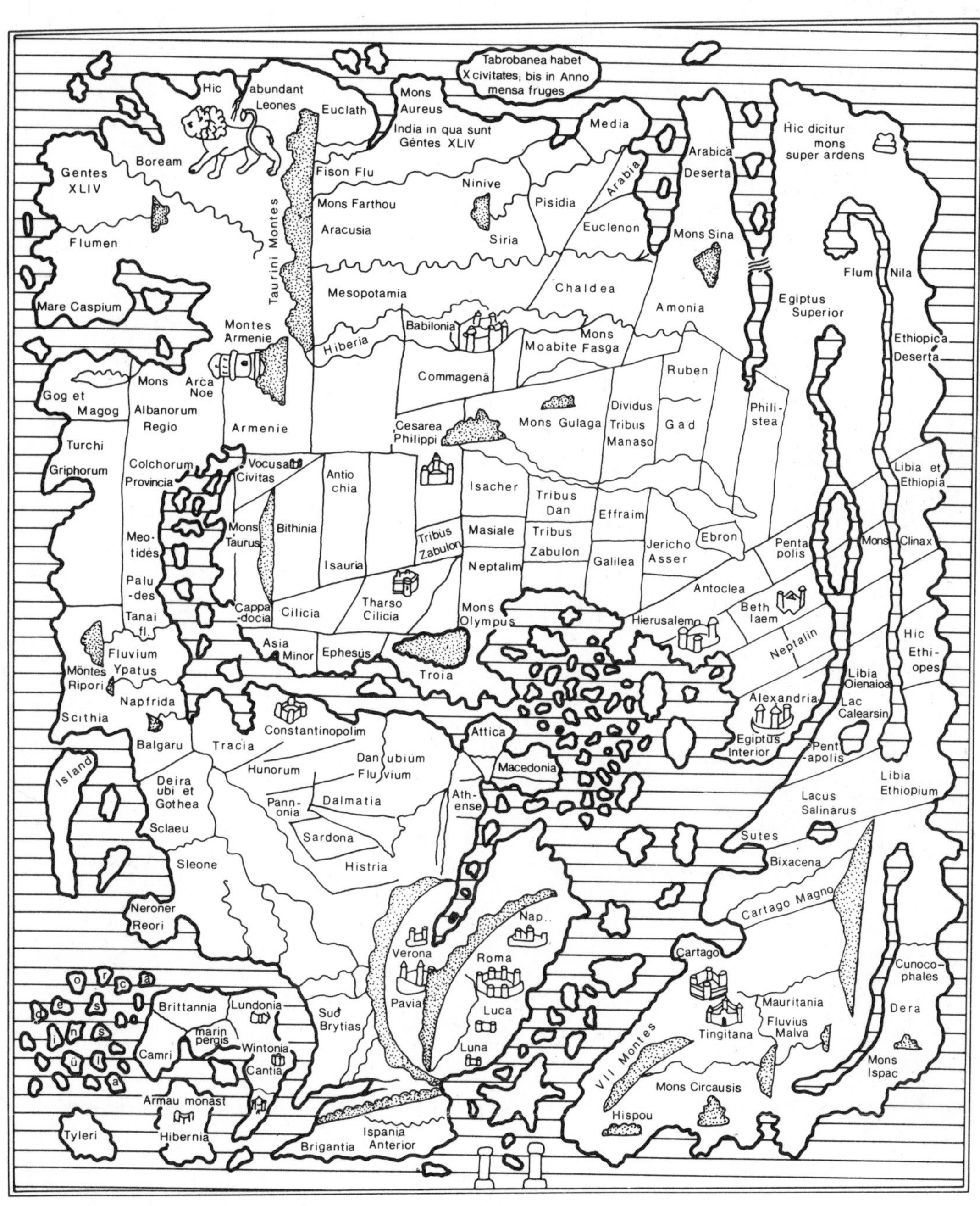

4 Diagram of the Cotton Tiberius world map

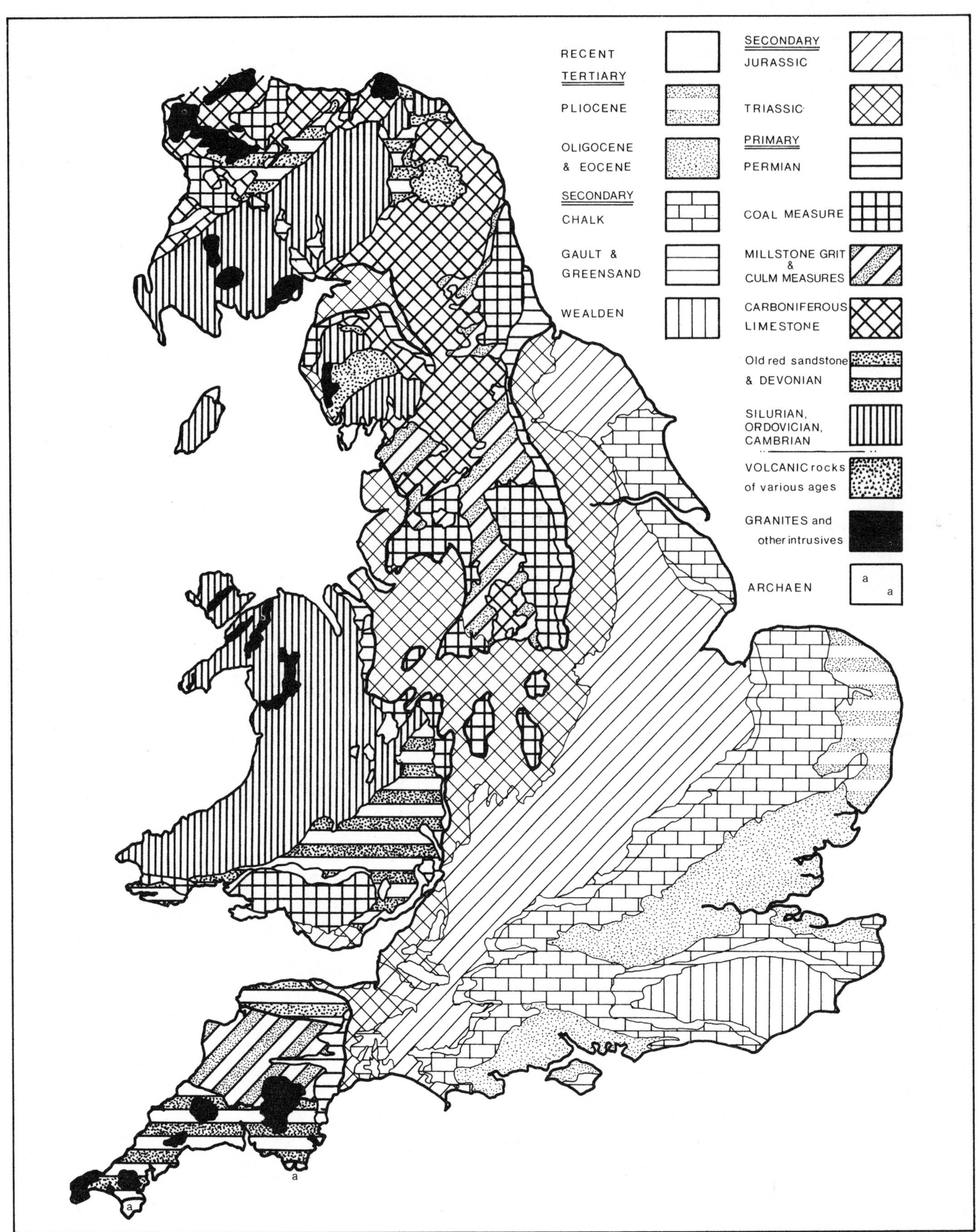

5 Simplified solid geology

The Background

Geology, Relief and Soil (5–9)

The picture revealed in the mapping of Anglo-Saxon England is often distorted, a distortion to which two factors have contributed: first, the distortion imposed by physical and geographic factors, for England was not a flat plain, uniformly vegetated, watered and peopled; and secondly, the bias that comes from the available evidence. Thus, an apparently significant distribution of an artefact or an event may only reveal the survival pattern or the retrieval pattern of the evidence.

The geographical constraints that affect all settlement in England are interrelated and often interact. Geology supplies the bare bones: in general, the older hard rocks are to the west and the softer sedimentary rocks to the east (map **5**). Patterns of erosion affect soil and relief, available minerals affect trade, and ridges such as the great Jurassic scarp control the routeways and also the provision of good building stone (maps **199** and **200**). However, there are large areas of England where the solid geology is unimportant, as it is overlaid by vast areas of fluvial or glacial drift (map **6**), often to a considerable depth.

The archaeology of Britain has typically been divided for all periods into that of highland and lowland zones (map **7**). But although this is as true for the Anglo-Saxon period as for any other, with the Celts holding the highland zone and the centres of Anglo-Saxon population in the lowland zone, it is clear that there are great differences not only within zones of relief (map **8**) but also in the configuration of the landscape. It remains true, nevertheless, that the economy and life of the highland zone marked out its settlement and later history from the more desirable lowland zone because of its high relief, hard rocks, poor soils, heavy rainfall and more extreme climate.

Map **9** is a simplification of the results of the Land Utilization Survey (1941) and shows the soils in broad categories. The quality of the land is the product of drift, solid geology, relief and rainfall: these soils are a key to settlement. Although map **9** indicates soil quality, it must be remembered that it is the result of **modern** research and therefore reflects those soils of most use for today's agricultural practices.

6 Drift-covered areas

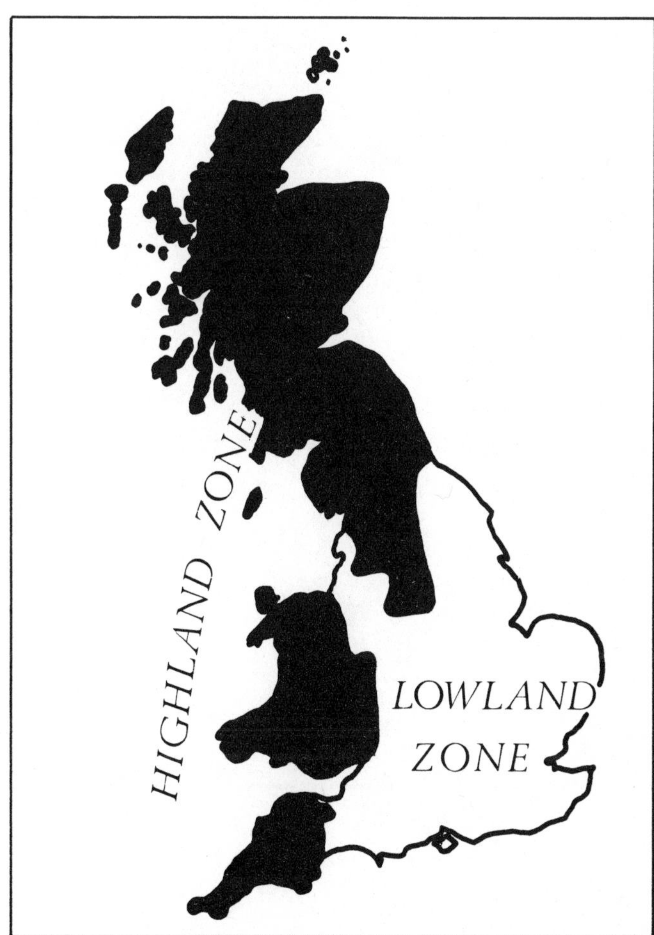

7 Highland and lowland zones

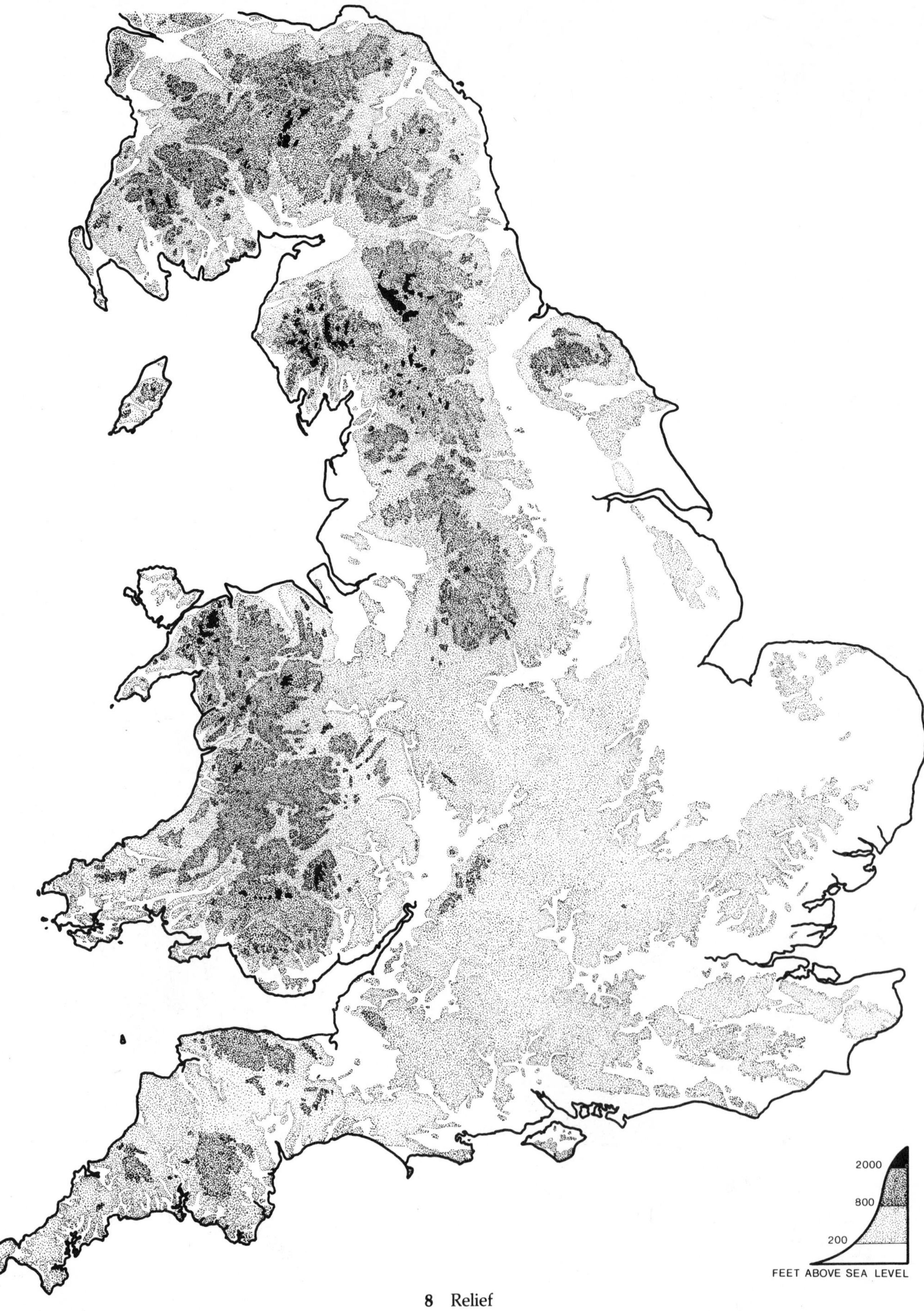
2000
800
200
FEET ABOVE SEA LEVEL

8 Relief

GOOD
Types A1 to G4
MEDIUM
Types G5 to AG6
POOR
Types G7 to H 10
FENS : This map shows present fertility so that drained areas are shown
0
MILES
50

9 Land quality

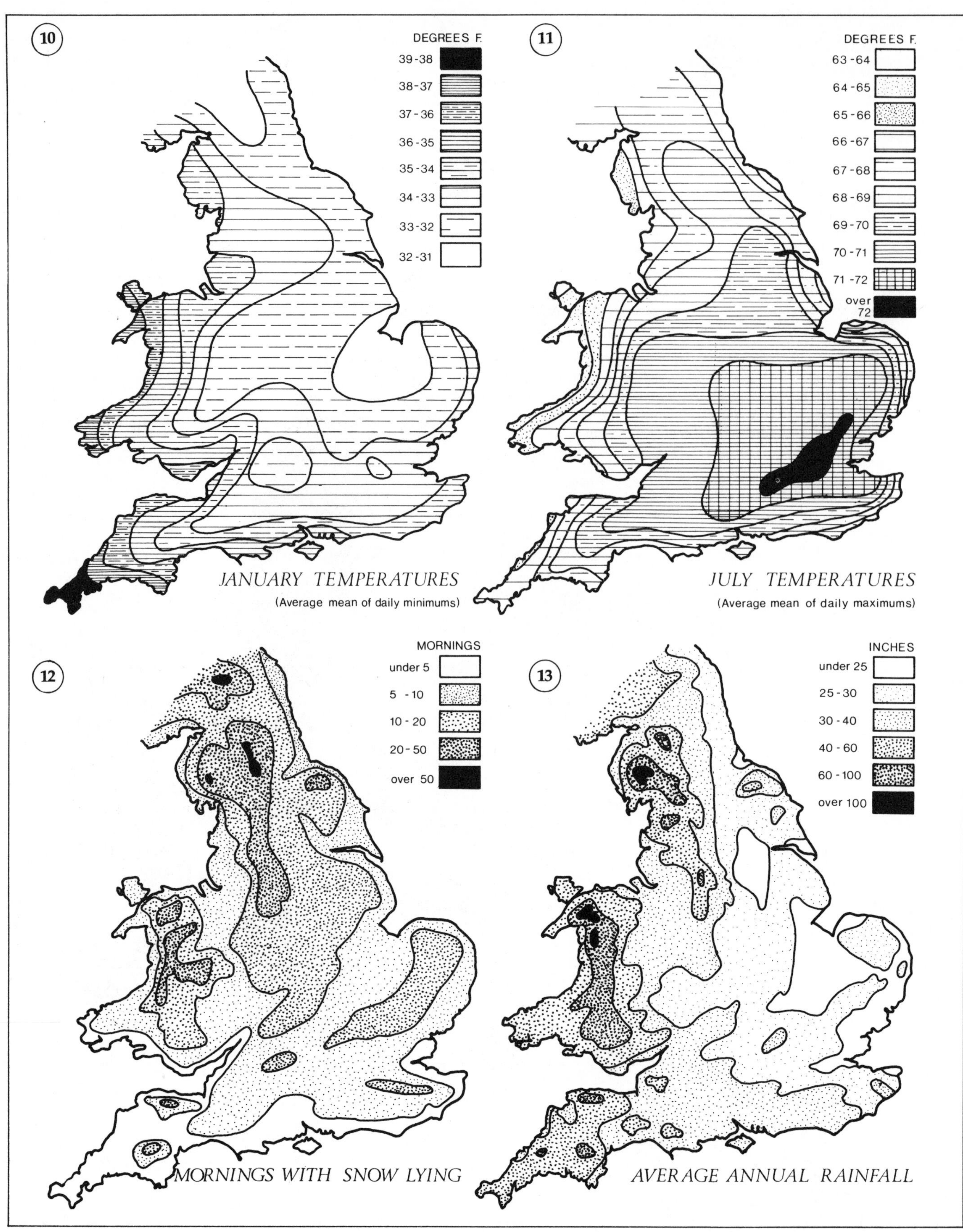
10
DEGREES F.
39-38
38-37
37-36
36-35
35-34
34-33
33-32
32-31
JANUARY TEMPERATURES
(Average mean of daily minimums)
11
DEGREES F.
63-64
64-65
65-66
66-67
67-68
68-69
69-70
70-71
71-72
over 72
JULY TEMPERATURES
(Average mean of daily maximums)
12
MORNINGS
under 5
5 - 10
10 - 20
20 - 50
over 50
MORNINGS WITH SNOW LYING
13
INCHES
under 25
25-30
30-40
40-60
60-100
over 100
AVERAGE ANNUAL RAINFALL

10–13 Climate

Climate (10–14)

It is now accepted that there have been major fluctuations in the climate both on a world scale and on a more local level in historic times. These changes have many important effects, and it should be understood by all those interested in the period that these variations have numerous ramifications. The Viking movements, agriculture, diet, coastline and trade, the early history of Greenland and the bone skates from York, the cultivation of the vine and the distribution of the sceatta coinage are all linked and modified by climatic development.

Interest in the subject is growing rapidly, and the present state of knowledge has recently been reviewed (Lamb 1978). Unfortunately for us, the comparison with the present state of British climate (maps **10–13**) is neither straightforward nor confined to one simple statement such as 'it was warmer', although it is possible to find statistics of one type that appear to summarize the overall trend for our period (AD 700–1066) and which demonstrate that it **was** warmer. The recovery of the Oxygen 18 isotopes from the Greenland icecap (**14**) provides further evidence. Because the layers in the ice can be dated, the isotope can be measured and related to specific years. It is believed that the production of Oxygen 18 is related to long-term trends in temperature and thus is a useful indicator of those trends. The physics may be beyond us, but the implications of this, and much else, in Lamb's latest work should be noted by everyone interested in the period.

In general, the pattern that emerges can be seen as building up to a period known as the medieval warm epoch, or 'Little Optimum', which took place from perhaps AD 950 to 1300, with variations around the world within those broad limits. There was then a shift of climate in the later Middle Ages towards the 'Little Ice Age', which controlled the entire early Modern period from Tudor times until the last century.

If we take it that the general trend from perhaps the sixth or seventh centuries was towards a drier and less stormy climate, we may see several climatic changes in the period c. AD 550 to c. 1180.

1 It was warmer: summer temperatures may have been one degree centigrade higher.
2 A Continental effect, with the depression track further to the north of the British Isles, meant that Britain was affected by Continental weather patterns — warmer in summer, much colder in winter — but the average for the year would have been higher than present-day averages.
3 Bog growth can be taken as an index of wetness. The Tregaron series shows a standstill or very slow growth between AD 900 and 1200, followed by rapid growth indicating a return to wet conditions.
4 There is some evidence for an increase in storminess in the North Sea after AD 1000.

'In general we can say that for a few centuries in the Middle Ages the climate regained something approaching the warmth of the warmest postglacial times' (Lamb 1978, 435).

The effects were numerous and included a higher tree line and the growth of crops and forests further north than either after 1300 or in the present day. Map **196**, showing the vineyards in England in the pre-Conquest period, provides a good illustration of the point.

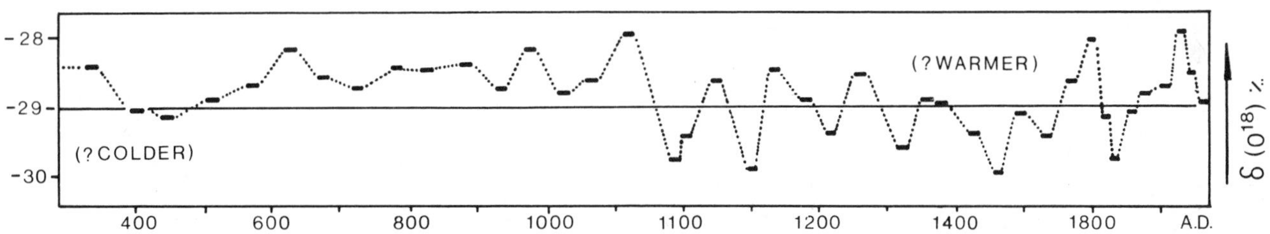

14 Oxygen isotope variations in the north-west Greenland icecap which are believed to represent broadly the course of temperature variations (from W. Dansgaard in Lamb 1978)

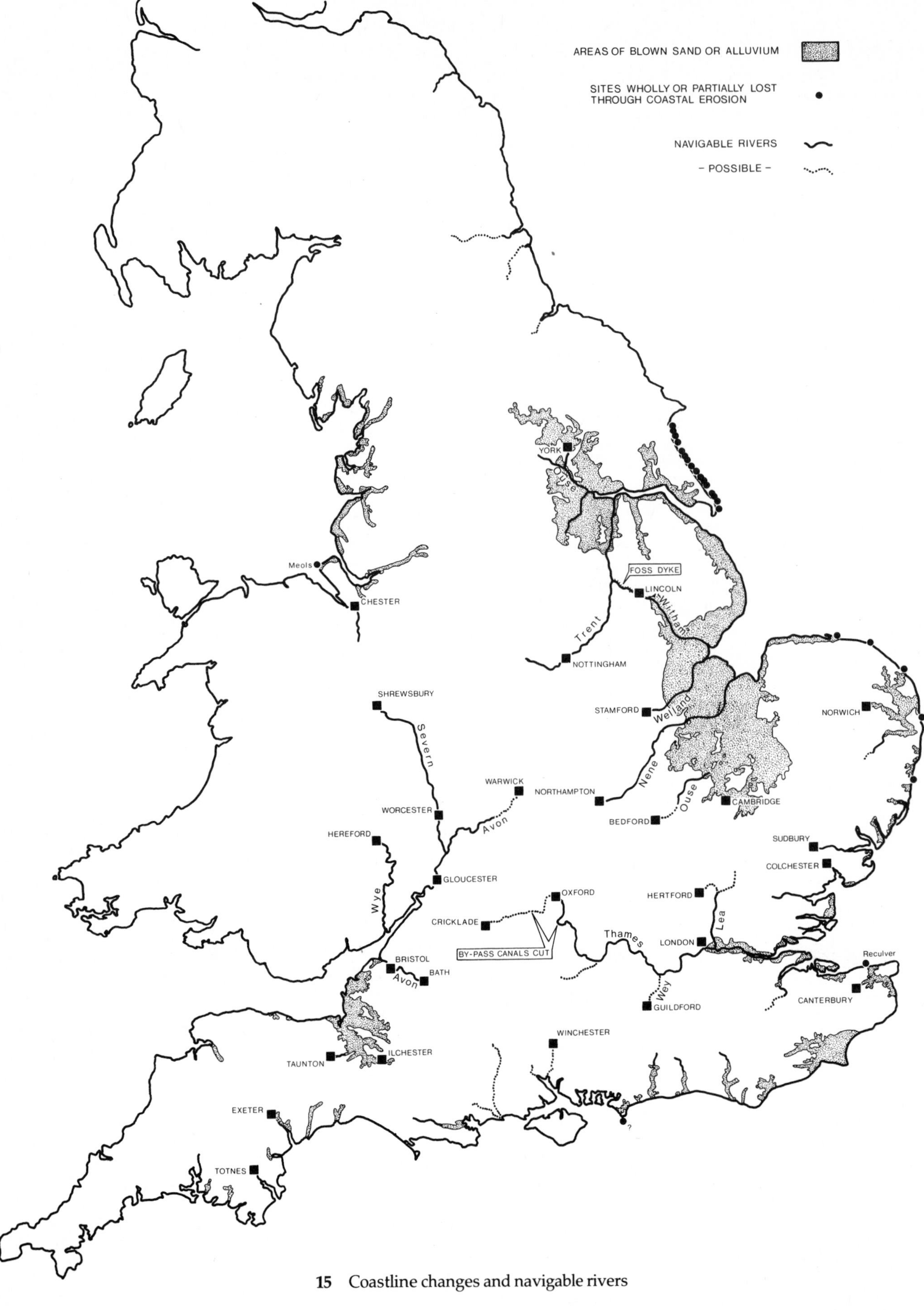
AREAS OF BLOWN SAND OR ALLUVIUM
SITES WHOLLY OR PARTIALLY LOST THROUGH COASTAL EROSION
NAVIGABLE RIVERS
- POSSIBLE -
YORK
Ouse
FOSS DYKE
LINCOLN
Witham
Trent
NOTTINGHAM
Meols
CHESTER
SHREWSBURY
Severn
STAMFORD
Welland
NORWICH
WARWICK
NORTHAMPTON
Nene
Ouse
CAMBRIDGE
BEDFORD
WORCESTER
Avon
HEREFORD
SUDBURY
COLCHESTER
GLOUCESTER
Wye
OXFORD
HERTFORD
Lea
CRICKLADE
Thames
LONDON
BY-PASS CANALS CUT
BRISTOL
BATH
Avon
Reculver
Wey
GUILDFORD
CANTERBURY
WINCHESTER
TAUNTON
ILCHESTER
EXETER
TOTNES

15 Coastline changes and navigable rivers

Coastline Changes and Navigable Rivers (15–16)

Widespread coastline changes (map **15**) have occurred between the Anglo-Saxon period and the present day, but they were very much a continuous process within the period, as may perhaps be demonstrated by the annal for 1014:

. . . and in this year on Michaelmas Eve [28 September] the great tide of the sea flooded widely over this country, coming up higher than it had ever done before, and submerging many villages and a countless number of people.

Although the 'coast' is simply that line along which the sea intersects the land, the causes of coastline changes can be complicated. In the Anglo-Saxon period there was a worldwide, eustatic rise in sea level as water from the icecaps and glaciers returned to the sea. This, of course, was also linked to the general rise in long-term averages in temperature discussed earlier. At the moment, water levels are rising at about 2 mm a year, and it can be seen that rises have been important at some earlier stages, leading to flooding of the land ('submergence' or 'marine transgression'). A lowering of the mean sea level ('emergence') is associated with the drying out of certain coastal flats. The subject is complex, as it also involves the questions of silting and man's interference with the shorelines. The data in **16** follow Fairbridge, as quoted in Bruce-Mitford (1975). Coupled to these changes in sea level are the tectonic changes in the land masses, with the southern part of the North Sea area tending to fall, whilst the North British area, centred on the West Grampians, tended to rise.

The navigable river pattern is fairly simple to reconstruct but it can lead to endless argument. What is navigable now may not have been so a millennium ago, and there is a problem in supplying an acceptable definition of 'navigable'. Minor streams in West Somerset may float a punt somewhere along their lengths after a wet February, but the navigable rivers in question are those thought to have been used regularly for the transport of goods and passengers.

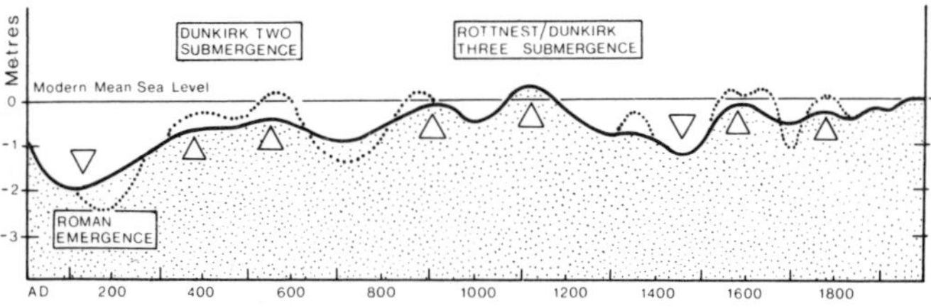

16 Sea level changes in the North Sea area. The possible extremes are shown by the dotted line

The Fens and the Wash (17–18)

There is in the Midland district of Britain a most dismal fen of immense size, which begins at the banks of the river Granta not far from the camp (**castello**) *which is called Cambridge* (**Gronte**) *and stretches from the south as far north as the sea. It is a very long tract, now consisting of marshes, now of bogs, sometimes of black waters overhung by fog, sometimes studded with wooded islands and traversed by the windings of tortuous streams. (Felix's* **Life of St Guthlac**, *early eighth century, quoted in Colgrave 1956, 87)*

The changes that have taken place in this area are enormous and mostly post-medieval, although the Anglo-Saxons were increasingly active here throughout the period (map **17**). The Fens themselves included great stretches of water (for example Whittlesea Mere in map **18** which, although shallow, was the largest body of fresh water in lowland Britain), which figure prominently in charters of the fenland monasteries because they represented an important resource for fish and fowl. The pattern of the coastline, but more particularly of the river systems, has changed greatly from that shown in Saxton's 1576 map (**18**). (It should be noted that present-day shorelines and river lines are shown throughout this atlas.)

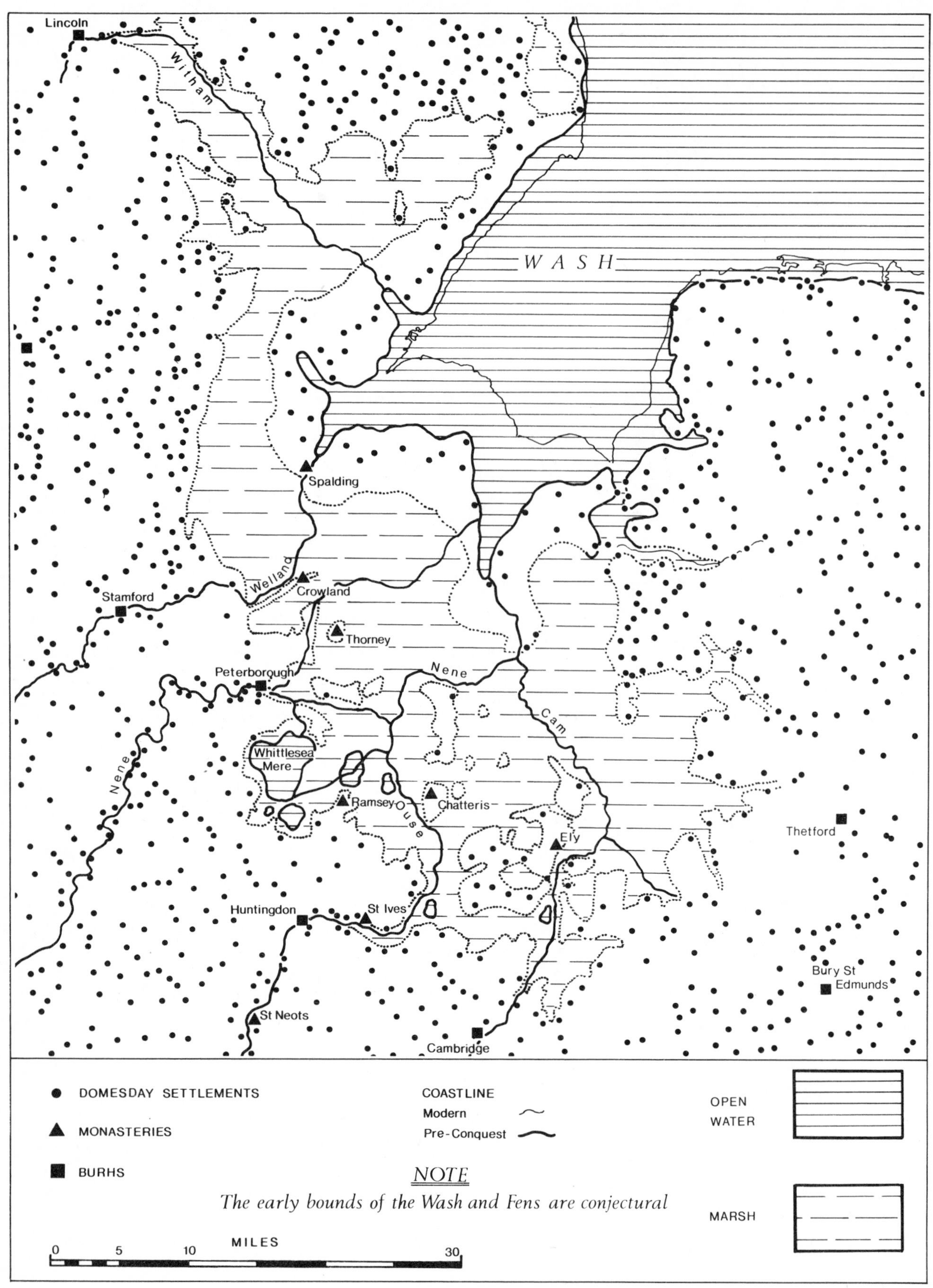
Lincoln
Witham
WASH
Spalding
Welland
Crowland
Stamford
Thorney
Peterborough
Nene
Cam
Whittlesea
Mere
Ramsey
Ouse
Chatteris
Ely
Thetford
Huntingdon
St Ives
Bury St
Edmunds
St Neots
Cambridge
DOMESDAY SETTLEMENTS
MONASTERIES
BURHS
COASTLINE
Modern
Pre-Conquest
OPEN
WATER
MARSH
NOTE
The early bounds of the Wash and Fens are conjectural
MILES
0
5
10
30

17 The Wash

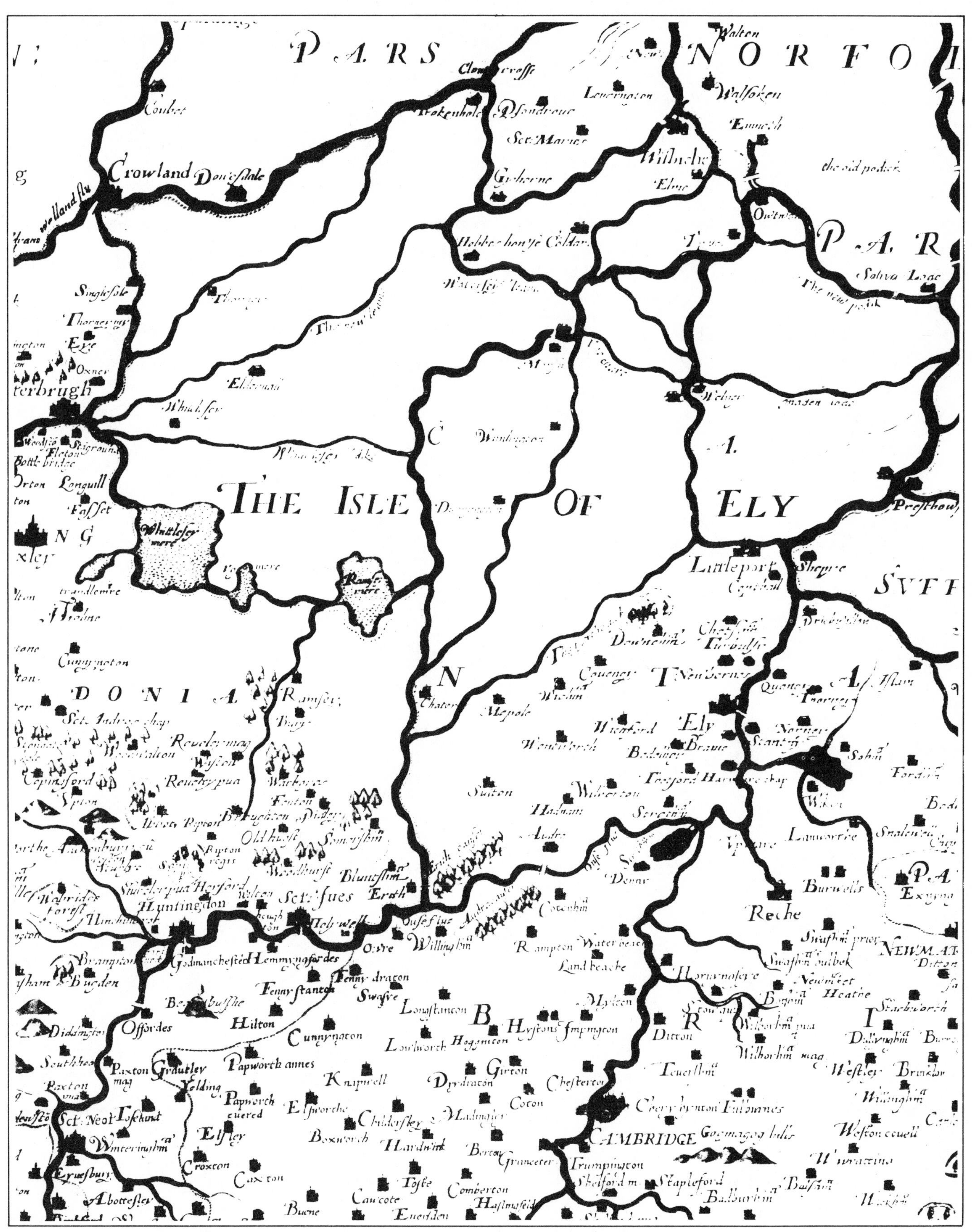

18 Whittlesea Mere and the rivers of the southern Fens according to Saxton (1576)

The Wantsum Channel (19–22)

On the east of Kent is the large Isle of Thanet containing according to the English way of reckoning, 600 families, divided from the other land by the river Wantsum, which is about three furlongs over, and fordable only in two places, for both ends of it run into the sea. (Bede's Ecclesiastical History, Book I, Cap. 25)

The Wantsum Channel (map **19**) would appear to have been an important part of the sheltered waterway system that ran from Ribe in Denmark to Quentovic in northern Gaul, and from the Alps to the Thames. The toll stations reflect this importance as does the concentration of finds of sceattas seen in maps **203** and **205**. Apart from the fact that this channel led to the important markets of Canterbury and into the Thames mouth, it may have avoided the dangers of the North Foreland. It can be assumed that the passage was made as the shipping was carried from the Downs and Sandwich up the Wantsum by the tide until they reached Sarre, where they waited until the tide fell and carried them north to the North Mouth.

Two important ports — Richborough at the early period and Sandwich at the later period — were situated to the south of the Wantsum Channel. Sandwich is described in the **Encomium Emmae Reginae** (c. 1041) as 'Sandwich which is the most famous of all the ports of the English'.

The dating of the closure of the channel as a passage for shipping is unclear, but the North Mouth is mentioned in connection with shipping and with Sandwich in the annal for 1052 (from the Anglo-Saxon Chronicle).

There are other cases of channels silting during this period: the important Limfiord in Jutland appears to have closed at this time, and there were major changes in the coastline of Frisia. The ninth century changes in the Rhine, which led to the abandonment of Dorestadt, are recorded in 864 (Brøndsted 1965, 47) as follows:

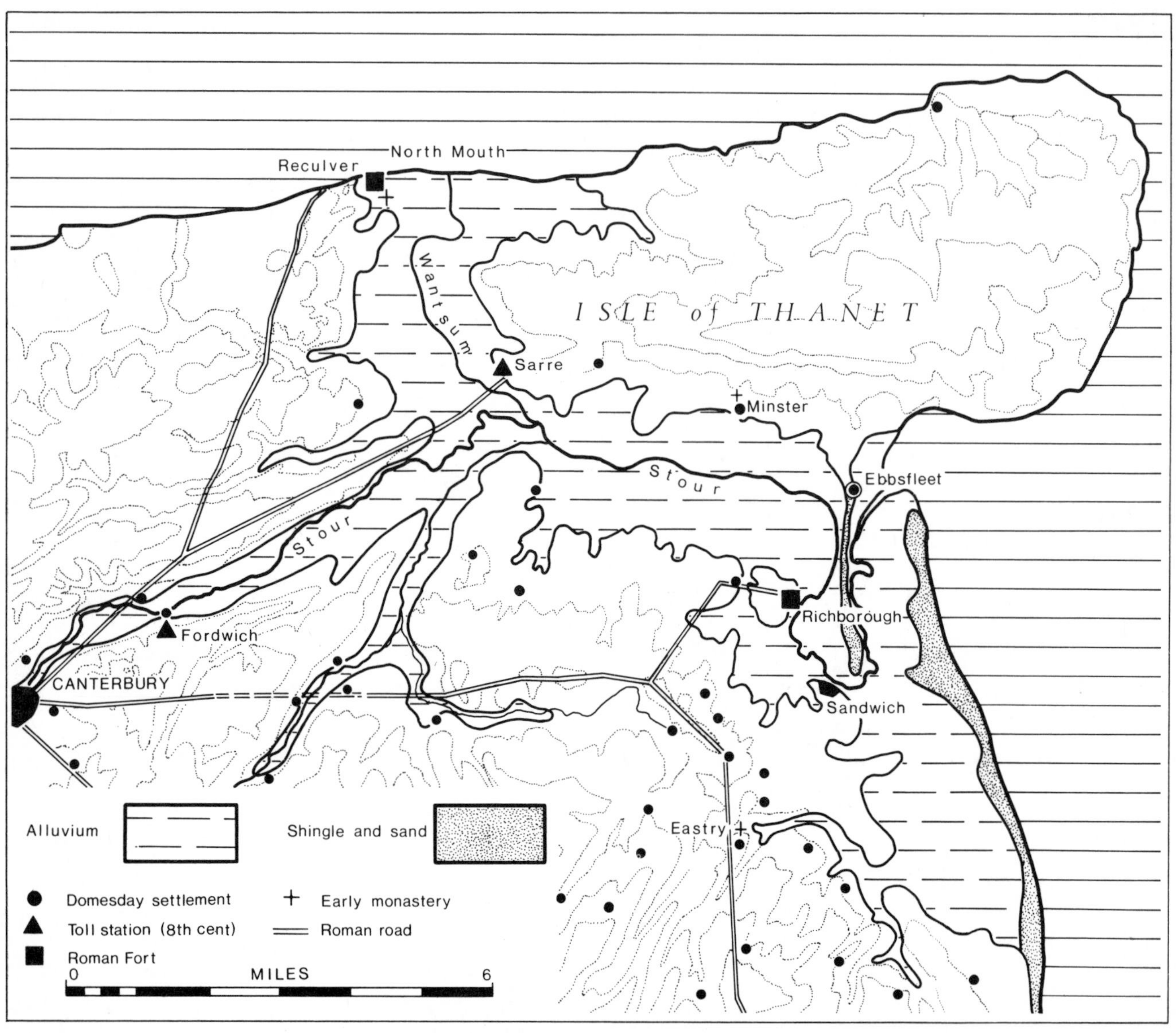

19 The Wantsum Channel. The earlier importance of the Channel is marked by the siting of the Roman forts at Richborough and Reculver

Strange portents were observed in the sky, and these were followed by plagues, gales, tidal waves, and floods. The waters of the Rhine were forced back by the sudden rush of the sea, drowning masses of people and animals in Utrecht and all over Holland. From then on, the River Lek was embanked with dikes, and the Rhine changed its course towards Utrecht, while at Katwijk it completely silted.

As yet there is no definitive work on the changes affecting much of the coast of South-east England, in the areas around Romney and Hastings, although there have been some brave attempts. To assist future work on the subject — and to indicate the nature of the problem maps **20** and **21** show two only partially successful efforts to reconstitute the pre-Conquest shoreline in the Rye area.

Great changes in the Dungeness area make it difficult to understand the early history of Appledore and Romney without some reconstruction of the coastline (map **21**). A model of the early course of the River Rother is also necessary when reading the annal for 892 and considering the site of Eorpeburnan (Davison 1972) (see map **150**).

The central part of Somerset was as waterlogged and marshy an area as the Fens. It was on the borders of these marshes that Alfred found refuge in 878, and the Somerset Levels (map **22**) were probably used by hunting parties from Cheddar in the tenth century. Early attempts at reclamation were made by the monastery at Glastonbury.

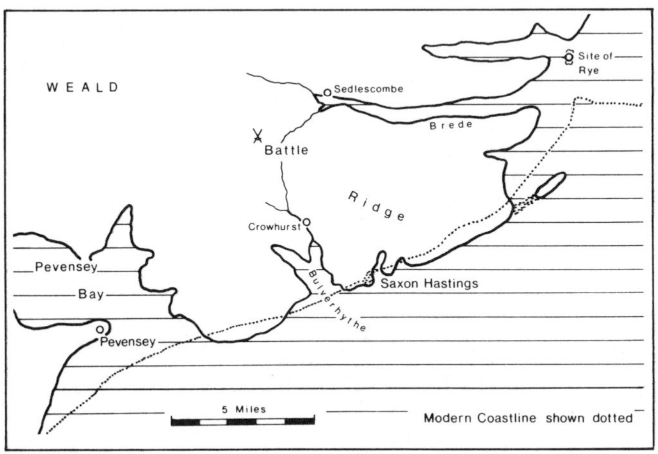

20 A reconstruction of the Hastings coastline in 1066 (Williamson 1959)

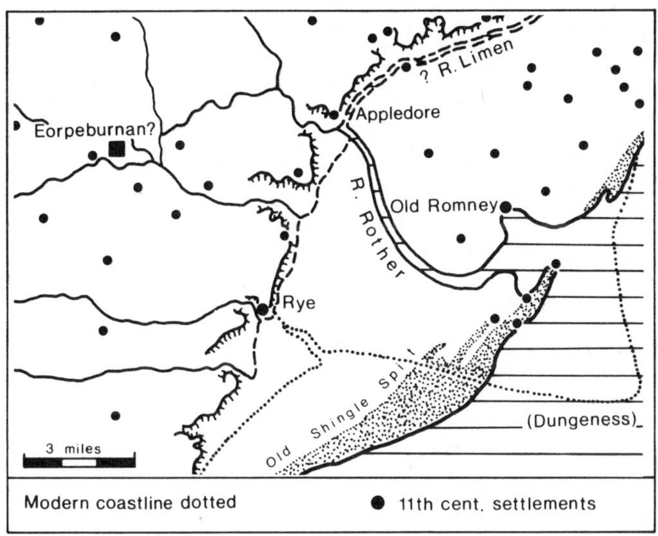

21 Early Dungeness (after Davison)

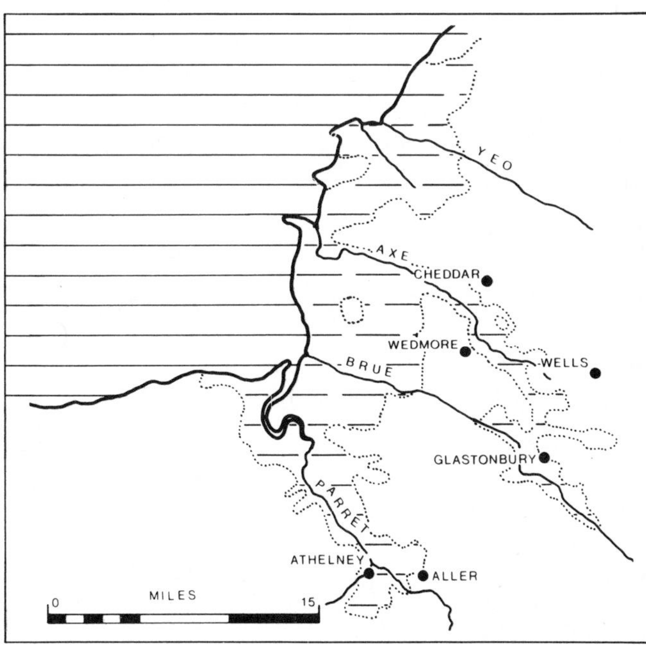

22 The Somerset Levels showing early medieval marine transgression (after Fowler 1972)

23 Alternative views of forest cover in Anglo-Saxon times (Stenton 1971 and Ordnance Survey 1935)

Forest (23–24)

No topographical feature of Anglo-Saxon England has come and gone with such rapidity as the great forest charted on many maps and influencing many interpretations of the events of the period. In 1935 the Ordnance Survey maps of Dark Age Britain and of Roman Britain were liberally covered with tracts of forest; in the latest version of the Ordnance Survey Map of Dark Age Britain (1966) this forest has apparently vanished:

The change . . . is seen in the abandonment of any attempt to restore natural woodlands on a geological basis. No apology is due for this. It has already been done on the third edition of the map of Roman Britain because wider knowledge of human distribution in that period shows that most of the natural wooded areas carried much larger populations than was thought possible thirty years ago. . . In any case the ancient equipment for cutting and removing timber was not greatly different from that which was commonly used in this country until as late as the 18th. century. . . .

Both approaches present problems: the first fill the map with tracts of impassable land, which deflected the reasoning of historians and archaeologists, while the second approach avoids the problem altogether. Map **23** therefore juxtaposes the 1935 view, which was most influential, and the Stenton view, which is milder. It should be noted that the two often bear little relation to one another. The matter should be treated as an open question and one which is not resolved here. The Domesday settlement evidence (maps **25–26**) is helpful and further evidence will come from the detailed place name work now being carried on

It is worth noting that the distribution of woodland in England today (map **24**) is unexpected and it is equally likely that actuality may belie our preconceptions for the Anglo-Saxon period. It is true that there were then important forests in England, that the country was more heavily wooded than in later periods, that the degree of forest cover decreased throughout the period. Our view of the nature of that forest has, however, changed from an impassable, damp oak forest to a canopy forest through which passage was possible and in which foraging animals provided a useful resource for man. The means do not yet exist to delineate many of these areas more closely, although there are signs that advances are being made (Sawyer 1978, 148).

Settlements and Population shown in Domesday Book (25–26)

One of the achievements of recent historical geography has been the compilation of **The Domesday Geographies of England** from Domesday Book. This work, edited by H.C. Darby, offers a view of the last days of Anglo-Saxon England as it was recalled by the jurors of 1086.

Most of England south of the Tees was covered and the majority of the settlements are included, although minor settlements are often considered under the name of the main estate (map **25**). We are given some idea of the true matrix into which we can fit our scraps from the charters and the Chronicle, and the calculated population distribution (map **26**) allows us to adjust our views of earlier periods and their settlements accordingly.

It is clear from these two maps that the constraints outlined in the preceding maps — those of geology, relief, land quality, highland and lowland zones, climate and coastline — combine to highlight the 1066 distributions. In map **25** the Wash, the Weald and Dartmoor can be identified as can the settlements following the streams in chalk areas of Wiltshire. It is a little more difficult to account for the areas of high population in map **26**.

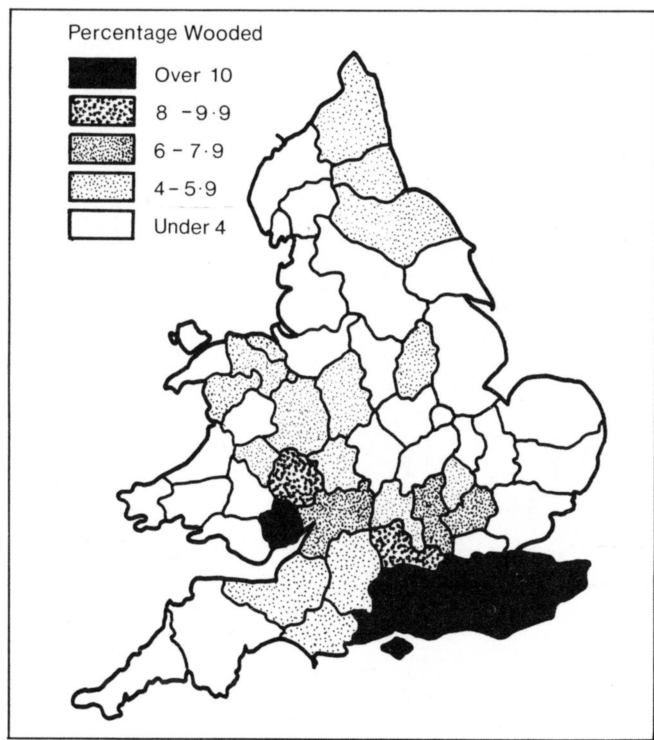

24 Proportion of shires wooded in 1947

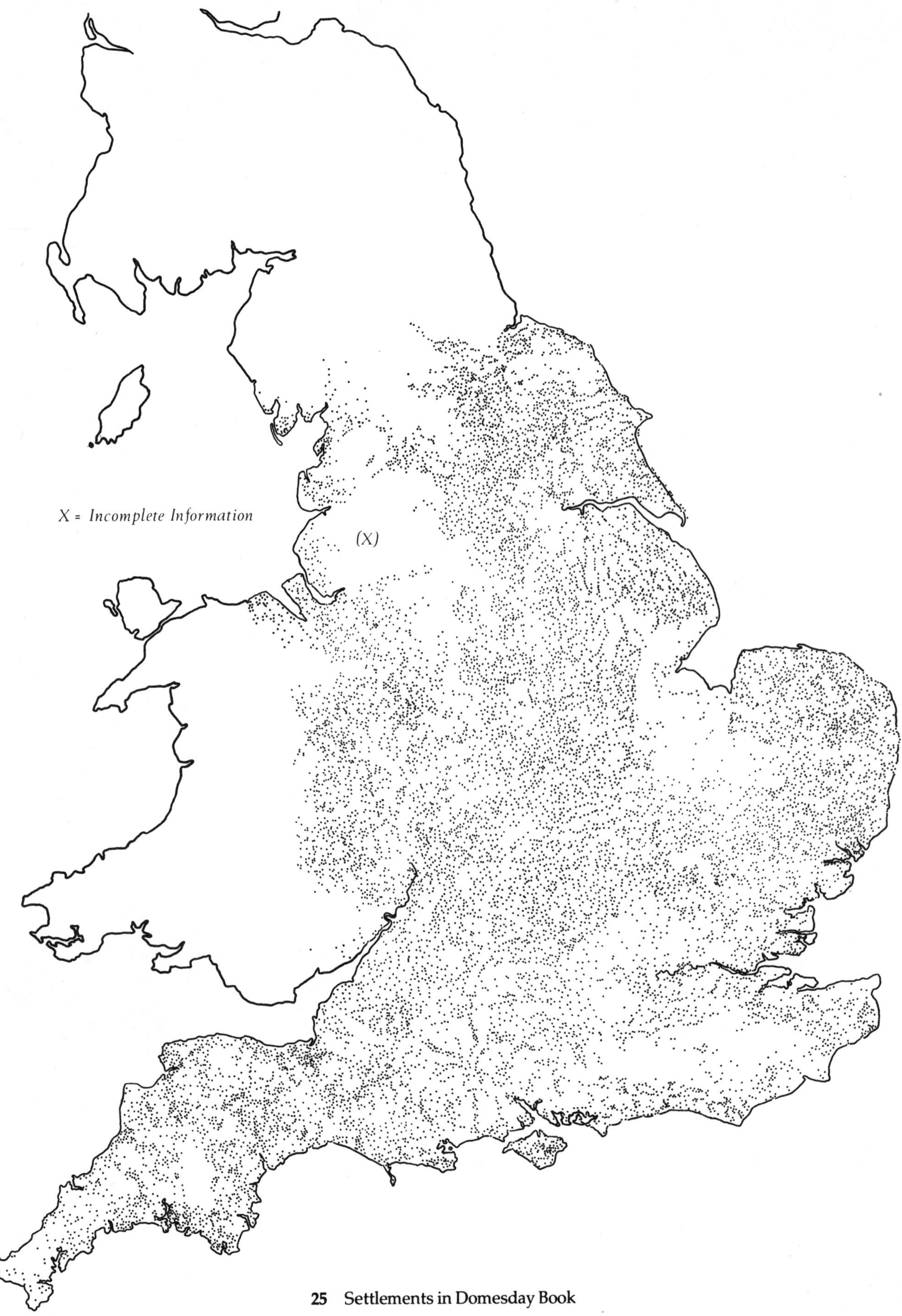

25 Settlements in Domesday Book

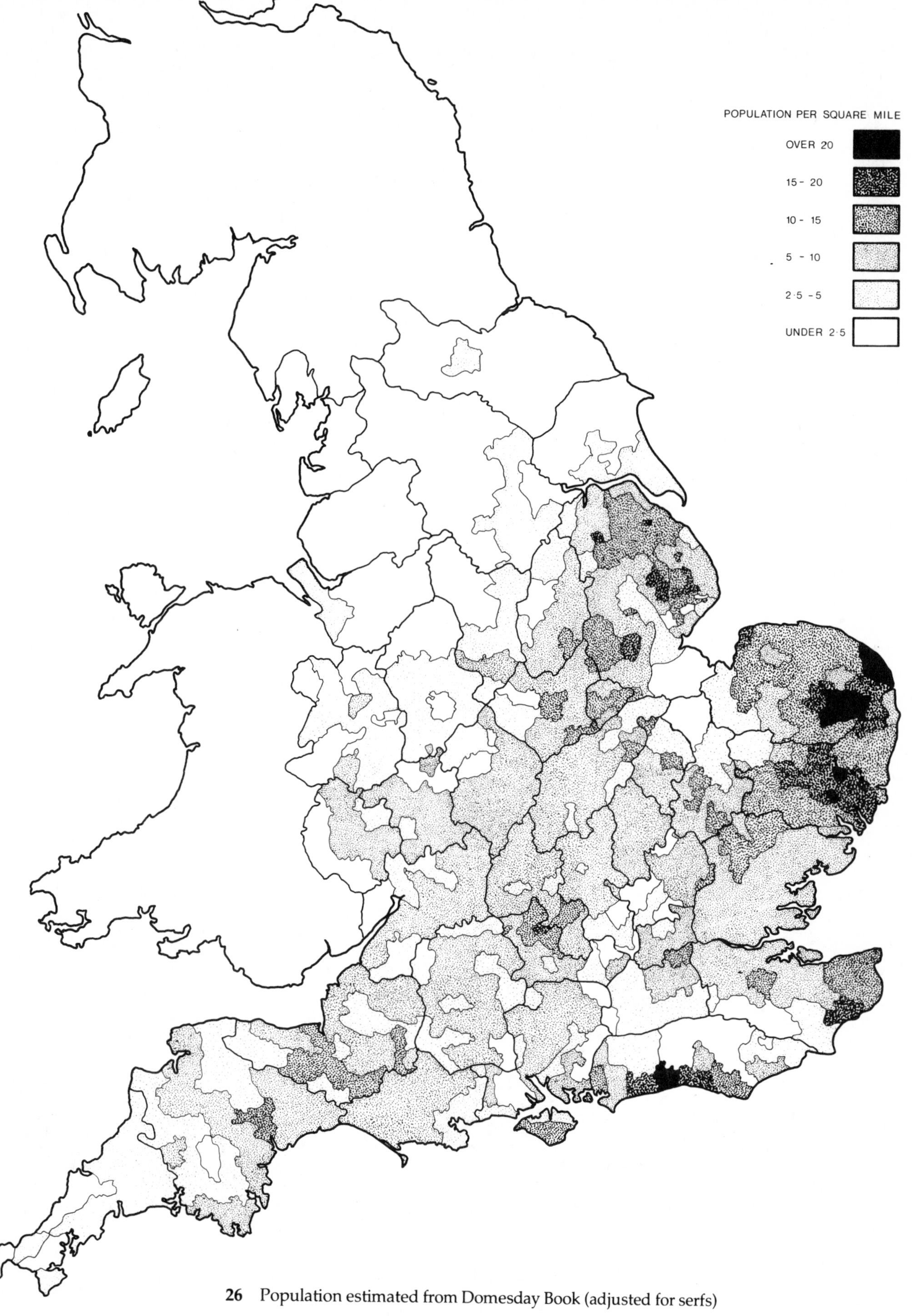

26 Population estimated from Domesday Book (adjusted for serfs)

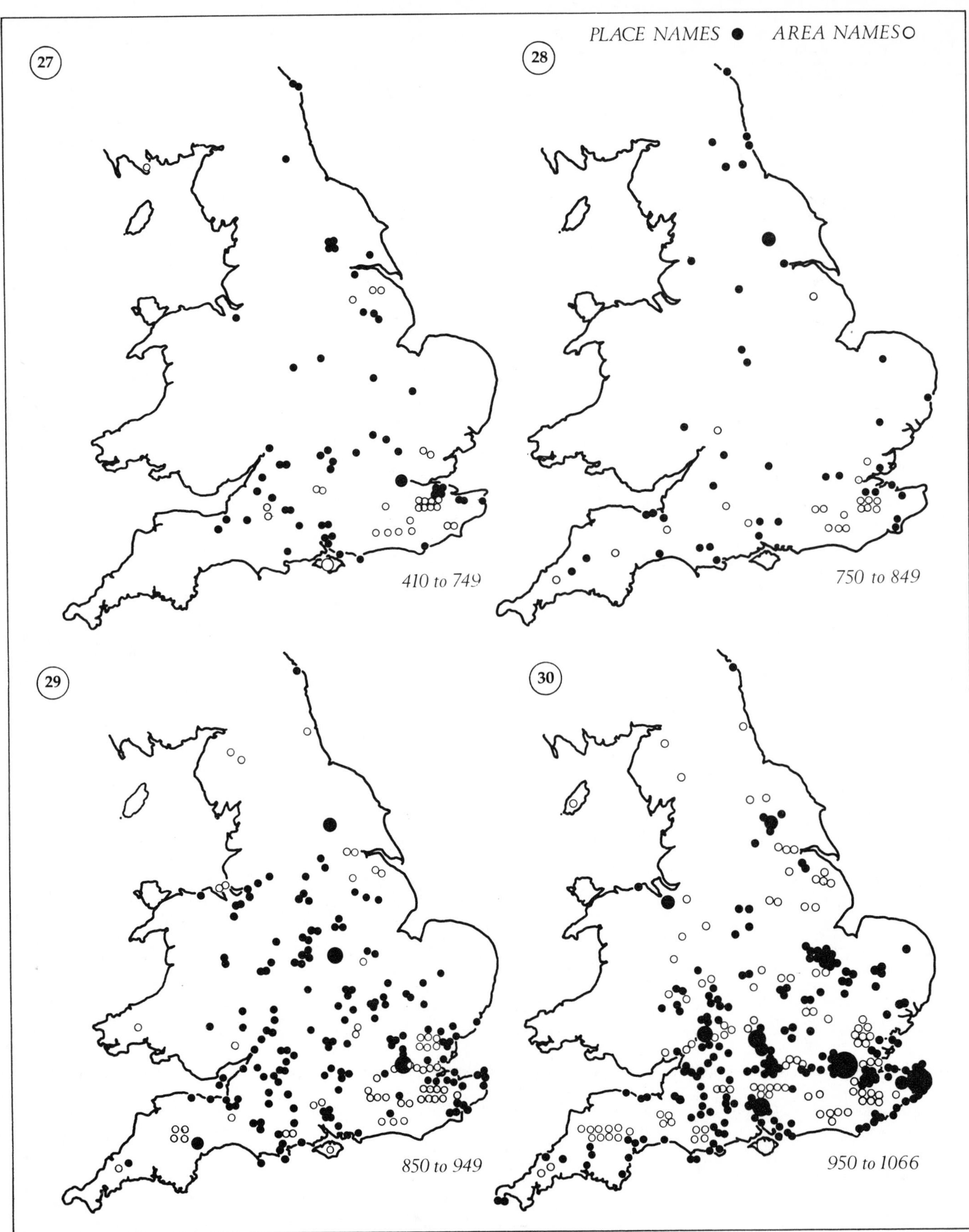

27–30 Places mentioned in the Anglo-Saxon Chronicle

Regional Bias in the Anglo-Saxon Chronicle (27–30)

The preceding set of maps has attempted to show some of the parameters within which the development and the life of Anglo-Saxon England took place. In particular it should have become apparent that there were vast differences between one part of the country and another. To ignore these differences and to treat the country as an homogeneous entity leads to serious misunderstandings.

The ensuing series of maps makes a similar point. It attempts to underline the range that the surviving evidence spans; it shows that the most important evidence is, not surprisingly, documentary but there are other valuable bodies of evidence; and that all these sources are subject to distortions. The major source for the history of the whole period is the Anglo-Saxon Chronicle and maps **27–30** show the geographical bias from period to period within the dates covered by this atlas. These maps are intended to elucidate points on the primary source for Anglo-Saxon studies from the end of the Age of Bede until the Conquest. The best introduction to these sources (for the Chronicle is a collection of parallel and complimentary documents drawn together from earlier materials in the reign of King Alfred and then developing separately in its several manuscripts) is in the foreword to **The Anglo-Saxon Chronicles: A Revised Translation,** edited by Dorothy Whitelock (1965).

Stenton has already pointed to the south-western bias at the early part of the era within the Chronicle and a southern, particularly a south-easterly, drift is visible in the later part of the period. It is clear from these maps that we cannot be certain that the omission of events or places from the record has any significance other than the interest of the author of a particular annal. These maps should also be viewed in conjunction with map **41**, the England of Bede, whose information affects map **27**, and is itself distorted, containing only places from the east of the country. Finally, these maps together with **31** and **35** should go some way to explaining why this atlas has so little to say about England north of the Humber.

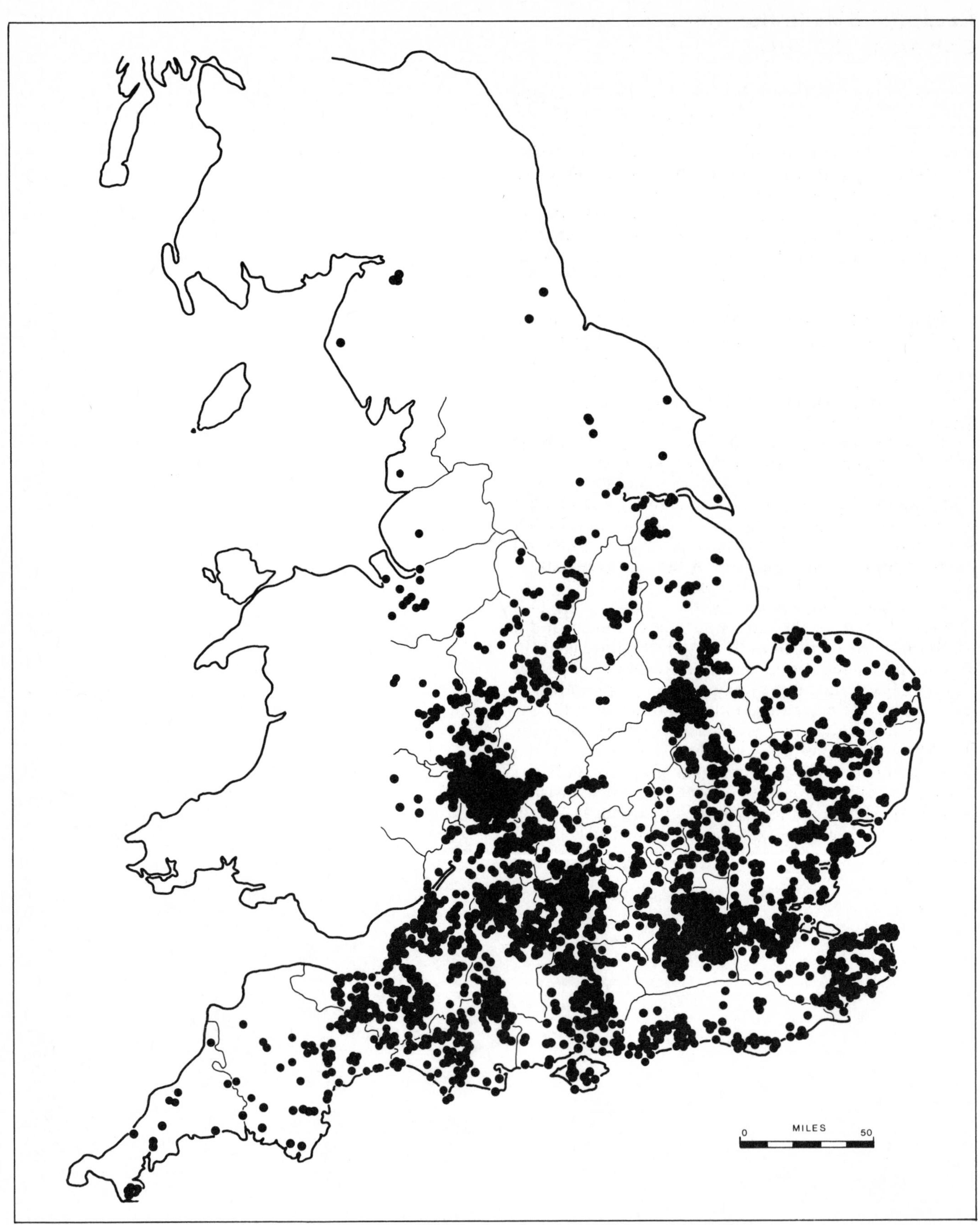

31 Distribution of estates mentioned in charters (after Goodier). All reputed charters, writs, leases and wills have been included

Charters as a Source of Evidence (31–35)

The land documents, wills, leases and writs, known collectively as charters, form the second most important Anglo-Saxon documentary source after the Chronicle, although the class of information is completely different. The Chronicle paints on a wide canvas whilst the charters deal with the particular: one talks of kings and battles, the other of fields and meadows.

The preponderance of the charters from a few houses is clearly reflected in map **31**. Worcester, the Canterbury and Winchester houses and Abingdon provide so many charters that the counties around them are well represented. Kent has the best coverage, whereas shires such as Lancashire or Herefordshire have practically none.

In map **31** the mention of a settlement is reflected by one dot, no matter how often that settlement is mentioned in subsequent charters. The map also includes all charters mentioned in Sawyer (1968) without any attempt to validate individual charters.

The general problem of the distribution of charters is reflected in the distribution of various categories of charters. Leases, for example, tend to be grouped around Worcester and lost and incomplete charters around Glastonbury. The problem is equally illustrated by the writs (map **32**), which replaced charters. Only a knowledge of the churches receiving the lands or rights makes any sense of an otherwise random distribution.

As a very large proportion of charters were in favour of, or granted by, the Church (see **33**), the vast majority of all documents come to us through the hands of the Church. When using documentary evidence we are in danger of seeing Anglo-Saxon England through stained glass windows.

One of the most interesting features of the charters is the whole category of intensely topographical information locked in the bounds. It is only recently that work has once again started on boundary clauses, which are such a rich source of every kind of evidence. In some areas the estate bounds interlock, allowing detailed work on the Anglo-Saxon landscape of several shires, for example Worcestershire (map **34**). Map **35** shows the distribution of all charter bounds, whether still attached to charters or not.

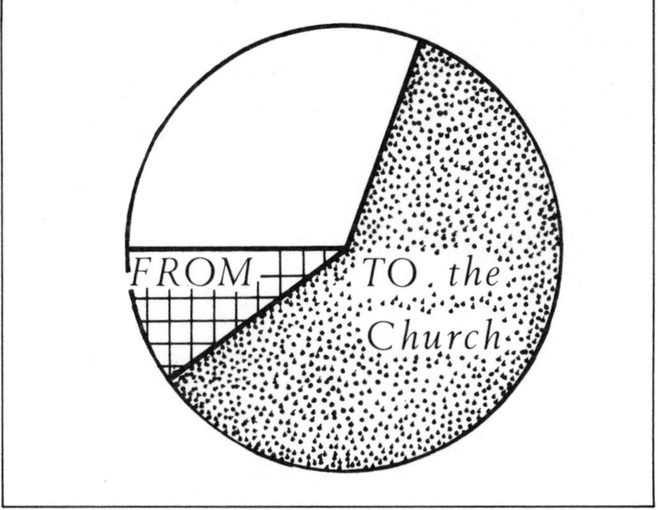

33 Proportion of charters issued by and to the Church

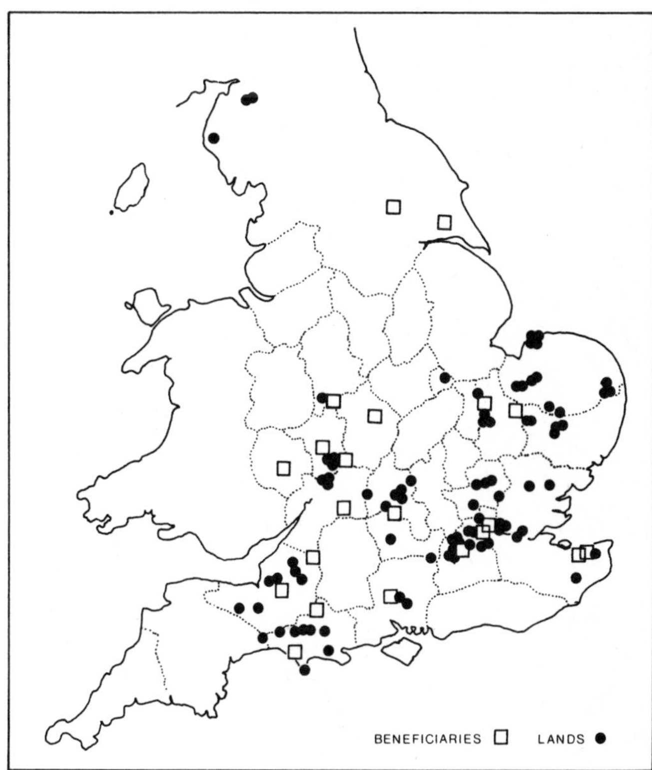

32 Distribution of beneficiaries and lands mentioned in alleged Anglo-Saxon writs

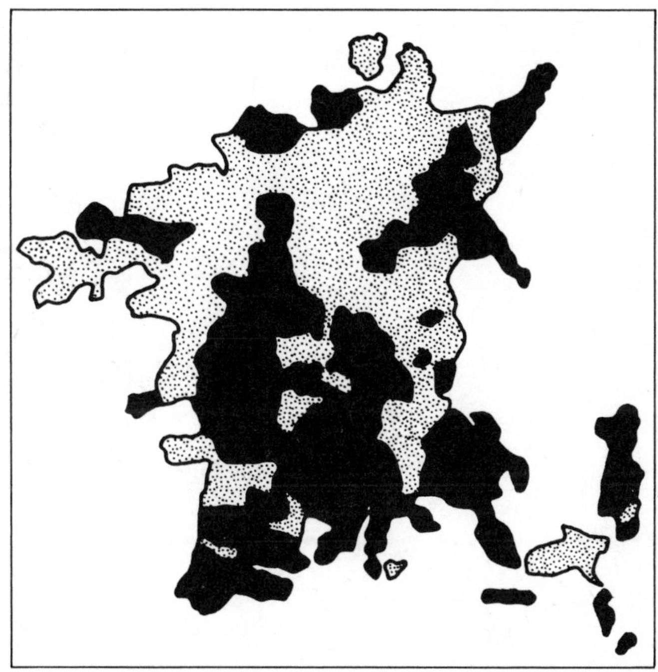

34 Worcestershire estates with detailed charter bounds shown solid (after Hooke)

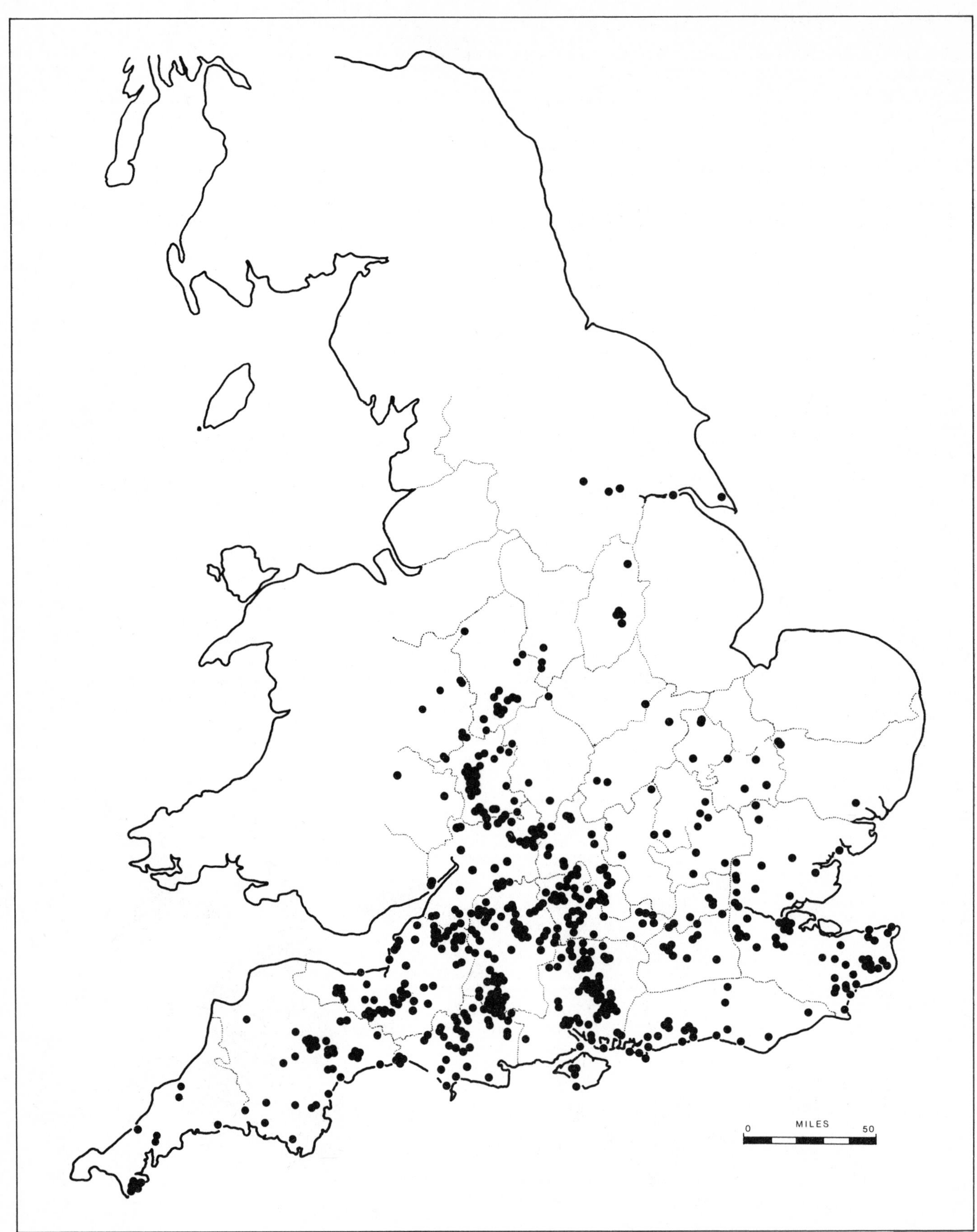

35 Distribution of charter bounds including detached bounds (after Goodier)

Chronological Bias: Charters and Anglo-Saxon Chronicle (36–37)

Geographical factors are not the only distortion in the major sources — there is also a chronological distortion. It would be reasonable to suppose either that all years are roughly equally represented by the charters or, rather more likely, that the later charters have survived better. The actual pattern (**36**) is therefore surprising: an enormous proportion of the charters was produced in the mid-tenth century, while the earlier period has a fairly uniform proportion of the charters produced, with a tailing off before the great wave of tenth-century charters. In the last years of the Anglo-Saxon monarchy there is a revival in the number of documents, particularly when writs are included.

This means that when we quote charter evidence on practically any subject we are probably quoting a tenth-century charter, and, from the evidence given above, a charter from a particularly limited part of the country. An awareness of the bias in the evidence will help to offset it.

If the number of words in the longest versions of the annals in the Anglo-Saxon Chronicle for a particular year are counted and then plotted in blocks of ten years it is possible to illustrate the very wide range of available evidence (**37**). This portrays the Chronicle as consisting of a steady background of annals with four enlarged portions which are, in effect, the 'Deeds of Alfred', the 'Deeds of Edward the Elder', 'The fall of Ethelred the Unready' and 'The reign of Edward the Confessor'. This severely restricts, for example, the available evidence for a discussion of the merits of kings such as Offa and Eadred. It is essential to remember that the Chronicle deals with a very narrow band of evidence, usually told from a fixed standpoint and often in a much abbreviated form.

Archaeology (38)

There has been an enormous expansion in the amount of money spent on archaeological excavations in Britain. Although much is to be hoped for from the growth of the subject, considerable care must be exercised when using archaeological evidence. Despite the discipline's claims to be 'scientific', map **38** shows how uneven is the spread of archaeological evidence which, in a most unscientific way, tends to leave large areas untested. Nevertheless it is cheering to note how much influence individual and group commitment has on the pattern. The map merely charts all Anglo-Saxon excavations, field-work and chance finds reported to **Medieval Archaeology** in the twenty-one years of its summaries.

What the map does not show is the large proportion of all funds spent on urban archaeology: town excavations form the bulk of all work that has been carried on in the last two decades.

Kings and Princes (39–40)

It is a rare individual who can recite the names of all the kings of Mercia, Wessex and England before the Conquest, yet on the names of kings we tend to hang our history. The charts in **39** and **40** may be of some assistance in this respect, but they have the more useful function of allowing us to see what kings and princes were contemporaries. The charts also show some trends in the development of Anglo-Saxon history: first, the extinction of the minor kingdoms and the supremacy of Mercia; followed by the rise of Wessex, so that by 860 there were only five kingdoms to be reckoned with (Mercia, Wessex, Northumbria, East Anglia and the Wales of Rhodri Mawr). Then come the Viking invasions; and the eventual union of the entire Anglo-Saxon kingdom.

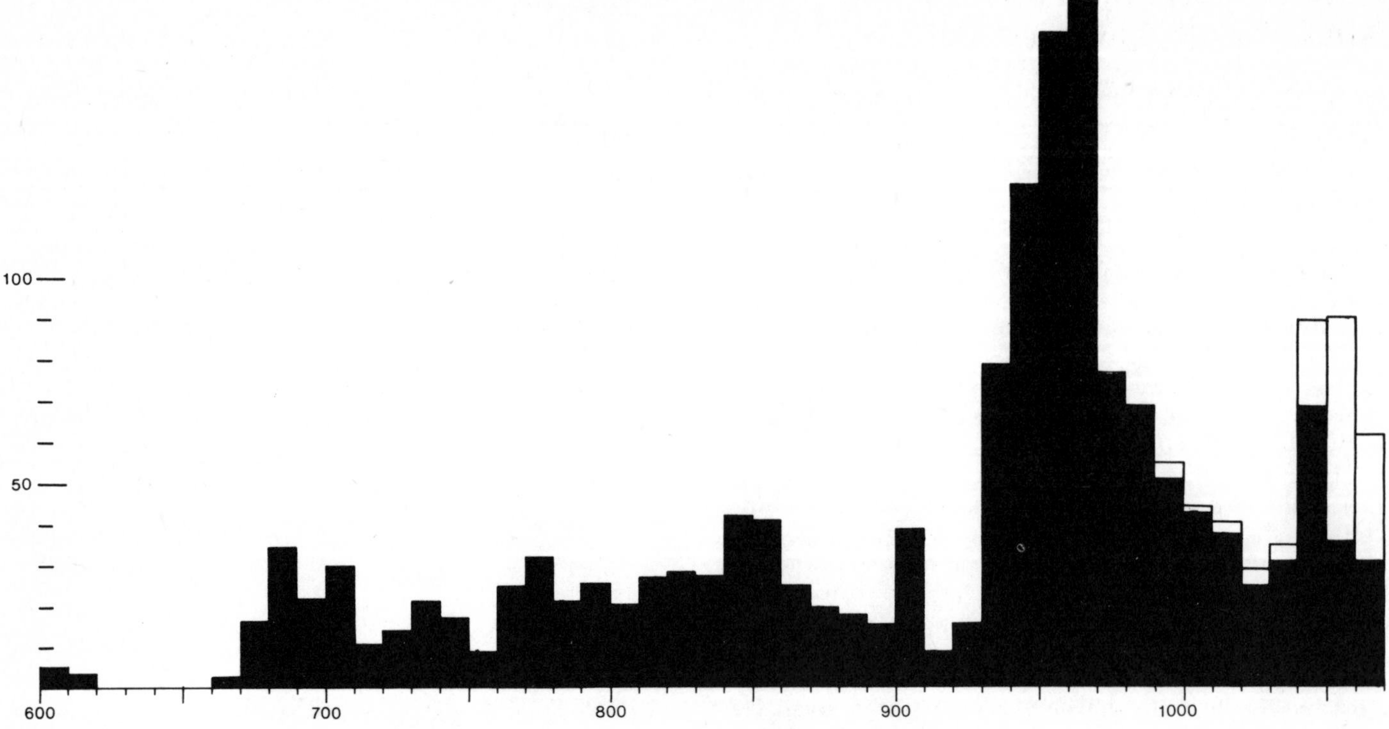

36 Anglo-Saxon charters: distribution by decades. Writs are shown in outline

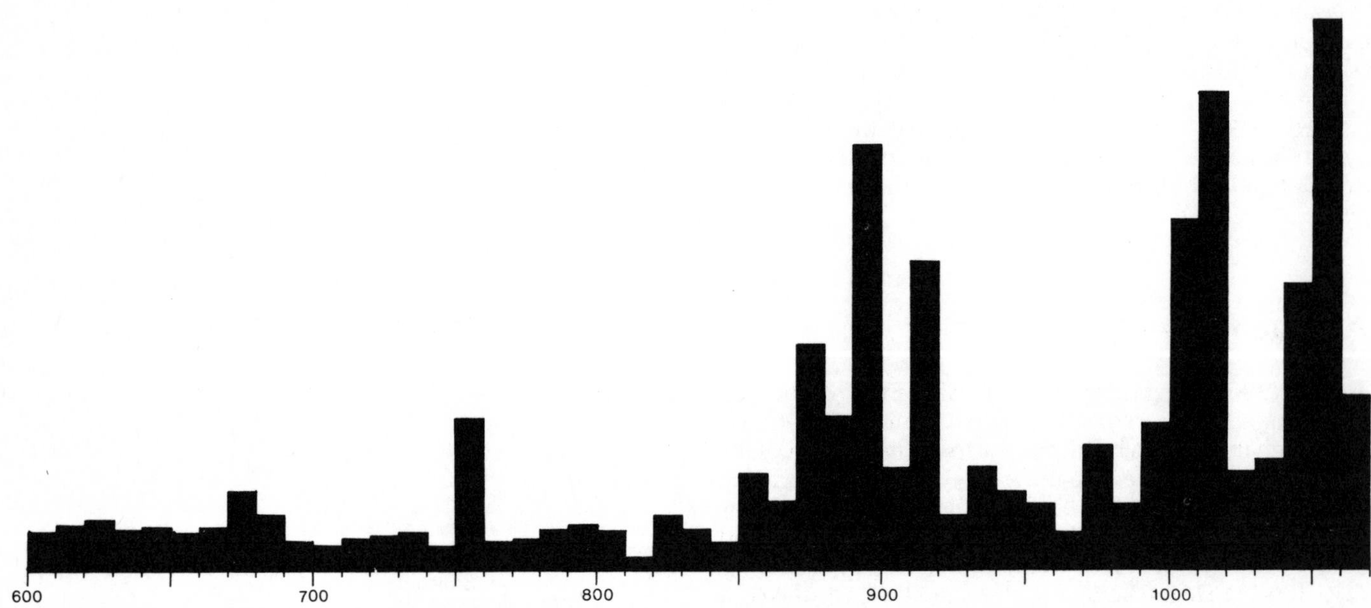

37 Comparative lengths of annals in the Anglo-Saxon Chronicle by decades

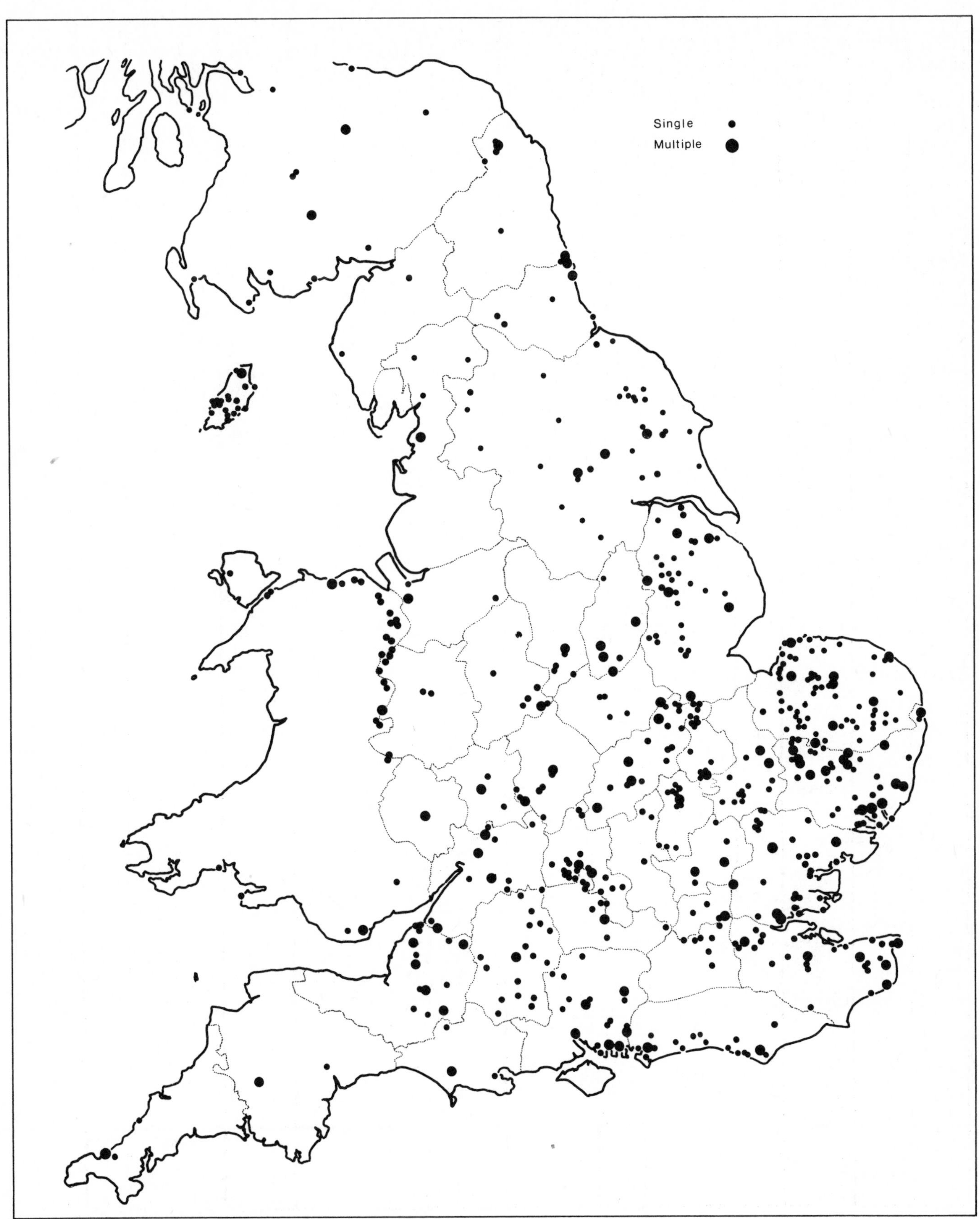

38 Archaeology of the Anglo-Saxon period. Excavations, field-work and chance finds reported in **Medieval Archaeology** 1957 to 1977

Years (scale): 710, 720, 730, 740, 750, 760, 770, 780, 790, 800, 810, 820, 830, 840, 850, 860, 870, 880

FRANKS: Pepin II · Charles Martel · Pepin the Short · CHARLE-MAGNE · Louis the Pious · Charles the Bald · Carloman

Northumbria: ALDFRITH · Eadwulf · OSRED · Coenred · OSRIC · Ceolwulf · EADBERT · Ethelwold Moll · ALCHRED · Ethelred I · ELFWALD I · Osred II · Etheired I · Osbald · Eardwulf · Elfwald II · EANRED · Redwulf · ETHELRED II · OSBERT · Aelle · Egbert I · Ricsige · Egbert II

Corn-wall

WESSEX: INE · ÆTHILHEARD · CUTHRED · Sigeberht · CYNEWULF · BEORHTRIC · EGBERT · (Athelstan) · ÆTHELWULF · ÆTHELBALD · ÆTHILBERHT · ÆTHELRED I · ALFRED

East Saxons: OFFA · Sælred · (Swebert) · Swith-red · Sige-ric · Sige-red

South Saxons: Nunna · Watt · Athel-stan · Ethel-bert · Osmund · Oswald · Oslac · Aldwulf

KENT: Wihtred · Eard-wulf · Eadbert · Ethel-bert II · Sigered · Ean-mund · Heabert · Egbert II · Eahl-mund · Eadbert · Baldred

Hwicce: Æthel-berht · Æthel-weard · Æthel-ric · Osred · Ean-berht · Uhtred · Ealdred

Magon-sætan: Merc-helm · Mild-frith

MERCIA: Æthelred · CENRED · CEOLRED · ÆTHELBALD · OFFA · Ecgfrith · CENWULF · Ceolwulf I · Beornwulf · Ludeca · WIGLAF · BEORHTWULF · BURGRED · Ceolwulf II · Æthelred & Æthelflæd

Lindsey: (Eatta) · Aldfrith

East Anglia: Aldwulf · Alfwold · Hun · Beonna · Alberht · Ethelred · Æthelberht · Athelstan · Ethelweard · EDMUND · ?Oswald · Guthrum

WALES: Arllechwedd · Arfon · LLeyn · POWYS · Ystrad Tywi · Ceredigion
Elise · Cadell · Cyngen (Powys) · Hywel · GWYN-EDD · Merfyn Frych · Cyngen · RHODRI MAWR · SEISY-LLWG · Gwygon

39 Kings and princes: chronology 700–880

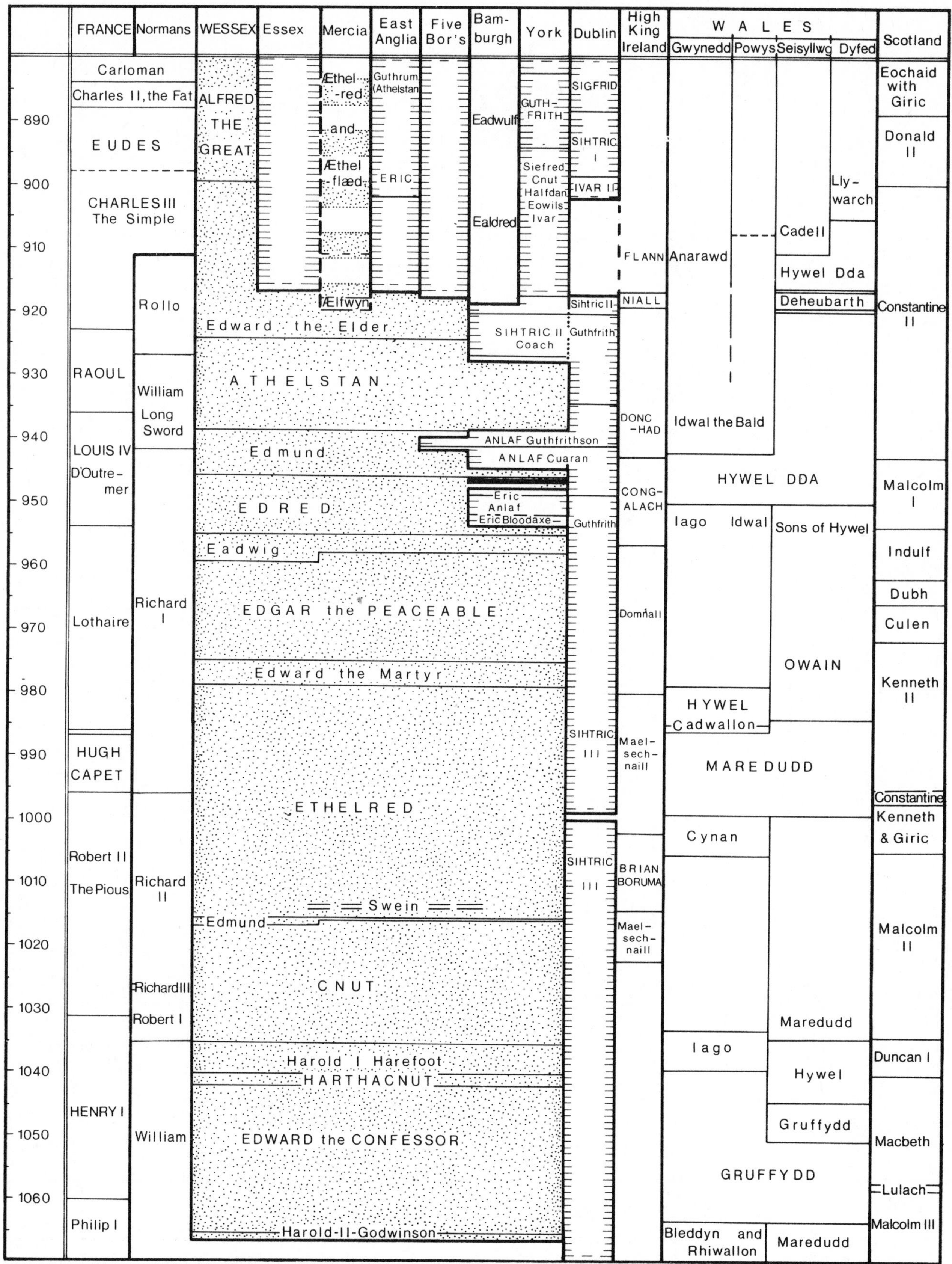

40 Kings and princes: chronology 880–1066

41 The England of Bede c.731. Places names from the **Ecclesiastical History**

The Events

From Bede to the Rise of Wessex (41–43)

The first century of the period covered by this atlas gives an appearance of great stability. Bede talks of an island in which the Anglo-Saxon portion was divided between a series of kingdoms, often referred to as the 'Heptarchy' under the sway or **imperium** of one kingdom (map **41**). The situation was by no means static but can overall be seen as the era of 'the supremacy of Mercia', the dominant kingdom (map **42**). The period does not lend itself to mapping but the itinerary of the Mercian kings is shown in map **145**; the disappearance of the minor kingdoms can be traced in outline in **39**; and places associated with the various campaigns can be found on maps **226–234**.

Essentially Anglo-Saxon England was divided between Northumbria and the area of Mercian domination, Southumbria, up until the reversal of Mercian fortunes following the battle of Ellendun in 825. There is still some dispute as to whether the collapse of Mercia was influenced by overcommitment to the campaigns and the final occupation of north Wales, but it cannot have been easy to conduct a war on two fronts nor to find the men both to hold down north Wales and to fight the West Saxons. The battle of Ellendun was to prove decisive as far as south-eastern England was concerned, as this became a permanent part of Wessex (map **43**). The submission of Mercia and of Northumbria, however, proved to be transitory. The final occupation by Wessex of Cornwall probably came with Athelstan but after the battle of Hingston Down in 838 the kings of Cornwall appear to have lost any freedom of action.

Two points should be made in relation to map **41** which shows England c. 731. First, in common with maps **27–30**, it reflects restrictions on the information available, or of interest to, Bede: the northern and eastern lands are well covered whilst the western and Celtic lands are ignored. The cluster of place names in Hampshire could, perhaps, be the result of the efforts of some particular correspondent of Bede's. Secondly, it is of interest for the study of the development of towns, to find that the nomenclature adopted for places was in the eighth century influenced more by their history than by their status. The appellation **civitas** was used for places with a known Roman ancestry, **urbs** for non-Roman towns. For a more accurate and extensive treatment see Campbell (1979, 52–3).

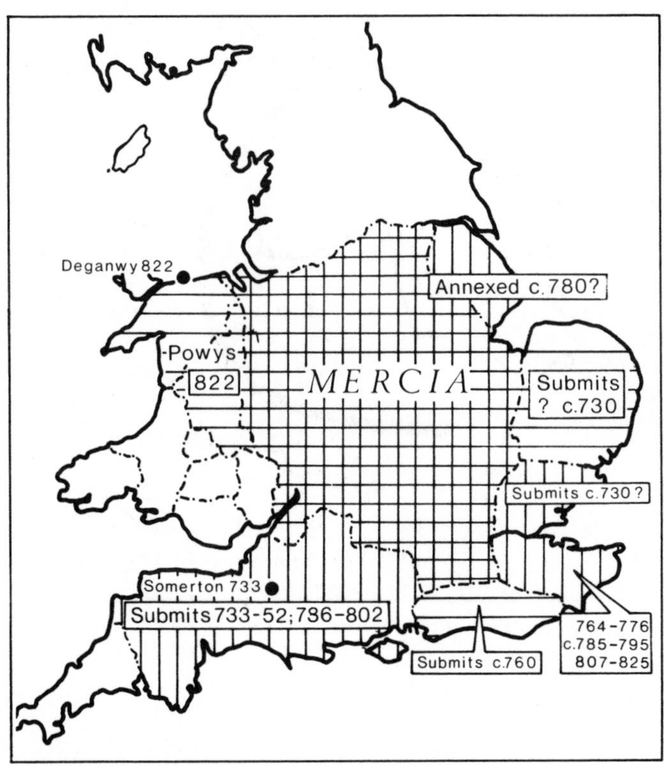

42 The supremacy of Mercia

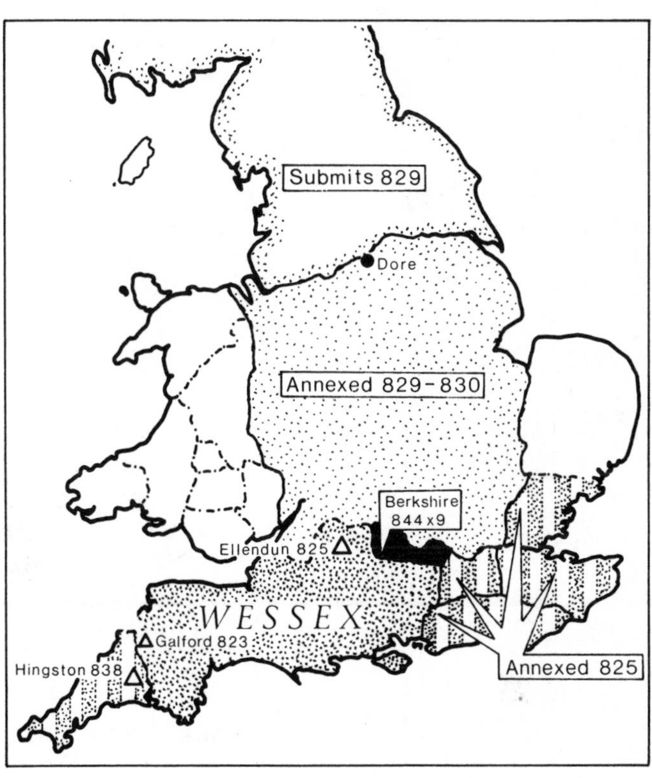

43 The rise of Wessex

The Vikings: Introduction (44–47)

It must be emphasized that this text makes no attempt to compete with the many excellent works dealing with the Vikings in Britain (Stenton 1971: Loyn 1977, etc.) or the large numbers of detailed studies of various aspects of their culture and impact (conveniently summarized in Wilson 1976, 393–404). These maps are a companion to such works, both insular and continental. Serious students should also consult, and evaluate, the series of important studies by A. P. Smyth (1975; 1977).

There were three Germanic groups in Europe — the Anglo-Saxons, the Continental Germans and the Scandinavians (map **44**). It was the latter group of Germanic peoples that expanded in this period and came to dominate Ango-Saxon history for more than two centuries. The Scandinavian expansion, loosely referred to as the 'Viking Age', had a great impact on the West and constitutes the dominant theme for the period 860 to 950 in England. The ramifications of the Viking impact cannot really be studied in isolation for England — even the British Isles is too limited an area. In fact, this study of the West European context could be criticized as too limited, for while the Vikings in eastern England were learning to come to terms with Edward the Elder, other Vikings were active on the shores of the Caspian. It is only possible to cover so much, and these Vikings have had to be left out, although, like Constantinople or Rome, they cannot be ignored by a student of Anglo-Saxon England.

During the whole of the period it is essential to bear in mind two factors. The first is the geographical separation of the Norse (Norwegian) areas of impact from the Danish areas. Dolley (1966) has illustrated their different areas of influence in the British Isles using coin finds (map **45**). Although there are areas of overlap on occasion (for example the early Norse expeditions to France before 820, or the Danish adventure linked with the name of Turgeis in Ireland in the 840s) the areas remain distinct. The same could be said for the Continent, for the line drawn by Dolley could be extended southwards so that mainland France is split, with the Loire and Brittany being, in the main, Norse and the Seine, Somme and Low Countries regions being Danish.

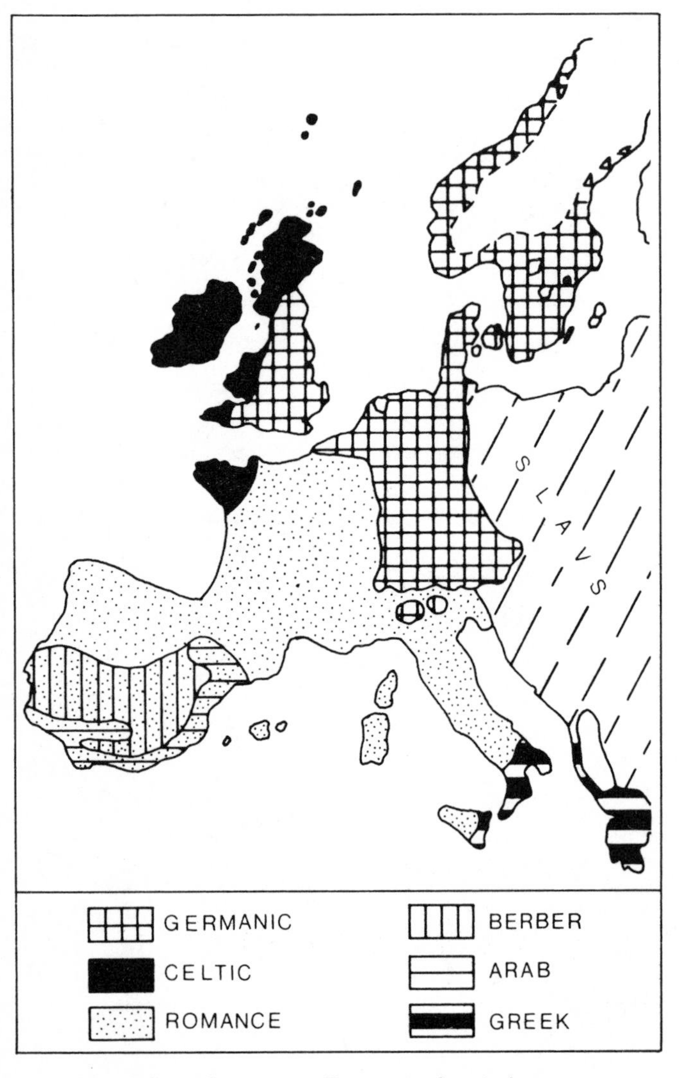

44 Ethnic divisions in Europe in the ninth century

45 Zones of Norse and Danish influence according to coin finds (after Dolley 1966)

KEY

△ Viking victory
▽ Viking defeat
□ Fort, Town, Winter quarters
▫ Non-viking fortification

	Germany-Low Countries	FRANCE	ENGLAND	IRELAND	WALES	Scotland	Northern Seas
780							
790							
			Lindisfarne				
			Donemuthan, MONKWEARMOUTH				
			Portland	Lambey	? Glamorgan	?Skye ?IONA	Years of the settlement of Orkney and Shetland
				Ulster, Inis Patrick		HEBRIDES	
	Frisian coast	Aquitaine					
800	Frisia	Charlemagne sets Guards	Tynemouth				
						Iona	
						Iona	
	Hedeby founded			INISMURRAY. SLIGO. ROSCOMMON		Kintyre	
		Pirates in the Channel					
810	Frisia						
		Charlemagne inspects defences	(Threat to Kent)	ULSTER			Faroes
				Connemara. West Coast. Lough			
				OWLESS			
820	Flanders	(repulsed on Seine) Aquitaine. Bouin					
				HOWTH. WEXFORD HARBOUR			
				CORK HARBOUR. BEGGARY ISLAND			DICUIL writes of Iceland and Faroes
				BANGOR			
				Skellig Michael, Bangor (Ards)			
				▽ULSTER △INIS-DAIMHLE		Iona	
				LOUTH: BREGH: LUSCA		Dalriada	
				FERNS; ULSTER			
830		▫Abb. of Noirmoutier builds Castrum				Abb. of IONA flees to Ireland	
				CONAILLI; LOUTH			
				ARMAGH: General pillaging in North			
				▽DERRY: CLONDALKIN; DROMISKIN			
	Frisia, Dorestadt, Utrecht			GLENDALOUGH: Slane; Fennor;			
	Dorestadt	Noirmoutier	Sheppey	Mungarit: Ormond: Dromin; Ferns			
	Frisia; Antwerp; Dorestadt		▽Carhampton	Bregh: Connacht: Tipperary: N. Deisi			
	Dorestadt; Walcheren			Fleet on Boyne: Bregh: Ui-Neill; Dublin			
	FLEET WRECKED OFF FRISIA		▽Hingston Down	△CONNACHT			
	Saxony			□LOUGH NEAGH: Ferris; All north: CORK		△Fortrenn	
840		Rouen, Seine	▽Southampton △Portland	□LOUGH NEAGH: LOUTH. ARMAGH			
		Rouen	Romney M.; Lindsey; E.Anglia; Kent	□Lough Neagh; □DUBLIN – Annagassan			
		Quentovic, Pas de Calais ⇒	London; Rochester; Southampton	FOUR FLEETS: CLONMACNOISE			
		Nantes; Noirmoutier	△Carhampton				
		SPAIN Aquitaine Quentovic		□Lough Ree, Clonfert		From Cluny to Dunkeld	
	Hamburg	Saintes Paris	▽Parret ▽Sandwich	Clonmacnoise: Lorrha: Terryglass			
	Frisia; Dorestadt	Noirmoutier; Aquitaine		Colooney; Baislic: △CONNACHT			
	Rhine	Brittany; Melle		IMLEACH – IUBHAIR		Tribute paid	
		Bordeaux		▽FORACH ▽Tomhrain killed ▽CORK			
		Perigueux		DUBLIN raided. 140 ships arrive			
850	Walcheren Fief	Somme: Seine; Therouanne ⇒	□Thanet Wrekin	Allied with Connacht (Danes)	S.WALES		
	Frisia; Ghent Saxony	Rouen; Beauvais; -	CANTERBURY: LONDON ▽Aclea	DUBLIN TAKEN BY DANES			
	Frisia; Scheldt	Seine; Beauvais; □Givoldi		Danes beat Norse (Carlingford L.)	Cyngen slain		
		Nantes; Noirmoutier	△Thanet	NORSE REGAIN CONTROL: Ulidians			
	Frisia; Saxony	Blois; Orleans; Tours; Angers					
	Frisia	Poitiers; Aquitaine Seine	□Sheppey	LOUGH CENDIN	Anglesey		
		Orleans; Tours; Blois Seine □Jeufosse		▽Glenn-Foichle: Lusca			
		Blois; Tours Seine; Paris		MUNSTER;			
	Frisia; Utrecht; Saxony	Dives; Chartres Bayeux; Evreux		ARRA			
	Frisia; Scheldt	Noyon; St.Valery; Amiens; Rhone; Beauvais		MEATH: MUNSTER			
860	Rhine	Nieuport; St.Bertin; Yser; Valence Somme ⇒	▽Winchester	▽WATERFORD			
		Therouanne; St.Omer, Paris □Oissel; Seine		MEATH			
	Saxony; Frisia	▫Pont de l'Arche Marne; Meaux; St. Feron		MEATH			
	Cologne; Dorestad □Nuits	Poitiers; Anjou; Garonne; Charente		NAS (Kildare) BOYNE VALLEY TOMBS			
	(Dorestadt flooded) Saxony	Aquitaine; Toulouse; St. Hilaire; Clermont	Thanet	CLONARD		FORTRIU	
		Chartres; Bourges; Poitiers; Orleans; Paris ⇒	East Anglia GREAT ARMY				
	□Yssel	Le Mans; Melun	York	▽LOUGH FEBHAIL; Aedh plunders Norse		PICTS	
	Rorik driven out of FRISIA	Bourges	△York; Mercia; □Nottingham			FORTRIU	
		Orleans ▫Le Mans & Tours fortified Charles the Bald	SIEGE OF NOTTINGHAM □York	▽CILL-Ua-nDAIGHRI		Strathclyde	
		▽Poitou	△Hoxne East Anglia □Thetford	ARMAGH			

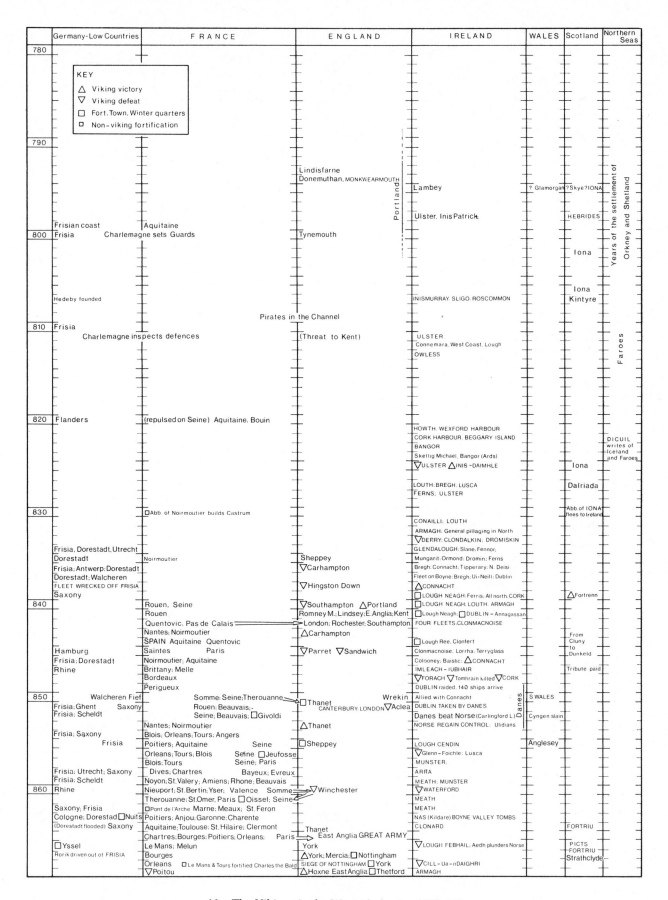

46 The Vikings in the West: chronology 780–869

The second factor is that many enterprises are linked together under the name **Viking**. To quote Brøndsted (1965, 31):

The Viking raids were inspired by several motives. On that account a mere chronological account of them would produce an obscure and contradictory pattern, and an attempt must therefore be made to classify them according to their varying motives and objectives. The Swedish scholar, Fritz Askeberg, has proposed a fourfold classification:

(1) Pirate raids conducted by individuals
(2) Political expeditions
(3) Colonizing ventures
(4) Commercial penetration

Such a division, as Askeberg himself points out, cannot be universally applicable, and many of the raids doubtless proceeded from mixed motives. But, so long as it is remembered that this classification is in no sense a chronological one, it serves to put the Viking period into perspective.

To some extent at least, these categories are modified by the Norse/Danish division: the scale of the Danish raids appears to have been larger, the raids involved greater numbers of participants, and more often than not the Danes when settling appeared to aim to take over as a ruling class. The Danes apparently attempted to gain some form of title to their lands, in the case of the Continent by taking the lands as fiefs from the emperor or king, in England by setting up, at least initially, a puppet king through whom they ruled.

The charts showing the chronology of the Vikings in the West (**46** and **47**) are, of necessity, simplified but together with the maps that follow they attempt to give some general picture of the ebb and flow of events in the West. What emerges very strongly is the interrelation of events in one country with events in another. For the Norse sphere of influence, the **Landnama** is closely linked to the 'forty years' rest' in Ireland, and periods of activity in France are periods of comparative rest in England. Thus the Great Army which comes together about 835 with the attacks on Frisia, moves to France and then to England, in each case leaving a period of rest behind it. Sometimes, as in the period 878 to 895, each move can be linked with a reverse in one country leading the Great Army to move on to fresh, and possibly easier, pastures. Although there is little evidence that the Great Army was used as an official title, on a par with Napoleon's **Grande Armée**, it is a useful concept for the principal conjunction of Danish forces, greater than the armies on the Seine, Somme or Loire. It is important to note that the army drew recruits from Scandinavian or Viking settlements, and that reinforcements, not being centrally directed, tended to follow success. Thus the Reconquest of the Danelaw made that area unpalatable to fresh Vikings just at the time that the settlement and expansion of Normandy drew recruits. The whole region was interlocked.

The army usually stayed in the West: it did not return home but consisted of groups who found their way West, joined, fought, made money, left and settled. The 'summer army' was a different, and rarer, phenomenon of lesser import. Although it did occasionally emerge, presumably largely though not exclusively from a Scandinavian base, the general weight of attack, certainly from 860, was from the army in the West. It is unlikely that armies of the size active at this time would have been welcome if they had returned **en bloc** to Scandinavia, several hundred ship-loads strong, practised in war, rich with booty, and led by men with royal pretensions. A returning army could be a most disruptive influence on the kingdoms of Scandinavia.

In the classic phase of Viking attacks on England, 830–95, the armies sailed not from Scandinavia but from France, Frisia or Ireland, and they can be recognized as groups operating there.

In the charts it should be noted that the right-hand side — covering Ireland, Wales, Scotland and the Northern Seas — deals in the main, with the area of Norse activity. The same symbols are used on both maps and charts in the following sections.

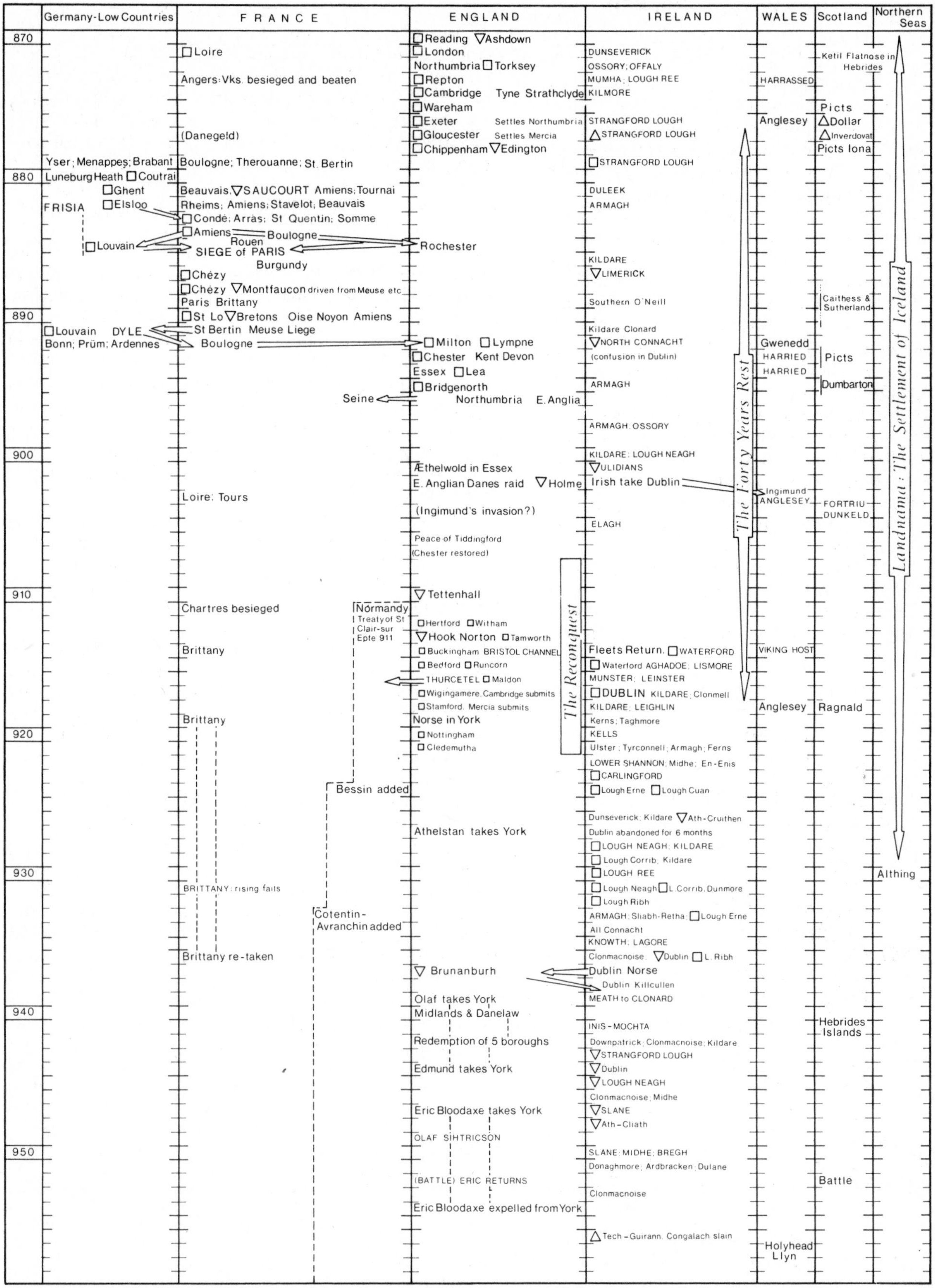

	Germany-Low Countries	FRANCE	ENGLAND	IRELAND	WALES	Scotland	Northern Seas
870			☐Reading ▽Ashdown				
871		☐Loire	☐London	DUNSEVERICK			
872			Northumbria ☐Torksey	OSSORY; OFFALY		Ketil Flatnose in Hebrides	
873		Angers: Vks. besieged and beaten	☐Repton	MUMHA; LOUGH REE	HARRASSED		
874			☐Cambridge Tyne Strathclyde	KILMORE			
875			☐Wareham			Picts	
876			☐Exeter Settles Northumbria	STRANGFORD LOUGH	Anglesey	△Dollar	
877		(Danegeld)	☐Gloucester Settles Mercia	△STRANGFORD LOUGH		△Inverdovat	
878			☐Chippenham ▽Edington			Picts Iona	
879	Yser; Menappes; Brabant	Boulogne; Therouanne; St. Bertin		☐STRANGFORD LOUGH			
880	Luneburg Heath ☐Coutrai						
881	☐Ghent	Beauvais ▽SAUCOURT Amiens; Tournai		DULEEK			
882	FRISIA ☐Elsloo	Rheims; Amiens; Stavelot; Beauvais		ARMAGH			
883		☐Condé; Arras; St Quentin; Somme					
884		☐Amiens Boulogne Rouen					
885	☐Louvain	SIEGE of PARIS	Rochester				
886		Burgundy		KILDARE			
887		☐Chézy		▽LIMERICK			
888		☐Chézy ▽Montfaucon driven from Meuse etc					
889		Paris Brittany		Southern O'Neill		Caithess & Sutherland	
890		☐St Lo ▽Bretons Oise Noyon Amiens					
891	☐Louvain DYLE	St Bertin Meuse Liege		Kildare Clonard			
892	Bonn; Prüm; Ardennes	Boulogne	☐Milton ☐Lympne	▽NORTH CONNACHT	Gwenedd		
893			☐Chester Kent Devon	(confusion in Dublin)	HARRIED	Picts	
894			Essex ☐Lea		HARRIED		
895			☐Bridgenorth	ARMAGH		Dumbarton	
896		Seine	Northumbria E. Anglia				
898				ARMAGH: OSSORY			
900				KILDARE: LOUGH NEAGH			
901			Æthelwold in Essex	▽ULIDIANS			
902			E. Anglian Danes raid ▽Holme	Irish take Dublin			
903		Loire: Tours			Ingimund ANGLESEY	FORTRIU	
904			(Ingimund's invasion?)			DUNKELD	
905				ELAGH			
906			Peace of Tiddingford				
907			(Chester restored)				
910			▽Tettenhall				
911		Chartres besieged; Normandy Treaty of St Clair-sur Epte 911					
912			☐Hertford ☐Witham				
913			▽Hook Norton ☐Tamworth				
914		Brittany	☐Buckingham BRISTOL CHANNEL	Fleets Return. ☐WATERFORD	VIKING HOST		
915			☐Bedford ☐Runcorn	☐Waterford AGHADOE; LISMORE			
916			THURCETEL ☐Maldon	MUNSTER; LEINSTER			
917			☐Wigingamere. Cambridge submits	☐DUBLIN KILDARE; Clonmell			
918			☐Stamford. Mercia submits	KILDARE; LEIGHLIN	Anglesey	Ragnald	
919		Brittany	Norse in York	Kerns; Taghmore			
920			☐Nottingham	KELLS			
921			☐Cledemutha	Ulster; Tyrconnell; Armagh; Ferns			
922				LOWER SHANNON; Midhe; En-Enis			
923				☐CARLINGFORD			
924		Bessin added		☐Lough Erne ☐Lough Cuan			
926				Dunseverick; Kildare ▽Ath-Cruithen			
927			Athelstan takes York	Dublin abandoned for 6 months			
928				☐LOUGH NEAGH; KILDARE			
929				☐Lough Corrib; Kildare			
930				☐LOUGH REE			Althing
931		BRITTANY: rising fails		☐Lough Neagh ☐L. Corrib, Dunmore			
932				☐Lough Ribh			
933		Cotentin-Avranchin added		ARMAGH: Sliabh-Retha; ☐Lough Erne			
934				All Connacht			
935				KNOWTH; LAGORE			
936		Brittany re-taken		Clonmacnoise; ▽Dublin ☐L. Ribh			
937			▽ Brunanburh	Dublin Norse			
938				Dublin Killcullen			
939			Olaf takes York	MEATH to CLONARD			
940			Midlands & Danelaw				
941				INIS-MOCHTA		Hebrides Islands	
942			Redemption of 5 boroughs	Downpatrick; Clonmacnoise; Kildare			
943				▽STRANGFORD LOUGH			
944			Edmund takes York	▽Dublin			
945				▽LOUGH NEAGH			
946				Clonmacnoise; Midhe			
947			Eric Bloodaxe takes York	▽SLANE			
948				▽Ath-Cliath			
949			OLAF SIHTRICSON				
950				SLANE; MIDHE; BREGH			
951				Donaghmore; Ardbracken; Dulane			
952			(BATTLE) ERIC RETURNS			Battle	
953				Clonmacnoise			
954			Eric Bloodaxe expelled from York				
956				△Tech-Guirann. Congalach slain			
957					Holyhead Llyn		

The Reconquest

The Forty Years Rest

Landnama: The Settlement of Iceland

47 The Vikings in the West: chronology 870–959

The Vikings in the West c. 789–850 (48–53)

The Viking Age opened with the contact of the Norse with the West. It seems apparent that they were using two routes, the most important being from Norway to Faroes, Shetland, Orkney, Western Isles and the western seaway. Although they occasionally probed the coasts of Frisia, England and France, the brunt of the attacks was taken by Ireland. It is quite possible that the Norse/Norwegian interest in the Loire area stemmed from their discovery that Irish trade was moving from southern Ireland to the saltpans around the coast of Aquitaine and the Vikings followed that established route which led them circuitously to France. The following of established paths and possibly using guides, as well as collecting sailing instructions, accounts for several 'discoveries', including, perhaps, Iceland.

The distribution of the raids in England at this period, together with the lesser problem of those in Wales, gives the impression that for the first forty years of the Danish and Norse raids England was a calm centre in a storm. This may well be a mistaken impression. The evidence from the chronicles is slim for the decades of Viking activity to 850 (compare **37**). The evidence from the one or two existing charters of the period does indicate threats to Kent in the first decades of the ninth century, as well as piracy in the Channel. There is a later record of heathens in the area of the Wrekin. These references alone should warn us of the sketchy nature of the Chronicle record.

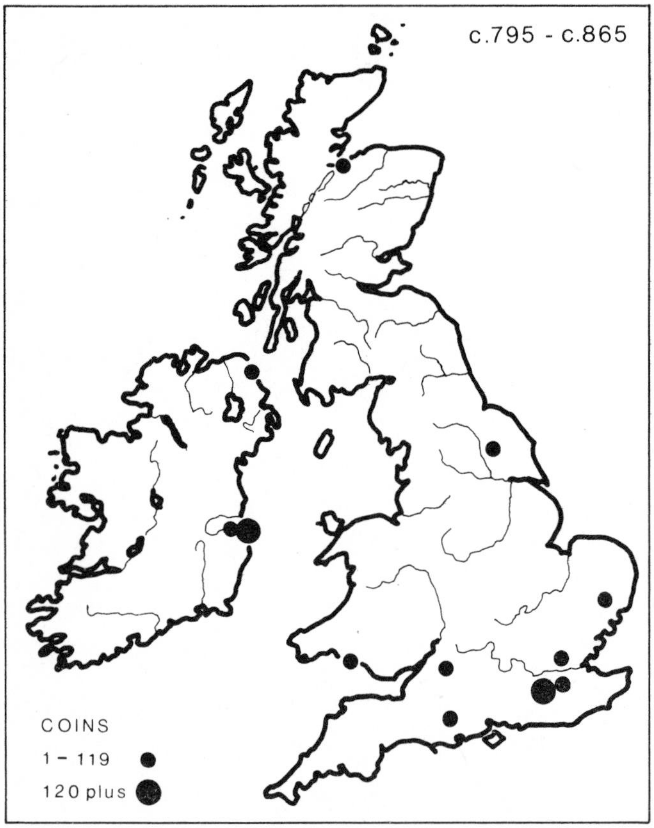

There is another form of evidence for the effect of the Vikings: the hoards of coins deposited, and not subsequently recovered by their owners, in the ninth and tenth centuries (map **48**). The deposition of these hoards may not always be linked to threats of war, for hoards are certainly also deposited in times of peace, but their increase is linked to times of uncertainty. Michael Dolley (1966) has carried out some very interesting research on these coin hoards and the patterns revealed certainly show that the general shape of the Chronicle account is right. It should be remembered that there is an increase in coin use during the whole of this period, resulting in more coin being available to hoard, and an increase in the areas (particularly in Ireland) using coin. Therefore we must expect more hoards at the end of the period than at the beginning.

The response of Charlemagne to the Vikings was vigorous: two of his tours of inspection are shown on map **49**, indicating that he saw the narrow seas as the point of greater danger. His use of coastal defence (beacons, fleets and forts) was to be followed fitfully by many Western rulers in the ensuing years.

Although the Danes had figured largely in the politics and diplomacy of Charlemagne and of Louis the Pious and although to read the chronicles of their reigns it would seem that the extensive coastal defences and fleets were built against them it is clear that the bulk of the campaigning in the West was Norse until about 834. The campaigns in Ireland increased in the 830s and it is to these campaigns we must look for a context to Hingston Down and Carhampton (map **50**). The attack on Sheppey on the other hand was an overspill from Frisia. The Frisian campaigns were a new departure and the defences were clearly overrun. The raids moved through the Straits of Dover.

The new era in Viking raids began with the sacking of Rouen in 840 (map **51**), and from this date we can detect a change in the character of Viking attack, with a pattern of widespread raiding on major centres, of considerable forays inland and of bases in the West either on islands or on rivers (map **52**). It should be noted that this new phase came after fifty years of very minor activity on the part of the Vikings, except in Ireland — and even there the raids had been minor compared with what was to follow.

For the British Isles the interaction of Viking raids in the West as a whole is vital. Some of the Viking adventures are of great interest, and invested with romance but of no significance for the Anglo-Saxons. The Greenland/Vinland expeditions, for example, are justly famous — but of no import to our studies. The well-known episodes in the Mediterranean may in fact only consist of three expeditions. That of 858–59 was the famous raid that continued into southern France and to Luna in Italy. The greatest impact of the Mediterranean adventures was in Moorish Spain (map **53**) where the Arabs reacted by founding a series of fortifications which have been identified by their **rapita** place names.

With the sacking of Paris in 845 the second phase of Viking raids was firmly under way (map **52**). The Norse were still active in the Western Isles and Ireland but it

48 Hoards of coins deposited c.795–c.865

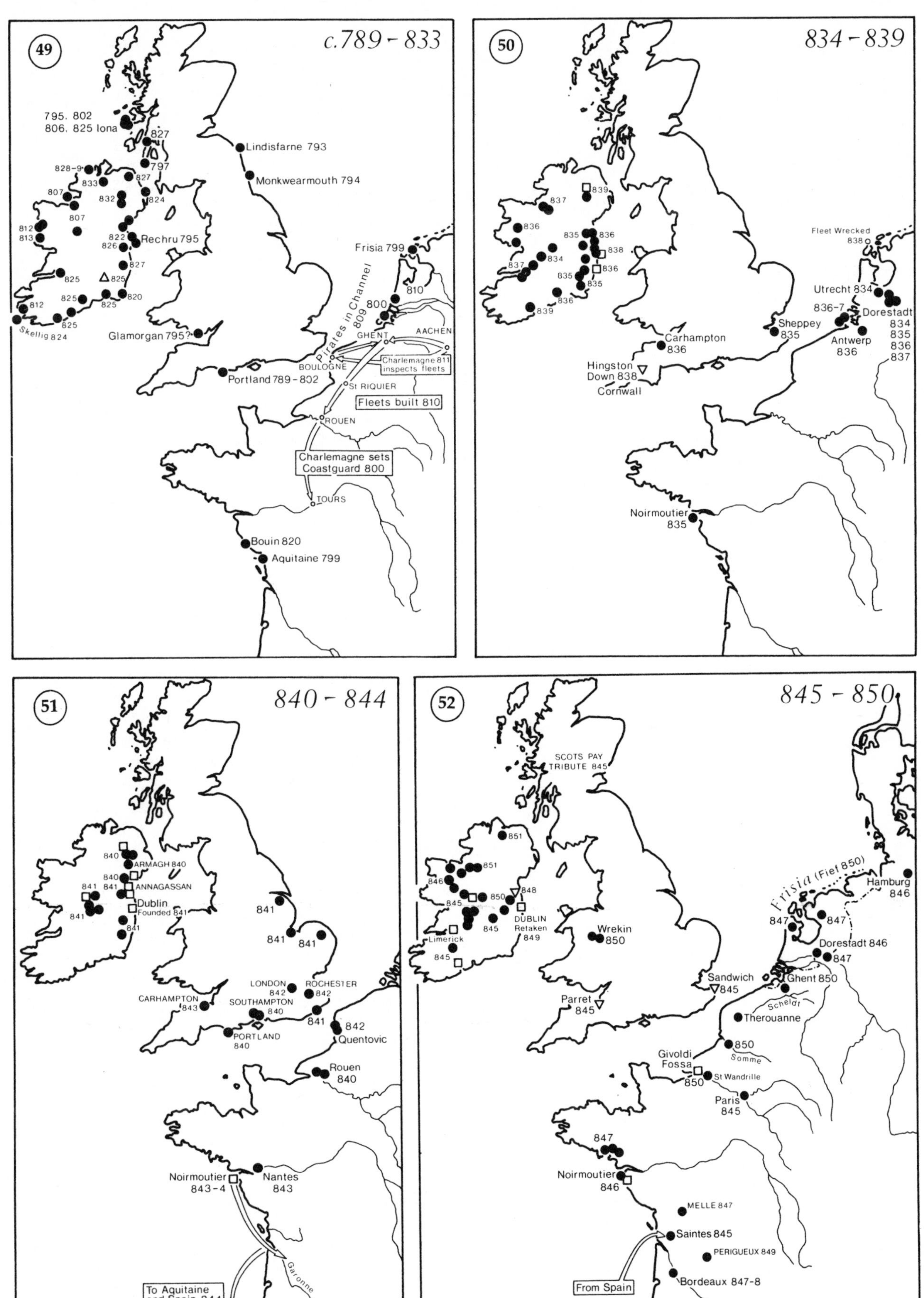
49
c.789 – 833
795. 802
806. 825 Iona
827
Lindisfarne 793
797
828–9
833
827
Monkwearmouth 794
807
832
824
807
812
813
822
826
Rechru 795
827
825
825
825
820
825
812
825
Skellig 824
Glamorgan 795?
Frisia 799
Pirates in Channel 809
810
800
GHENT
AACHEN
BOULOGNE
Charlemagne 811 inspects fleets
Portland 789 - 802
St RIQUIER
Fleets built 810
ROUEN
Charlemagne sets Coastguard 800
TOURS
Bouin 820
Aquitaine 799
50
834 – 839
839
837
836
835
836
838
834
836
837
835
835
836
839
Fleet Wrecked 838
Utrecht 834
836–7
Dorestadt
834
835
836
837
Sheppey 835
Antwerp 836
Carhampton 836
Hingston Down 838
Cornwall
Noirmoutier 835
51
840 – 844
840
ARMAGH 840
840
841 841
ANNAGASSAN
841
Dublin Founded 841
841
841
841
841
LONDON 842
ROCHESTER 842
CARHAMPTON 843
SOUTHAMPTON 840
841
842
Quentovic
PORTLAND 840
Rouen 840
Noirmoutier 843-4
Nantes 843
Garonne
To Aquitaine and Spain 844
52
845 – 850
SCOTS PAY TRIBUTE 845
851
851
846
850
848
845
DUBLIN Retaken 849
845
Limerick
845
Wrekin 850
Frisia (Fiet 850)
Hamburg 846
847
847
Dorestadt 846
847
Sandwich 845
Ghent 850
Scheldt
Parret 845
Therouanne
850
Somme
Givoldi Fossa 850
St Wandrille
Paris 845
847
Noirmoutier 846
MELLE 847
Saintes 845
PERIGUEUX 849
From Spain
Bordeaux 847-8

49–52 The Vikings in the West c.789–850. For key to symbols on these and later Viking maps, see **46**

was the Danish semi-permanent armies operating from bases that were typical of this phase. There were also a number of armies in the Seine and Loire (and in the Somme a little later) which, together with the lack of fixed purpose on the part of the Carolingians, gave the second phase its character.

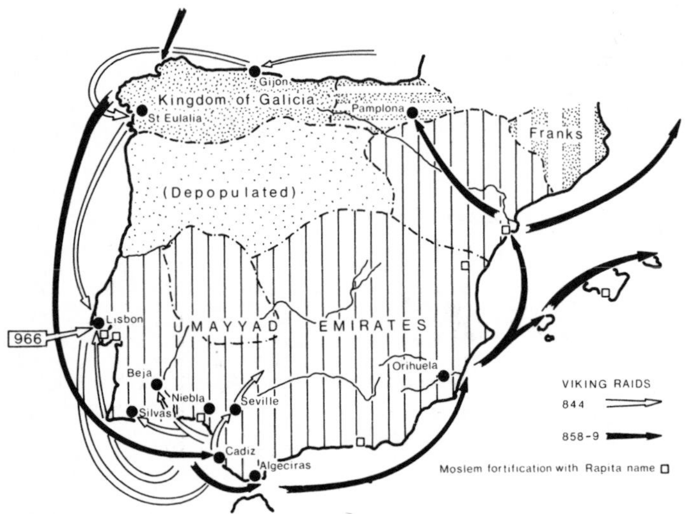

53 The Vikings in Spain

The Vikings in the West 851–878 (54–57)

The Danish armies roamed widely over the West and finally came into conflict with the Norse in Ireland in 851 (map **54**). Here the Vikings were distinguished as the 'black foreigners' (the Danes) and the 'white foreigners' (the Norse). At this stage it is already possible to discern the beginning of a process that was to absorb the Vikings into Irish life as the 'Hiberno-Norse', Vikings who had never seen Scandinavia and who came to dominate Irish commercial life. In the battles between Dane and Norwegian the native Irish came to take part as allies and to raid their Celtic neighbours for a share of the booty.

There had already been some raids into England by the Danes but they appear to have led to reverses which helped to keep England clear of the armies. The activities of the Norse are probably in evidence in the west of England. Yet it is possible that the full tally of raids has not been passed down to us. For the latter half of the 850s (map **55**) attention was concentrated on the campaigns in the Seine and the Somme where Carolingian resistance was at its most feeble. Although the bases at Jeufosse and Oissel were deep inside Carolingian territory, there seems to have been no concerted effort to dislodge them. This failure is usually attributed to the internecine struggles of the Carolingian Royal House: it has been said that to Charles the Bald, fighting for his throne against his brothers, the attacks of the Danes were like the buzzing of a wasp in the hair of a man being strangled. Yet the effects on trade, the towns, the peasantry, tax returns, in fact on every form of life in this, the richest part of France (compare map **211**) must have been considerable.

The overspill of Danes into England is shown by the raid of 860 when the Danes on the Somme were paid to attack and remove those on the Seine. Instead they sailed for England and attacked Winchester before sailing to the Seine. The northern armies were drawn off in 866 to England (map **56**), the result for France being a period of eleven years during which northern France had a respite and only the mainly Norse Loire army was active (map **57**). A significant factor accounting for these movements was Charles the Bald's vigorous defence of his realm before the fleets sailed for England. The series of bridge works at Pont de l'Arche, les Ponts de Cé and elsewhere were only part of his efforts — efforts which often failed but which certainly contributed to the increasing difficulties facing the Danes.

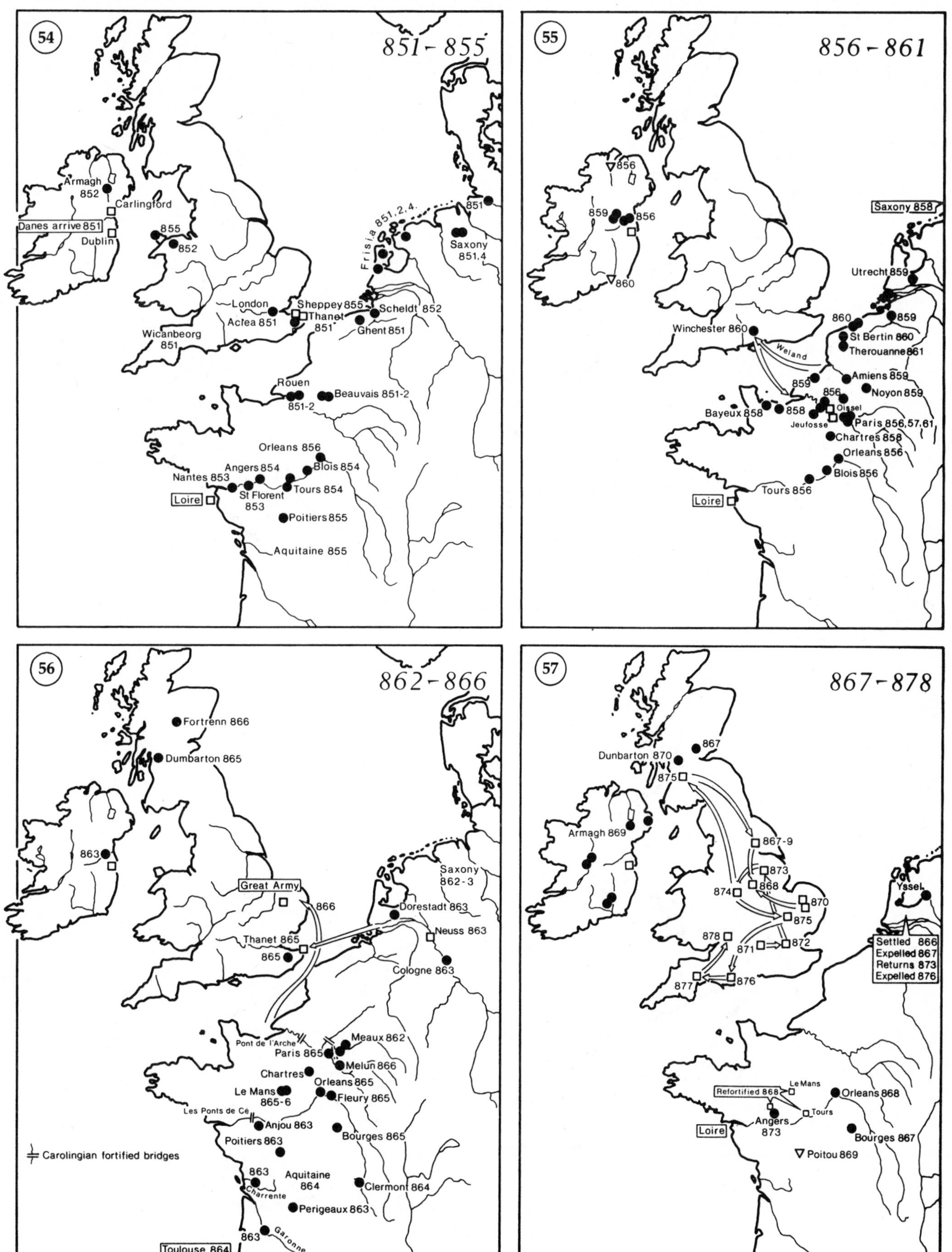

54–57 The Vikings in the West 851–878

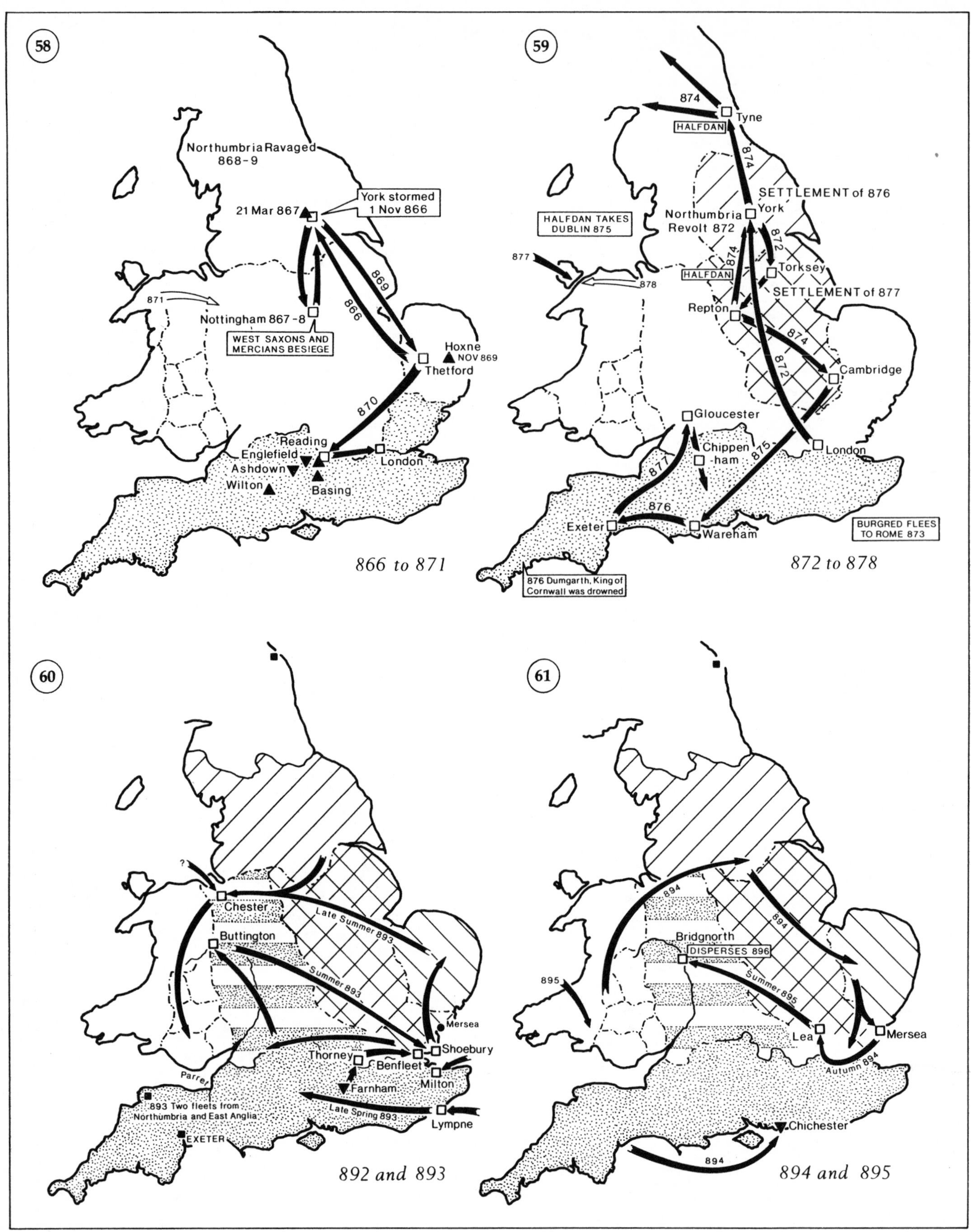

58–61 The Vikings in England 866–895

The Vikings in England 866–895 (58–61)

No part of the Anglo-Saxon story is better known than the epic of Alfred the Great and the Danes: it is well covered in Stenton and in most other general works, and most of the evidence is contained in Asser and the Chronicle which can be read easily and consecutively. While it is not necessary to recount the events here, certain points need to be stressed. The account we have is Wessex based and throws little light on the role of Mercia, particularly in the early stages, nor on the transfer of power in Mercia to the West Saxons. The Danes' intention of becoming the ruling elite is shown by their appointment of puppet rulers in at least three kingdoms: only later did they start to farm the land. Even then the role of Danish peasant farmers may have been limited, unlike the Norse whose peasant farming can be detected in the north and west at a later date.

The political impact of the Danish wars (maps **58** and **59**) was immense. By the close of 879 the map of England had been transformed: the south and west were Saxon; soon (probably by 880, certainly soon after) to be West Saxon was the protected state of the Ealdormanry of Mercia; the east and central northern areas were a series of Danish states, namely East Anglia, Danish Mercia and York; and in the far north the rump of the Kingdom of Northumbria, known to the Irish at least as being ruled by the King of the North Saxons, known to the West Saxons (and through their writings to posterity) as ruled by the Ealdorman of Bamburgh.

The final set of raids (maps **60** and **61**) was more spectacular than damaging. Close investigation shows them to be the raids of an army that had split many times, lost many men to the new settlements and been defeated in a series of battles from Ethandun to Saucourt and the Dyle. The campaigns consisted of armies operating in the marginal land of Essex, where their bases were built after moving from the south-east. The raids then swept across the whole of middle England. The apparent ease with which the raiders moved is deceptive for they were always travelling along the no-man's-land between the new Danish settlements and the lands controlled by the West Saxons. The West Saxon heartland had already been fortified by a series of **burhs** (fortified centres) and the army of King Alfred had been reorganized. Although the process of **burh**-building is not well documented for these years, it was certainly going on. Charles the Bald had similarly been re-fortifying towns in 868 and indeed this had been a general response against the Vikings throughout the area: the **rapitas** in Spain, the **burhs** in Wessex, the fortified bridges and towns in the lands of Charles the Bald are all evidence of the same trend. It may well be that the obsession of the Chronicle with the movements of the Danish army in France from 878 to 892 stemmed from anxiety as the West Saxons raced to complete their fortifications before the next blow fell.

The Vikings in the West 879–896 (62–64)

The Vikings who left for France in 879 were only part of the Danish armies and they had suffered a serious reverse in England. The movements of this army in the next twelve years were those of a body of men now known to be fallible (map **62**). Although they devastated large parts of the north of France and a new army in 880 and in 883 had successes in the lands of the East Franks, they also received disastrous checks at Saucourt and the Dyle, from the Bretons and in front of Paris (map **63**). When they finally re-entered England they were a very battered force and even the arrival of an army from the Loire to assist them was less hopeful than at first appeared for they too were defeated before they set out (map **64**).

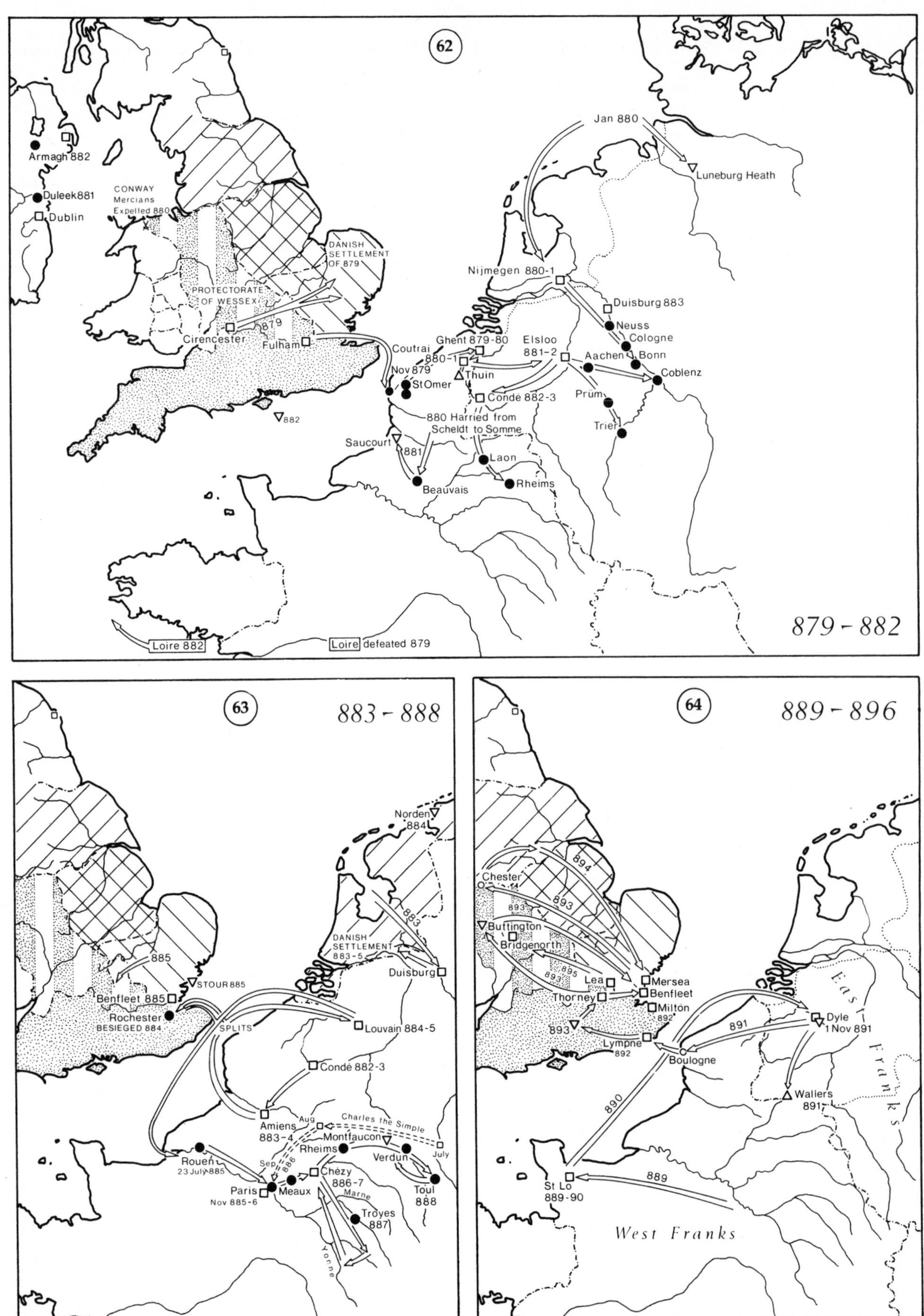
62
879 - 882
Jan 880
Luneburg Heath
Armagh 882
Duleek 881
Dublin
CONWAY
Mercians
Expelled 880
DANISH
SETTLEMENT
OF 879
PROTECTORATE
OF WESSEX
879
Cirencester
Fulham
Nijmegen 880-1
Duisburg 883
Neuss
Cologne
Bonn
Coblenz
Aachen
Elsloo
881-2
Ghent 879-80
880-1
Coutrai
Nov 879
St Omer
Thuin
Conde 882-3
Prum
Trier
882
880 Harried from
Scheldt to Somme
Saucourt
881
Beauvais
Laon
Rheims
Loire 882
Loire defeated 879
63
883 - 888
Norden
884
883
DANISH
SETTLEMENT
883-5
Duisburg
885
STOUR 885
Benfleet 885
Rochester
BESIEGED 884
SPLITS
Louvain 884-5
Conde 882-3
Amiens
883-4
Aug
Charles the Simple
July
Montfaucon
Rheims
Verdun
Toul
888
Sep
886
Rouen
23 July 885
Paris
Nov 885-6
Meaux
Chezy
886-7
Marne
Troyes
887
Yonne
64
889 - 896
894
Chester
893
893
Buttington
Bridgenorth
895
893
Lea
Mersea
Benfleet
Milton
892
Thorney
893
Lympne
892
Boulogne
891
Dyle
1 Nov 891
East Franks
Wallers
891
890
St Lo
889-90
889
West Franks

62–64 The Vikings in the West 879–896

Scandinavian Coins and Graves (65–67)

The Scandinavian settlement of large parts of England was in general a short-lived phenomenon. Nevertheless, when the last Viking kingdom disappeared in 954, real and long-lasting effects were to be seen, not in independent Danish kingdoms, but in the settlement of peoples with language, laws and a separate form of organization loosely referred to as the Danelaw. The limits of the Danelaw are very hard to fix (see maps **174–177**) but some of the results of the settlement can be charted.

The northern settlements do show quite well on the map of coin hoards listed by Dolley (map **65**), the Yorkshire area being particularly well represented. The strangest point to emerge from Dolley's listings is the lack of material from Ireland, from which one can only deduce that the 'forty years' rest' was a time of limited activity in the area. (For a full discussion of the hoard material see Dolley (1966) and several more recent articles by the same author.)

When the comparative material from the Continent is considered (map **66**) the number of graves in Britain looks more impressive. There are only two inhumations (a man at Antum and a woman at Pitres) and a cremated ship-burial in the Cruguel mound on the Ile de Groix.

The distribution of Scandinavian artefacts is surprisingly limited and consists of very few finds; the number of burials (map **67**) is small, particularly for the area of Danelaw, although the small number of pagan burials of the Viking Age may suggest the swift adoption of Christian practices or at least of Christian burial places by the Viking settlers (Wilson 1976, 394).

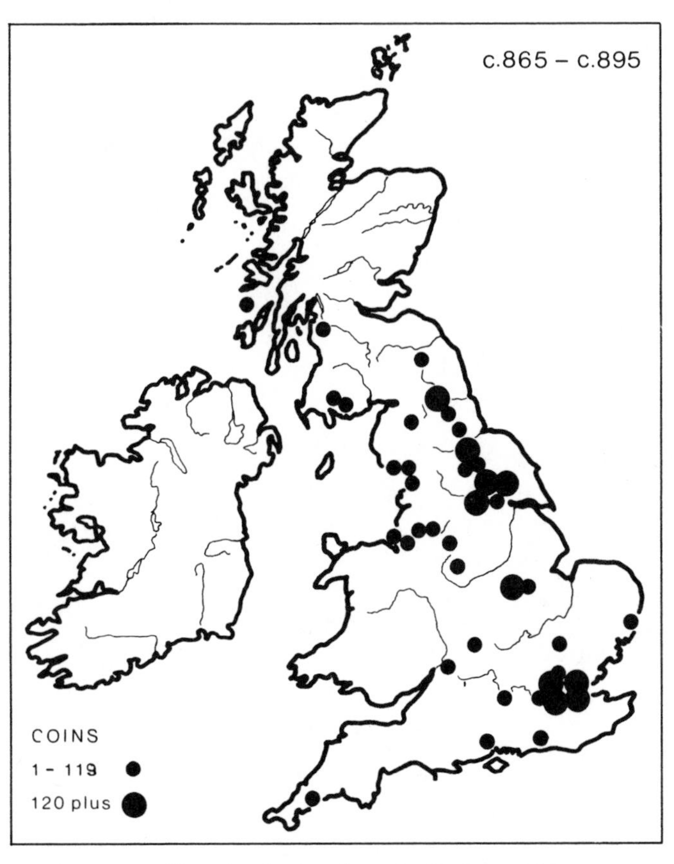

65 Hoards of coins deposited c.865–c.895

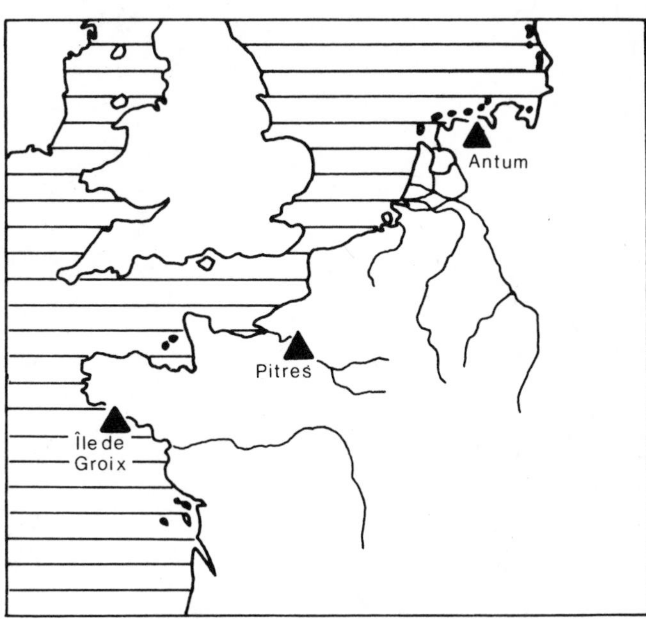

66 Viking graves in western Europe

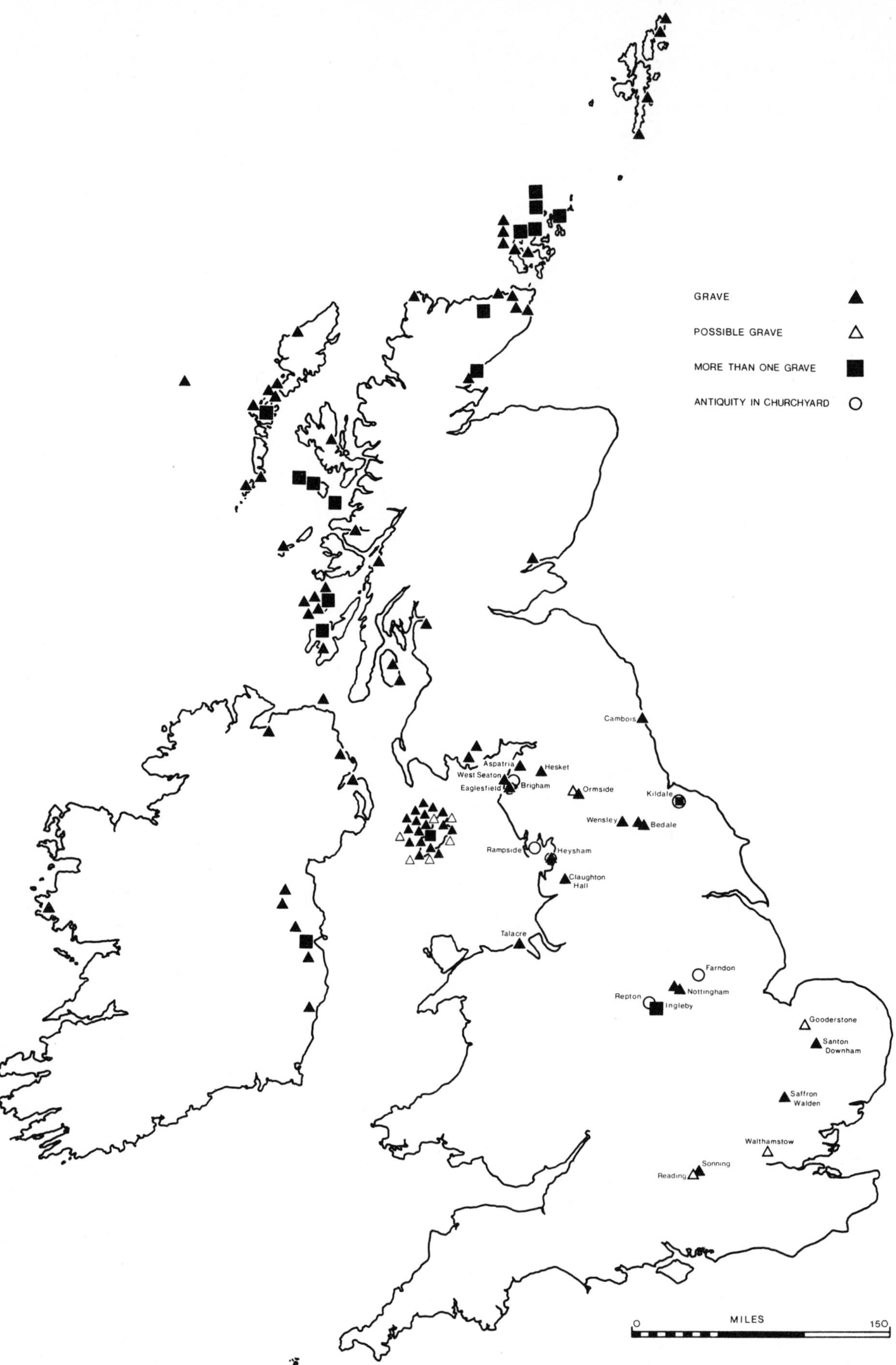

67 Scandinavian graves of the Viking age (after Wilson)

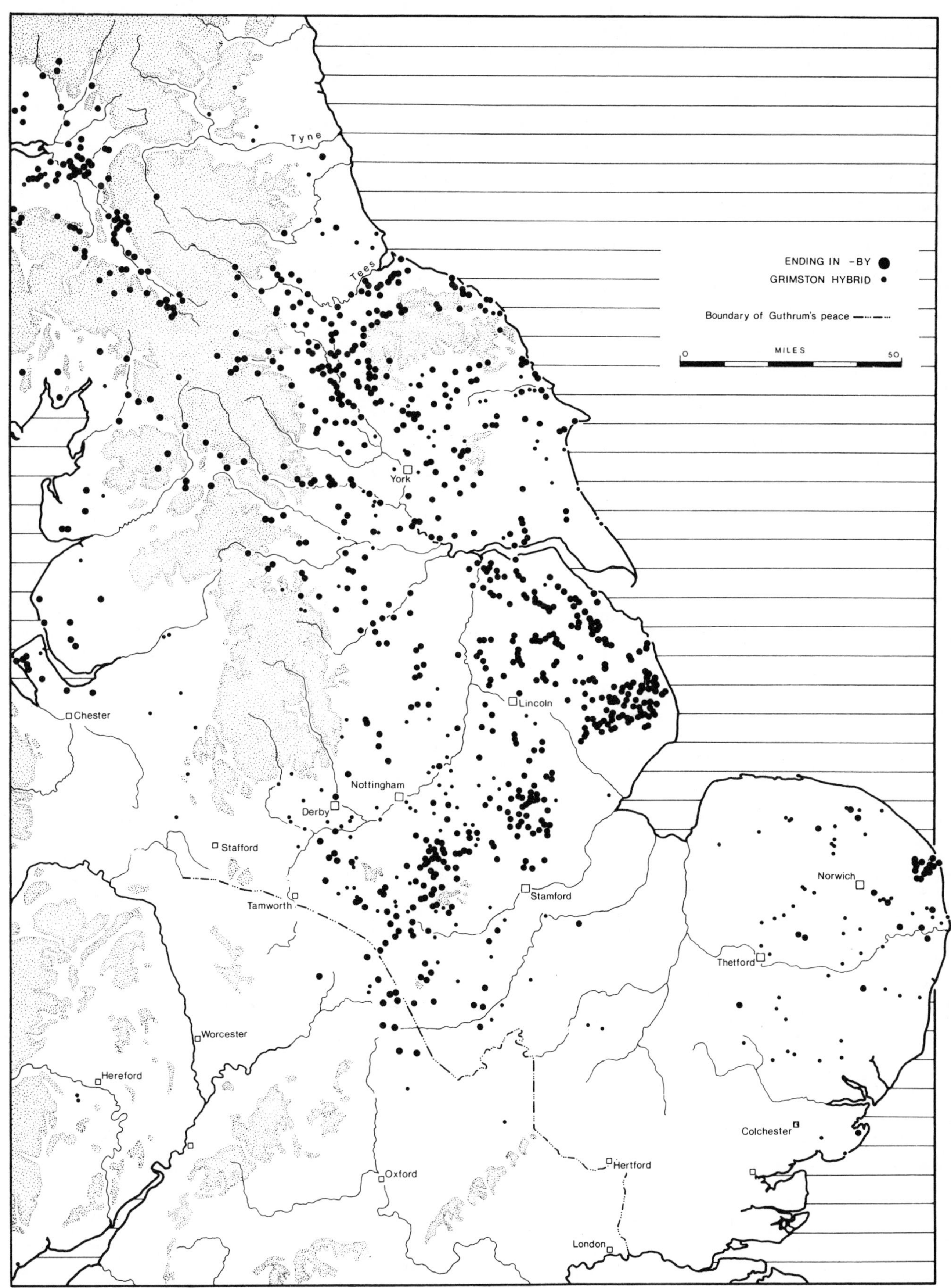

68 Scandinavian place names of eastern England

Scandinavian Place Names (68–69)

The place name evidence for Anglo-Saxon England is extensive but not well represented in this volume for, in general, it tends to illustrate themes not touched on here. It should also be noted that the English Place Name Society volumes have yet to cover the whole country.

The evidence (map **68**) does illustrate the Danish settlement beautifully and indicates a varying density of place names (and therefore **perhaps** a varying density of Scandinavian settlers). The heartland of the Danish settlement of eastern England lies to the east of the Pennines between the Tees and the Nene, and map **68** indicates the area remaining under the rule of the Ealdorman of Bamburgh (Ordnance Survey 1973).

Scandinavian place names associated with the Norse settlements are also quite extensive in the north-west of England and the far north of Scotland but surprisingly sparse in Ireland (map **69**).

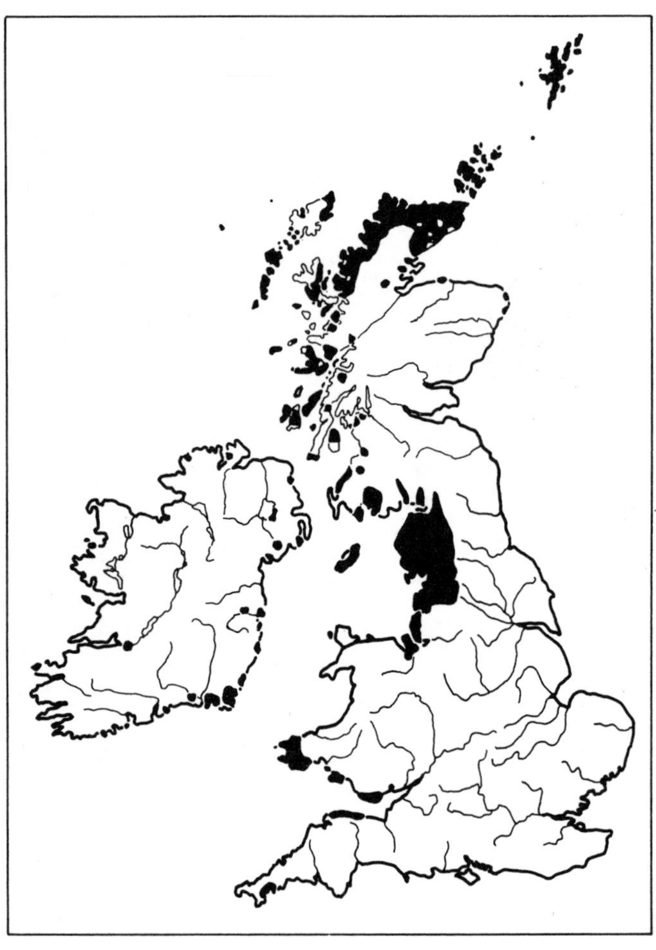

69 Scandinavian place names in the north and west

Mercia 880–906 (70)

The extent and strength of the ealdormanry of Mercia under the overlordship of Alfred and his son Edward the Elder is difficult to judge, but Mercia is the key to an understanding of the Danelaw. A careful mapping of the available evidence does offer a few pointers towards the limits of the surviving Mercian state (map **70**). The places disposed of by charter by the rulers of Mercia (marked on the map as 'places with charter') define a considerable area of influence. In the south and west of the old kingdom of Mercia it is clear that, from at least the early 880s, the areas of the former sub-kingdoms of the Hwicce and of the Magonsætan (indicated by a dotted line, as is the shire of Middlesex) were included together with much land to the north of the lower Thames valley. The northern limits are defined nebulously by the necessity for Cheshire to have formed part of Mercia if any sense is to be made of the north Welsh campaign of 881 and the lands bought in Derbyshire would likewise argue for all of Staffordshire and Cheshire to be included. The distribution of Scandinavian place names makes this likely. The frontier to the east is more problematic, but the map suggests that the 'boundary between Alfred's and Guthrum's kingdoms' had little lasting significance. The question of the extent of the Danelaw is raised by this map, as by **174–177** and **68**. There may be at least six methods of defining this area with little evident correlation between them. Interestingly, from the evidence gathered here it would appear that Gloucester was, for a time, the important centre in Mercia.

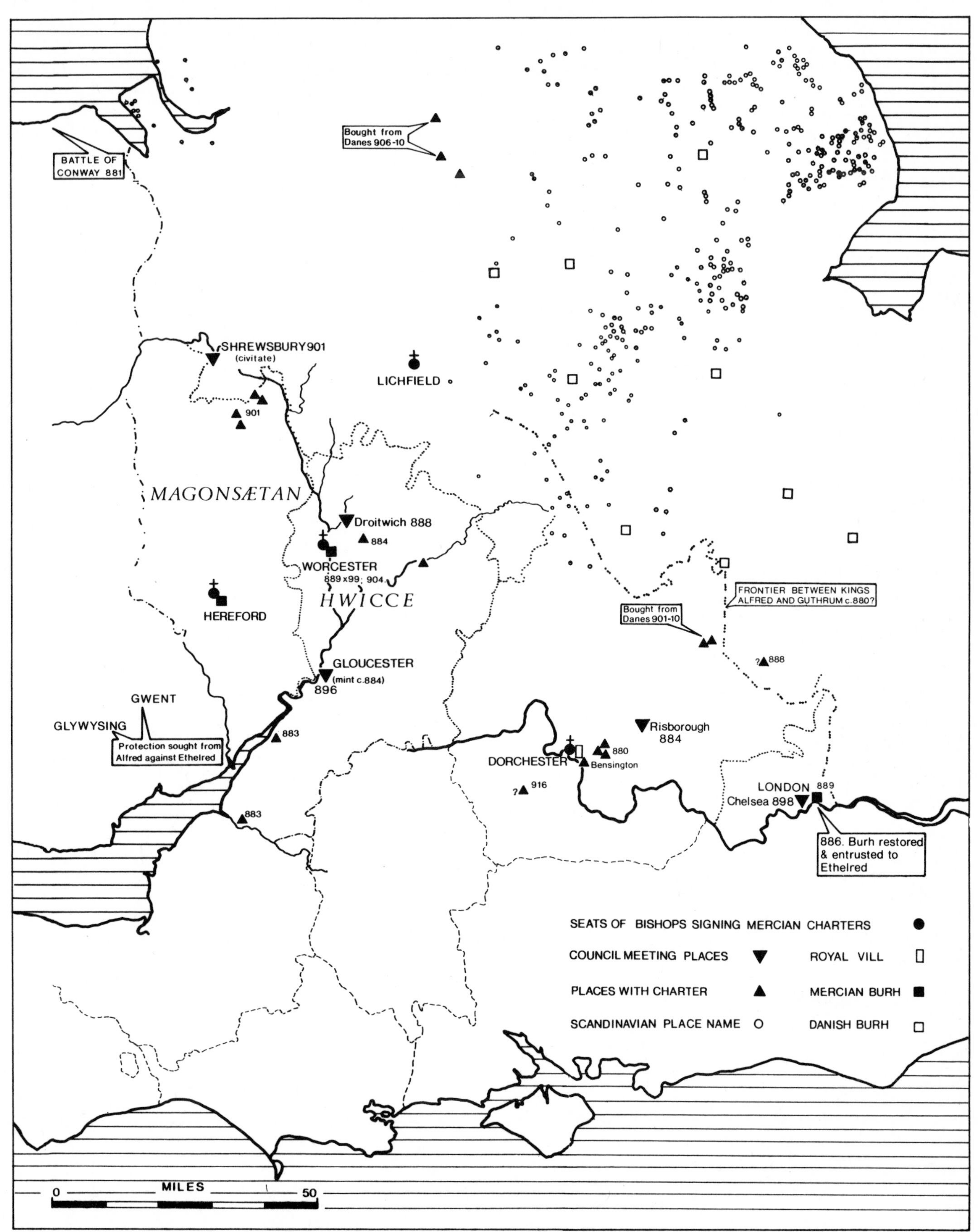
BATTLE OF CONWAY 881
Bought from Danes 906-10
SHREWSBURY 901
(civitate)
901
LICHFIELD
MAGONSÆTAN
Droitwich 888
884
WORCESTER
889 x 99; 904
HWICCE
HEREFORD
GLOUCESTER
(mint c.884)
896
GWENT
GLYWYSING
Protection sought from Alfred against Ethelred
883
883
FRONTIER BETWEEN KINGS ALFRED AND GUTHRUM c.880?
Bought from Danes 901-10
?888
Risborough
884
880
DORCHESTER
Bensington
?916
LONDON 889
Chelsea 898
886. Burh restored & entrusted to Ethelred
SEATS OF BISHOPS SIGNING MERCIAN CHARTERS
COUNCIL MEETING PLACES
ROYAL VILL
PLACES WITH CHARTER
MERCIAN BURH
SCANDINAVIAN PLACE NAME
DANISH BURH
0
MILES
50

70 Mercia 880–906 and the itinerary of Æthelred and Æthelflaed

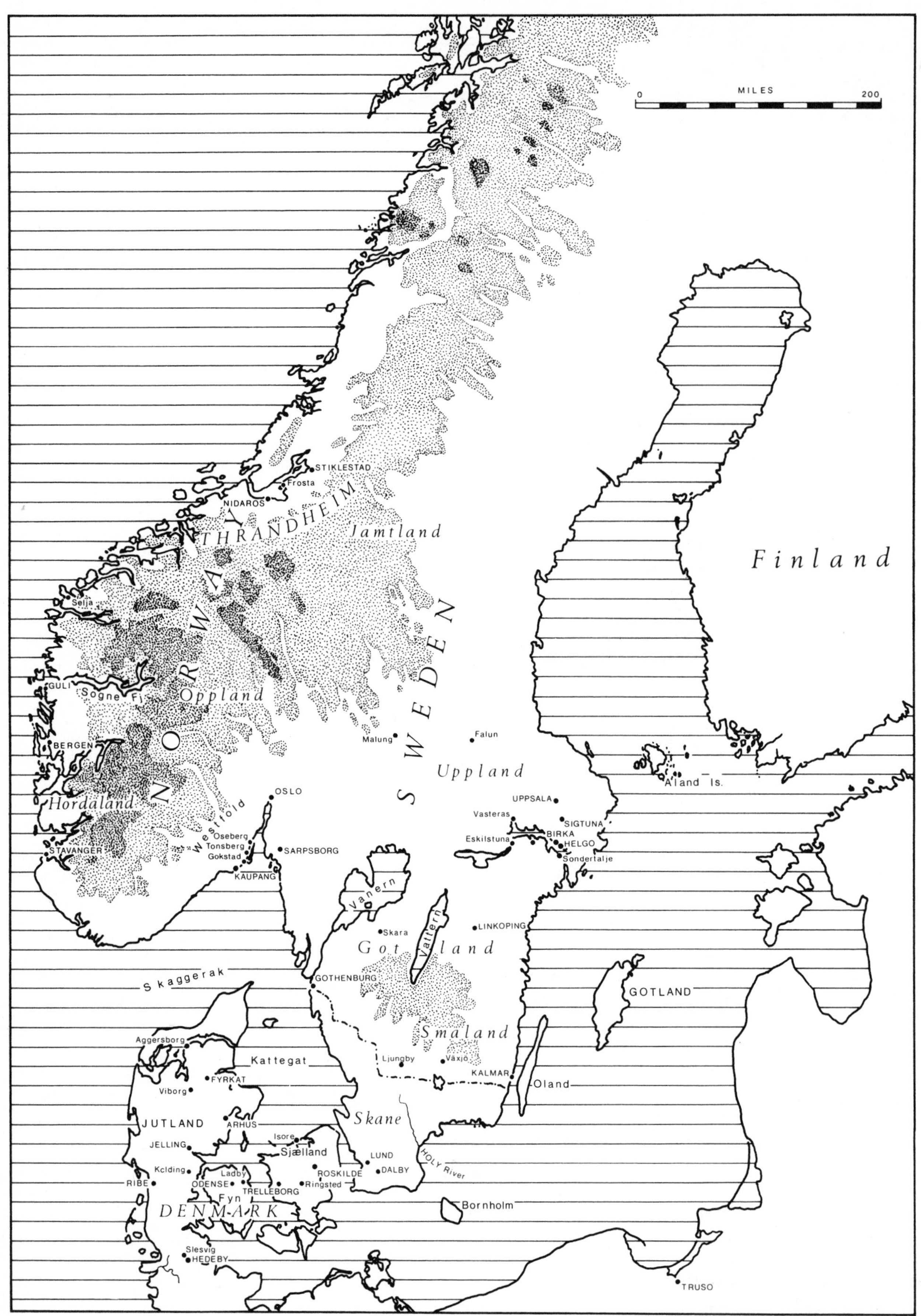

0 MILES 200
Finland
STIKLESTAD
Frosta
NIDAROS
THRANDHEIM
Jamtland
NORWAY
SWEDEN
Selja
GULI
Sogne Fj
Oppland
BERGEN
Hordaland
Westfold
Oseberg
Tonsberg
Gokstad
STAVANGER
KAUPANG
OSLO
SARPSBORG
Malung
Falun
Uppland
UPPSALA
Vasteras
SIGTUNA
BIRKA
Eskilstuna
HELGO
Sondertalje
Aland Is.
Vanern
Vattern
Skara
LINKOPING
Gotland
GOTHENBURG
Skaggerak
GOTLAND
Smaland
Aggersborg
Kattegat
Ljungby
Växjö
KALMAR
Oland
FYRKAT
Viborg
JUTLAND
ARHUS
Skane
Isore
JELLING
Sjælland
LUND
DALBY
HOLY River
Kolding
Ladby
ROSKILDE
RIBE
ODENSE
TRELLEBORG
Ringsted
Fyn
DENMARK
Bornholm
Slesvig
HEDEBY
TRUSO

71 Scandinavia

Scandinavia (71–72)

The homelands of the Vikings — Denmark (which included Skane), Sweden and Norway — are very different regions and have differing histories during the period. They are linked by a common language and tradition which gave the Viking the ability to operate with Vikings of another country. Map **71** shows a number of places important for the study of Scandinavian history, without defining them as settlement, fort, town, etc. The relief is indicated and the approximate frontier between Sweden and the Danish province of Skane is shown. The map is intended to assist the reader in general rather than to make any specific point.

It is clear that the areas available near home for Norse and Dane settlement were limited, particularly those areas suitable for farming in Norway where snow often covers the ground for too extensive a period (map **72**). It should be noted that even this limited area is swiftly affected by small climatic variations. In Iceland, similarly, only a limited part of the total area is available for farming. The harsh and restricted environment may explain why peasant farmers were prepared so readily to move out to colonize the Faroes, Shetland, Iceland and beyond.

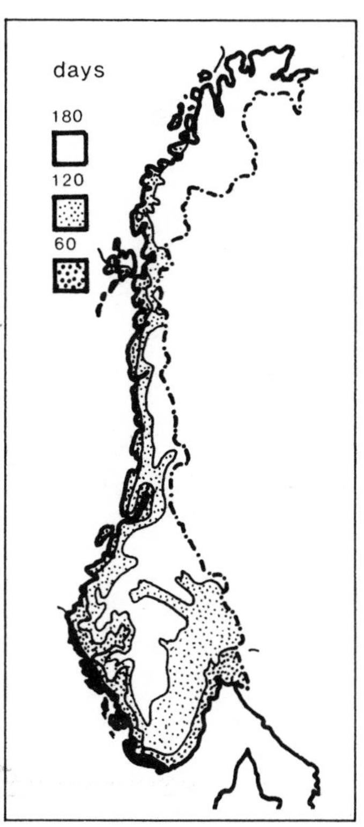

72 Snow cover in Norway

Ireland (73)

It is surprising that the Saga literature of Iceland is part of Europe's cultural and historical heritage whilst the rich and varied sources from Ireland (map **73**) in the same period are largely unknown or, worse, ignored. The English student of the Anglo-Saxon period will know all about the Vinland Sagas or even the **Landnámabók** yet few have read the Chronicles of Ireland which contain much more direct information on England, Wales and Scotland and give a vast amount of information on the Vikings, not least on their raids into England. Irish sources often supply direct causal effects for events in England in the Viking age.

The series of Viking settlements around the coasts of Ireland provided the base for a string of raids on England and also provided the 'other half' of the Viking kingdom of Dublin and York.

Lough Foyle
COLERAINE
Dal Riata
AILECH
KILMACRENEN
DERRY
DUNGIVEN
RAPHOE
Mourne
Bann
Ulaid
CONNOR
Ui Neill
ANTRIM
Belfast L.
Bangor
Lough Neagh
TULACH OC
MAGBILE
CRAEB TULCHA
ULADH
Strangford
DROMORE
Lough Erne
CLOGHER
ARMAGH
DRUMCLIFF
Argialla
DOWNPATRICK
KILLALA
RATHMULCAH
Clones
Breifne
Conaille
Carlingford Lough
KILMORE
LOUTH
CONNACHTA
Annagassan
Mayo
GRANARD
Boyne
Ui Briuin Ai
Kells
KNOWTH
Brega
ROSCOMMON
ARDAGH
MIDE
TARA
CONG
Tuam
Lough Ree
LAGORE
CLONARD
ATHLONE
UISNECH
CLONCURRY
Clontarf
Lough Corrib
DUBLIN
(Atha Cliath)
Liffey
CLONMACNOISE
DURROW
Llamain
Rathangan
NAS
CLONFERT
KILDARE
Ui Maine
AILEEN
BIRR
Glen Mama
Barrow
Glendalough
WICKLOW
TOMGRANEY
Loch Derg
AGHABOE
RAITH BILE
MAGNADAIR
ARKLOW
Nore
LAIGIN
KILLALOE
Dal Cais
OSRAIGE
DINN RIG
ARD LADRANN
GABRAN
LIMERICK
(Luimneach)
Slaney
FERNS
Shannon
Eoganacht
St Mullins
Cashel
EMLY
Suir
WEXFORD
MUMHA
WATERFORD
(Port Lairge)
Blackwater
LISMORE
Loch Lein
Deisi
ARDMORE
Lea
CORK
SKELLIG
Desmuma
VIKING (HIBERNO-NORSE) TOWNS
MILES
0
70

73 Ireland

Iceland (74–78)

Iceland drew off many Norse and Viking settlers and so gave Ireland the 'forty years' rest'. Traders and poets passed to and fro and the Sagas record the doings of many of the figures of North European history. The area in which all this happened is constricted both by surface conditions and by weather factors to the coastal strip and to the west of the island (**74**). The **Landnámabók** recounts the taking of the island by Viking settlers and lists all the original settlements. When these settlements are mapped (**75**) one can see immediately the importance of access to the sea and the colonization of all the shores and the valleys of the west.

Without denigrating the achievements of the age, it is likely that access to Iceland (**76** and **77**) and travel generally in the North Atlantic (**78**) area was comparatively easy at the time due to the climatic amelioration.

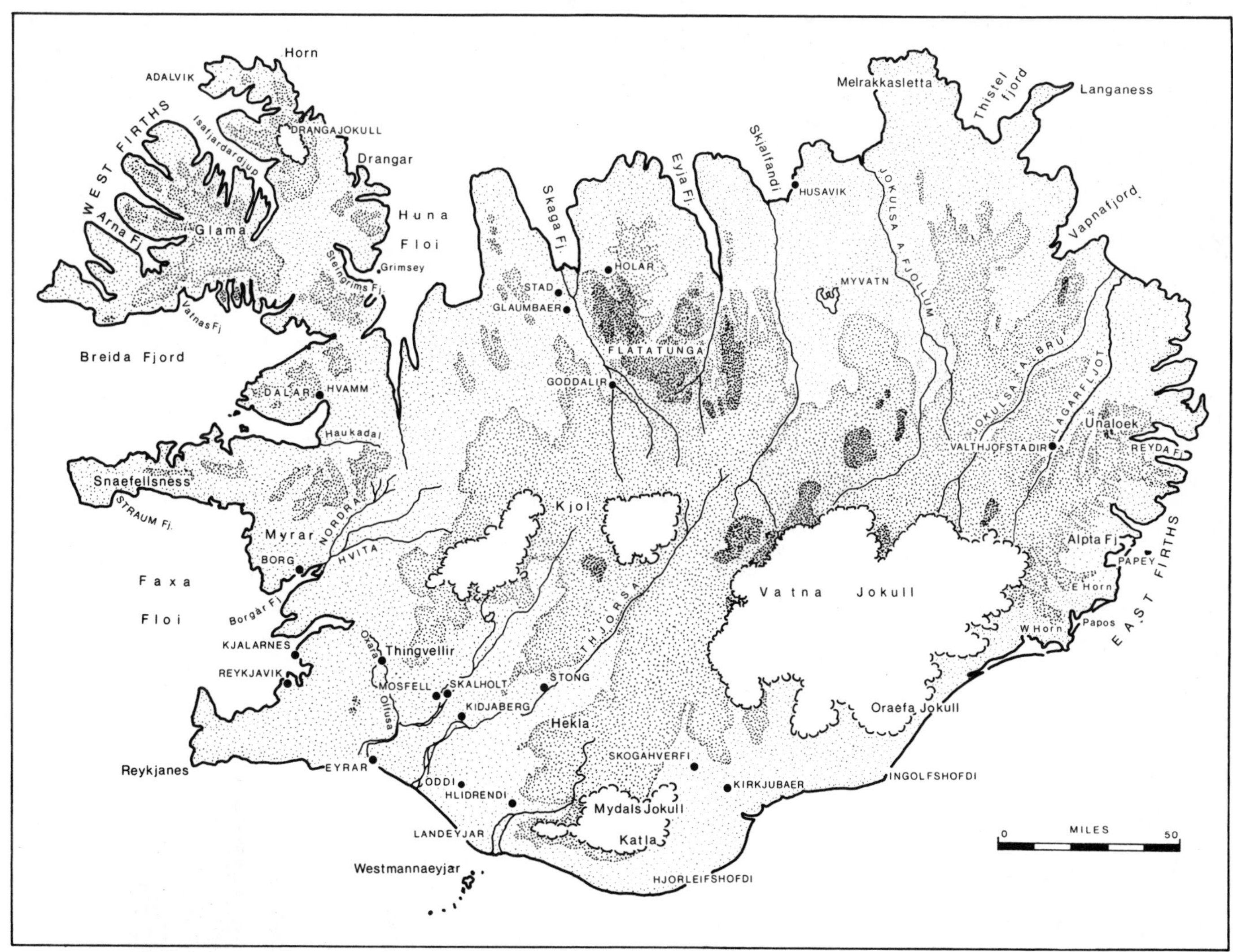

74 Iceland

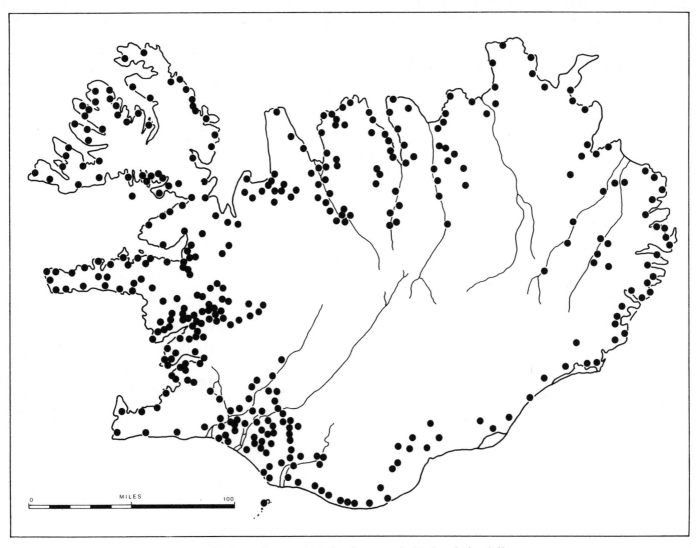

75 Early settlements in Iceland as recorded in **Landnámabók**

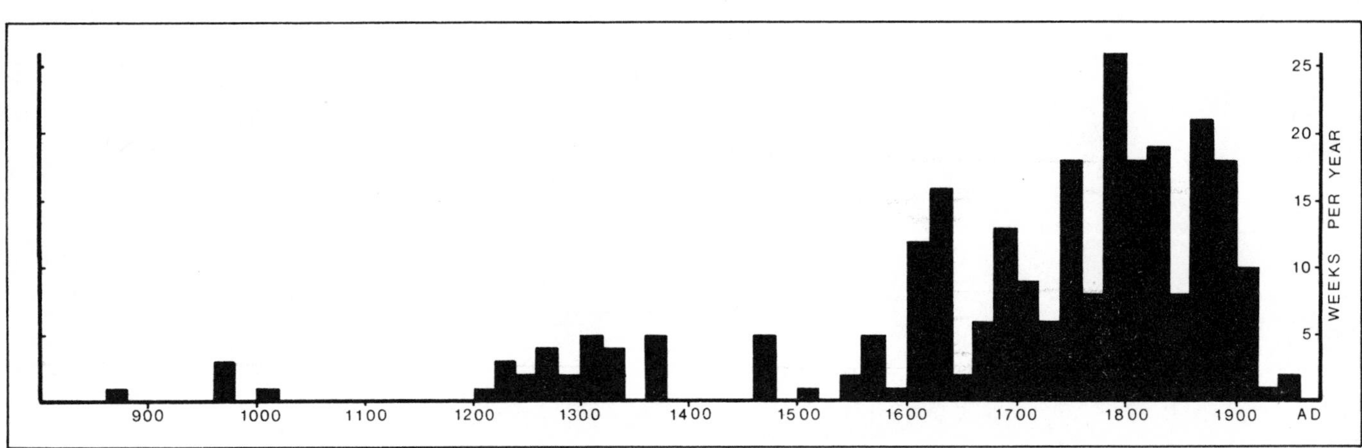

76 Ice-free days on Iceland's coasts 860 to the present (after Koch). Weeks per year shown as twenty-year averages

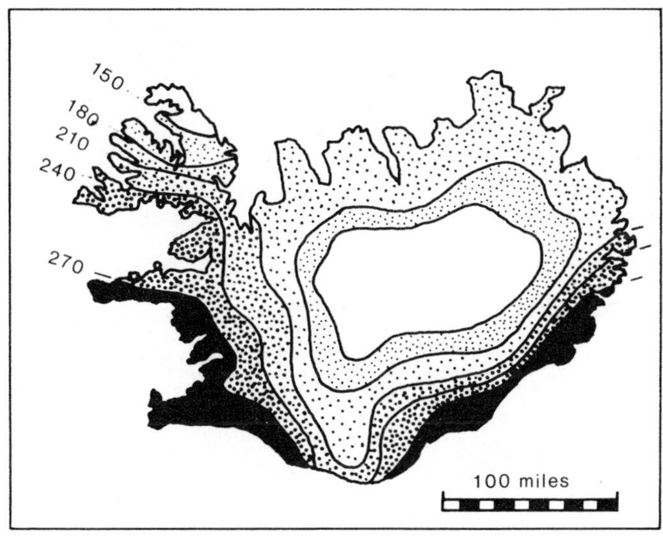

77 Snow cover in Iceland

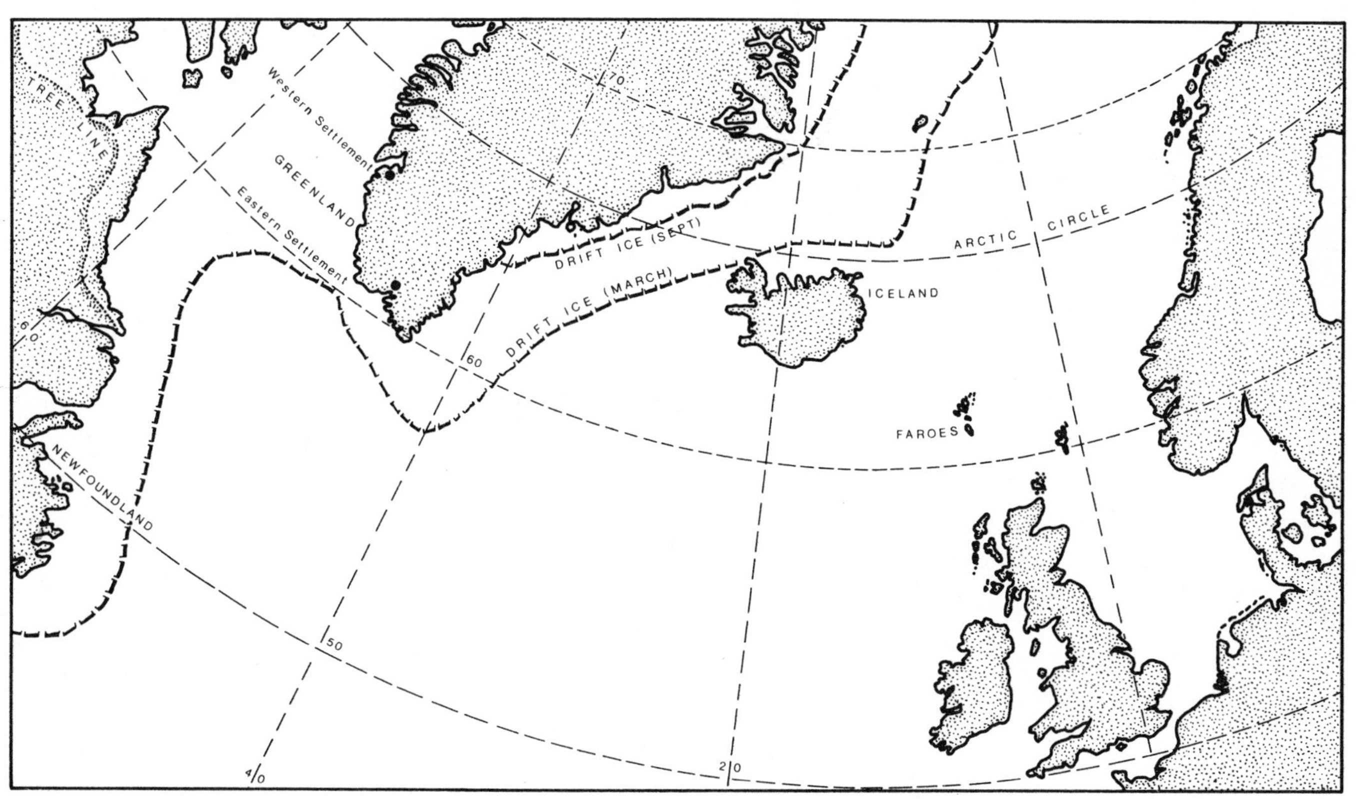

78 The Norse Atlantic

Viking Trade (79–80)

The areas under the control of the Vikings were quite large by the close of the ninth century, the links between them were strong and both the Danish areas and the later Hiberno-Norse successor kingdoms in Northumbria had strong economic and political links with Ireland and the Western Isles. The hoards of coins of the Vikings of East Anglia and of Northumbria mark these areas out (map **79**). Particular emphasis is shown in the Isle of Man and Dublin areas.

The Vikings in the British Isles were part of a much larger economic and trade area using coinage, particularly as bullion. Sawyer has recently discussed in some detail his thesis that the supply of Arabic silver and then its denial had great consequences on the flow of Vikings to the West (Sawyer 1971). It should be noted that much of the silver in areas such as the south Baltic must have reached there as a result of trade out of Scandinavia (map **80**).

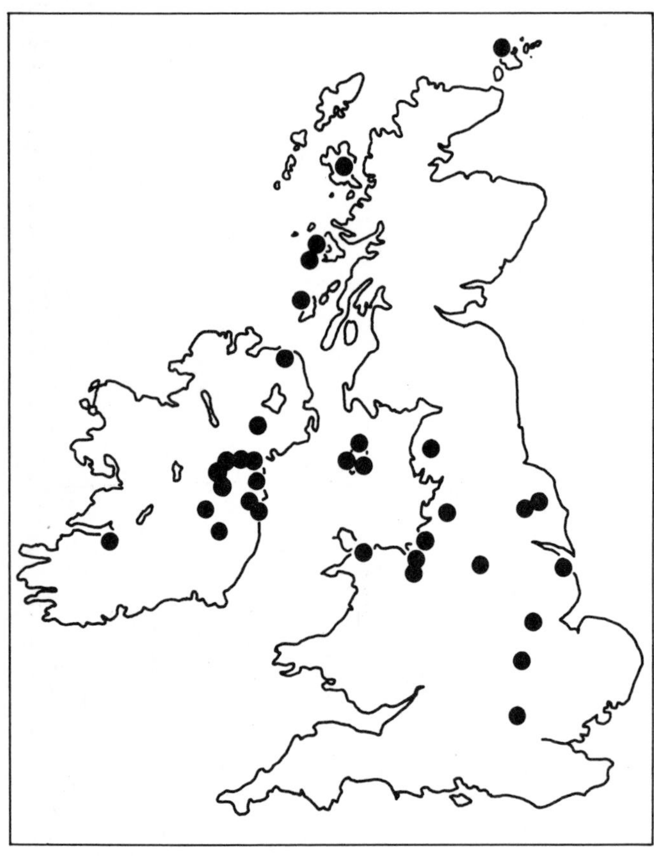

79 Hoards containing coins of the Vikings of East Anglia and Northumbria

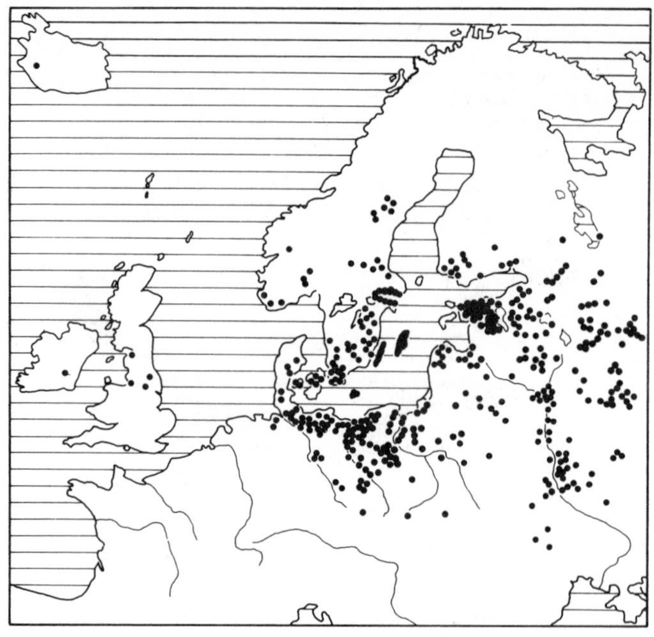

80 Finds of Arabic coins of the Viking Age (after Oxenstierna 1967)

The Reconquest 902–921 (81–98)

The campaigns of 892–95 had left a strengthened Wessex facing a series of Danish settlements with no major Danish army roaming the area. This was the setting for the Reconquest. Patrick Wormald (personal communication) remarks that he is rather unhappy with the traditional use of the term 'Reconquest' of the Danelaw. The West Saxons may have attempted to represent their efforts as precisely that. In sober fact, the campaigns represented a West Saxon conquest, and it is far from clear that all Mercians and East Anglians saw their arrival and domination as the happiest answer to their problems. If the word is to stand, and for convenience it must, then we should realize that its use is tendentious.

The disposition of coin hoards for the period c.895–c.965 (map **81**) shows a significant concentration in the eastern part of England, clearly reflecting dangerous times. In the decade 895–905 the initiative passed to Edward the Elder. The raids back and forth did not disguise the fact that the underlying strength of Wessex was increasing (map **83**). The fortified centres, **burhs**, meant that the West Saxons could not suffer a sudden catastrophic collapse such as followed the Danish invasion in 878. Other factors must have affected the Danish areas. The lack of reinforcements, the ageing of the original force and the process of absorption from below, with the swift loss of language and religion, made the Danes more likely to compromise with the West Saxons in order to hold on to their lands.

The areas of the southern armies appear to have given rise to the formation of what were later to be recognized as the shires of the east Midlands. A clue is to be found in the peace of Tiddingford (map **82**), for treaties were often at this period negotiated on the frontiers, as at Dore or Billingsley. Tiddingford does not stand on the so-called frontier of Guthrum (see map **70**). Although the peace was negotiated in 906 the river on which the site stands forms the later shire boundary, which in turn may reflect the army of Bedford's area of control. It is therefore arguable that many of the shires were laid out before 920 in the east Midlands. Tiddingford stands at the point where the Herepath crosses the River Ousel.

These small armies, centred on one **burh**, were too small to face the West Saxons and even the larger units of East Anglia and Essex do not seem to have been either strong enough or sufficiently ready to coordinate their efforts with others to survive.

The pattern of the campaigns was hardly dashing — it was a process of slowly strengthening the West Saxon and Mercian areas with **burhs**, then fortifying the frontier areas with more **burhs**, and finally pushing the **burhs** forward far enough to force the Danes to react. The forced attacks of the Danes on the West Saxon and Mercian defences were always failures, as were their more wide-ranging attacks, and the policy of allowing them to continue to hold their lands after the transfer to sovereignty appears to have made submission preferable to defeat.

The Reconquest was a slow process to begin with. Although the southern Danelaw was gradually eroded, only limited gains were made before 916 (maps **83–90**). The Mercian policy was similar and coordinated with the West Saxons but it was complicated by the fact that considerable efforts had to be made to control the Welsh frontier at the same time. Finally there were the dramatic campaigns of 917 (maps **91–94**) as a result of which the Danelaw submitted in a chain reaction as the surrender of neighbouring armies isolated the surviving armies and exposed their flanks to West Saxon attack.

The final stage of the Reconquest was denied to the West Saxons by two factors, the death of Æthelflaed and the arrival of the Dublin Norse in the Kingdom of York. However, after 917, the pattern of states that had subsisted since 878 disappeared. The Danish states south of the Humber had been amalgamated into the West Saxon Kingdom and the Danish Kingdom of York, along with the lands of the Ealdorman of Bamburgh, became the Hiberno-Norse Kingdom of York linked with Dublin (maps **95–98**).

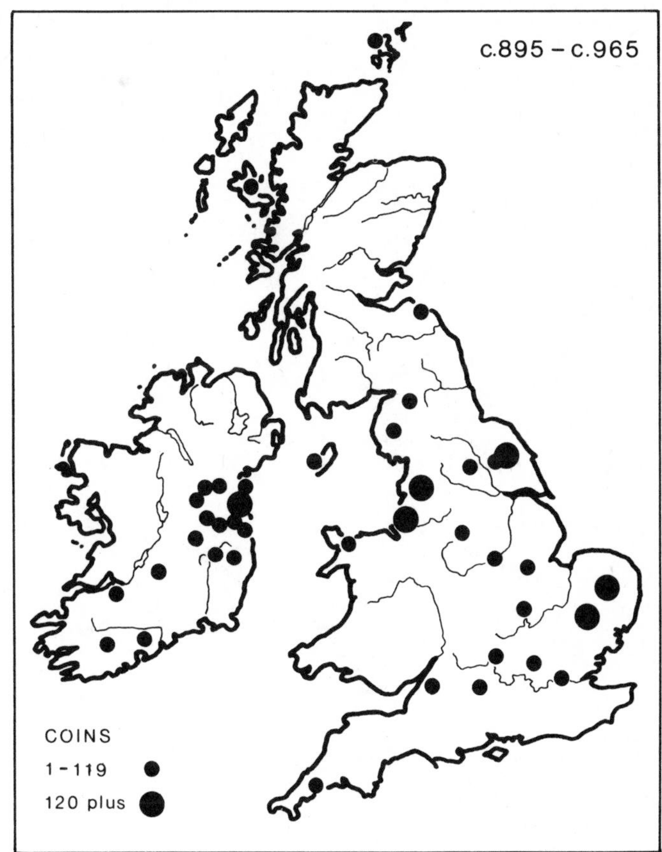

81 Hoards of coins deposited c.895–c.965

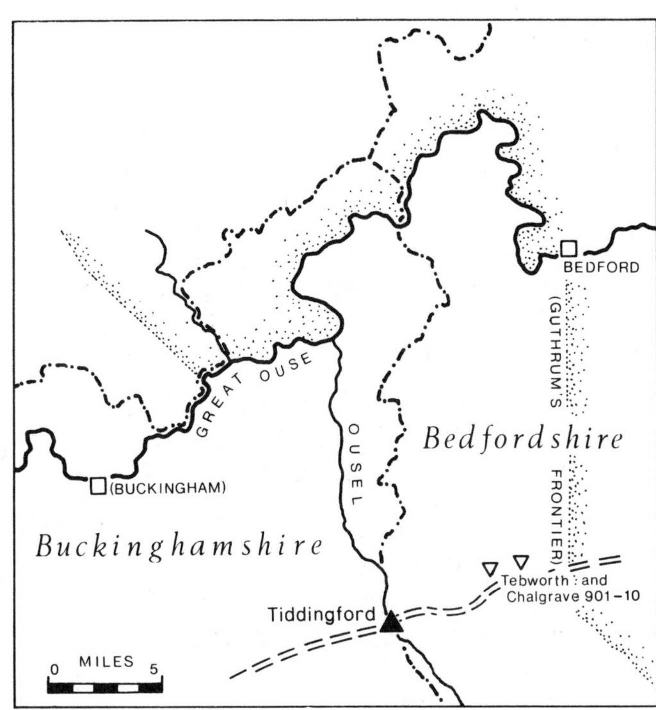

82 The Peace of Tiddingford 906

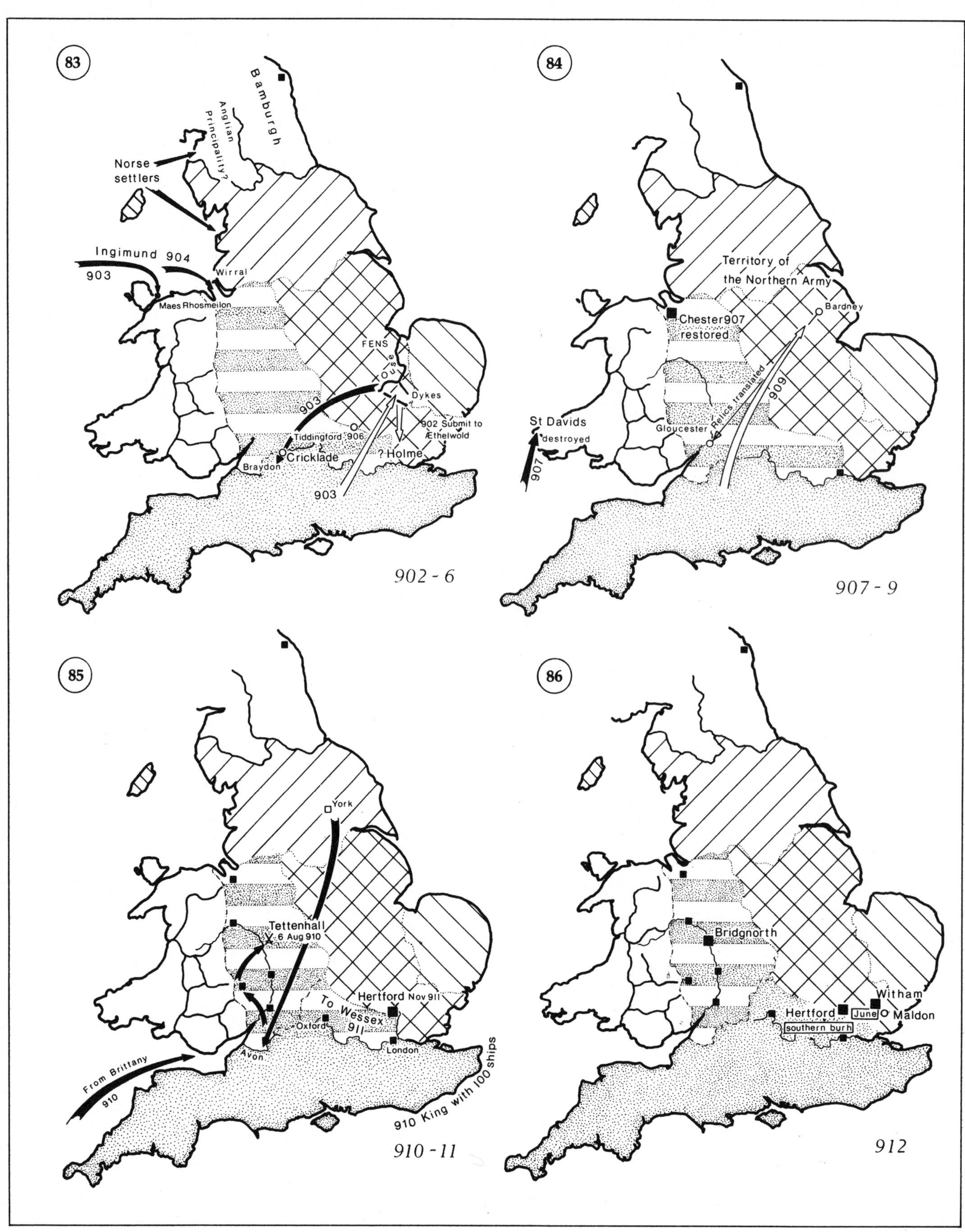

83–86 The Reconquest 902–912. Viking movements shown in black on this and subsequent maps

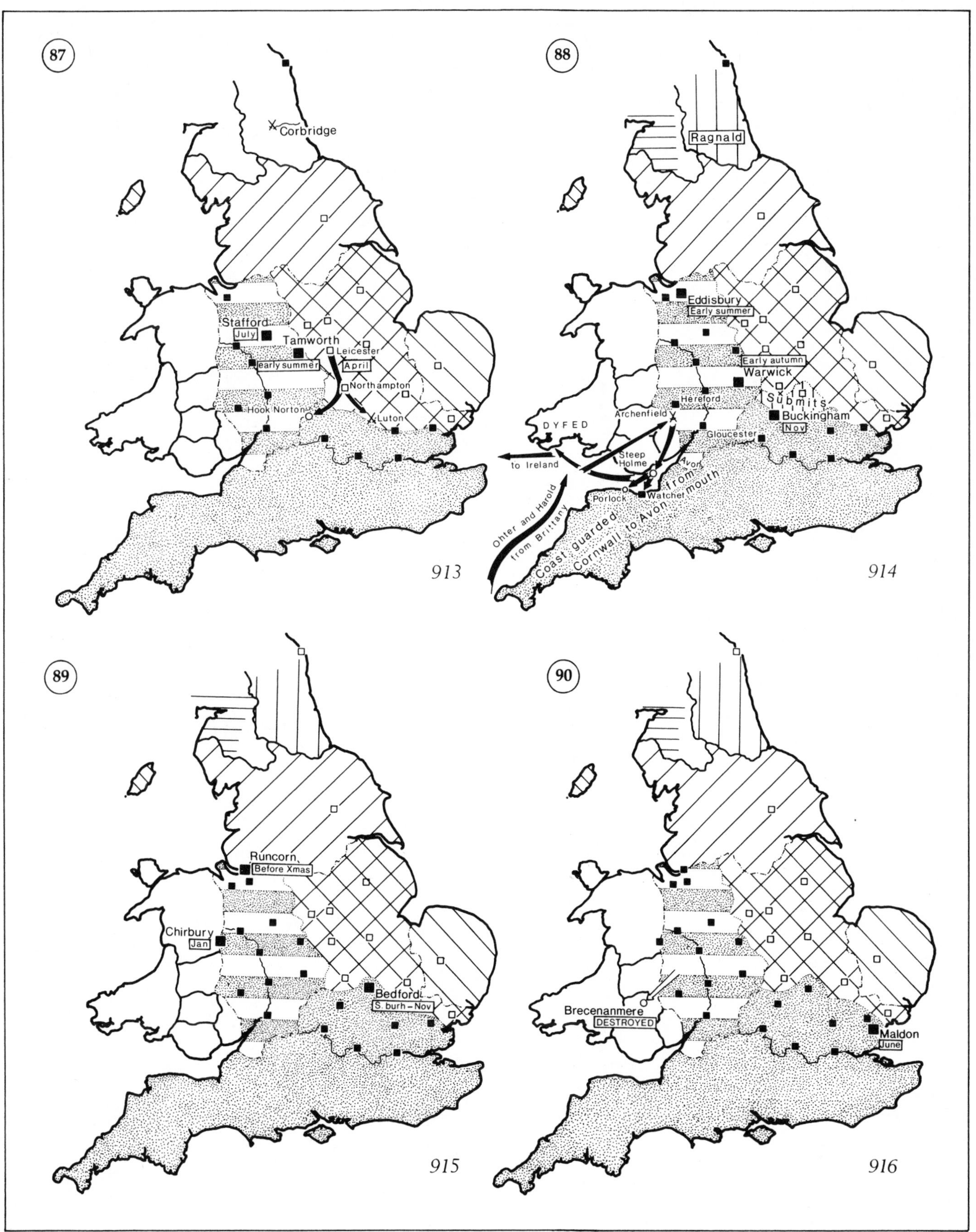

87–90 The Reconquest 913–916

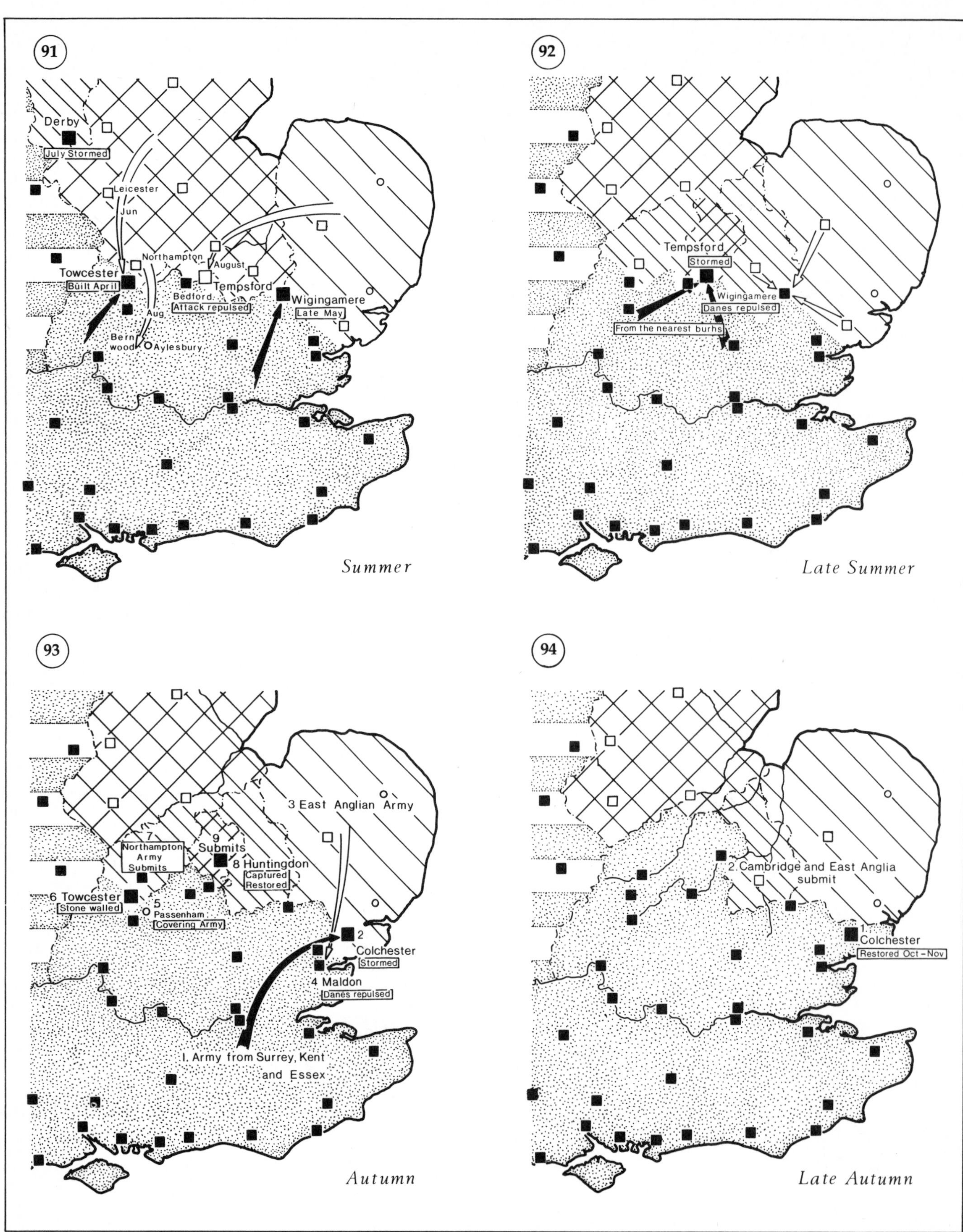

91–94 Campaigns of 917

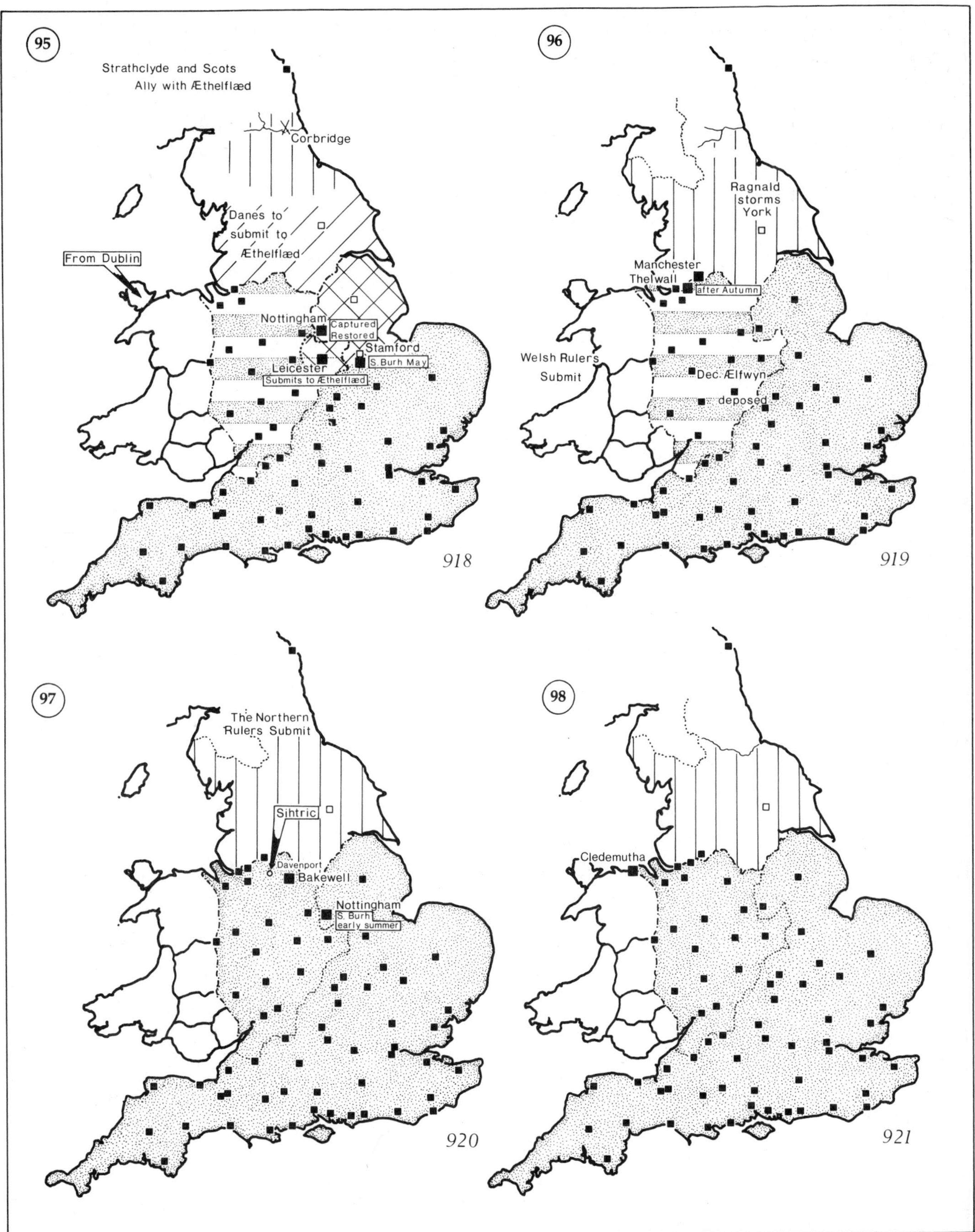

95
Strathclyde and Scots
Ally with Æthelflæd
Corbridge
Danes to
submit to
Æthelflæd
From Dublin
Nottingham
Captured
Restored
Stamford
S. Burh May
Leicester
Submits to Æthelflæd
918
96
Ragnald
storms
York
Manchester
Thelwall
after Autumn
Welsh Rulers
Submit
Dec. Ælfwyn
deposed
919
97
The Northern
Rulers Submit
Sihtric
Davenport
Bakewell
Nottingham
S. Burh
early summer
920
98
Cledemutha
921

95–98 The Reconquest 918–921

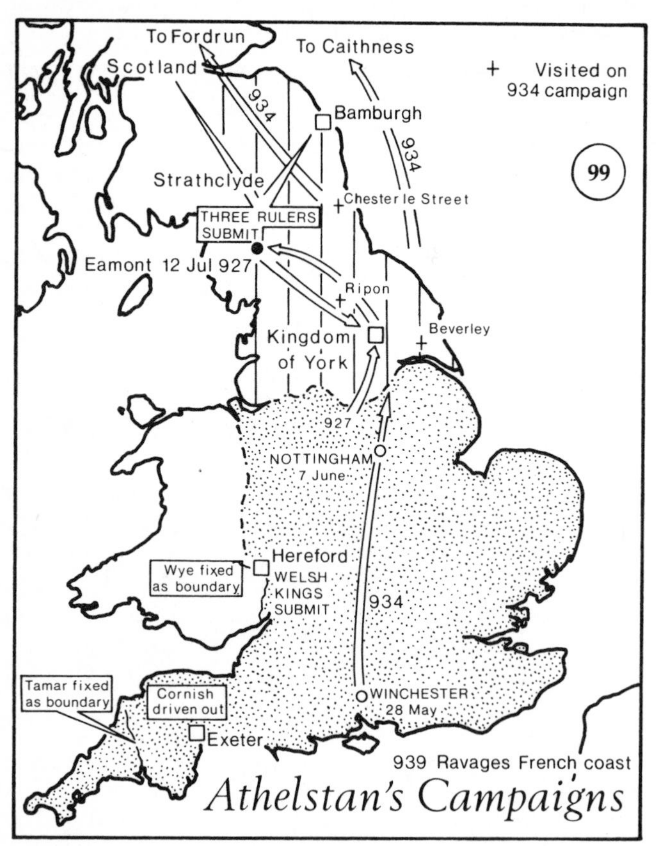
To Fordrun
To Caithness
Scotland
Visited on 934 campaign
934
Bamburgh
934
99
Strathclyde
Chester le Street
THREE RULERS SUBMIT
Eamont 12 Jul 927
Ripon
Beverley
Kingdom of York
927
NOTTINGHAM 7 June
Wye fixed as boundary
Hereford
WELSH KINGS SUBMIT
934
Tamar fixed as boundary
Cornish driven out
WINCHESTER 28 May
Exeter
939 Ravages French coast
Athelstan's Campaigns

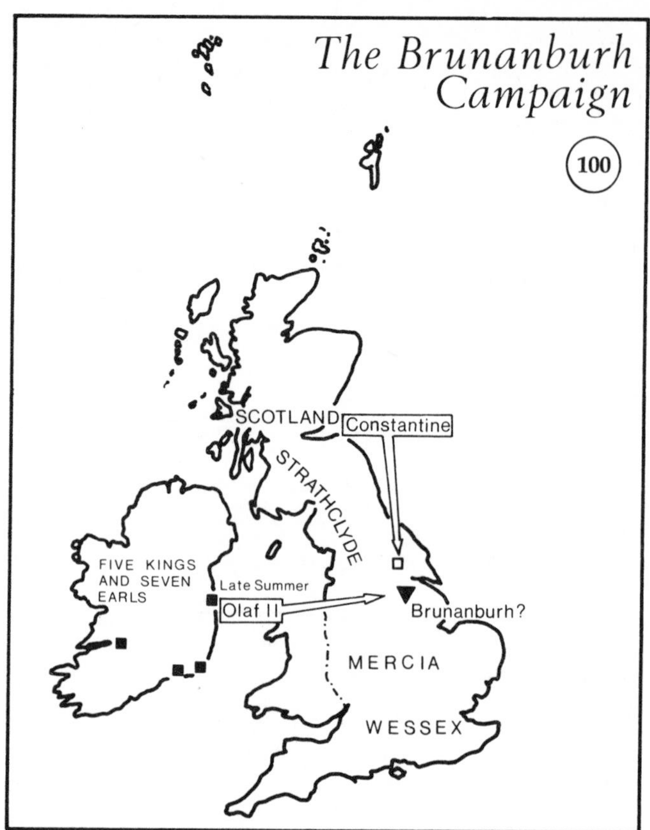
The Brunanburh Campaign
100
SCOTLAND
Constantine
STRATHCLYDE
FIVE KINGS AND SEVEN EARLS
Late Summer
Olaf II
Brunanburh?
MERCIA
WESSEX

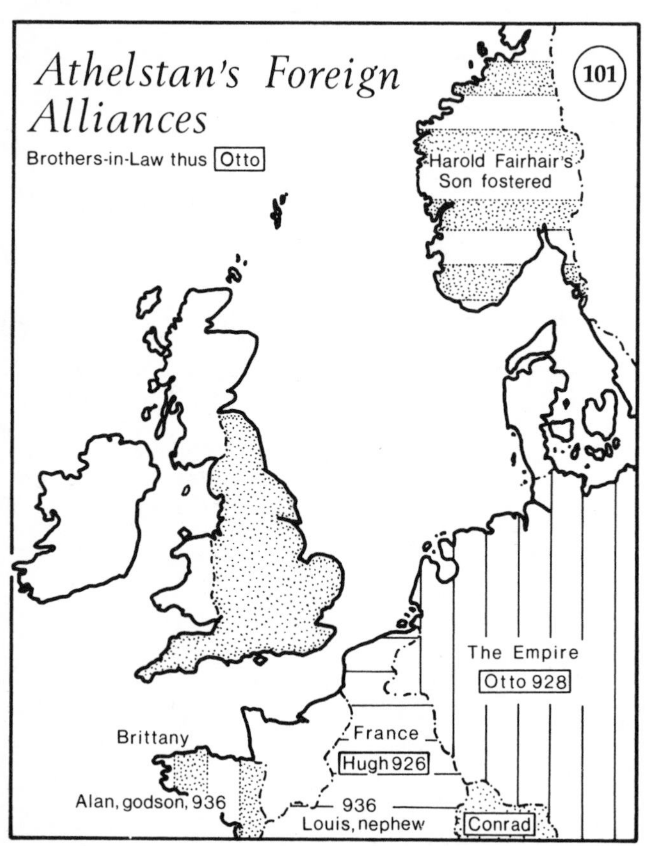
Athelstan's Foreign Alliances
101
Brothers-in-Law thus Otto
Harold Fairhair's Son fostered
The Empire
Otto 928
France
Hugh 926
Brittany
Alan, godson, 936
936
Louis, nephew
Conrad

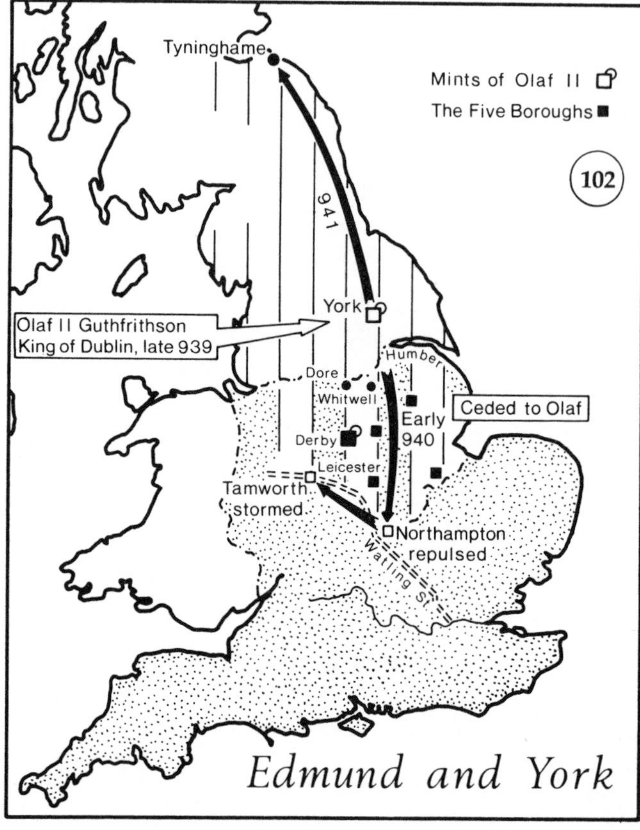
Tyninghame
Mints of Olaf II
The Five Boroughs
102
941
York
Olaf II Guthfrithson King of Dublin, late 939
Humber
Dore
Whitwell
Ceded to Olaf
Early 940
Derby
Leicester
Tamworth stormed
Northampton repulsed
Watling St.
Edmund and York

99–102 From Athelstan to Eric Bloodaxe 924–954

From Athelstan to Eric Bloodaxe 924–954 (99–102)

Athelstan began his reign by putting the frontiers of his kingdom in order on all sides and followed this up with an alliance with York (map **99**). The situation appeared to be lost when the great combination of Celtic and Viking powers faced him at Brunanburh but his victory there set a West Saxon king firmly over a Kingdom of England (map **100**). Athelstan went on to become a monarch of European stature, forming alliances both within and beyond the British Isles (map **101**).

The kingdom nearly disintegrated with his death as Olaf Guthfrithson recovered the Danelaw and Northumbria up to Dunbar. The situation was soon remedied, not least because the Danish settlers had had nearly twenty years of West Saxon rule and preferred it to that of the heathen Norse. There was to be a final upsurge of the Norse Kingdom of York with Eric Bloodaxe and Olaf Sihtricson but after Eric's death in 954 the adventure begun in East Anglia in 866 was over (map **102**).

The Submission to Edgar, Chester 973 (103–105)

The events surrounding Edgar's coronation in Bath and the submission at Chester created a scene of medieval splendour which had an impact on the imagination of the time and on that of succeeding generations. His coronation was the consummation of the expansion charted in the preceding maps. Ælfric wrote in his life of Swithun (Skeat 1881):

> *. . . King Edgar*
> *furthered Christianity, and built many monasteries,*
> *and his kingdom still continued in peace,*
> *so that no fleet was heard of,*
> *save that of the people themselves who held this land;*
> *and all the kings of the Cymry and the Scots*
> *that were in this island, came to Edgar*
> *once upon a day, being eight kings,*
> *and they all bowed themselves to Edgar's rule*

The identification of the realms and kings that submitted has been discussed by Stenton (1971, 369–70). Mapping these events and the kingdoms involved sheds an interesting light on the whole affair (map **103**). The best list is provided by Florence of Worcester. Maccus, King of many Islands, expanded his kingdom by occupying Anglesey (in the Welsh Annals he and his brother are 'The Sons of Maccus'). Anglesey was part of Iago's kingdom of Gwynedd and Iago was under the protection of Edgar. After the coronation at Bath Edgar took his fleet (presumably around Wales, for he is recorded as founding St Mary's at Bangor) to Chester. This great fleet must have had a profound effect on Maccus: he and the other sub-kings came to a ceremony of submission. The map makes it clear that the island kingdom was greatly exposed in the face of such a combination, and the cession to Lothian at about this time may well have been linked to securing an alliance against Maccus and the Vikings in the Irish Sea area. We know very little about the state of the Border area at this, or any other early, time; but the distribution of place names (map **104**) makes it clear that the Anglian kingdom of Northumbria had extended far to the north, including the region around present-day Edinburgh, although the Anglian presence in the Solway and Galloway regions is less marked. It may well be that in these areas Anglian names are overlain by later additions.

The hoard evidence (map **105**) supports the general idea of a realm at peace, with only the raids around Chester and a few coastal sites in the latter part of the period showing up.

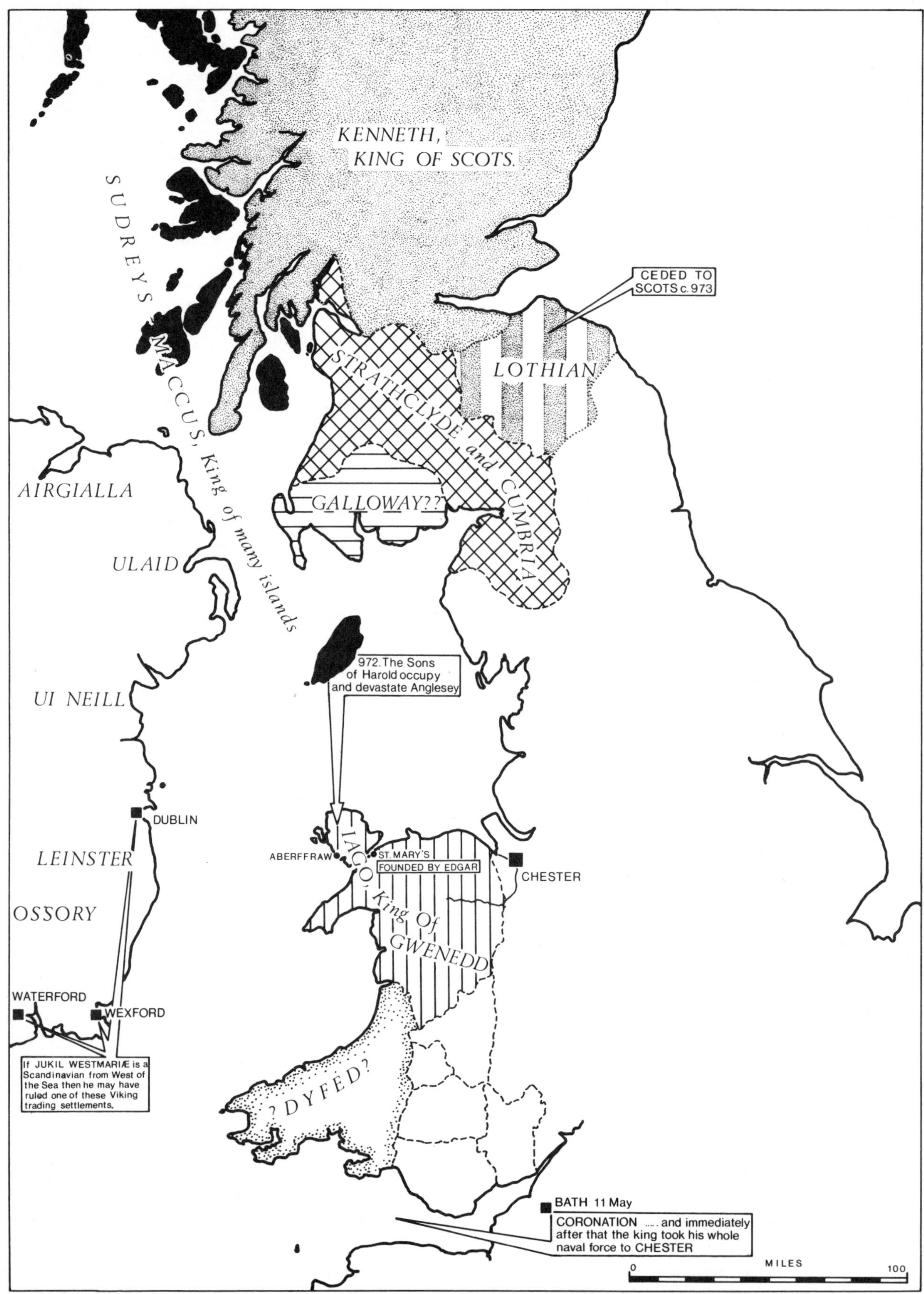

103 The submission to Edgar, Chester 973. Sub-kingdoms stippled

104 Anglian place names in Scotland (McNeill and Nicholson 1975)

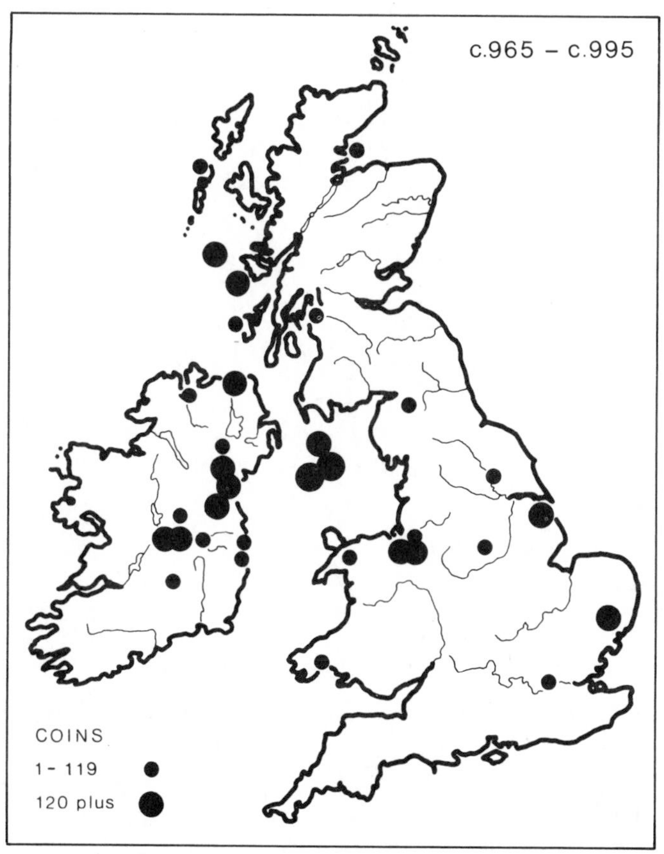

105 Hoards of coins deposited c.965–c.995

The Wars of the Reign of Ethelred the Second (106–129)

The maps that follow are mainly designed to draw together the information carried in the Anglo-Saxon Chronicle and Florence of Worcester and to augment it with the information from the Welsh sources; they may be a useful aid when following the account in the Chronicle or Stenton.

The chronicler's thoroughly gloomy account, heavily biased against Ethelred, is certainly distorted, at least for the early period. The hoard maps (**106**) gives the impression that the Viking raids were on a rather more restricted scale than the Chronicle would indicate. As Dolley has highlighted, the map also shows a contraction of the Viking sphere of influence in Ireland.

The poetic account of the battle of Maldon of 991 (maps **107** and **109**) equally belies the atmosphere of weakness and defeatism conjured by the Chronicle, and it is hard to detect a dying society in the voluminous works of Aelfric.

In maps **108–129** only the places relevant to the years dealt with or to the understanding of those events have been included. It is important to realize that the white areas are not empty and that maps for a particular year should be used together with the maps of mints, towns or churches later in the book.

The renewed Viking attack on England started with sporadic raids around the coast (maps **108–111**), but it is clear that there were two completely different sets of raids: those in the east, which were to prove decisive, and those in the west originating in Ireland with the Hiberno-Norse, which belong to a pattern that Edgar the Peaceable's reign had merely interrupted. These acts of Irish piracy were to continue at odd moments until the Conquest and particularly bedevilled the Welsh and Scots coasts. It is clear from their positioning that the eastern sets of raids were in all probability mounted from the Low Countries (see maps **112–115**) but they were not connected with any general renewal of Viking activity. In fact the scale and direction of these new attacks was very different from those of the Heroic Age. They may have contained an element of Danish imperialism; certainly the Danish kings were soon involved and the war brought out considerable numbers of combatants on both sides. The Danish raids did not take place every year. When the raiders did appear, the English response was very positive, notwithstanding the defeatist tone of the chronicler of this section of the Anglo-Saxon Chronicle, who has tainted our view of the period and certainly omitted or played down successes in the first part of the wars (maps **116–119**). Ethelred made great efforts to reorganize army, fleet and fortifications. In every other branch of Anglo-Saxon life of which we have knowledge the Danish incursions seem to have had little effect until 1006, by which time the English had been resisting steadily for a quarter of a century.

The chronicler's bias against Ethelred led him to decry all the king's moves, which has in turn affected later judgements of history. For example, the campaign against Man and Cumbria in 1000 (map **115**) is often seen as inexplicable or pointless. Yet it was probably part of an English attempt to squeeze the Dublin Vikings who had been thrown out after the defeat at Glen Mama but were still in the Irish Sea region, pehaps in the areas of Norse control known to have existed in Cumbria and Galloway, or in the Isle of Man. The claim (see map **122**) that the shires overrun by 1011 included the whole of south-east England is disproved by the preceding maps and appears to be simple exaggeration.

The second phase of the Viking attack (maps **120–129**) involved some of the most awe-inspiring Viking fighters, including the dreaded Jomsvikings and figures such as Thorkell the Tall, but even then there was no sudden English collapse. They resisted even after seven more years of disasters, which the chronicler would have us believe were unrelieved. It was only the death of Edmund Ironside that finished the campaigns and gave Cnut the kingdom, thirty-six years after the attack on Chester in 980.

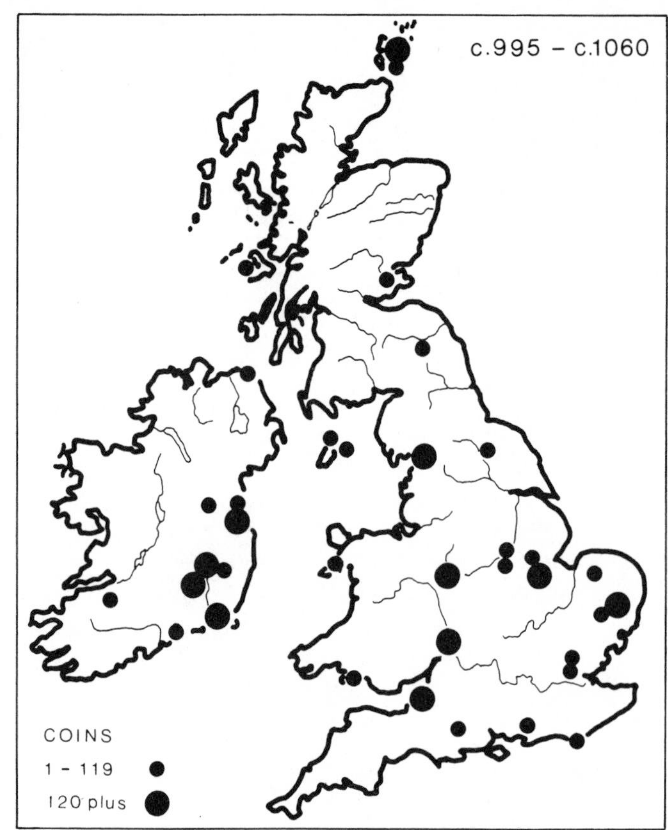

106 Hoards of coins deposited c.995–c.1060

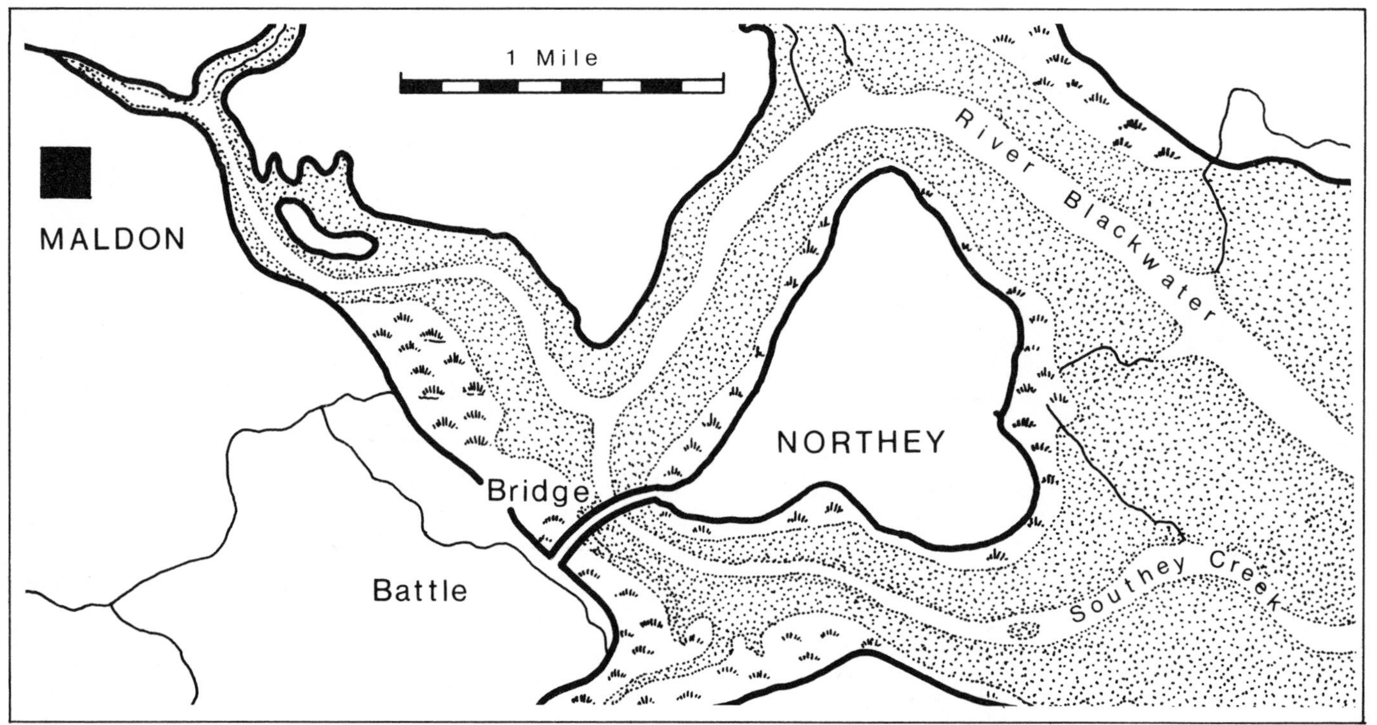

107 The Battle of Maldon 991

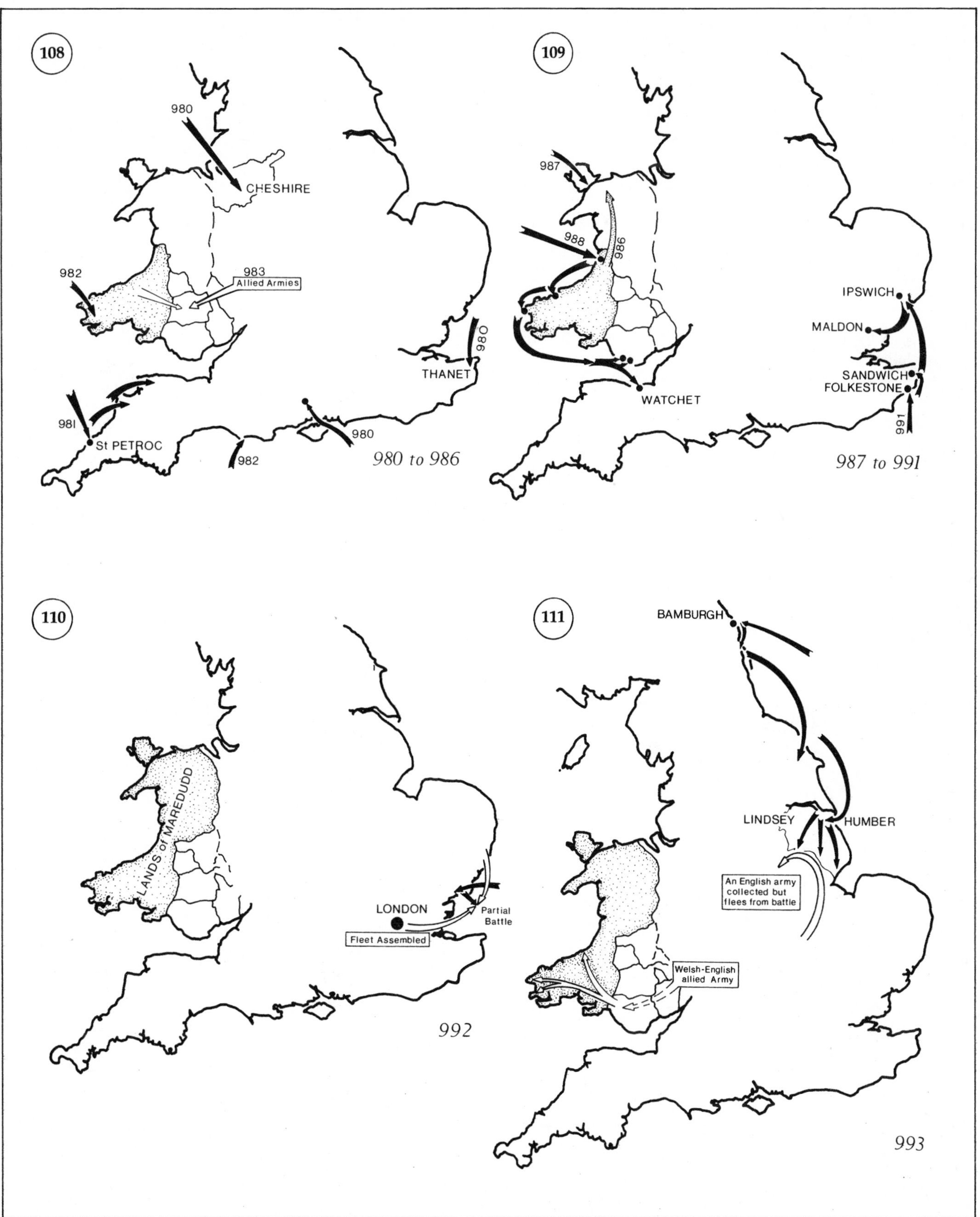

108–111 Ethelred II: the earliest attacks 980–993. Viking movements shown in black on this and subsequent maps

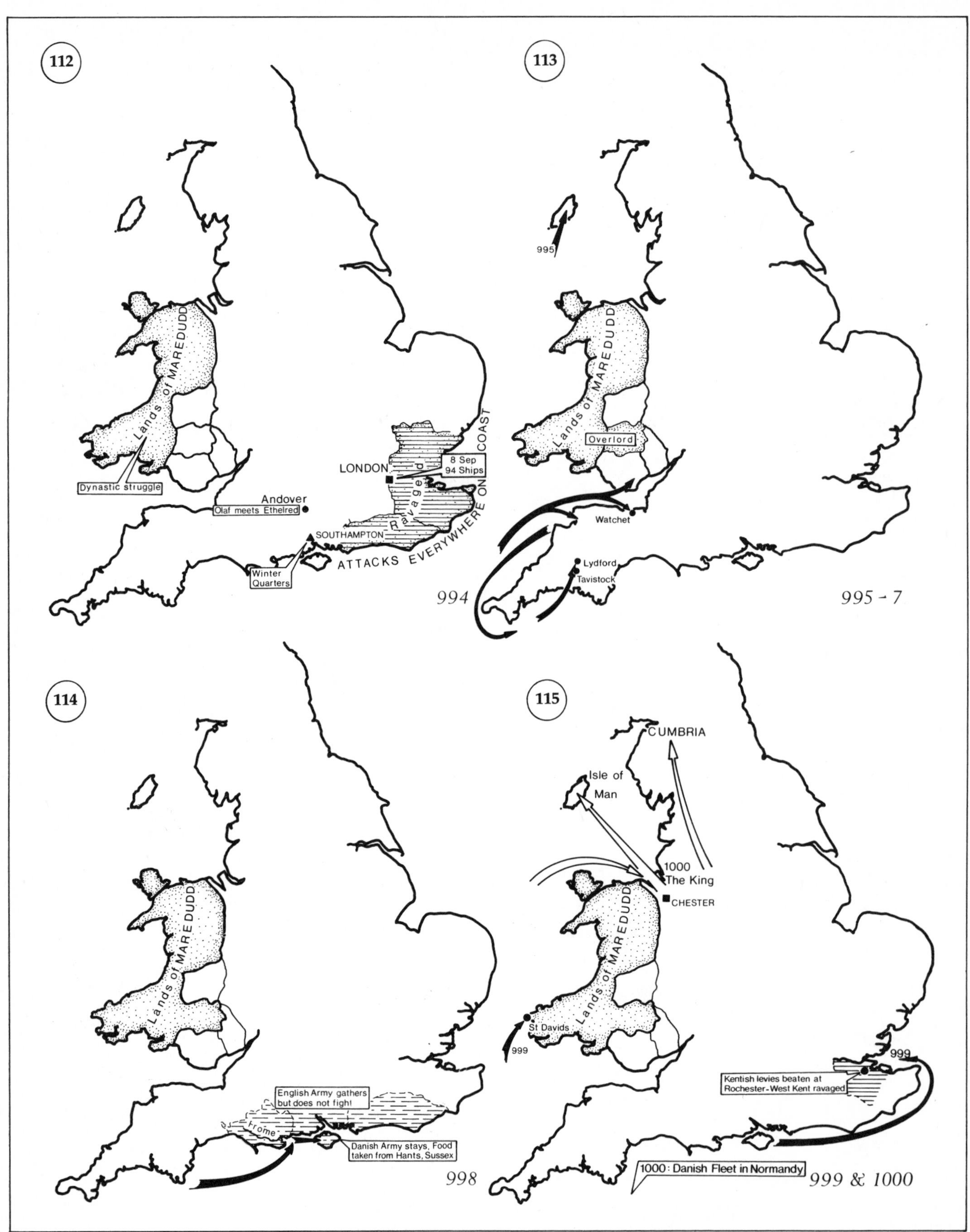
112
Lands of MAREDUDD
Dynastic struggle
Andover
Olaf meets Ethelred
LONDON
8 Sep
94 Ships
Ravaged
SOUTHAMPTON
Winter
Quarters
ATTACKS EVERYWHERE ON COAST
994
113
995
Lands of MAREDUDD
Overlord
Watchet
Lydford
Tavistock
995 - 7
114
Lands of MAREDUDD
English Army gathers
but does not fight
Frome
Danish Army stays, Food
taken from Hants, Sussex
998
115
CUMBRIA
Isle of
Man
1000
The King
CHESTER
Lands of MAREDUDD
St Davids
999
999
Kentish levies beaten at
Rochester-West Kent ravaged
1000: Danish Fleet in Normandy
999 & 1000

112–115 Raids and campaigns 994–1000

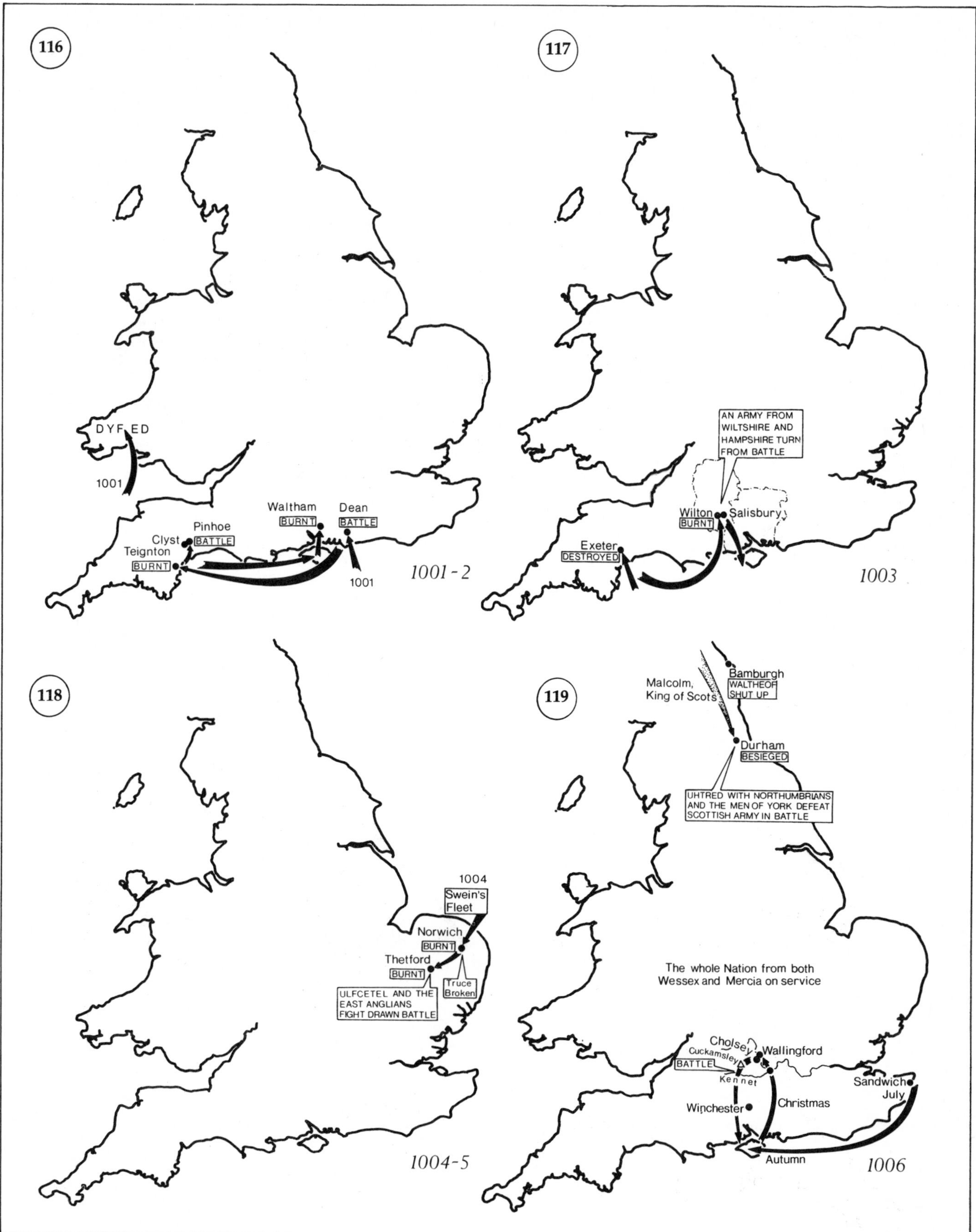

116
DYFED
1001
Waltham
BURNT
Dean
BATTLE
Pinhoe
Clyst
BATTLE
Teignton
BURNT
1001
1001-2
117
AN ARMY FROM WILTSHIRE AND HAMPSHIRE TURN FROM BATTLE
Wilton
BURNT
Salisbury
Exeter
DESTROYED
1003
118
1004
Swein's Fleet
Norwich
BURNT
Thetford
BURNT
Truce Broken
ULFCETEL AND THE EAST ANGLIANS FIGHT DRAWN BATTLE
1004-5
119
Malcolm, King of Scots
Bamburgh
WALTHEOF SHUT UP
Durham
BESIEGED
UHTRED WITH NORTHUMBRIANS AND THE MEN OF YORK DEFEAT SCOTTISH ARMY IN BATTLE
The whole Nation from both Wessex and Mercia on service
Cholsey
Cuckamsley
Wallingford
BATTLE
Kennet
Sandwich
July
Winchester
Christmas
Autumn
1006

116–119 Raids and campaigns 1001–1006

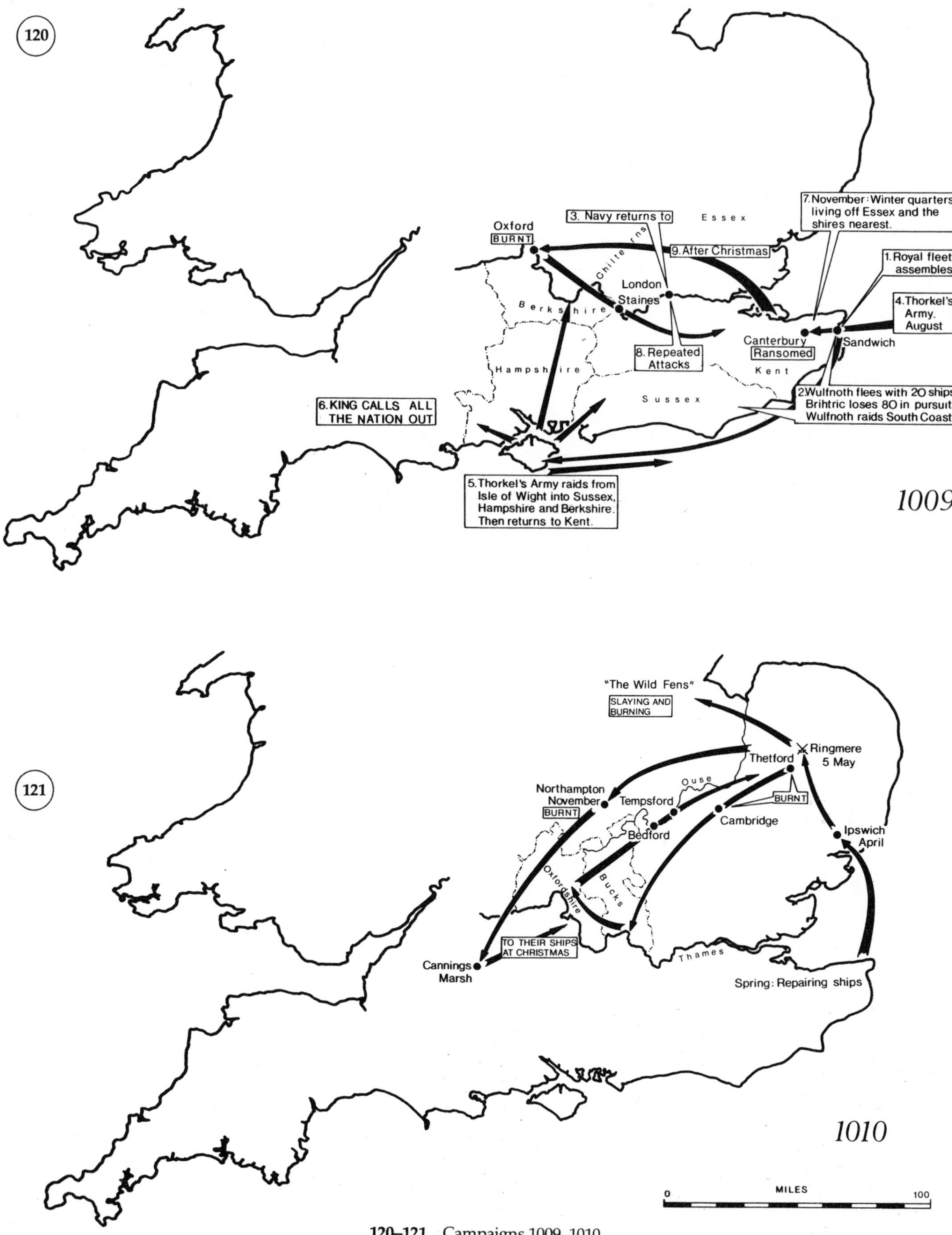

120
Oxford
BURNT
3. Navy returns to
Essex
7. November: Winter quarters living off Essex and the shires nearest.
9. After Christmas
1. Royal fleet assembles
London
Staines
Berkshire
Chilterns
4. Thorkel's Army. August
Canterbury
Ransomed
Sandwich
8. Repeated Attacks
Hampshire
Kent
Sussex
2. Wulfnoth flees with 20 ships Brihtric loses 80 in pursuit. Wulfnoth raids South Coast.
6. KING CALLS ALL THE NATION OUT
5. Thorkel's Army raids from Isle of Wight into Sussex, Hampshire and Berkshire. Then returns to Kent.
1009
"The Wild Fens"
SLAYING AND BURNING
121
Ringmere 5 May
Thetford
Ouse
Northampton November
BURNT
Tempsford
BURNT
Cambridge
Bedford
Ipswich April
Oxfordshire
Bucks
TO THEIR SHIPS AT CHRISTMAS
Cannings Marsh
Thames
Spring: Repairing ships
1010
0 MILES 100

120–121 Campaigns 1009–1010

122

123

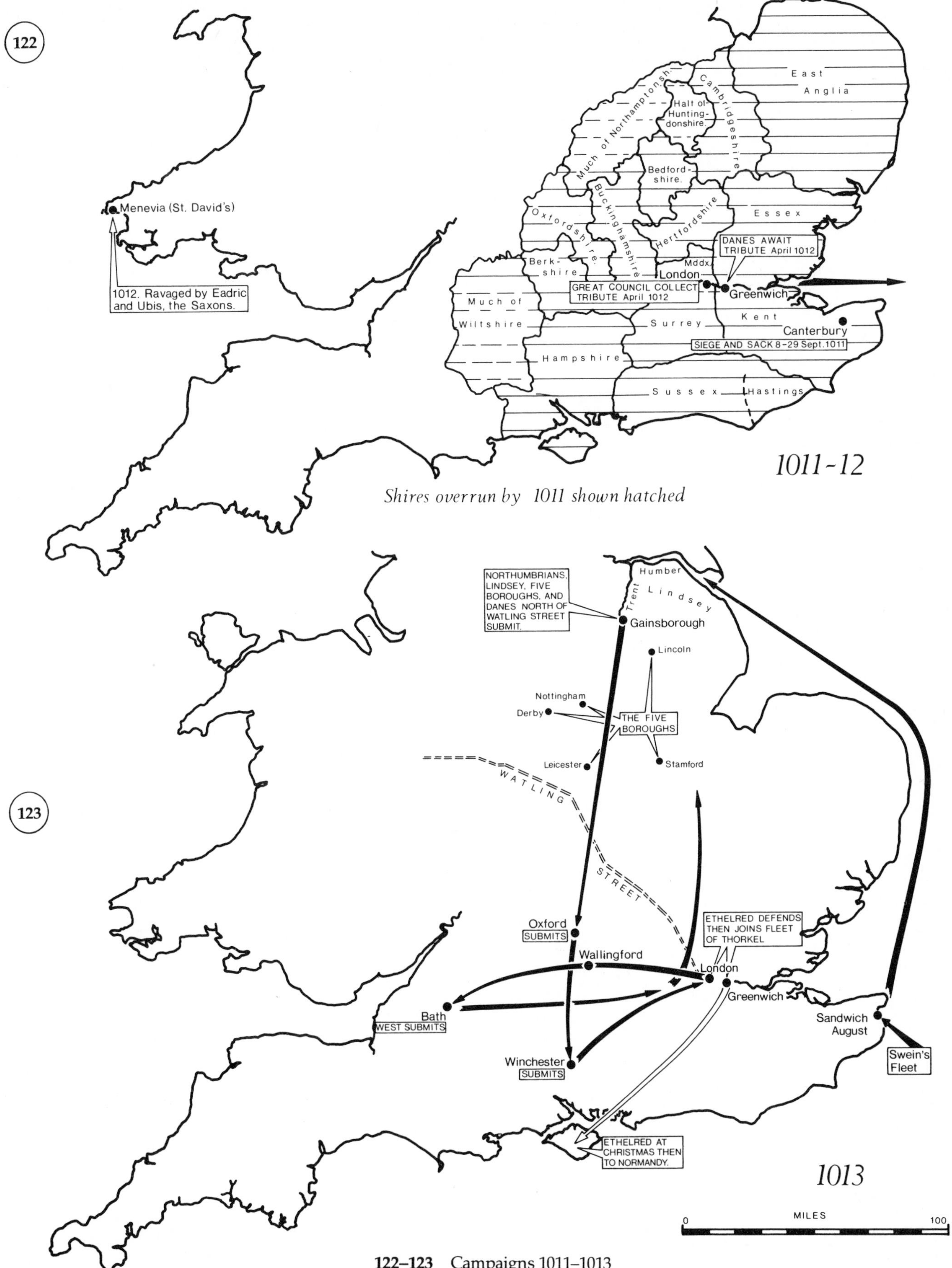

Menevia (St. David's)
1012. Ravaged by Eadric and Ubis, the Saxons.
East Anglia
Much of Northamptonsh.
Half of Huntingdonshire
Cambridgeshire
Bedfordshire.
Buckinghamshire
Oxfordshire.
Hertfordshire
Essex
Berkshire
Mddx.
London
DANES AWAIT TRIBUTE April 1012
GREAT COUNCIL COLLECT TRIBUTE April 1012
Greenwich
Much of Wiltshire
Surrey
Kent
Canterbury
SIEGE AND SACK 8-29 Sept. 1011
Hampshire
Sussex
Hastings
1011-12
Shires overrun by 1011 shown hatched
NORTHUMBRIANS, LINDSEY, FIVE BOROUGHS, AND DANES NORTH OF WATLING STREET SUBMIT.
Humber
Trent
Lindsey
Gainsborough
Lincoln
Nottingham
Derby
THE FIVE BOROUGHS
Leicester
Stamford
WATLING STREET
Oxford
SUBMITS
Wallingford
ETHELRED DEFENDS THEN JOINS FLEET OF THORKEL
London
Greenwich
Bath
WEST SUBMITS
Sandwich August
Swein's Fleet
Winchester
SUBMITS
ETHELRED AT CHRISTMAS THEN TO NORMANDY.
1013
MILES
0
100

122–123 Campaigns 1011–1013

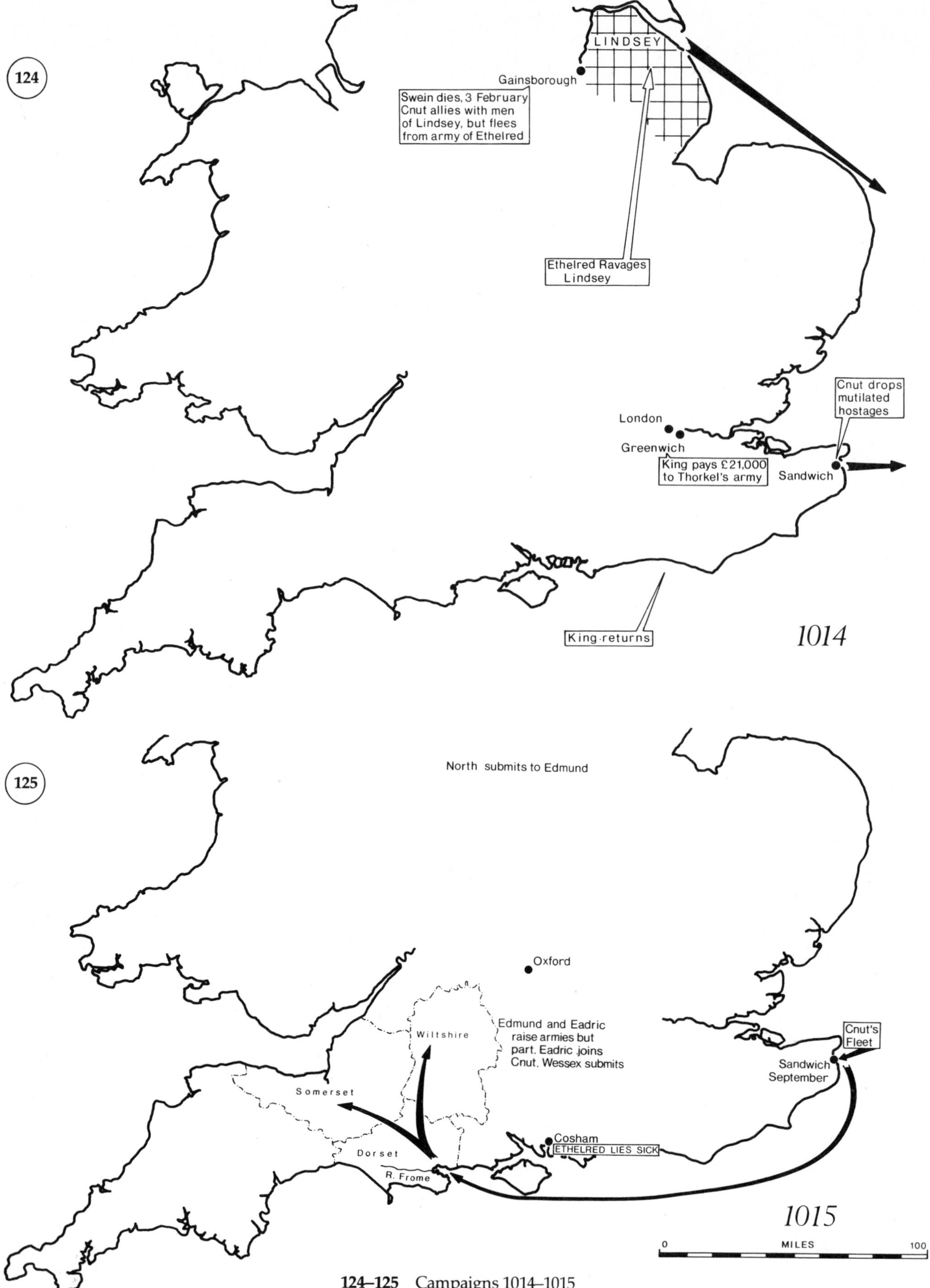
124
LINDSEY
Gainsborough
Swein dies, 3 February
Cnut allies with men
of Lindsey, but flees
from army of Ethelred
Ethelred Ravages
Lindsey
London
Greenwich
King pays £21,000
to Thorkel's army
Cnut drops
mutilated
hostages
Sandwich
King returns
1014
125
North submits to Edmund
Oxford
Edmund and Eadric
raise armies but
part. Eadric joins
Cnut. Wessex submits
Wiltshire
Somerset
Dorset
R. Frome
Cosham
ETHELRED LIES SICK
Cnut's
Fleet
Sandwich
September
1015
0
MILES
100

124–125 Campaigns 1014–1015

126–129 Campaigns of 1016 and Peace of Alney

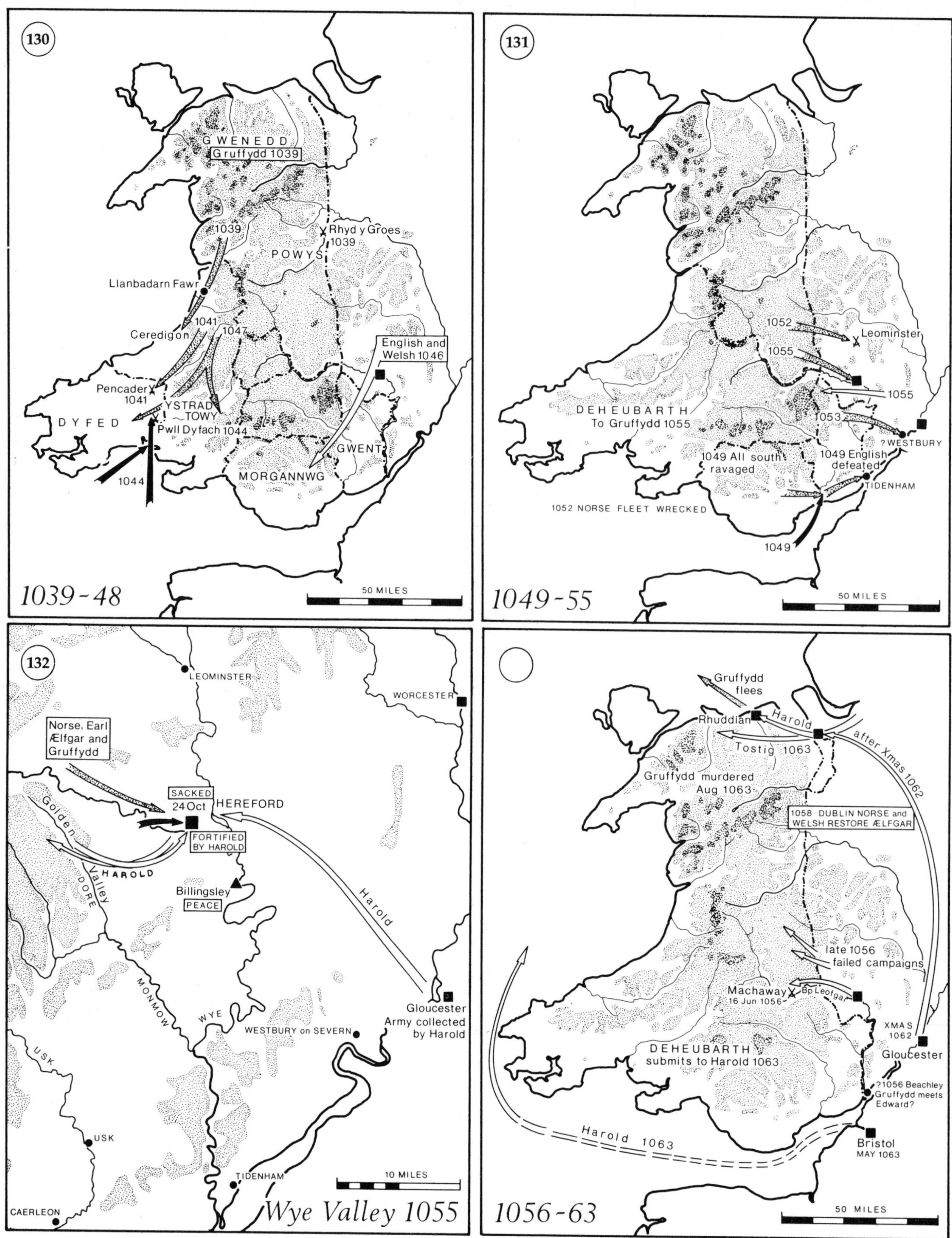

130
GWENEDD
Gruffydd 1039
1039
Rhyd y Groes 1039
POWYS
Llanbadarn Fawr
1041
1047
Ceredigon
English and Welsh 1046
Pencader 1041
YSTRAD TOWY
DYFED
Pwll Dyfach 1044
GWENT
1044
MORGANNWG
1039-48
50 MILES
131
1052
Leominster
1055
1055
DEHEUBARTH To Gruffydd 1055
1053
? WESTBURY
1049 All south ravaged
1049 English defeated
TIDENHAM
1052 NORSE FLEET WRECKED
1049
1049-55
50 MILES
132
LEOMINSTER
WORCESTER
Norse, Earl Ælfgar and Gruffydd
SACKED
24 Oct
HEREFORD
Golden Valley
FORTIFIED BY HAROLD
HAROLD
DORE
Billingsley
PEACE
Harold
MONMOW
WYE
Gloucester Army collected by Harold
WESTBURY on SEVERN
USK
USK
TIDENHAM
10 MILES
CAERLEON
Wye Valley 1055
Gruffydd flees
Rhuddlan
Harold
Tostig 1063
after Xmas 1062
Gruffydd murdered Aug 1063
1058 DUBLIN NORSE and WELSH RESTORE ÆLFGAR
late 1056 failed campaigns
Machaway
16 Jun 1056
Bp Leofgar
XMAS 1062
Gloucester
DEHEUBARTH submits to Harold 1063
?1056 Beachley Gruffydd meets Edward?
Harold 1063
Bristol MAY 1063
1056-63
50 MILES

Wales (130–134)

After the conclusion of the Danish Wars, in the period 1016–66, there were no great campaigns apart from those of Cnut in Scandinavia. But it was a period of significant developments in Anglo–Welsh relations, which have too often been ignored. The rise of Gruffydd ap Llywelyn to become the eventual ruler of all Wales was a long one, his skirmishes with the English were many and he made skilful use of the rivalries of the English houses and of the interventions of the Vikings from Ireland. Gruffydd finally sacked a major English town and escaped retribution, going on to rule all Wales from his palaces and to own a fleet. It took the most powerful man in England, Harold, to bring about his downfall and then only after several unsuccessful forays into Wales (maps **130–133**).

The whole episode commands a considerable amount of attention in the Chronicle, where indeed it is the only Welsh episode to be treated at length. The story illustrates the resources that the Welsh threat could absorb and the attention it could demand and may provide some measure of the troubles Wales posed for the Mercian kingdom in earlier centuries. Maps **181** and **182** show the concentrations of lands held by Harold and the Leofric families on the border, which perhaps reflects the attention that the earls had to pay to the Welsh problem.

Waste estates are noted in many shires in the Domesday Book and are sometimes attributable to historic events. Significantly, there is a concentration of waste places recorded TRE, i.e. in 1066, along the Welsh border (map **134**). Whilst these places may have become waste for a variety of reasons, as in other shires far from the border, the concentration does suggest that the raids recorded for the reign of Edward the Confessor had an effect and may have been the cause of most waste vills. Certainly the four waste vills due to King Caraduach cannot be attributed to any other cause.

130–133 Wales 1039–1063

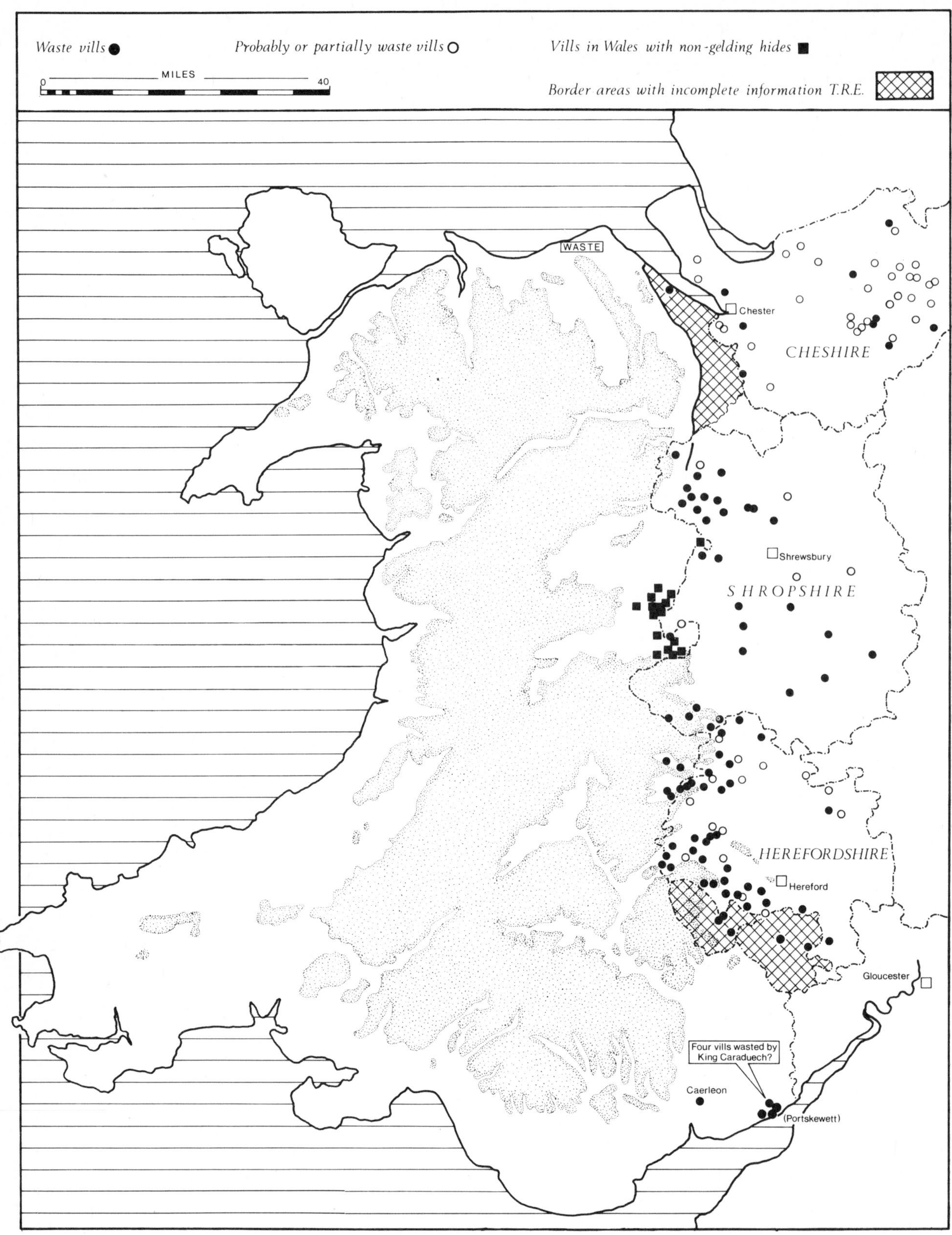

134 Domesday waste in 1066 as an indicator of previous Welsh raids. High ground stippled

Administration

The Administrative Implications of Offa's Dyke (135)

The materials for the reconstruction of the administration of Anglo-Saxon England are extremely sketchy. It is easy therefore to fall into the trap of believing that the administration was rudimentary and to concentrate attention only on the surviving documents, the laws and the charters. However to gain some perspective on the strength of the Anglo-Saxon administrative machinery, it is essential to look at its achievements, for example the frontier system known as Offa's and Wat's Dykes (map **135**). The dykes are longer than the more famous Roman Antonine and Hadrian's Walls added together: they run from sea to sea, cutting off the Welsh peninsula from Mercia. There can be little doubt that the larger dyke was built at the command of Offa; the shorter but stronger dyke must belong to the same period. The dykes are roughly 149 miles long, the probable height of the rampart was some 24 feet above the ditch bottom, and the ditch was some 6 feet deep.

The number of men required to build the dykes and the effort of directing and maintaining them on the border of the Mercian kingdom must have been considerable. The enterprise shows the degree of organization an early medieval society could attain. The whole of England was assessed in tax units which were linked conceptually to the productive capacity of the land. These were hides in most of the country, sulungs in Kent and, later in the Danelaw, carucates. It is probable that the system was to order so many men from a hide-unit, with their tools and food, under the organization of their ealdormen to appear on a given day at a predetermined point on the dyke line. Difficult stretches would already have been marked out with a small bank and ditch; for the rest, a line of marking rods sufficed. This basic system was used by the Carolingians for works such as the great bridge at Pont de l'Arche and was general in northern Europe. As long as there was some idea of the tax possibilities of the realm and its constituent parts then a building project or a tax could be assessed in terms of men or of money and divided first by the total, to arrive at a figure such as one man from every ten hides, or a penny from every hide. The total was divided between shires or **regiones,** the shire reeve or ealdorman would then pass the assessment down to the hundred meeting or its predecessor, and finally the collection would be made and returned back up through the system. Little was needed in the way of book-keeping. That there were some royal memoranda is not in question. Surprisingly, amongst so little in the way of secular documentation, we even have two surviving examples.

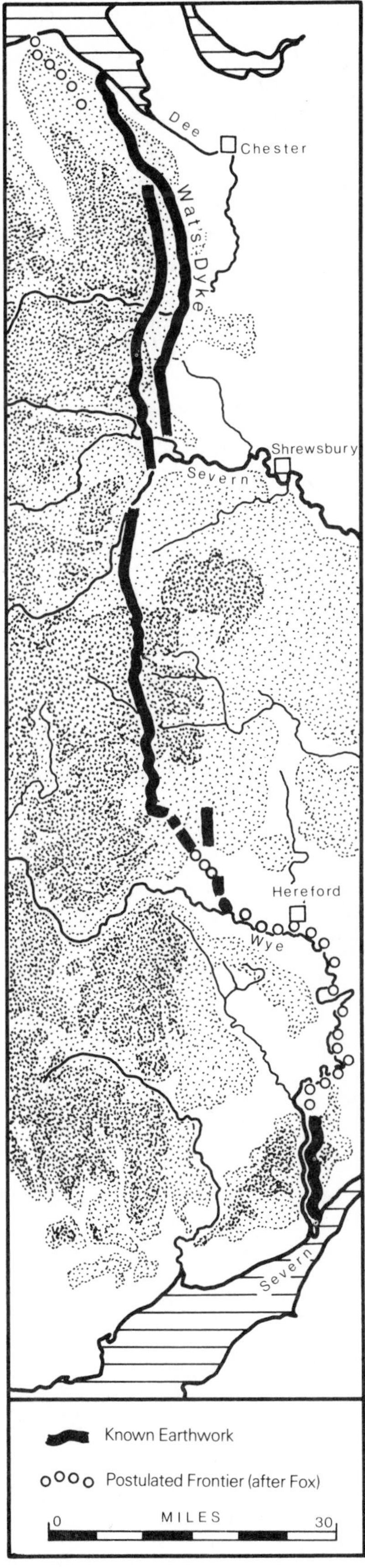

135 Offa's dyke

136 The Tribal Hidage: place names from Harleian MS 3271

The Tribal Hidage (136–138)

One document, known since the days of Maitland as the 'Tribal Hidage', exists in a tenth-century manuscript but there can be no doubt that the exemplar comes from the days of the Mercian Supremacy. Where it should be placed within that period is a subject of debate still awaiting satisfactory elucidation. In the meantime it is safest to reckon it an 'ancient tribute-list of the Mercian kings . . . it should probably be attributed to the reign of Wulfhere, Æthelbald, or Offa. Its great age, to which much of its obscurity is due, shows that it must have been intended to serve some practical purpose' (Stenton 1971, 43, 295–7, 300–1). The names of the various **regiones**, provinces and kingdoms are often obscure and their exact location a matter of dispute (Davies and Vierck 1974; Hart 1971). Map **136** and the diagram and list (**137–138**) offer the information as it stands; further discussion is better left to the authorities cited. Some of the early kingdoms that appear are well known — we can attach other information to them and in some cases even chart their frontiers — whereas others are known only from this list.

137

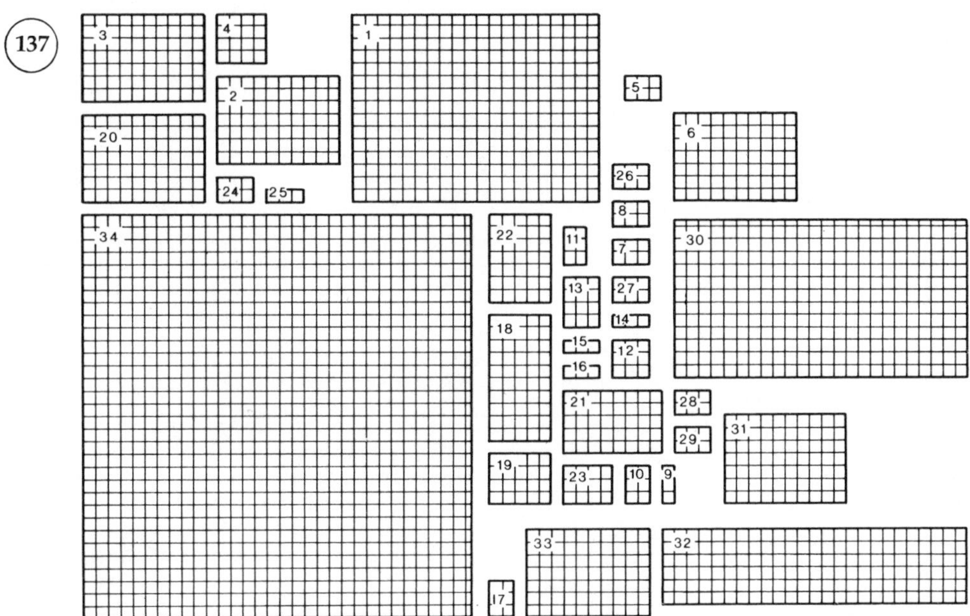

138

		Hundreds of Hides
1	MYRCNA LANDES	300
2	WOCEN SÆTNA	70
3	WESTERNA	70
4	PECSÆTNA	12
5	ELMEDSÆTNA	6
6	LINDES FARONA and Heathfeld land	70
7	SOUTH GYRWA	6
8	NORTH GYRWA	6
9	EAST WIXNA	3
10	WEST WIXNA	6
11	SPALDA	6
12	WIGESTA	9
13	HEREFINNA	12
14	SWEORDORA	3
15	GIFLA	3
16	HICCA	3
17	WIHTGARA	6
18	NOXGAGA	50
19	OHTGAGA	20
	TOTAL	66,100

		Hundreds of Hides
20	HWINCA	70
21	CILTERN SÆTNA	40
22	HENDRICA	35
23	UNECUNG GA	12
24	AROSÆTNA	6
25	FÆRPINGA	3
26	BILMIGA	6
27	WIDERIGGA	6
28	EAST WILLA	6
29	WEST WILLA	6
30	EAST ENGLE	300
31	EAST SEXENA	70
32	CANTWARENA	150
33	SUTH SEXENA	70
34	WEST SEXENA	1000
	TOTAL	247,700

137–138 The Tribal Hidage: comparative assessments and listing

Early Kingdoms (139–143)

At the opening of the period covered by this atlas, England south of the Humber was organized in some degree with reference to the central kingdom of Mercia. By the reign of Æthelbald there was allied kingdoms, subject and tributory kingdoms, provinces and **regiones**. The allied, subject and tributory kingdoms were themselves divided, in the case of Wessex from an early stage, into shires.

One of the these kingdoms was that of Lindsey, one of the few early kingdoms of which the bounds can be accurately drawn (map **139**). These bounds and the early history of the kingdom have been discussed by Stenton (1970, 127–35). The 'island' of Lincoln was cut off on two sides by river valleys and on the other two by the sea and the Humber estuary. Within this isolation the kingdom managed to survive independently into the eighth century, while to the south the rest of present-day Lincolnshire was part of Middle Anglia. The kingdom had to exist under an overlord, which by the middle of the eighth century was Mercia. The kings of Lindsey became permanent tributory kings under Offa and were finally absorbed into the Mercian nobility by 800.

The bounds of the other kingdoms are sometimes embedded to some extent in the dioceses which were originally founded to serve individual kingdoms. It is therefore possible to postulate the extent of the kingdom of the East Saxons by comparing it with the diocese of London (map **140**). There are problems, however, as the northern boundary of Middlesex and the coincident limit of the diocese of London reflect only the edge of the holdings of the Abbey of St Albans. However the map is useful, as the kingdom included the whole of Essex and Middlesex and the eastern fringe of Hertfordshire. The Middlesex and Hertfordshire portions were probably lost between 735 and 755 as a result of pressure from Æthelbald, but it is clear that Middlesex was firmly in the Kingdom before 730, when Bede referred to London as its metropolis, and the Thames would appear to have formed the frontier with Wessex in 704–706, when a meeting was held in Brentford. This would suggest that Wessex had some hold over Surrey at the time. Although no East Saxon king was of national rather than local importance, the kingdom survived in its truncated form into the ninth century when it appears to have been incorporated into Wessex.

Among the longest lasting of the minor kingdoms were the Hwicce and the Magonsætan (map **143**). Although their independence disappeared in the eighth century they remained as territorial units in the eleventh century when their ealdorman still led the group to battle. The grouping had thus survived the Danish wars and the incorporation into Wessex, and even the division of Mercia into shires in the first half of the tenth century. This territorial unity must have been aided by the fact that the Magonsætan were also the people served by the bishopric of Hereford whilst the Hwicce were served by the bishopric of Worcester. As the map shows, the later division of the area into shires cut across these early kingdoms.

That the use of the diocesan boundaries is an acceptable approach towards the reconstruction of the early boundaries is shown by the distribution of charters issued by the kings of the Hwicce. In map **141** the charters of the kings of Hwicce are plotted in relation to the later diocesan boundary of the bishopric of Worcester and the two clearly correlate. At one time, as the map shows, there was also jurisdiction over Bath, a fact born out by the intineraries of the Mercian kings; a certain fluidity in the boundaries is only to be expected.

This fluidity was operating upon the Hwicce and the Magonsætan at the end of the ninth century, when it would appear that there was some extension of Saxon control into the areas of the Welsh kingdoms. The Welsh kings finally abrogated authority over the area known as Archenfield sometime after 900 — when the series of Welsh charters dealing with the area ceases (Davies 1978, 26). When the authority of the old divisions broke down as a result of the Danish wars the dioceses of Hereford and Worcester seem to have taken responsibility for areas which originally belonged to the Wrocensetnan and the Tomsætan (map **142**). These two peoples are named after the Wrekin and the Tame (in the same way that one must assume the Magonsætan were named after the old Roman site at Kenchester, Magnis).

The few charter references which allow us to guess at the extent of these areas put some part within the dioceses representing the Hwicce and the Magonsætan. This same evidence points to the Tomsætan as a large unit. The evidence of map **142** must act as a caution against drawing frontiers too uncritically using apparently early materials (Ford 1976, 281).

There is a series of articles discussing these kingdoms (Finberg 1961, 167–81, 217–24; Smith 1965; M. Wilson 1968). They had ceased to function at all independently by 750 although the names of their kings were still recorded into the last years of the eighth century when, like many other small divisions, they were absorbed into Mercia.

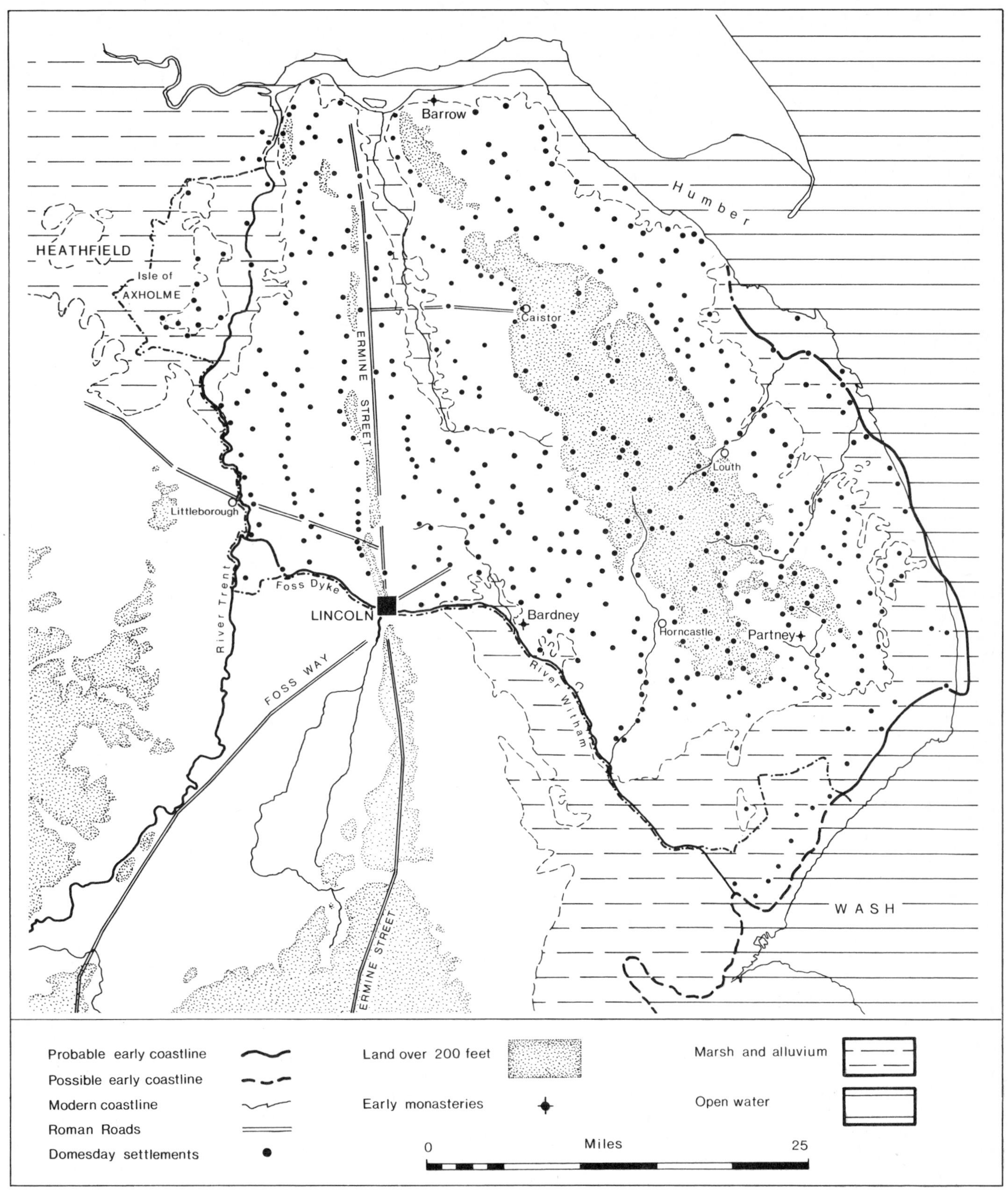
Barrow
Humber
HEATHFIELD
Isle of
AXHOLME
Caistor
ERMINE STREET
Louth
Littleborough
Foss Dyke
LINCOLN
Bardney
Horncastle
Partney
River Trent
FOSS WAY
River Witham
ERMINE STREET
WASH
Probable early coastline
Possible early coastline
Modern coastline
Roman Roads
Domesday settlements
Land over 200 feet
Early monasteries
Marsh and alluvium
Open water
0
Miles
25

139 Early Lindsey

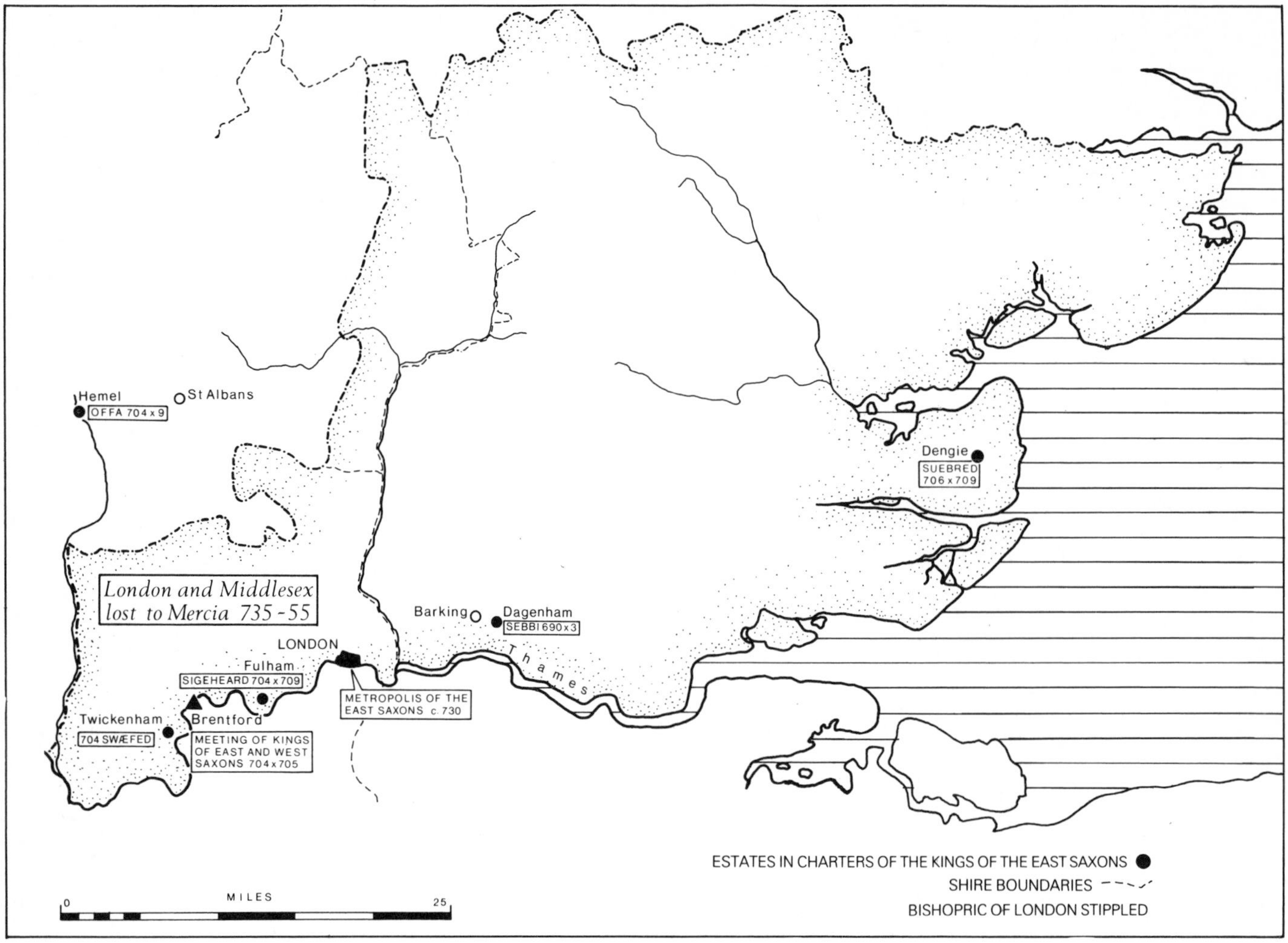

Hemel
OFFA 704 x 9
St Albans
London and Middlesex lost to Mercia 735-55
LONDON
Fulham
SIGEHEARD 704 x 709
Twickenham
704 SWÆFED
Brentford
MEETING OF KINGS OF EAST AND WEST SAXONS 704 x 705
METROPOLIS OF THE EAST SAXONS c. 730
Barking
Dagenham
SEBBI 690 x 3
Thames
Dengie
SUEBRED 706 x 709
ESTATES IN CHARTERS OF THE KINGS OF THE EAST SAXONS
SHIRE BOUNDARIES
BISHOPRIC OF LONDON STIPPLED
0 MILES 25

140 The Kingdom of the East Saxons

Lands
Beneficiaries
0 Miles 25

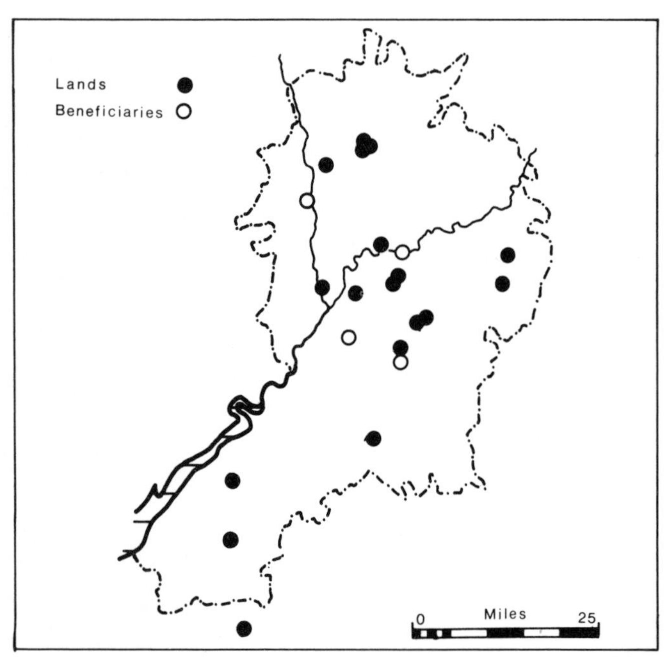

141 Charters of the kings of Hwicce

Wirksworth 835
Repton 835
Breedon 848
Trent
Aston 963
Lichfield
Wrekin
Tamworth
Leicester
Plaish 963
Severn
Tame
Crofton 849
Worcester
0 Miles 25
WROCENSETNAN
Lands in
TOMSÆTAN
Lands in
Lands associated with Hunbert
Bound of medieval dioceses of Worcester and Hereford

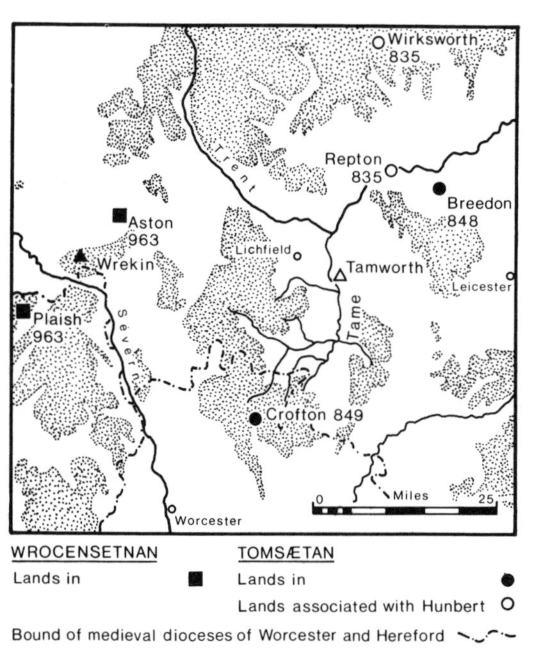

142 The Tomsætan and Wrocensetnan

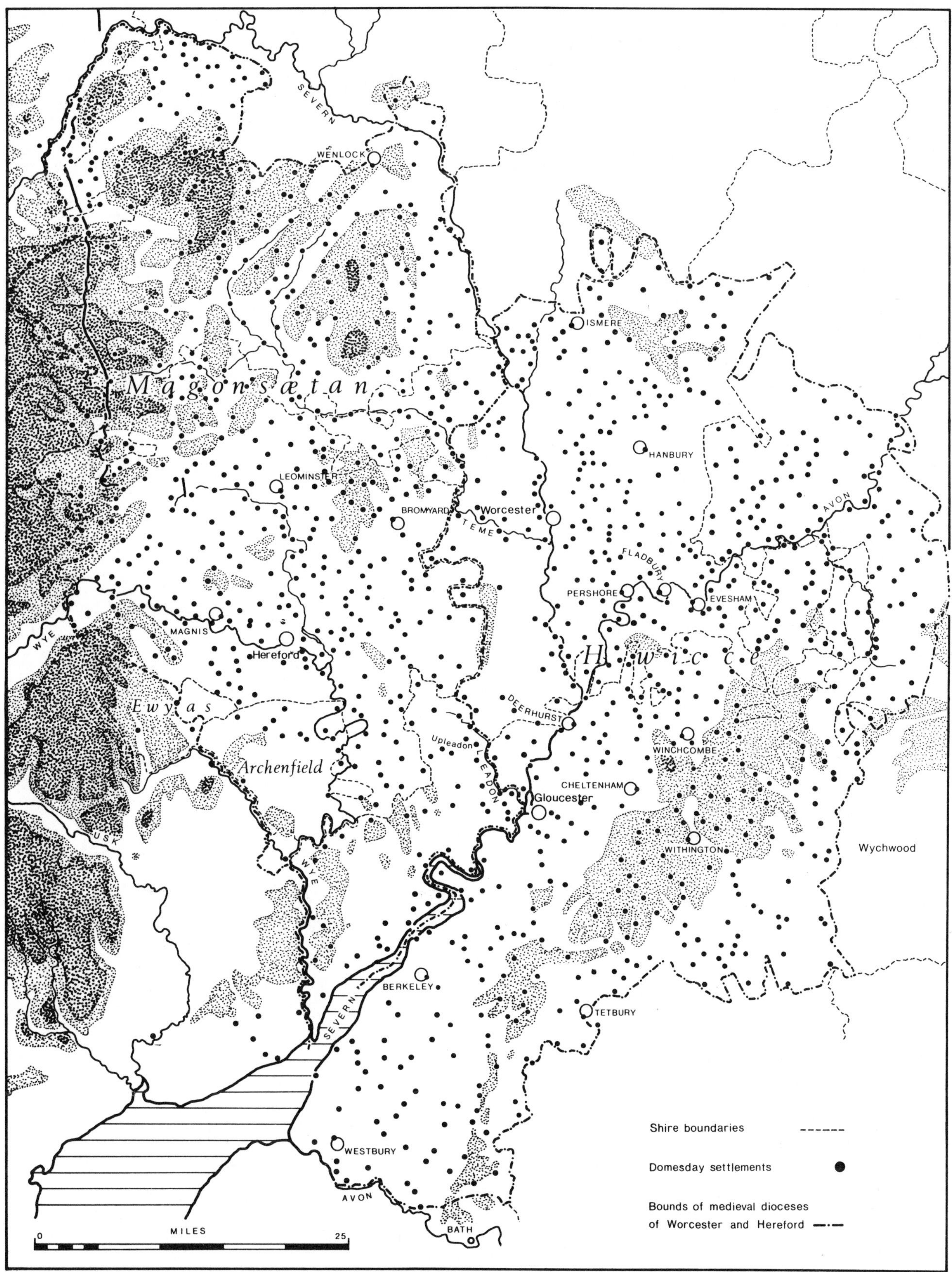

143 The Kingdoms of the Magonsætan and Hwicce

The Itineraries of the Early Kings (144–148)

Itineraries of rulers of the early medieval period in Europe have often been drawn and found useful by scholars. Examples are the itineraries of Charlemagne (map **144**) and Henry the Fowler. Such material becomes increasingly common after the Conquest. It is a little less certain that the effort will produce any clear results for the more fragmentary movements of the Anglo-Saxon kings. However the maps have been compiled, and although they are not exhaustive, they show some interesting patterns which may have important implications and inferences. All the itineraries show civil rather than military movements.

The itinerary of the Mercian kings (map **145**) reveals little that is new, as it is substantially the same as the map of 'the Mercian Kingdom' in Stenton (1971, 201), although the version here does bring out the importance of Tamworth rather more strongly. The itinerary of West Saxon kings (map **146**) has several interesting features: first, the Berkshire area is bereft of meetings, which, taken with the Mercian map, opens up the question of exactly where the frontier between the two kingdoms was up to 850, as does the fact that Bath was a place that Mercian kings visited. The West Saxon kings showed an early preference for the four shires of Hampshire, Wiltshire, Dorset and Somerset, a preference which continued into the late tenth century when all England was theirs to choose from.

Alfred the Great showed an interest in all parts of his kingdom which is reflected both in his itinerary (map **147**) and in his will (map **148**). The evidence suggests that the king held east Cornwall in his own hands, perhaps as a relatively deserted band between him and whatever remained of the Cornish state to the west of Bodmin Moor.

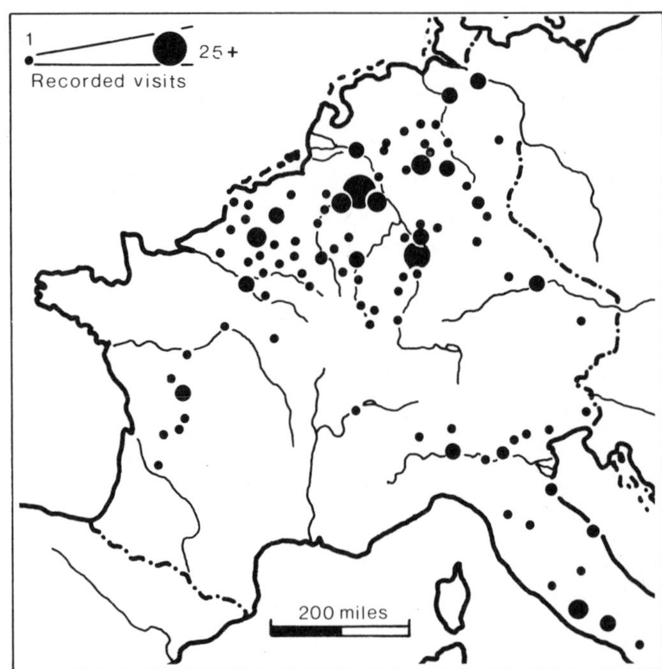

144 The itinerary of Charlemagne

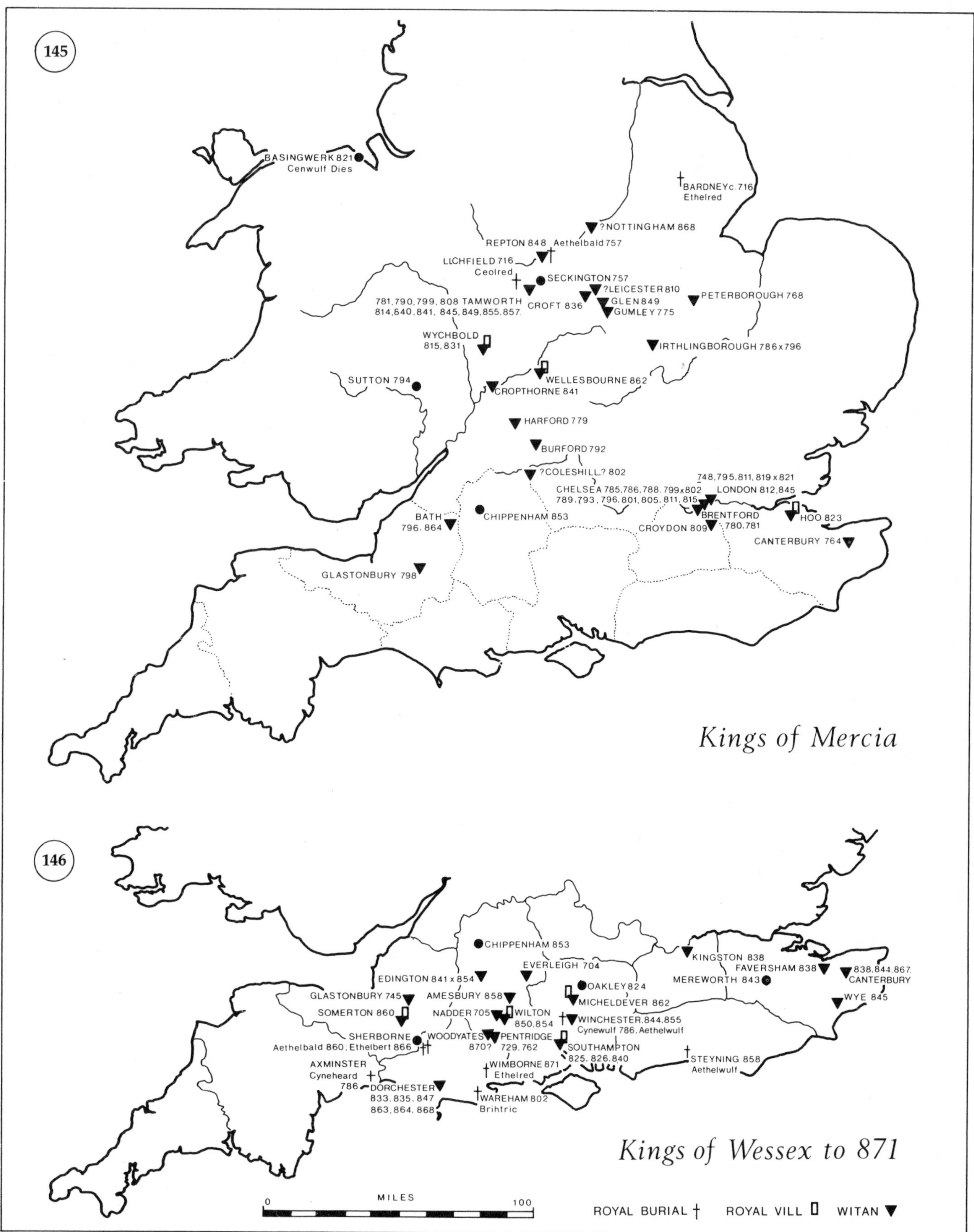
145
BASINGWERK 821
Cenwulf Dies
BARDNEY c. 716
Ethelred
?NOTTINGHAM 868
REPTON 848 Aethelbald 757
LICHFIELD 716
Ceolred
SECKINGTON 757
?LEICESTER 810
781, 790, 799, 808 TAMWORTH
814, 640, 841, 845, 849, 855, 857.
CROFT 836
GLEN 849
GUMLEY 775
PETERBOROUGH 768
WYCHBOLD
815, 831
IRTHLINGBOROUGH 786 x 796
SUTTON 794
WELLESBOURNE 862
CROPTHORNE 841
HARFORD 779
BURFORD 792
?COLESHILL,? 802
748, 795, 811, 819 x 821
CHELSEA 785, 786, 788, 799 x 802
789, 793, 796, 801, 805, 811, 815
LONDON 812, 845
BATH
796, 864
CHIPPENHAM 853
BRENTFORD
780, 781
HOO 823
CROYDON 809
CANTERBURY 764
GLASTONBURY 798
Kings of Mercia
146
CHIPPENHAM 853
EVERLEIGH 704
KINGSTON 838
FAVERSHAM 838
838, 844, 867
CANTERBURY
EDINGTON 841 x 854
MEREWORTH 843
OAKLEY 824
GLASTONBURY 745
AMESBURY 858
MICHELDEVER 862
WYE 845
SOMERTON 860
NADDER 705
WILTON
850, 854
WINCHESTER, 844, 855
Cynewulf 786, Aethelwulf
SHERBORNE
Aethelbald 860; Ethelbert 866
WOODYATES
870?
PENTRIDGE
729, 762
SOUTHAMPTON
825, 826, 840
STEYNING 858
Aethelwulf
AXMINSTER
Cyneheard
786
WIMBORNE 871
Ethelred
DORCHESTER
833, 835, 847
863, 864, 868
WAREHAM 802
Brihtric
Kings of Wessex to 871
0
MILES
100
ROYAL BURIAL
ROYAL VILL
WITAN

145–146 Itineraries of the Kings of Mercia and of Wessex to 871

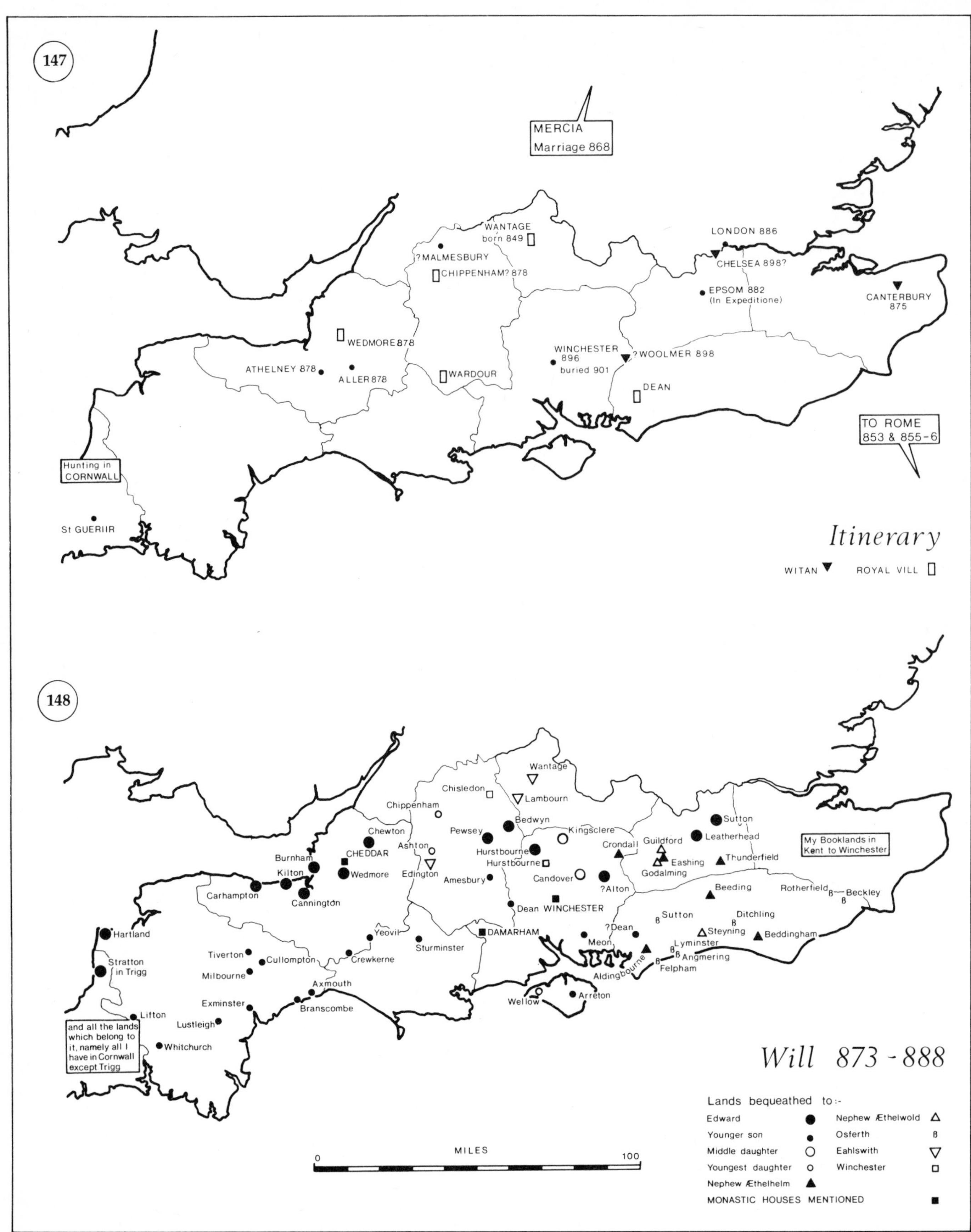
147
MERCIA
Marriage 868
WANTAGE
born 849
?MALMESBURY
CHIPPENHAM? 878
WEDMORE 878
ATHELNEY 878
ALLER 878
WARDOUR
WINCHESTER
896
buried 901
?WOOLMER 898
DEAN
LONDON 886
CHELSEA 898?
EPSOM 882
(In Expeditione)
CANTERBURY
875
TO ROME
853 & 855-6
Hunting in
CORNWALL
St GUERIIR
Itinerary
WITAN
ROYAL VILL
148
Wantage
Chisledon
Lambourn
Chippenham
Chewton
Pewsey
Bedwyn
Kingsclere
Ashton
Burnham
CHEDDAR
Hurstbourne
Hurstbourne
Crondall
Guildford
Sutton
Leatherhead
Eashing
Thunderfield
Godalming
My Booklands in
Kent to Winchester
Kilton
Wedmore
Edington
Amesbury
Candover
?Alton
Carhampton
Cannington
Dean
WINCHESTER
Beeding
Rotherfield
Beckley
Sutton
Ditchling
Steyning
Beddingham
Hartland
Yeovil
Sturminster
DAMARHAM
?Dean
Meon
Lyminster
Angmering
Felpham
Aldingbourne
Stratton
in Trigg
Tiverton
Cullompton
Crewkerne
Milbourne
Axmouth
Exminster
Branscombe
Wellow
Arreton
Lifton
and all the lands which belong to it, namely all I have in Cornwall except Trigg
Lustleigh
Whitchurch
Will 873 - 888
Lands bequeathed to :-
Edward
Younger son
Middle daughter
Youngest daughter
Nephew Æthelhelm
Nephew Æthelwold
Osferth
Eahlswith
Winchester
MONASTIC HOUSES MENTIONED
MILES
0
100

147–148 The itinerary and will of Alfred the Great

The Burghal Hidage (149–153)

The survival of this royal memorandum is of great importance in the study of the development of towns and fortifications under Alfred the Great and his children. It consists of a list of West Saxon **burhs**, fortified places, set out in order around southern England, omitting Kent, London and most of Mercia (**150–153**). The places are each assigned a number of hides and a concluding paragraph allows one to deduce the length of defended wall (**149**), so that we can be certain what places were defended at a given time, 919 (for a discussion of the date and other important points see Brooks 1964). This conversion from the tax assessment in hides to length of wall is obviously of great import if it is possible to confirm the exact extent of a defended area at a fixed moment of time (Hill 1969), and the figures given in the text can be checked against the actual lengths, giving a surprising degree of accuracy. In fact the whole document is a piece of early mathematics which can be seen to work, from the complex conversion table to the totals at the end of the second version of the text. If the correlation apparently demonstrated in **149** is correct we have much to learn of the early history of Exeter and Chichester which show such a deviation from the norm.

Thus the one document allows us to examine the early topography of a town, know that it was walled at a given time, at the king's command and that there was an area of a known size dependent in some way on it.

The Burghal Hidage stands alone in importance and it is doubtful even now if we have realized its full significance in relation to the development of royal government as well as in the more urban field. (Loyn 1971, 117)

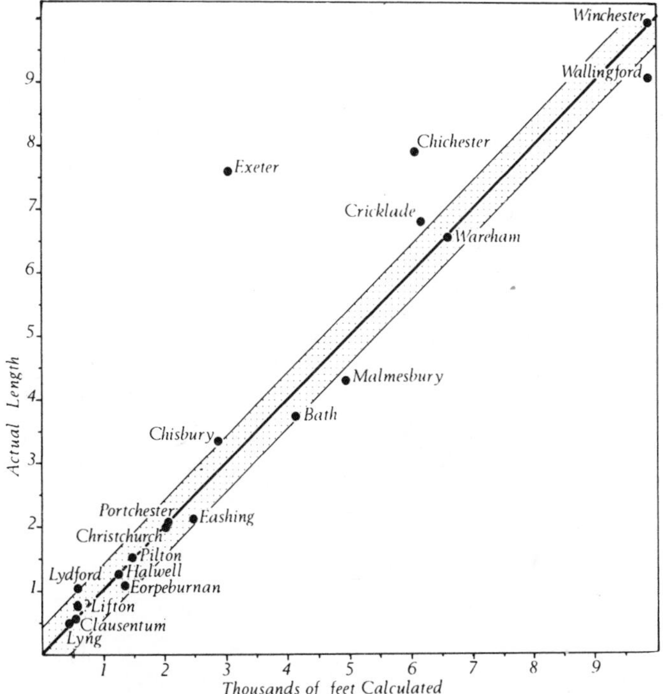

149 The Burghal Hidage: correlation of wall lengths. The stippled area represents the 'rounding up' of 50 hides

The Itineraries of the Kings of England from Edward the Elder to Cnut (154–163)

In the whole of the tenth century, when the King of the West Saxons was, with interruptions, King of all England, it is remarkable how rarely he is to be seen travelling outside of the south of England, and more particularly the four heartland shires of Wessex. This may have some general relevance apart from a very sensible preference for the better part of England. It explains how the remark that Ethelred II was 'eating his foodrents' in Shropshire in 1006 was meant to be ironic, for no other king is known to have been in that shire in the preceding century. More generally, however, it is clear that it must tell us something of the nature of royal administration. Only Athelstan (map **155**) appears to have spent any considerable portion of his time in Mercia and it follows that the whole realm had to be administered from the centre of Wessex where the king decided to be. It should be noted that it was not from the towns, Winchester or Dorchester, that the king mainly ran his affairs but from estates in the countryside, Cheddar, **sede regali**, Frome or Amesbury. If Edgar the Peaceable (map **160**) wished to administer his kingdom from Cheddar he would need a skilled household, dependable subordinates in the outlying regions and good communications. There is little here of the king travelling restlessly, grazing the pastures of his estates and eating up his foodrents. This is a sophisticated system and not run from 'a box under the bed'.

There is a change apparent with the stress of the Danish Wars, and about AD 1000 a drift in the centre of affairs towards the Thames Valley is noticeable with some indication of the special links that Ethelred had with London (map **162**). But for Ethelred and Cnut (maps **162–163**) there seems little attempt to travel the heartlands of the Midlands. One thing which puzzles me, and for which I have yet to find an explanation, is the insistance on the part of successive kings that they be consecrated at Kingston upon Thames, a place which is neither in Wessex nor the heart of Mercia.

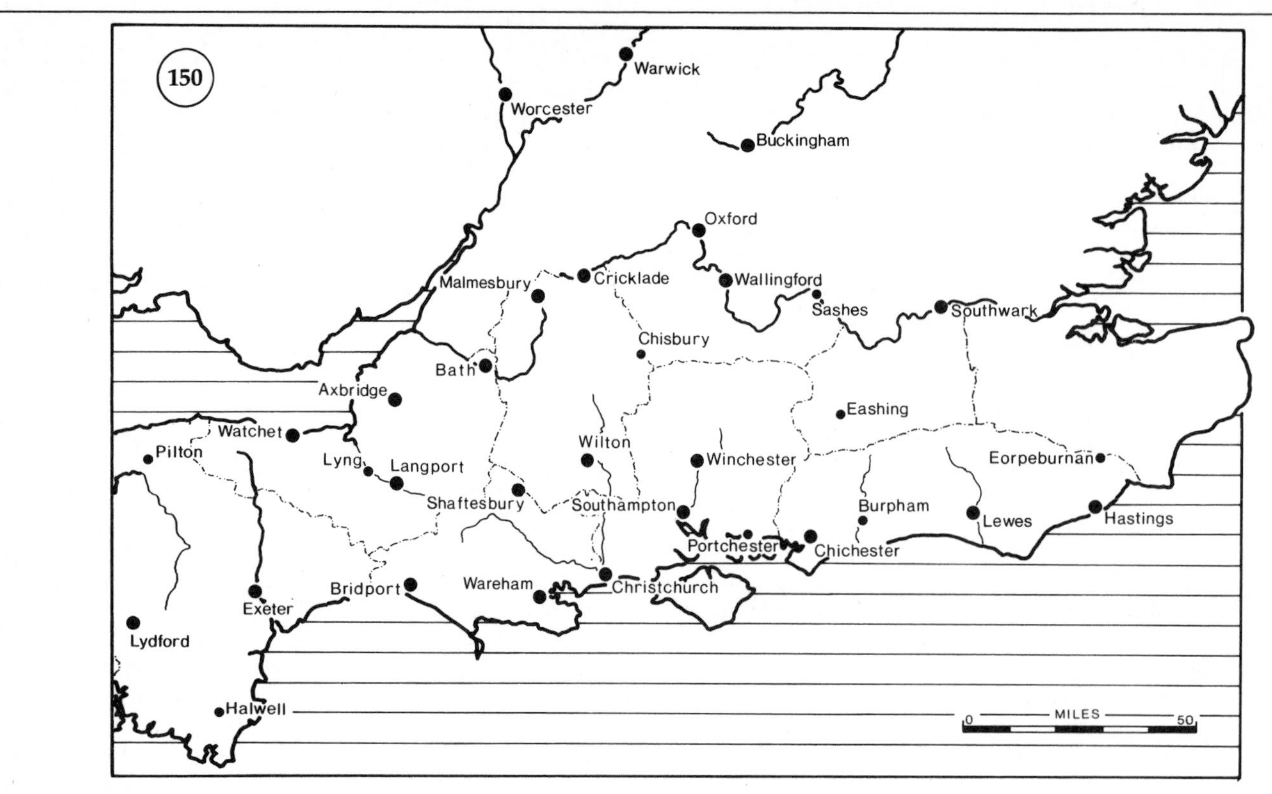

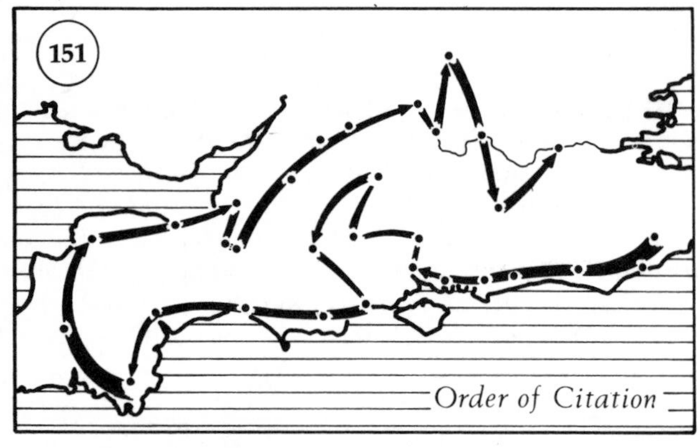

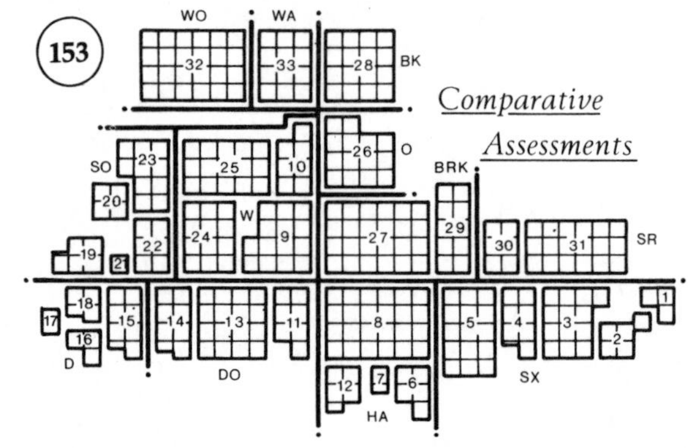

152

		ASSESSMENT (HIDES)	EQUIVALENT (FEET)
1	EORPEBURNAN	324	1336
2	HASTINGS	500	2062
3	LEWES	1300	5362
4	BURPHAM	720	2972
5	CHICHESTER	1500	6187
6	PORTCHESTER	500	2062
7	SOUTHAMPTON	150	619
8	WINCHESTER	2400	9900
9	WILTON	1400	5775
10	CHISBURY	700	2887
11	SHAFTESBURY	700	2887
12	CHRISTCHURCH	470	1939
13	WAREHAM	1600	6600
14	BRIDPORT	760	3135
15	EXETER	734	3028
16	HALWELL	300	1237
17	LYDFORD	140	577
18	PILTON	360	1485
19	WATCHET	513	2116
20	AXBRIDGE	400	1650
21	LYNG	100	412
22	LANGPORT	600	2475
23	BATH	1000	4125
24	MALMESBURY	1200	4950
25	CRICKLADE	1500	6187
26	OXFORD	1400	5775
27	WALLINGFORD	2400	9900
28	BUCKINGHAM	1600	6600
29	SASHES	1000	4125
20	EASHING	600	2475
31	SOUTHWARK	1800	7425
	TOTAL FOR WESSEX	27.070	
32.	WORCESTER	1200	4950
33	WARWICK	2400	9900

150–153 The Burghal Hidage

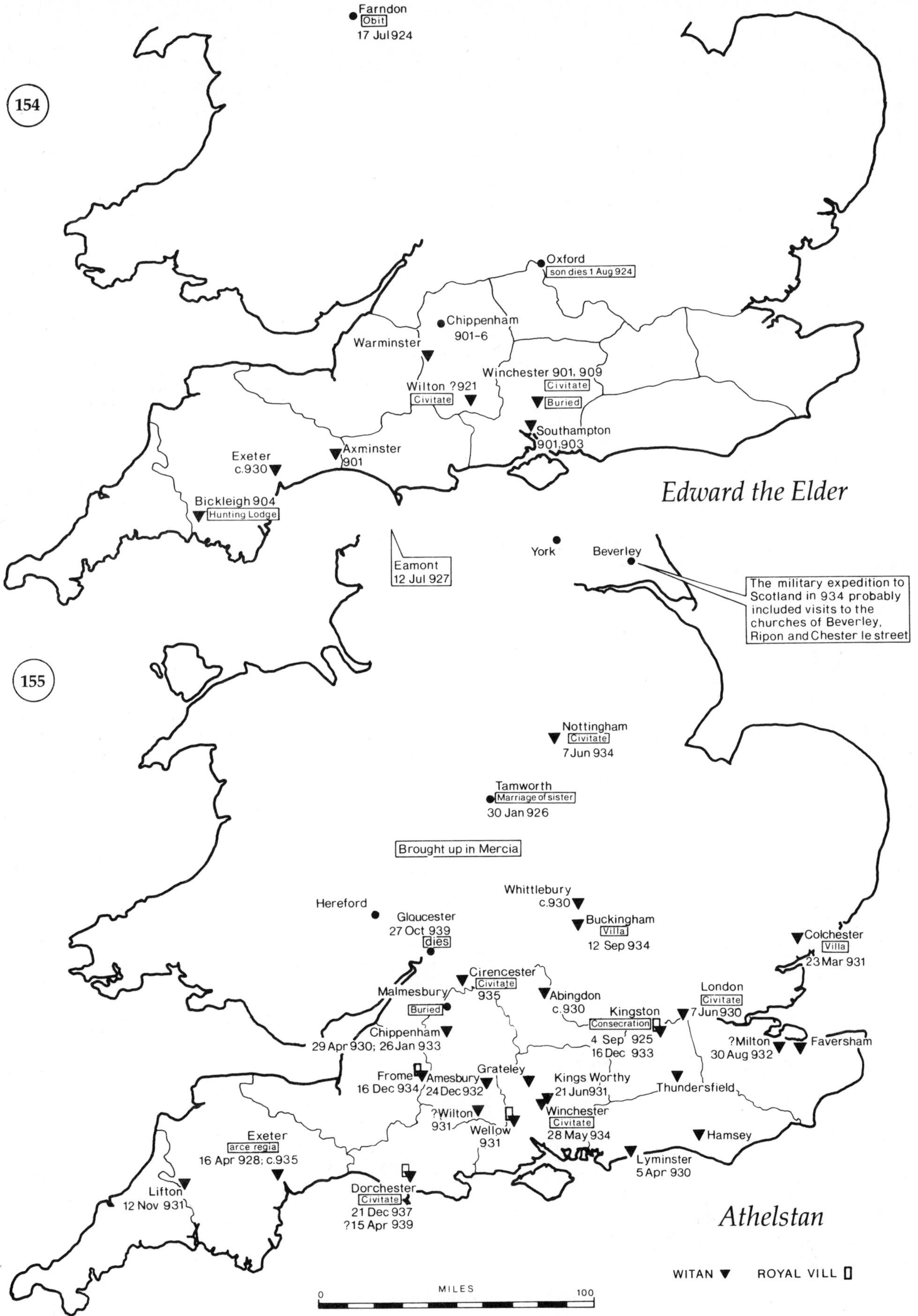
154
Farndon
Obit
17 Jul 924
Oxford
son dies 1 Aug 924
Chippenham
901-6
Warminster
Winchester 901, 909
Civitate
Buried
Wilton ?921
Civitate
Southampton
901,903
Axminster
901
Exeter
c.930
Bickleigh 904
Hunting Lodge
Edward the Elder
Eamont
12 Jul 927
York
Beverley
The military expedition to Scotland in 934 probably included visits to the churches of Beverley, Ripon and Chester le street
155
Nottingham
Civitate
7 Jun 934
Tamworth
Marriage of sister
30 Jan 926
Brought up in Mercia
Whittlebury
c.930
Hereford
Gloucester
27 Oct 939
dies
Buckingham
Villa
12 Sep 934
Colchester
Villa
23 Mar 931
Cirencester
Civitate
935
Malmesbury
Buried
Abingdon
c.930
London
Civitate
7 Jun 930
Kingston
Consecration
4 Sep 925
16 Dec 933
Chippenham
29 Apr 930; 26 Jan 933
?Milton
30 Aug 932
Faversham
Grateley
Frome
16 Dec 934
Amesbury
24 Dec 932
Kings Worthy
21 Jun 931
Thundersfield
?Wilton
931
Wellow
931
Winchester
Civitate
28 May 934
Hamsey
Exeter
arce regia
16 Apr 928; c.935
Lyminster
5 Apr 930
Lifton
12 Nov 931
Dorchester
Civitate
21 Dec 937
?15 Apr 939
Athelstan
WITAN
ROYAL VILL
MILES
0
100

154–155 Itineraries of Edward the Elder and Athelstan

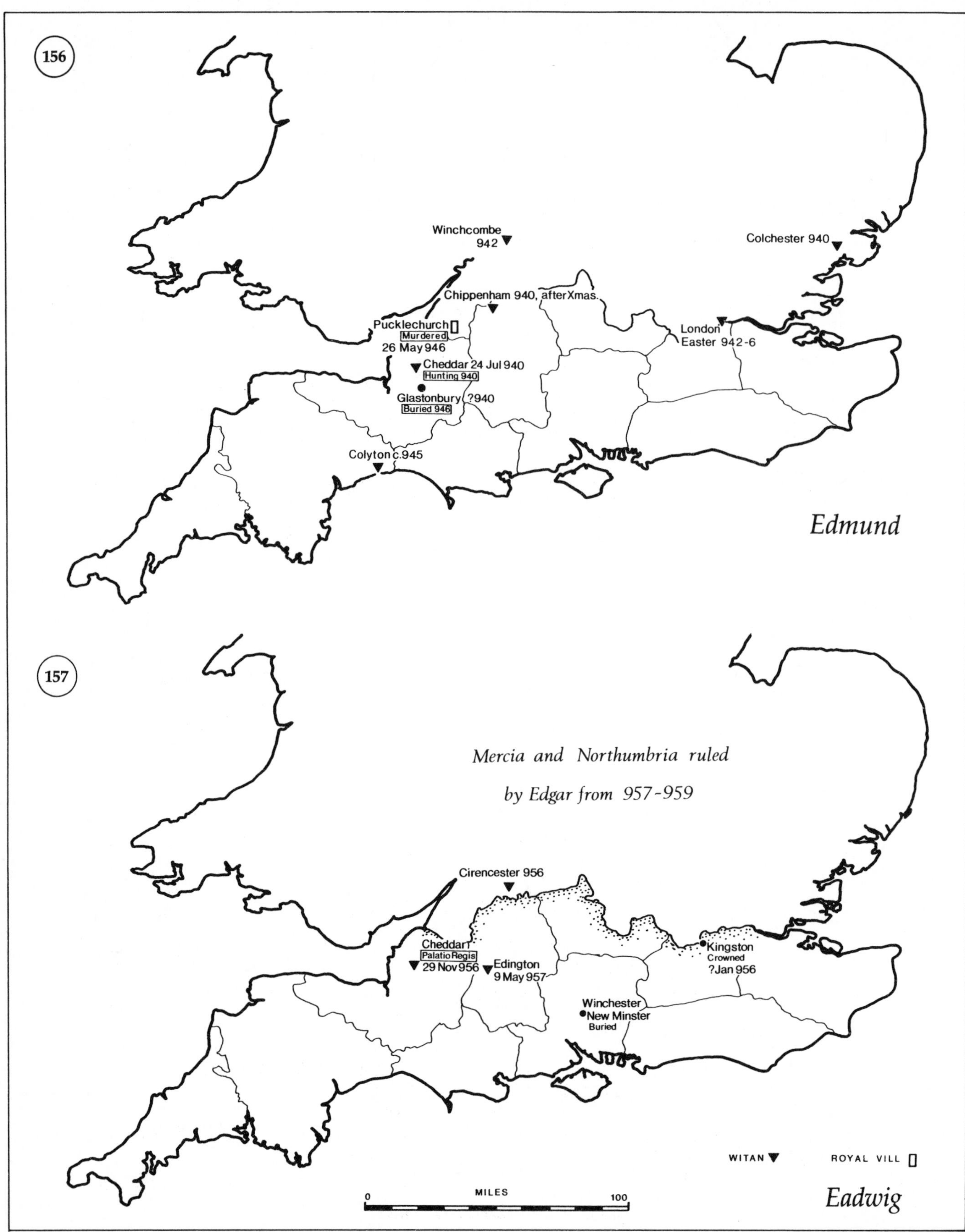
156
Winchcombe
942
Colchester 940
Chippenham 940, after Xmas.
Pucklechurch
Murdered
26 May 946
London
Easter 942-6
Cheddar 24 Jul 940
Hunting 940
Glastonbury ?940
Buried 946
Colyton c.945
Edmund
157
Mercia and Northumbria ruled
by Edgar from 957-959
Cirencester 956
Cheddar
Palatio Regis
29 Nov 956
Edington
9 May 957
Kingston
Crowned
?Jan 956
Winchester
New Minster
Buried
WITAN
ROYAL VILL
0
MILES
100
Eadwig

156–157 Itineraries of Edmund and Eadwig

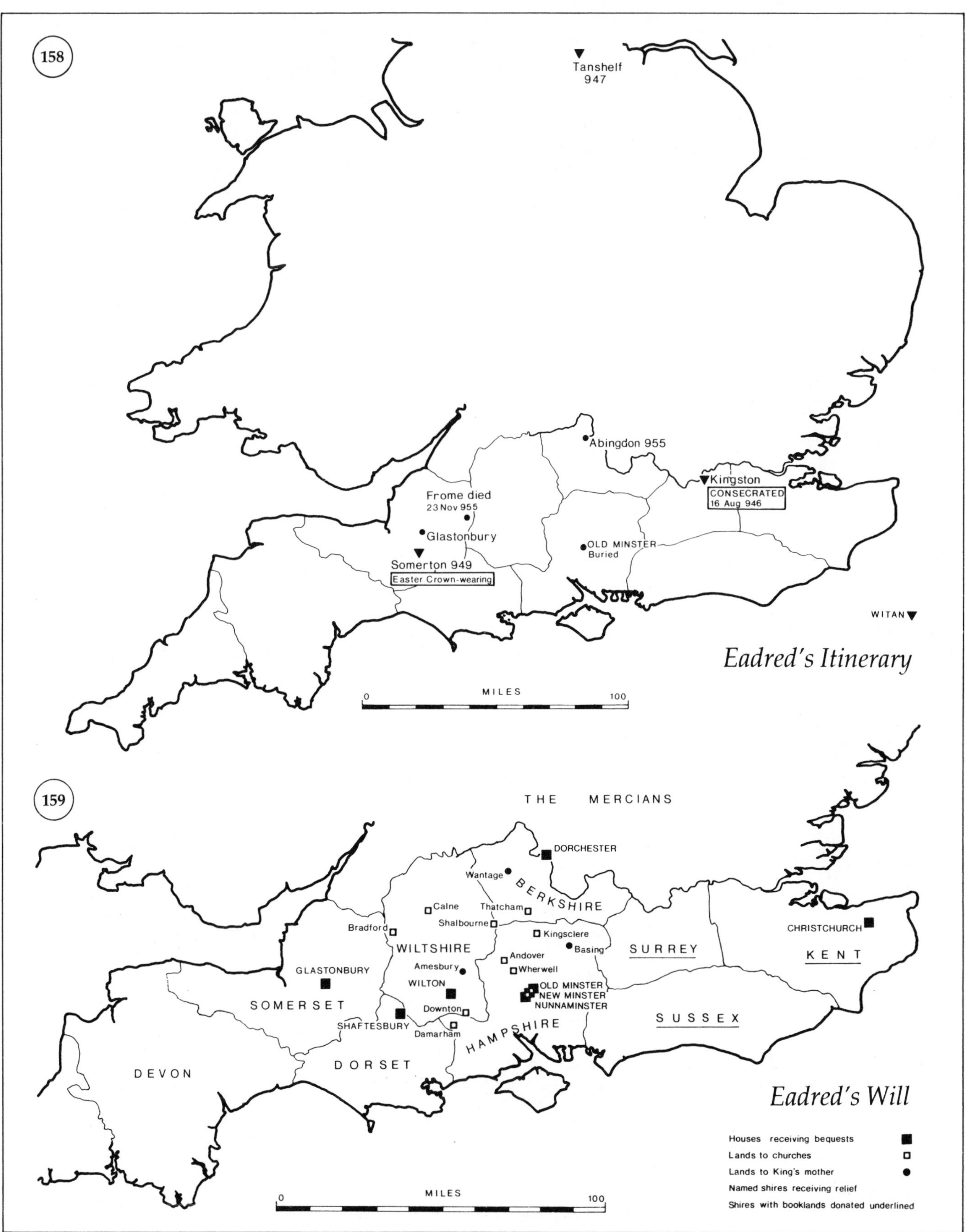
158
Tanshelf
947
Abingdon 955
Kingston
CONSECRATED
16 Aug 946
Frome died
23 Nov 955
Glastonbury
Somerton 949
Easter Crown-wearing
OLD MINSTER
Buried
WITAN
Eadred's Itinerary
MILES
0
100
159
THE MERCIANS
DORCHESTER
Wantage
BERKSHIRE
Calne
Thatcham
Shalbourne
Bradford
Kingsclere
Basing
SURREY
CHRISTCHURCH
KENT
WILTSHIRE
Andover
Wherwell
Amesbury
WILTON
GLASTONBURY
OLD MINSTER
NEW MINSTER
NUNNAMINSTER
SOMERSET
Downton
SHAFTESBURY
Damarham
HAMPSHIRE
SUSSEX
DORSET
DEVON
Eadred's Will
Houses receiving bequests
Lands to churches
Lands to King's mother
Named shires receiving relief
Shires with booklands donated underlined
MILES
0
100

158–159 Itinerary and will of Eadred

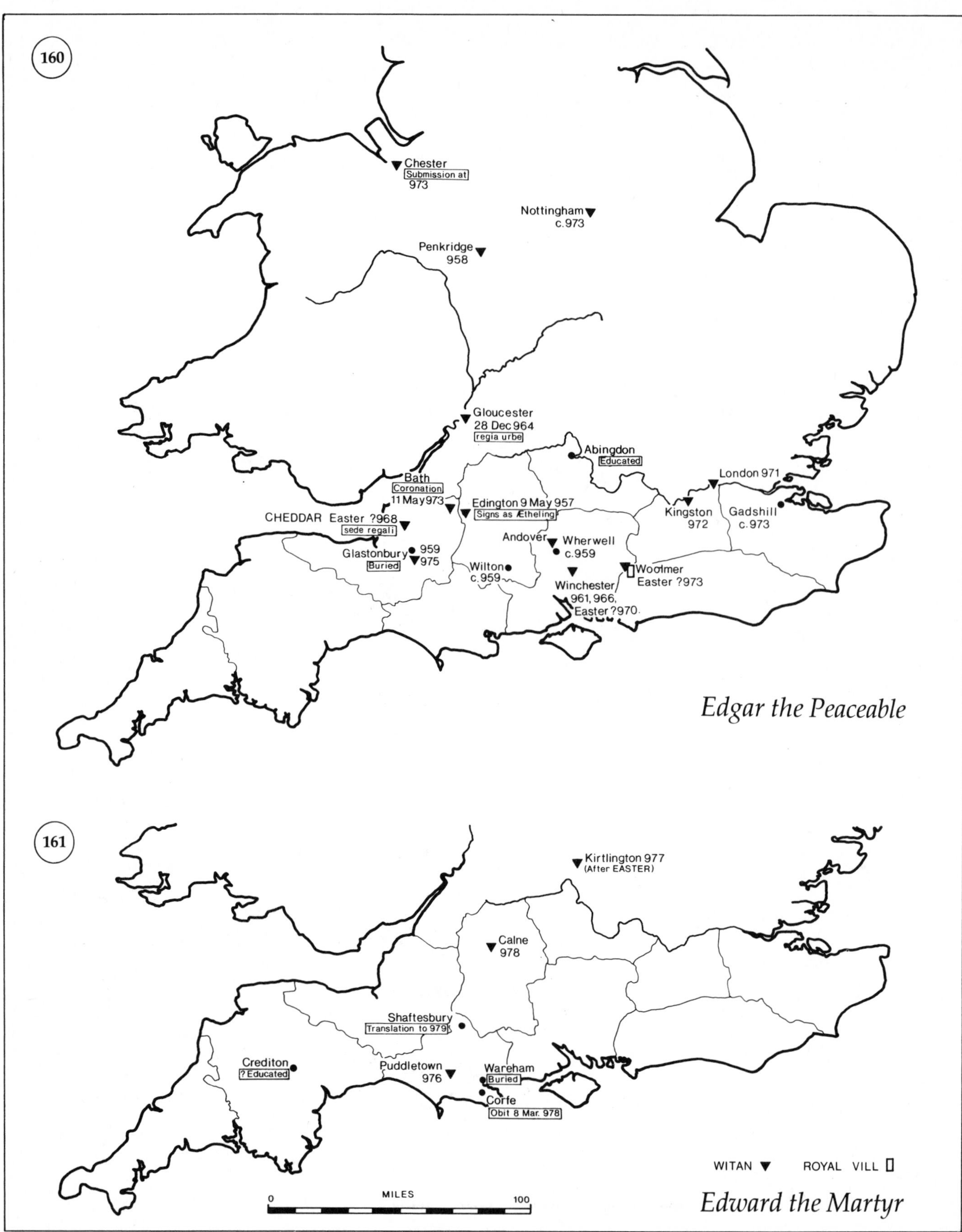

160–161 Itineraries of Edgar the Peaceable and Edward the Martyr

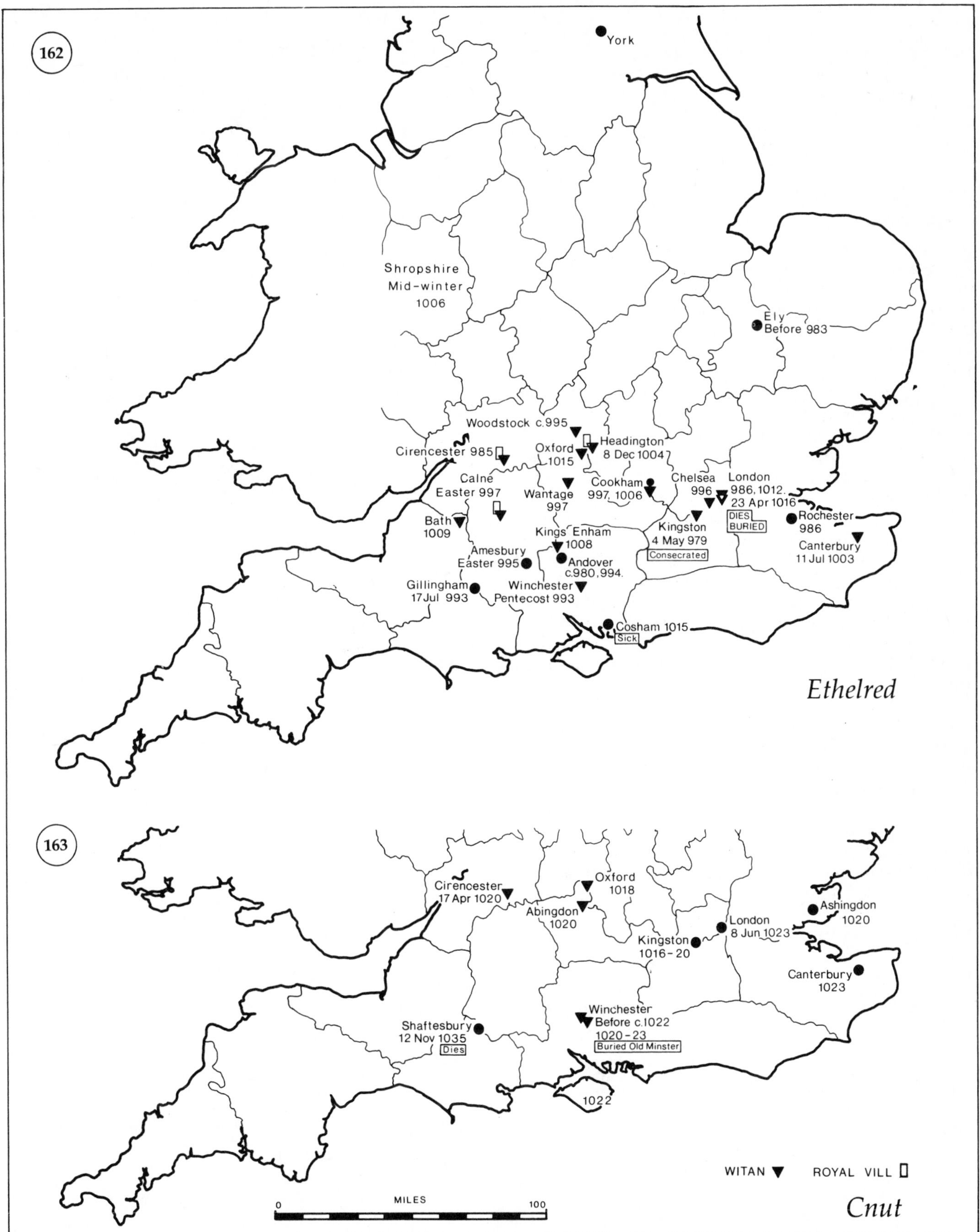
162
York
Shropshire
Mid-winter
1006
Ely
Before 983
Woodstock c.995
Headington
8 Dec 1004
Cirencester 985
Oxford
1015
Calne
Easter 997
Wantage
997
Cookham
997, 1006
Chelsea
996
London
986, 1012,
23 Apr 1016
DIES
BURIED
Rochester
986
Bath
1009
Kings Enham
1008
Kingston
4 May 979
Consecrated
Canterbury
11 Jul 1003
Amesbury
Easter 995
Andover
c.980, 994.
Gillingham
17 Jul 993
Winchester
Pentecost 993
Cosham 1015
Sick
Ethelred
163
Cirencester
17 Apr 1020
Oxford
1018
Abingdon
1020
Ashingdon
1020
London
8 Jun 1023
Kingston
1016-20
Canterbury
1023
Winchester
Before c.1022
1020-23
Buried Old Minster
Shaftesbury
12 Nov 1035
Dies
1022
WITAN
ROYAL VILL
0
MILES
100
Cnut

162–163 Itineraries of Ethelred and Cnut

The Fleet (164–166)

1008 *In this year the king ordered that ships should be built unremittingly over all England, namely a warship from 310 hides, and a helmet and corselet from eight hides. (Anglo-Saxon Chronicle)*

The importance of the fleet in late Anglo-Saxon England is often overlooked, but it was active from the days of the kings of Wessex, through the reigns of Alfred the Great and Athelstan to its high point during the reign of Edgar the Peaceable, where it could be seen as an instrument of policy as well as a fighting machine. The fleet was part of a defensive scheme that included the army, which could be called upon in several stages, the **burhs** in which the population sheltered, the **herepaths**, along which the armies moved, and the beacon system which warned the various parts of the system and the fleet.

The evidence for the beacon system has yet to be fully worked out but it appears to be a direct ancestor of the Armada system, the Hampshire portion of which is shown in map **164** with the beacons for which Anglo-Saxon evidence could be inferred named in heavy type. Where these documents (Robertson 1939, no. 72) fit with the evidence for a coastwatch (for example Sawyer, charter no. 1363) is difficult to determine. The first document is a list of those estates belonging to the church of St Paul's in London which sent men to ship; the second is constructed from a letter where another bishopric, that of Sherborne, is complaining that whereas he should have 300 hides to provide a ship, he has lost 33 of those hides.

The administration that lay behind the fleet pre-dates the order of 1008 noted in the Chronicle entry above (Whitelock 1955) as the St Paul's document (map **165**) shows. The involvement of the bishops would appear to be an administrative convenience, but all landowners were liable. The stipulation that a ship should come from 300 hides with a crew of helmeted and armoured men would lead to a figure of some 90 ships and 3,380 armed sailors from Wessex alone (map **166**), and there would be other fleets from the other parts of the kingdom. The threat they were facing could hardly have been a small one.

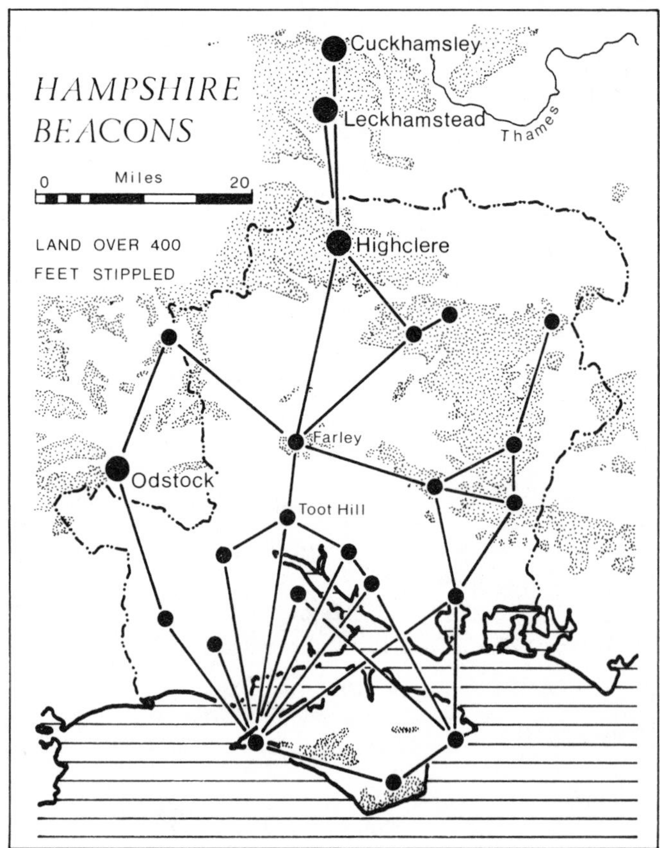

164 Hampshire beacons

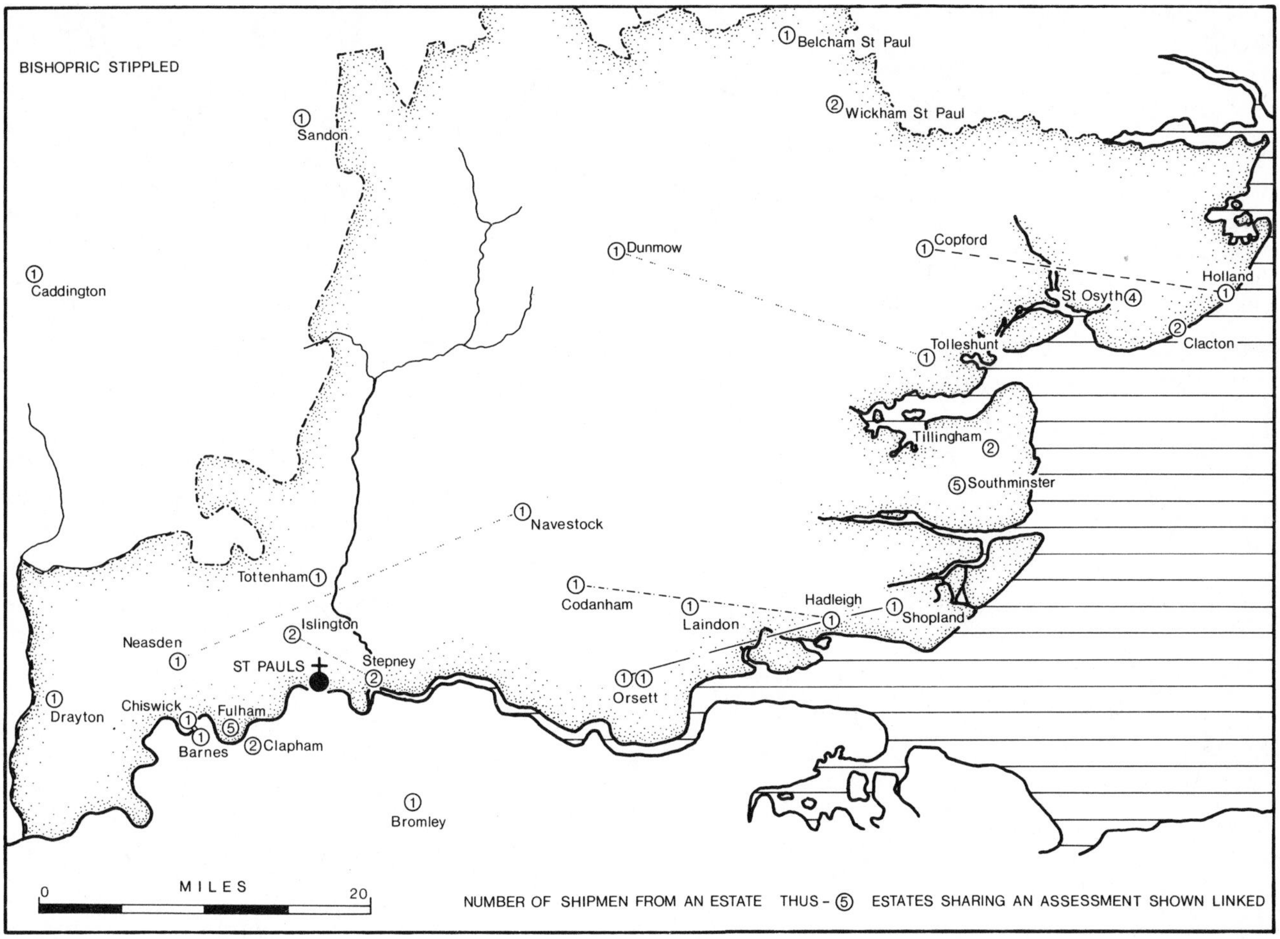

BISHOPRIC STIPPLED
1 Belcham St Paul
2 Wickham St Paul
1 Sandon
1 Caddington
1 Dunmow
1 Copford
Holland 1
St Osyth 4
2 Clacton
Tolleshunt 1
Tillingham 2
5 Southminster
1 Navestock
Tottenham 1
1 Codanham
1 Laindon
Hadleigh 1
1 Shopland
2 Islington
Neasden 1
ST PAULS
Stepney 2
1 1 Orsett
1 Drayton
Chiswick 1
Fulham 5
1 Barnes
2 Clapham
1 Bromley
MILES
0
20
NUMBER OF SHIPMEN FROM AN ESTATE THUS - 5
ESTATES SHARING AN ASSESSMENT SHOWN LINKED

165 Manning a ship from St Paul's Estates 995 × 998

BISHOPRIC STIPPLED
9 ?HOLCOMBE ROGUS?
SHERBORNE
Clifton Maybank 6
2 Trill
Bubbancumbe 1
7 Up Cerne
3 Dibberford
2 Alton Pancras
5 Hewish
5 Bockhampton
1 Wool
'33 hides that are lacking from the three
hundred hides that other bishops had for their diocese.'
PLACES FROM WHICH SHIP-SCOT HAS, OR MAY BE, LOST WITH HIDATION THUS - 3
MILES
0
20

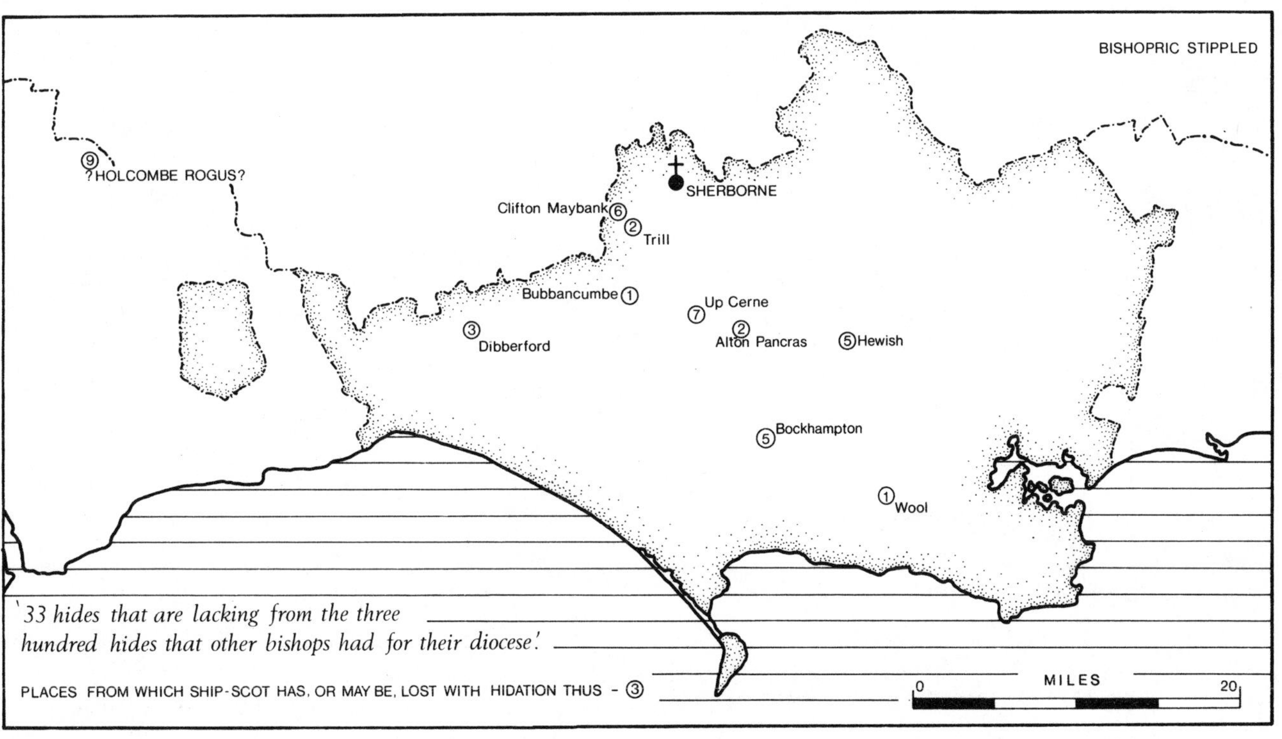

166 Ship-scot for the Bishop of Sherborne 1001 × 1012

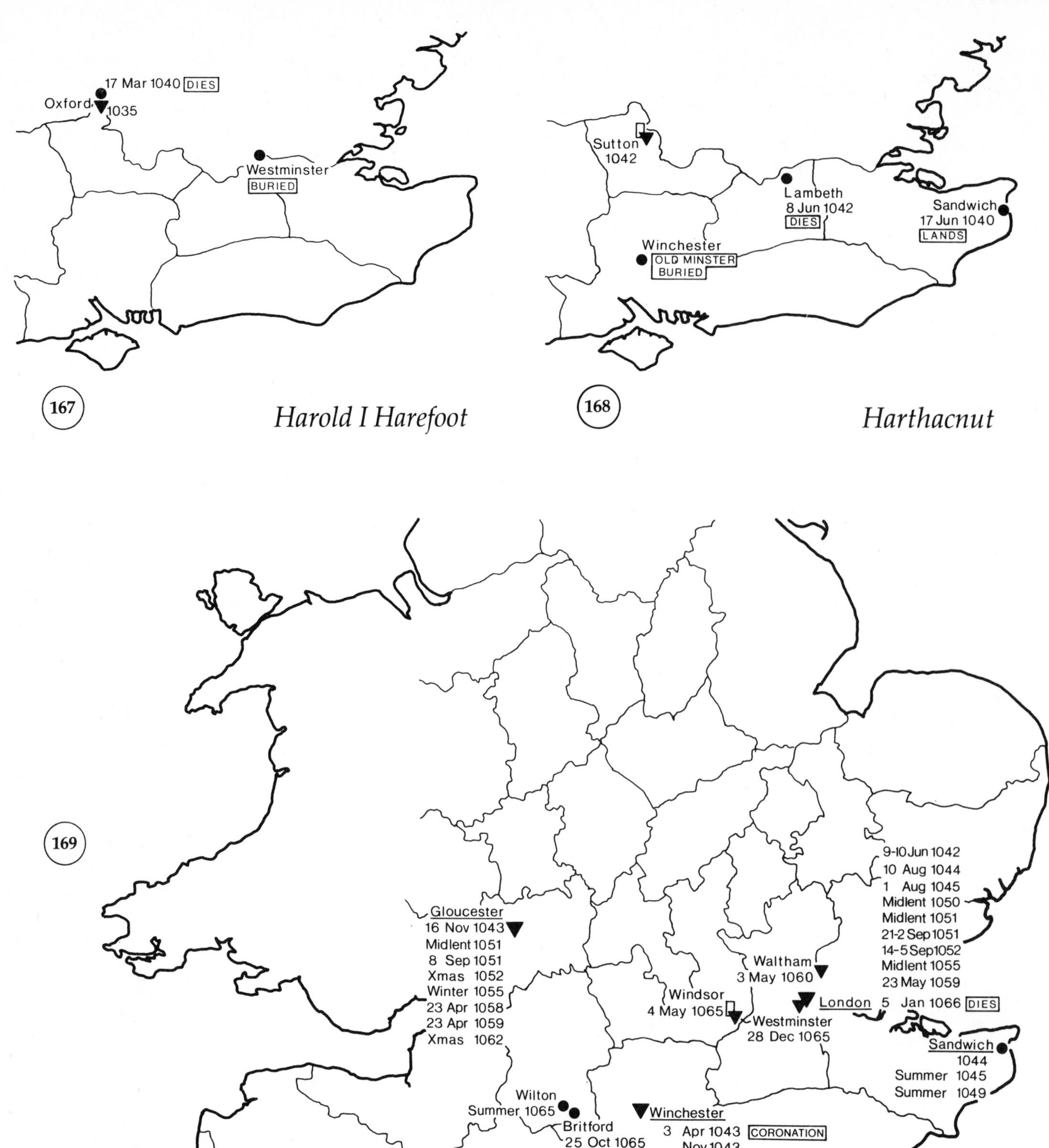

167–169 Itineraries of Harold I Harefoot, Harthacnut and Edward the Confessor

Itineraries of Harold I Harefoot, Harthacnut and Edward the Confessor (167–170)

The small amount of evidence for the reigns of Harold I Harefoot (map **167**) and Harthacnut (map **168**) is hardly enough to sustain the argument that their movements were similar to those of Ethelred and Cnut, with an axis along the Thames Valley.

It is clear that when Cnut died there was a division of the kingdom between Harthacnut's followers and those of Harold. The Chronicle records 'Earl Leofric and almost all the thegns north of the Thames chose Harold to the regency of all England'. There is further information in Florence of Worcester: 'the kingdom of England was divided by lot, and the north part fell to Harold, and the south to Harthacnut.' This situation, which lasted from late in 1035 until 1037, is reflected by the pattern of mints striking in the name of the absent Harthacnut (map **170**).

The itinerary of Edward the Confessor (map **169**) differs from the itineraries of his predecessors in that the king had three urban centres, London, Gloucester, and on a rather smaller scale, Winchester. Perhaps the years spent abroad coupled with the Danish interregnum broke with the traditions of the past and the hunting lands of Somerset had no childhood memories for Edward (he was born at Islip) or perhaps his father had already broken with the past. It is notable that he was crowned at Winchester and not at the traditional site at Kingston.

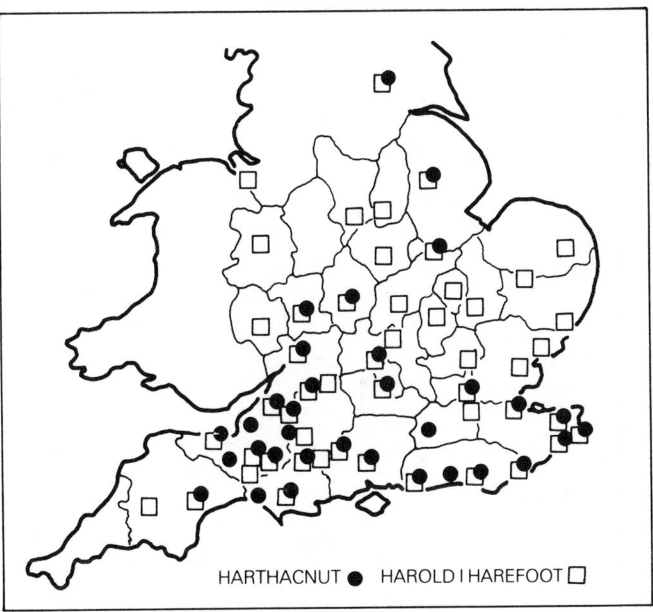

170 Mints for the 1035–1040 issue

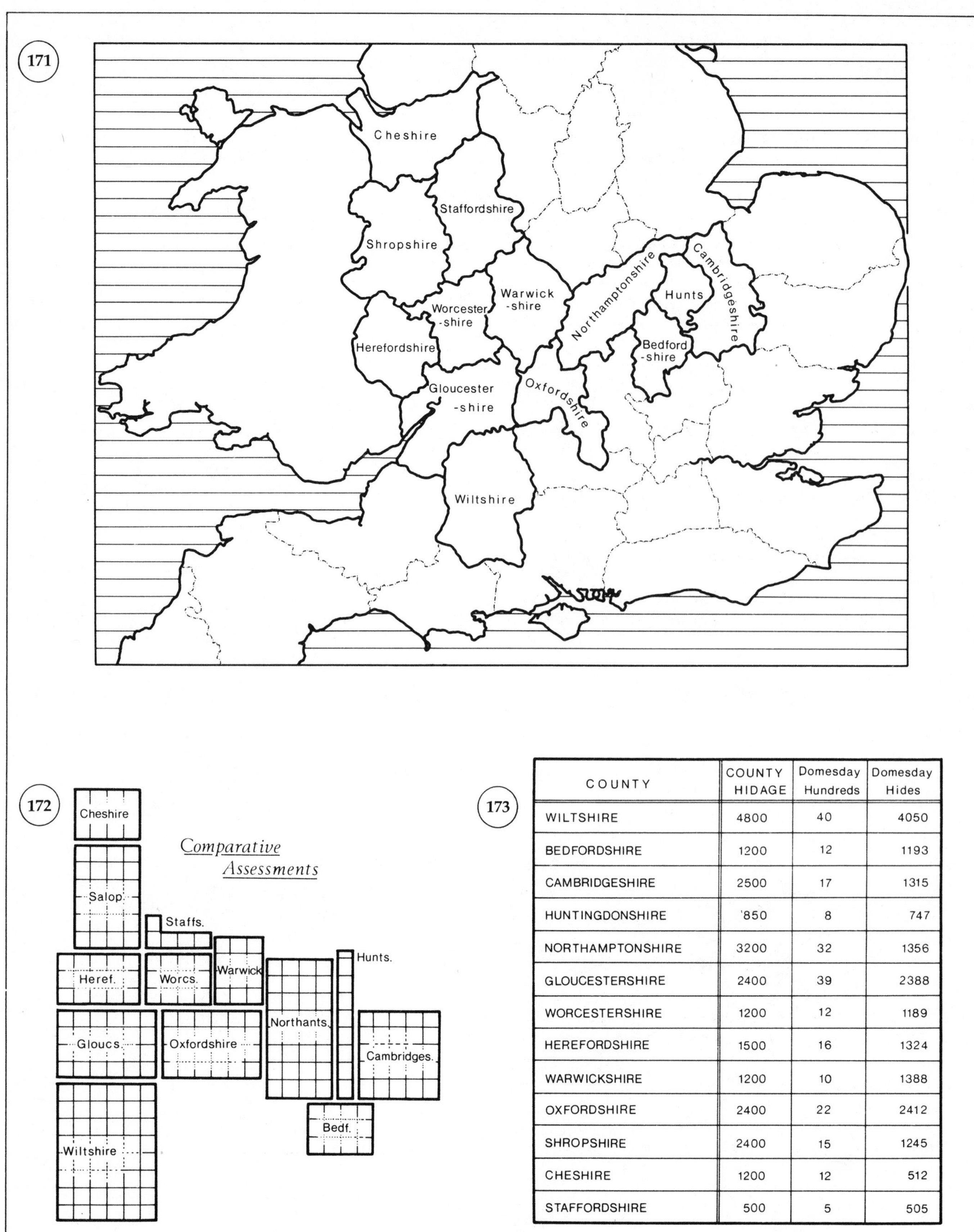

COUNTY	COUNTY HIDAGE	Domesday Hundreds	Domesday Hides
WILTSHIRE	4800	40	4050
BEDFORDSHIRE	1200	12	1193
CAMBRIDGESHIRE	2500	17	1315
HUNTINGDONSHIRE	850	8	747
NORTHAMPTONSHIRE	3200	32	1356
GLOUCESTERSHIRE	2400	39	2388
WORCESTERSHIRE	1200	12	1189
HEREFORDSHIRE	1500	16	1324
WARWICKSHIRE	1200	10	1388
OXFORDSHIRE	2400	22	2412
SHROPSHIRE	2400	15	1245
CHESHIRE	1200	12	512
STAFFORDSHIRE	500	5	505

171–173 The County Hidage

The County Hidage (171–173)

Recent work by David Austin has cast doubt on whether the document known as the 'County Hidage' is pre-Conquest, or even if it contains any pre-Conquest material. Whatever it is, the document is interesting, as it deals with an area of Midland England and assigns hidages which are considerably at odds with the Domesday assessments (**171–173**). On balance it may represent a tradition of early assessments and has therefore been included. As the document has often been quoted it is useful to have the information set out. The figures follow Austin whose appraisal appears sound. For another view see Sawyer (1978, 228–9).

Law and Land (174–178)

In late documents we are told that England was divided into three laws, the West Saxon, the Mercian and the Danelaw (map **174**). From this comes the expression for the area of Danish and Scandinavian settlement and influence, the 'Danelaw'. The versions of the 'Law' divisions attached to the county hidage represent the largest extent of the Danelaw in any of the versions known to us, as even London, Middlesex and Buckinghamshire are included.

The Domesday Book contains other indicators of Danish influence. The smallest area of the Danelaw is represented by those shires (map **175**) which were divided into the wapentake rather than the hundred. The area where the tax unit was the carucate and not the hide (map **176**) is rather larger, including Norfolk and Suffolk, whilst the area where land units were counted not in fives, as in the south, but in the Scandinavian twelves is an amalgam of both areas (map **177**). Division into these groups is not always clear cut, as in Essex, where there are a few groups of five-hide units.

These permanent alterations in the legal traditions of the land do not fit comfortably with other definitions of the territory of the Danelaw, such as the treaty line between Alfred and Guthrum (map **70**) or the distribution of place names (**68**) or graves (**67**).

In the first half of the tenth century the old divisions of Mercia were abolished by the West Saxons, who then proceeded to shire the area in their hands. This would seem to have been part of the organization of the defences, for each shire was designed to contribute to, and be protected by, the **burh** within it. Thus the shires of the West Midlands received the names of their **burhs**: Gloucestershire, Warwickshire and so on. One of these shires was set up around Winchcombe but the shire was annexed to Gloucestershire during the ealdormanry of Eadric Streona 'who tore up shires as if they were paper'. That this is not the whole story is clear from map **178**, which shows that the work of Eadric Streona in the early years of the eleventh century involved the inclusion of large areas of lands belonging to the church of Worcester into that shire thus giving the whole area the patchwork effect that survived into this century. The map itself is based on Cotton Tiberius A xiii, Hemming's Cartulary, which contains the earliest surviving charter collection (as opposed to individual charters). Although the cartulary is biased against Eadric, it is an essential source for the period and area.

The reconstruction of the shire of Winchcombeshire has been attemped (Finberg 1961, 228–35) but it is likely that this shire ran to the north of the boundary of Gloucestershire and reached the Severn.

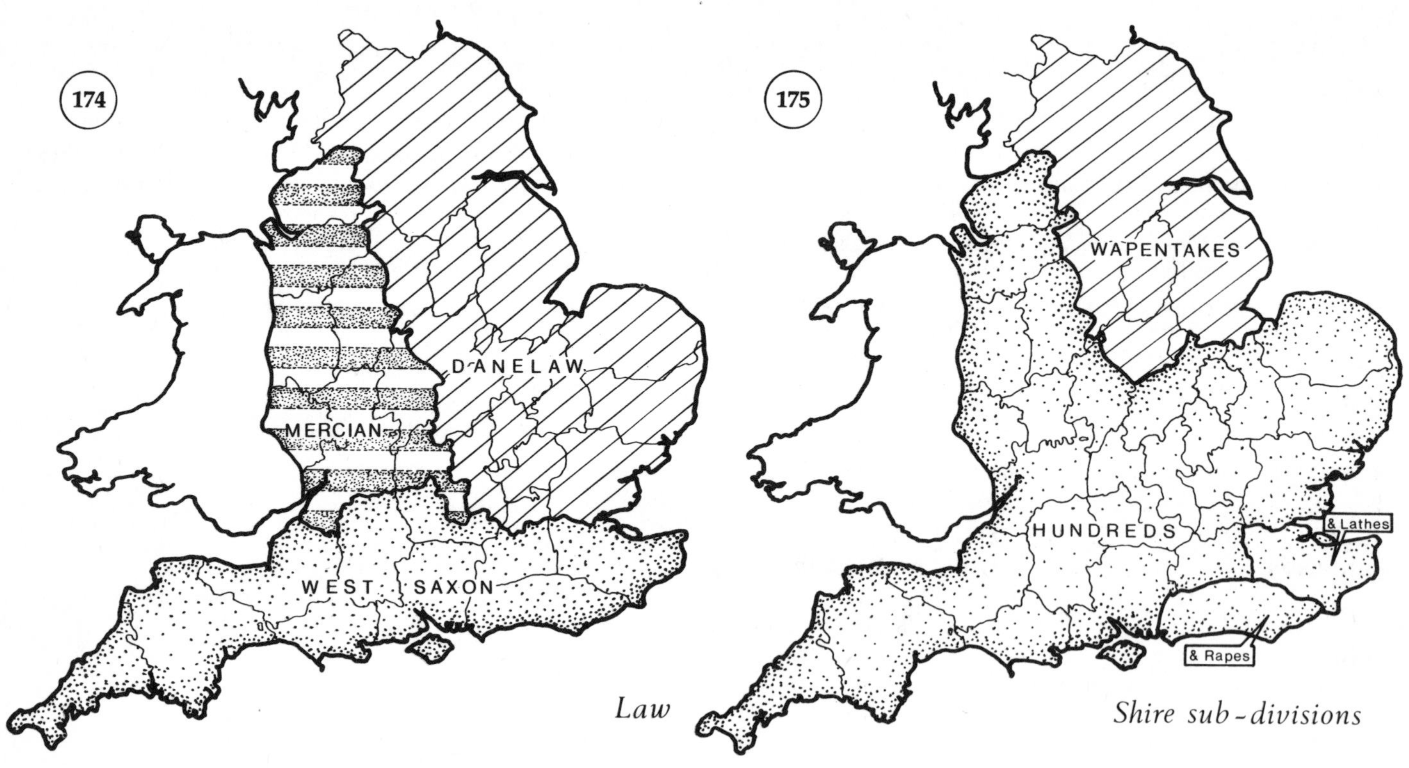

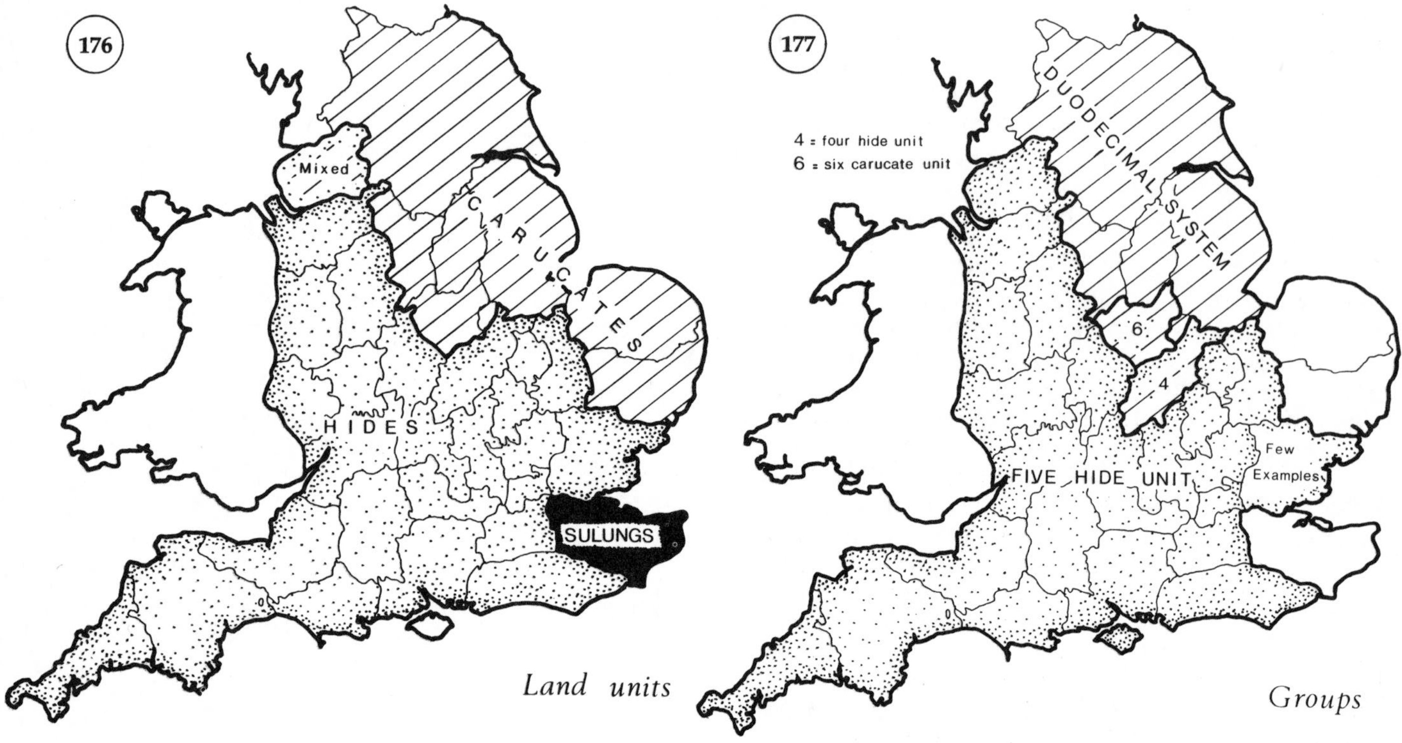

174–177 Law and land

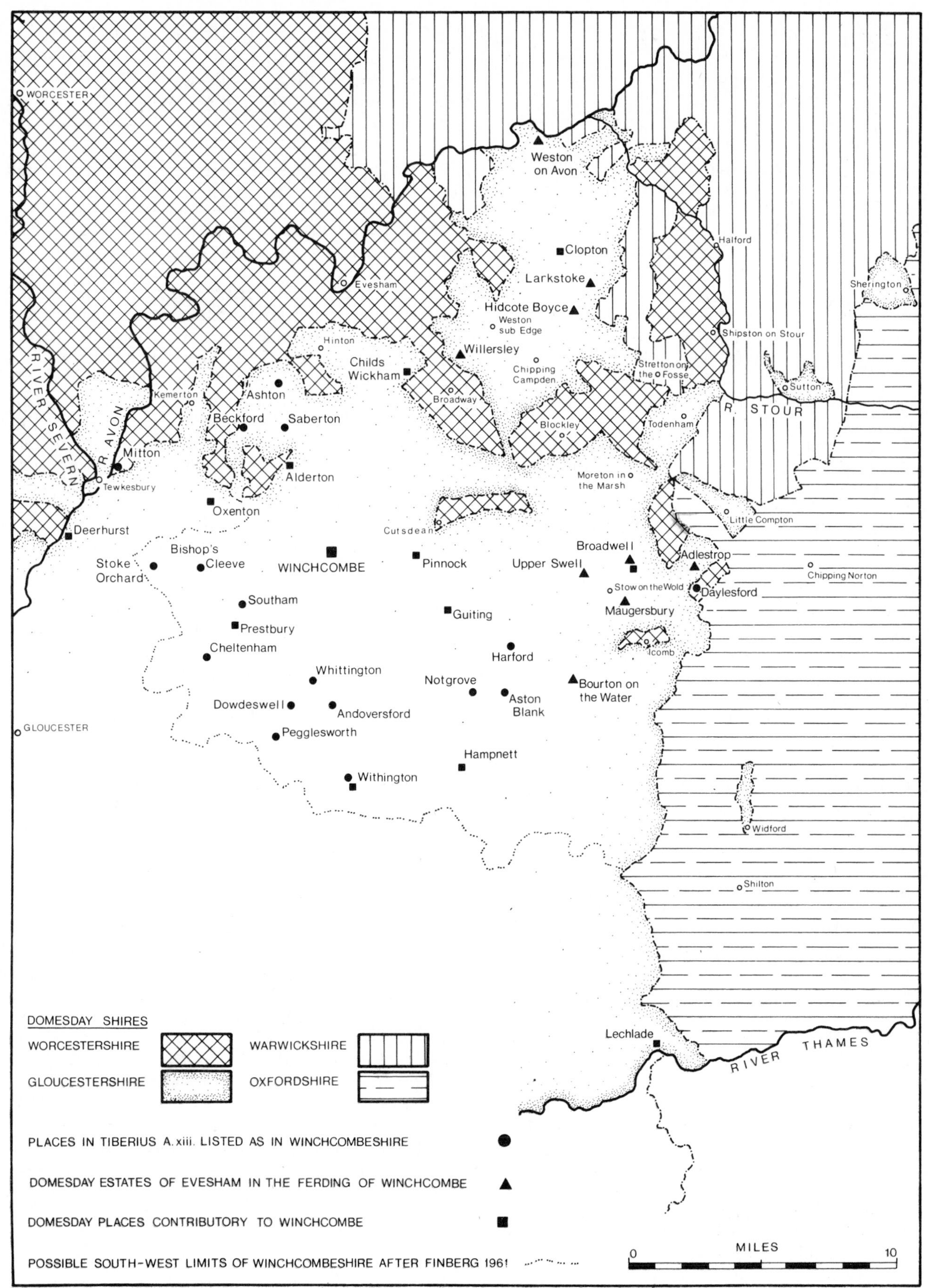

WORCESTER
Evesham
Weston on Avon
Clopton
Larkstoke
Halford
Hidcote Boyce
Weston sub Edge
Sherington
Shipston on Stour
Hinton
Willersley
Childs Wickham
Chipping Campden
Stretton on the Fosse
Sutton
Kemerton
Ashton
Broadway
R. STOUR
RIVER SEVERN
R. AVON
Beckford
Saberton
Blockley
Todenham
Mitton
Alderton
Moreton in the Marsh
Tewkesbury
Oxenton
Little Compton
Cutsdean
Deerhurst
Bishop's Cleeve
Broadwell
Stoke Orchard
WINCHCOMBE
Pinnock
Upper Swell
Adlestrop
Chipping Norton
Stow on the Wold
Daylesford
Southam
Guiting
Maugersbury
Prestbury
Cheltenham
Icomb
Harford
Whittington
Notgrove
Bourton on the Water
Aston Blank
Dowdeswell
Andoversford
GLOUCESTER
Pegglesworth
Hampnett
Withington
Widford
Shilton
Lechlade
RIVER THAMES
DOMESDAY SHIRES
WORCESTERSHIRE
WARWICKSHIRE
GLOUCESTERSHIRE
OXFORDSHIRE
PLACES IN TIBERIUS A.xiii. LISTED AS IN WINCHCOMBESHIRE
DOMESDAY ESTATES OF EVESHAM IN THE FERDING OF WINCHCOMBE
DOMESDAY PLACES CONTRIBUTORY TO WINCHCOMBE
POSSIBLE SOUTH-WEST LIMITS OF WINCHCOMBESHIRE AFTER FINBERG 1961
MILES
0
10

178 North-east Gloucestershire showing changes in shire boundaries

Landholding in 1066 (179–187)

The Domesday Survey used juries of local men to reconstruct the ownerships of a particular district in January of 1066, as this was the time of legal probity before the usurper Harold and the disturbances which followed. We therefore have an accurate statement of the holdings of the late Anglo-Saxon monarchy, the earls, the church and the thegns. Although it is at the end of the period, it allows us to examine the eleventh century and also to see patterns extending back at least to the monastic revival and, in the case of the king's holdings, back to the West Saxon state.

The major secular landholders in 1066, TRE, the time of King Edward, were the king himself (**179**), the Queen (**180**), the widespread Godwin family (**181**) (of which Queen Edith was a member), and the family of Leofric (**182**). When these holdings are calculated in value, as in **183**, then it will be seen that the holdings of the king, in demesne lands, are almost equalled by the holdings of the Godwin family. The holdings of Harold II, Godwinson, must have been enormous as they brought together both sets of lands. It is a moot point, however, whether the kings of the first half of the tenth century had fewer lands than Edward the Confessor; it is quite possible that the holdings of Athelstan, incorporating the royal holdings of Wessex, Mercia and Northumbria, were considerably larger than Edward's. It was the mid-tenth century 'reforms' that may have dissipated the royal domain.

In 1066 Harold held the largest individual holding and it may have been larger, as it is not known who actually held those lands entered in Domesday as belonging to Earl Godwin (who had died in 1053). These lands were mainly in Sussex and were possibly administered by Harold along with his own. The Leofric family holding compares badly with the Godwin family total.

The earldoms were mapped by Freeman (1870) and Barlow (1970, 358–9) as a useful aid to the understanding of the late Saxon office of earl (maps **184** and **185**). The mapping is based on the addressing of the royal writs and it can be appreciated that this information is far from complete, especially when one is attempting to follow changes in a short period (see map **32**). From the reign of Cnut the holdings of the family of Godwin are paramount in the south, with the family of Leofric in control in the midlands. The earldom of Northumbria followed its own line of descent for most of the period. It would be possible to map all the earls' holdings in Domesday but the two, lands of Earl Harold, map **181**, and the lands of the Leofric family, map **182**, appear to be the most informative. When the two are compared, the clear division of responsibility for the important Welsh border region can be seen.

The values of the holdings shown in **183** should be seen in relation to the strength of the Church. On **249** the total income of Church holdings is something in excess of £9,550, larger than the king's holdings and the holdings of the house of Godwin combined. These figures do not include the amounts for the lands of the bishops, houses of secular canons or parish churches.

There are other ways of showing the vast holdings of the Church at the close of the reign of Edward the Confessor, and it is arguable that the proportion had not changed greatly in the eleventh century. One way is to arrange the holdings into a 'pie' diagram (**186**) for two typical shires, and it can be seen that the Church forms the largest block of holdings.

A second way is to take two other shires and equate Domesday holdings with ecclesiastical parishes of the early nineteenth century, marking the owner of the holding. The resultant cartoon (map **187**) may not be correct in detail but it is extremely informative in general. In these shires there were perhaps unusually large holdings of the church of Winchester around Taunton, the monastery of Glastonbury's extensive holdings in east Somerset, the Bath Abbey estates, the lands of the church of Malmesbury, the bishop of Ramsbury's holdings north of Bedwyn and the nunnery of Wilton's holdings in south Wiltshire. Against this it should be remembered that this was the home area of the tenth-century kings, although the estates in south Wiltshire had passed to the church since Alfred's day, and one must assume a similar diminution of the royal demesne around Cheddar and Axbridge. The map does show the attempts of the kings to increase their revenue from the royal estates by the founding, mainly in the eleventh century, of the small market centres, **ports**, on their lands.

Maps **179–182** show distributions of demesne lands only, and in some cases the size of the holdings has been calculated from the ploughlands. Carucates have been treated, together with sulungs, in the same way as hides. The attempt has been to create the visual image, and a close similarity would have been achieved using values; however, it is felt that the value of the lands in the south-west is still underrated.

The lands of the king do show a concentration in the south and west, with northern Mercia not well represented. The large estates in Wiltshire, Somerset and Dorset show up well, but the king has a series of estates in the Thames valley. The value of royal rights in the towns and from various other dues are not shown.

The queen's dower lands in Somerset are shown and there are some unexplained holdings in Hereford and Worcester; the dower lands in the Thames valley date back at least to the birth of Edward the Confessor but the western holdings are probably more ancient. Winchester was held to be the queen's morning gift.

The succession of earldoms held by Harold are well represented on the map showing his lands and it is complemented by the lands of the Leofric family which covers those shires not covered by Harold, although the Leofric estates are also to be found around London, presumably to give them a base when called south on royal business.

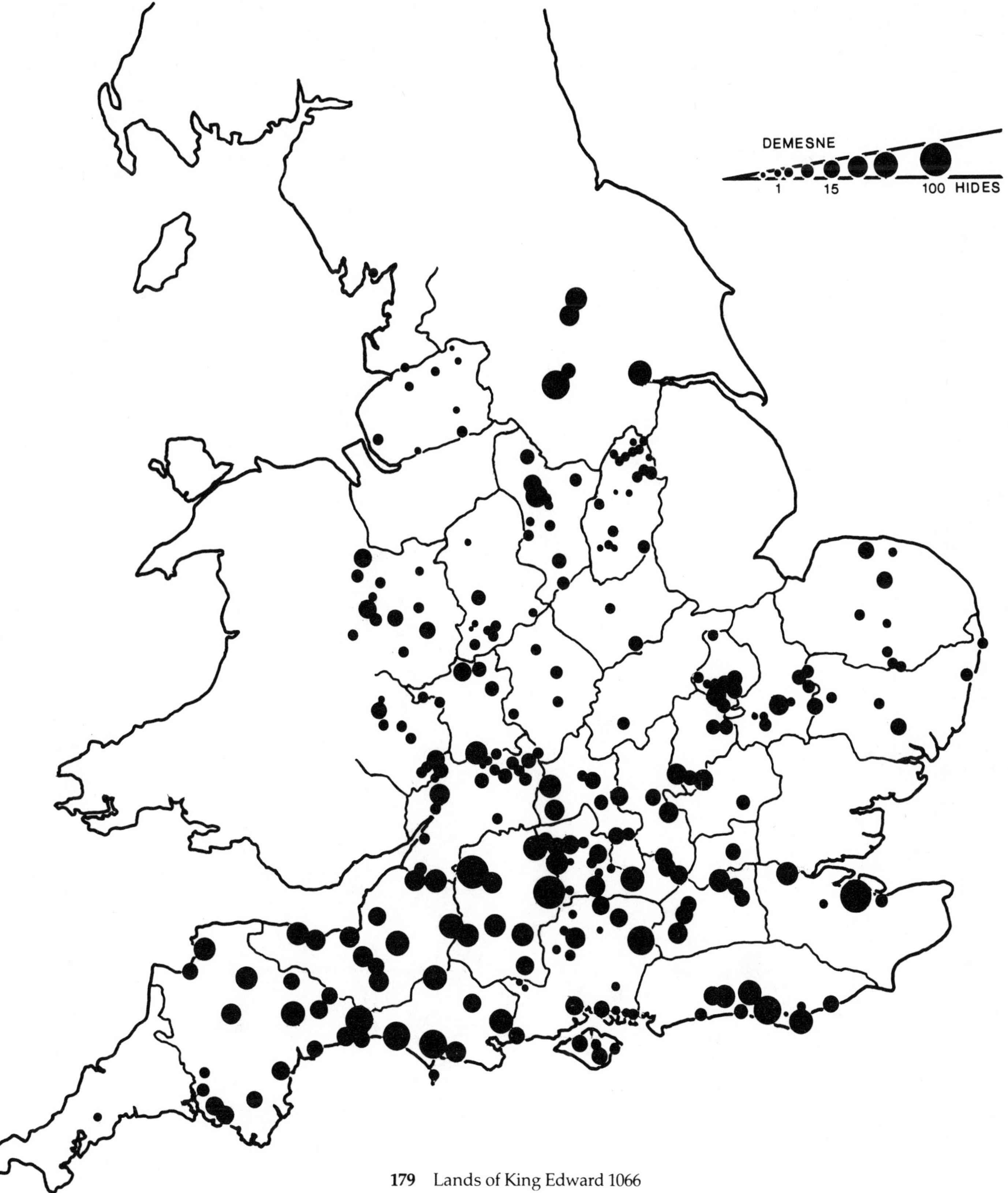

179 Lands of King Edward 1066

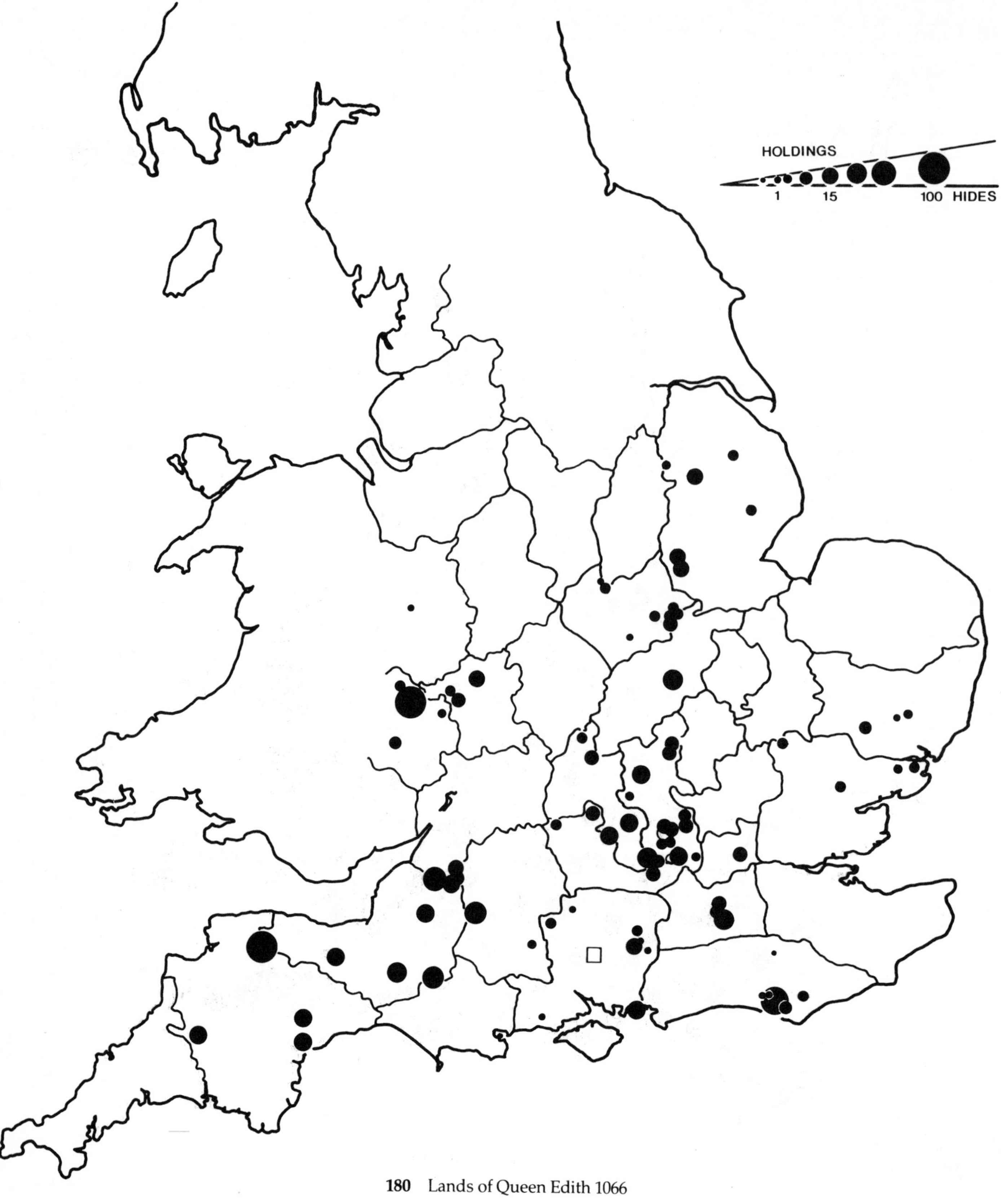

180 Lands of Queen Edith 1066

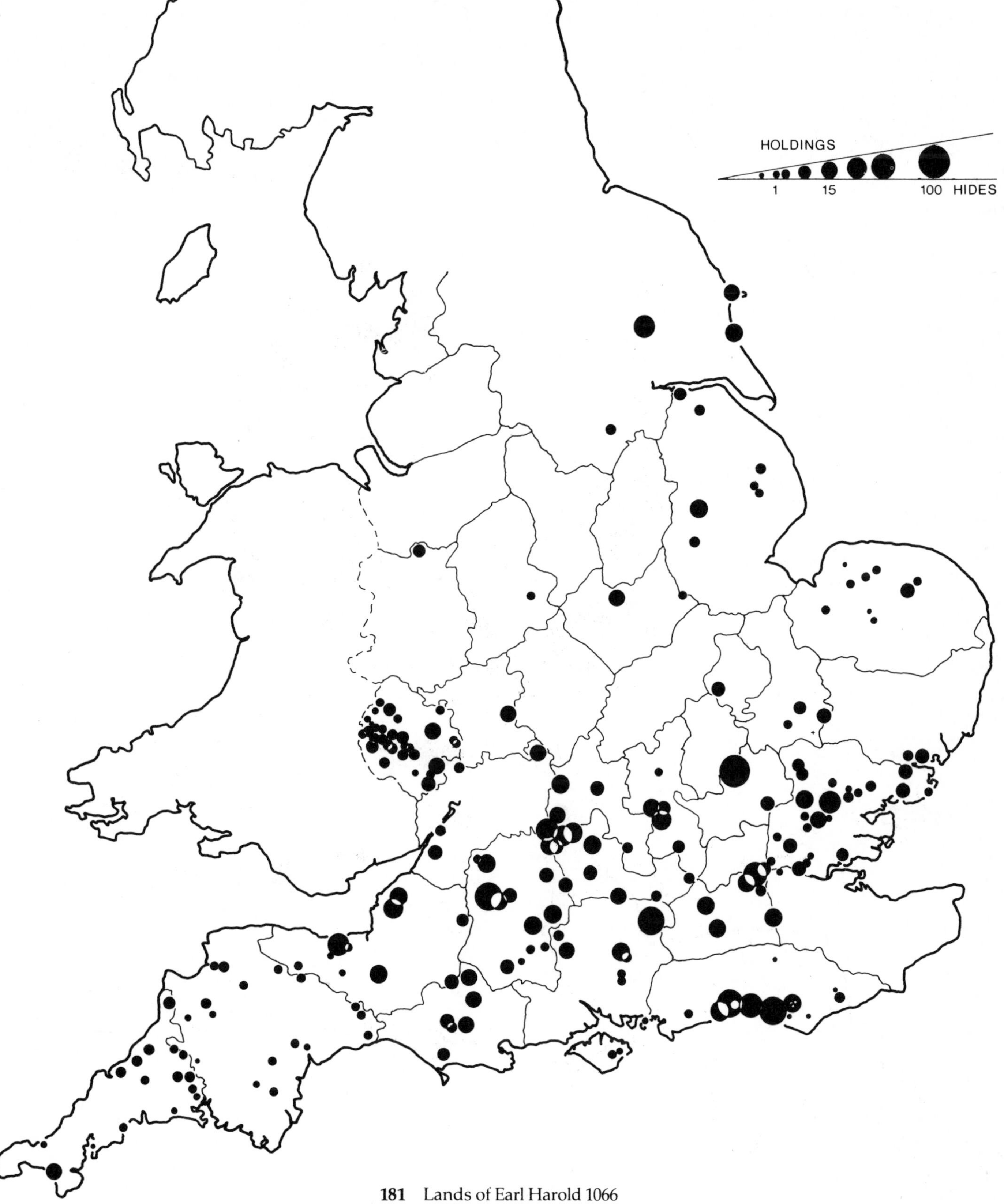

181 Lands of Earl Harold 1066

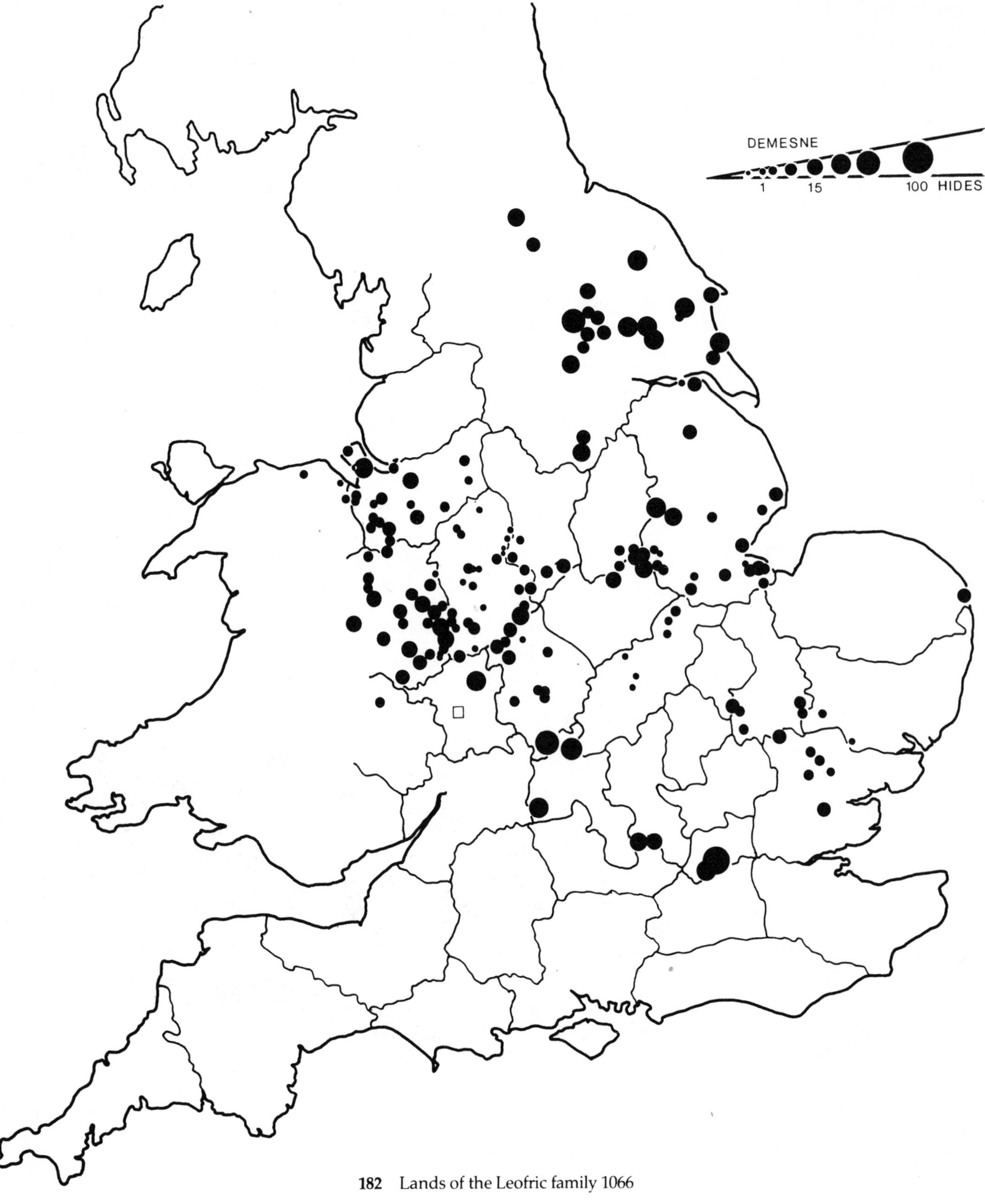

182 Lands of the Leofric family 1066

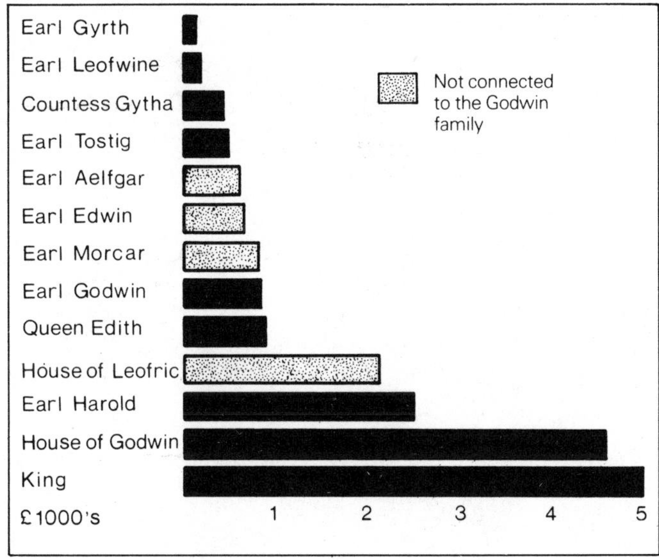

183 Value of lands held by the king and leading families in 1066

184 Earldoms in 1045 (after Freeman 1869–75)

185 Earldoms in 1065 (after Freeman 1869–75)

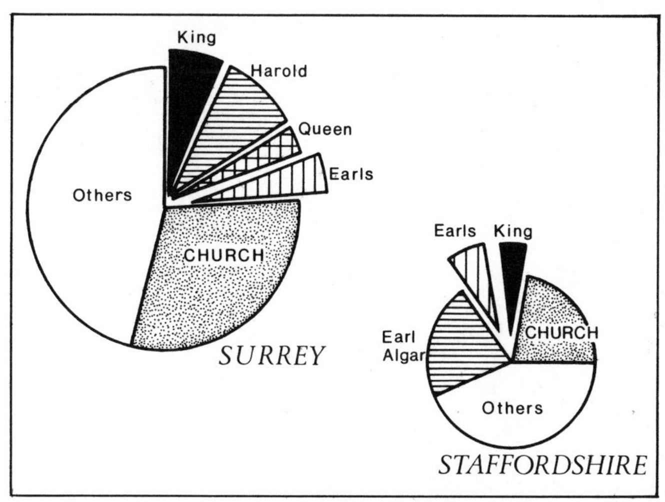

186 The proportional holdings of demesne lands in the shires of Staffordshire and Surrey in 1066

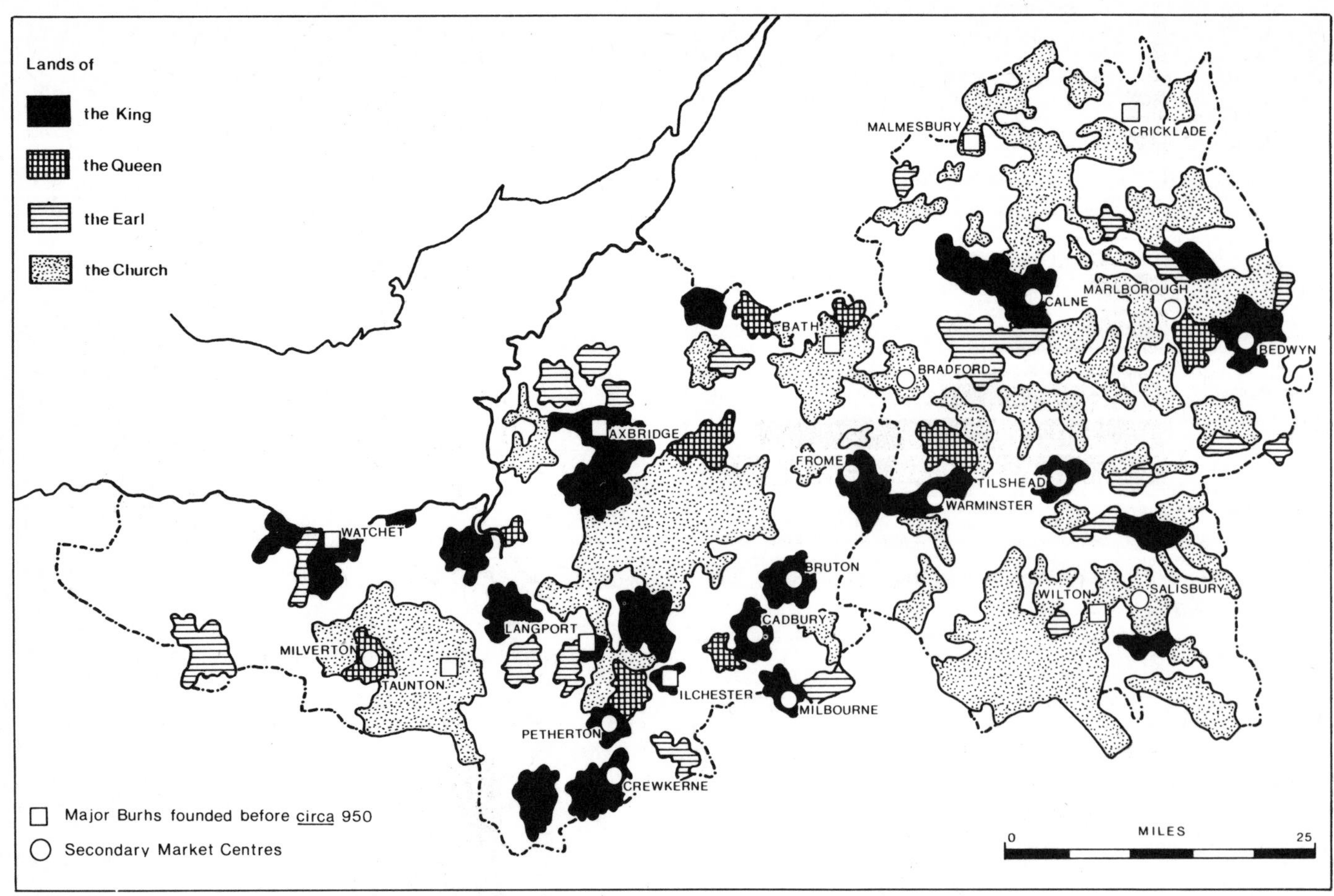

187 Landowners and markets in Somerset and Wiltshire in 1066

The Economy

Research into the early medieval period has progressed beyond the point where it is possible to believe in the extremely simple economy once postulated for the period. It was once, wrongly, supposed that most estates, vills, villages or settlements were self-sufficient. Everything needed on the estate was produced on the estate, trade was limited to a tiny amount of luxury goods for the nobility and the king, the surplus of any estate was eaten up by the king, noble or bishop travelling with his retinue 'eating up his rents'. The village sat in the middle of its fields; beyond, the meadow; beyond that the waste and finally the great wild wood. In fact, the charter bounds show that many estates had their fields abutting and one of the commonest features on the boundaries was the road, way or path with its bridge or ford — all indicating frequent movement from place to place. Common sense shows that many commodities were unavailable on the 'average' estate — few of them would have been naturally endowed with supplies of iron, salt, lead, hone and building stone, wine, fish, flax, antler and the hundred and one requirements of the late Saxon economy. Many of these commodities are the product of specialist communities — charcoal, metals, salt and fish spring readily to mind. The following maps highlight those parts of the economy that can be charted but it should always be remembered that from the time of Offa onwards estates had to find an increasing part of their taxes, dues and renders in coin: the only way to obtain this was by the export of goods or services.

Before embarking on discussion of the economic life of Anglo-Saxon England the limitations of the evidence should be clearly recognized, as these are inherent in distribution maps in particular and should be borne in mind when using this section. The problems of one of the most important classes of evidence (pottery and ceramics) are such that it has been decided not to attempt to cover an extremely difficult and rapidly expanding subject. The situation has recently been summarized (Hurst 1976) and sounds the warning that in the last two decades the earlier distributions and received truths have been torn up and discarded. The warning note sounded in Hurst's paper applies to much else in the study of the economy but it should be remembered that pottery was being made and traded from many centres in middle and late Saxon England. There was also a thriving import trade from many centres from the Rhineland to Aquitaine. All this has developed so rapidly that maps drawn in 1958 have now to be discarded.

Minerals, Salt and Lime (188–192)

There is a unique charter reference to an iron mine in Kent as early as 689 (see map **188**). The rest of the evidence is scattered but with the collation of archaeological and Domesday evidence TRE the pattern emerges of widespread ironworking. It would be fatuous to add a map of iron artefacts as this would simply show excavated settlements where the soil conditions are suitable for the preservation of iron. The spread of ironworking must have been extensive due to the widespread sources of iron; the blooms of iron would then be traded to those areas lacking their own sources.

The same range of evidence that is available for iron can be used for salt even though archaeological evidence is lacking (map **189**). The importance of salt in the early economy is obvious and it is not surprising that it is widely represented in the charter evidence. Three areas can be recognized for supply and distribution: the important Droitwich brine springs serving most of Midland England through a series of pre-Conquest saltways, a pattern confirmed by the Domesday evidence; the east and south served by coastal saltpans (it should be noted that there are none in the Bristol Channel, presumably due to the turbid and silty waters); and the perhaps later Saltwichs of Cheshire serving the north.

It becomes clear from contrasting the availability of limestone and chalk with the known pre-Conquest mortared stone buildings (map **190**) that some lime would have to be moved considerable distances to the mainly religious building sites.

The evidence for lead-working comes both from archaeology, in that it is a common find on archaeological sites of the period, and from charter mentions, either of a mine in the bounds at Stoke Bishop or of lead renders as at Wirksworth (map **191**). It was known abroad and was used in England for roofs and, more importantly, for the construction of brine vats in the salt-making process, an example of the interlocking of two specialist communities. It is usually thought that silver was obtained by the cupellation process from lead but it should be noted we have no evidence for it in England, nor do we have evidence of the working of lead in the Mendips or the far north.

There are claims, though I do not know their basis, for the working of the Shropshire copper deposits and there is the inferential evidence that the Trewhiddle hoard was found in a tinstream for the working of that metal (map **192**). However, apart from the fact that the metals are found in use as objects or slag, we have no evidence for the sources of these metals in England at the time

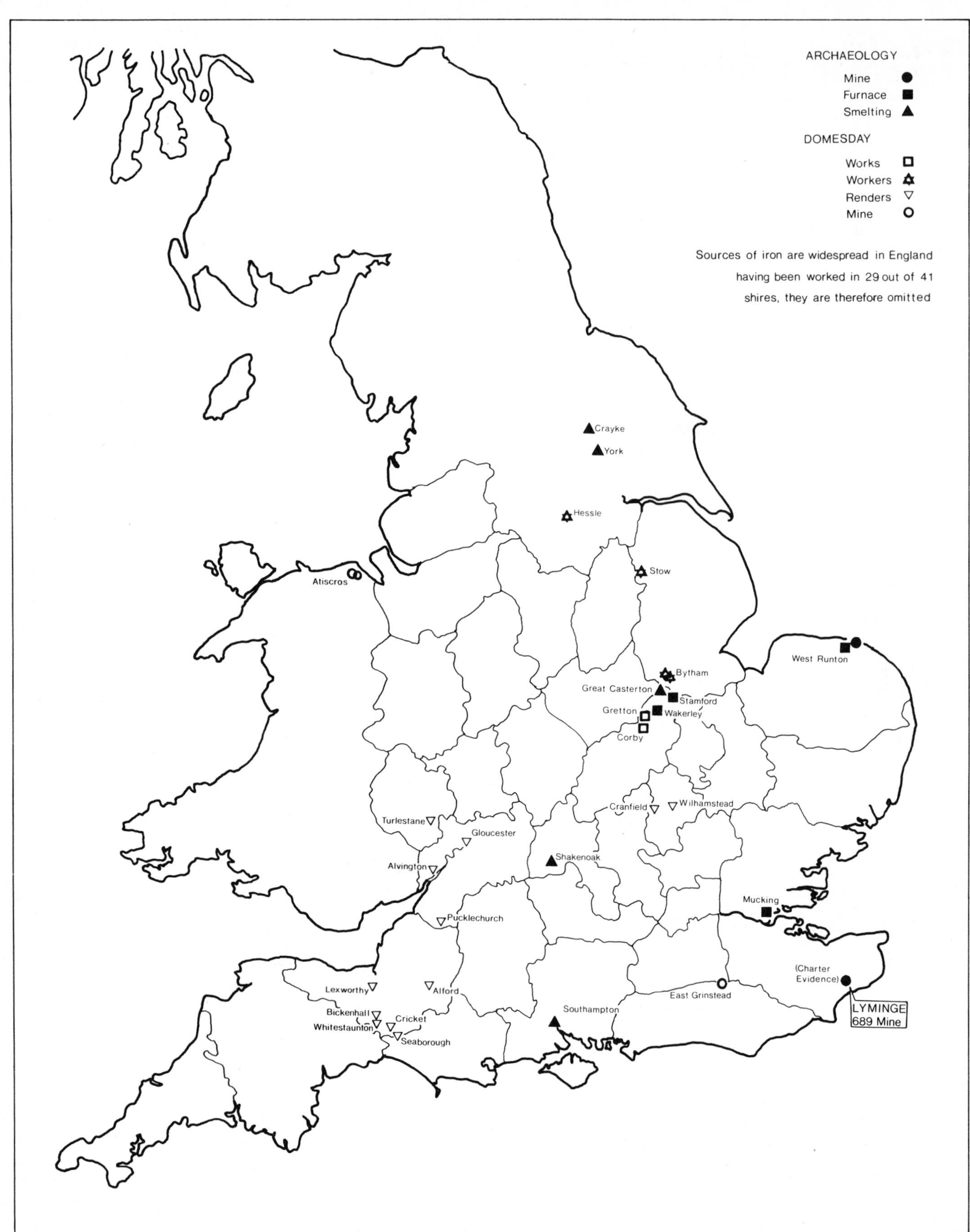
ARCHAEOLOGY
Mine
Furnace
Smelting
DOMESDAY
Works
Workers
Renders
Mine
Sources of iron are widespread in England having been worked in 29 out of 41 shires, they are therefore omitted
Crayke
York
Hessle
Stow
Atiscros
West Runton
Bytham
Great Casterton
Stamford
Gretton
Wakerley
Corby
Cranfield
Wilhamstead
Turlestane
Gloucester
Shakenoak
Alvington
Mucking
Pucklechurch
(Charter Evidence)
LYMINGE
689 Mine
Lexworthy
Alford
East Grinstead
Southampton
Bickenhall
Cricket
Whitestaunton
Seaborough

188 Iron

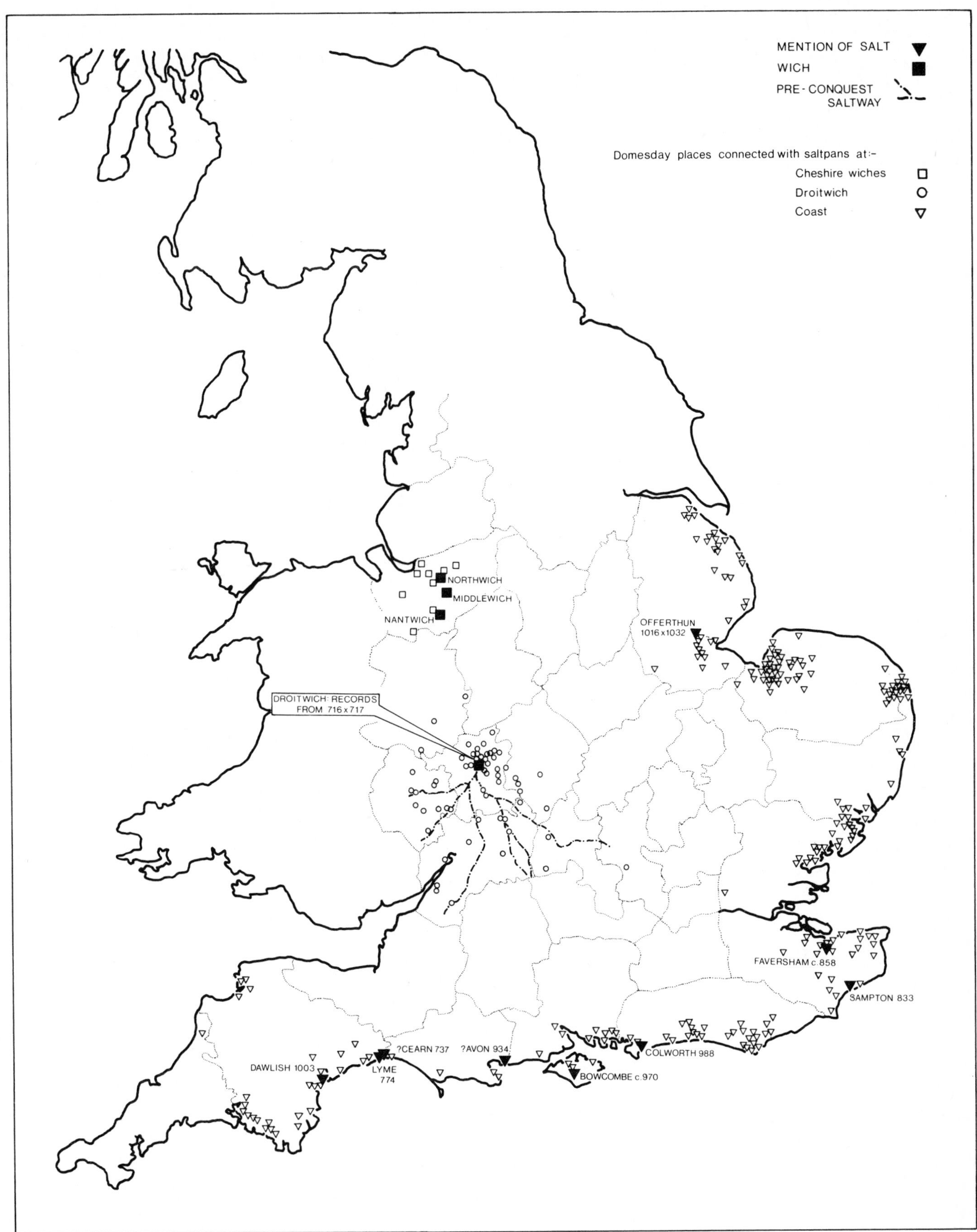
MENTION OF SALT
WICH
PRE-CONQUEST SALTWAY
Domesday places connected with saltpans at:-
Cheshire wiches
Droitwich
Coast
NORTHWICH
MIDDLEWICH
NANTWICH
OFFERTHUN 1016 x 1032
DROITWICH: RECORDS FROM 716 x 717
FAVERSHAM c.858
SAMPTON 833
?CEARN 737
?AVON 934
COLWORTH 988
DAWLISH 1003
LYME 774
BOWCOMBE c.970

189 Salt

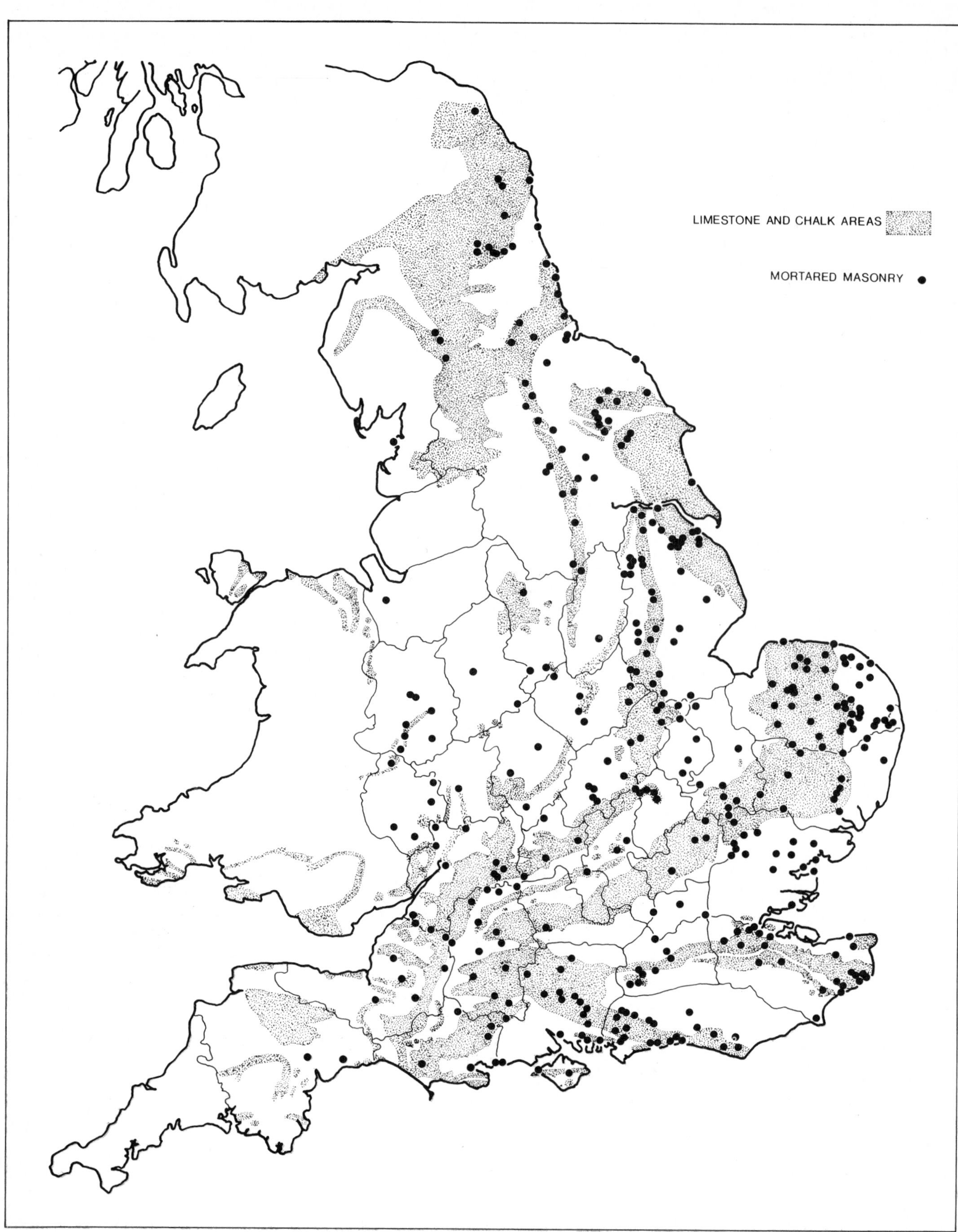
LIMESTONE AND CHALK AREAS
MORTARED MASONRY

190 Lime

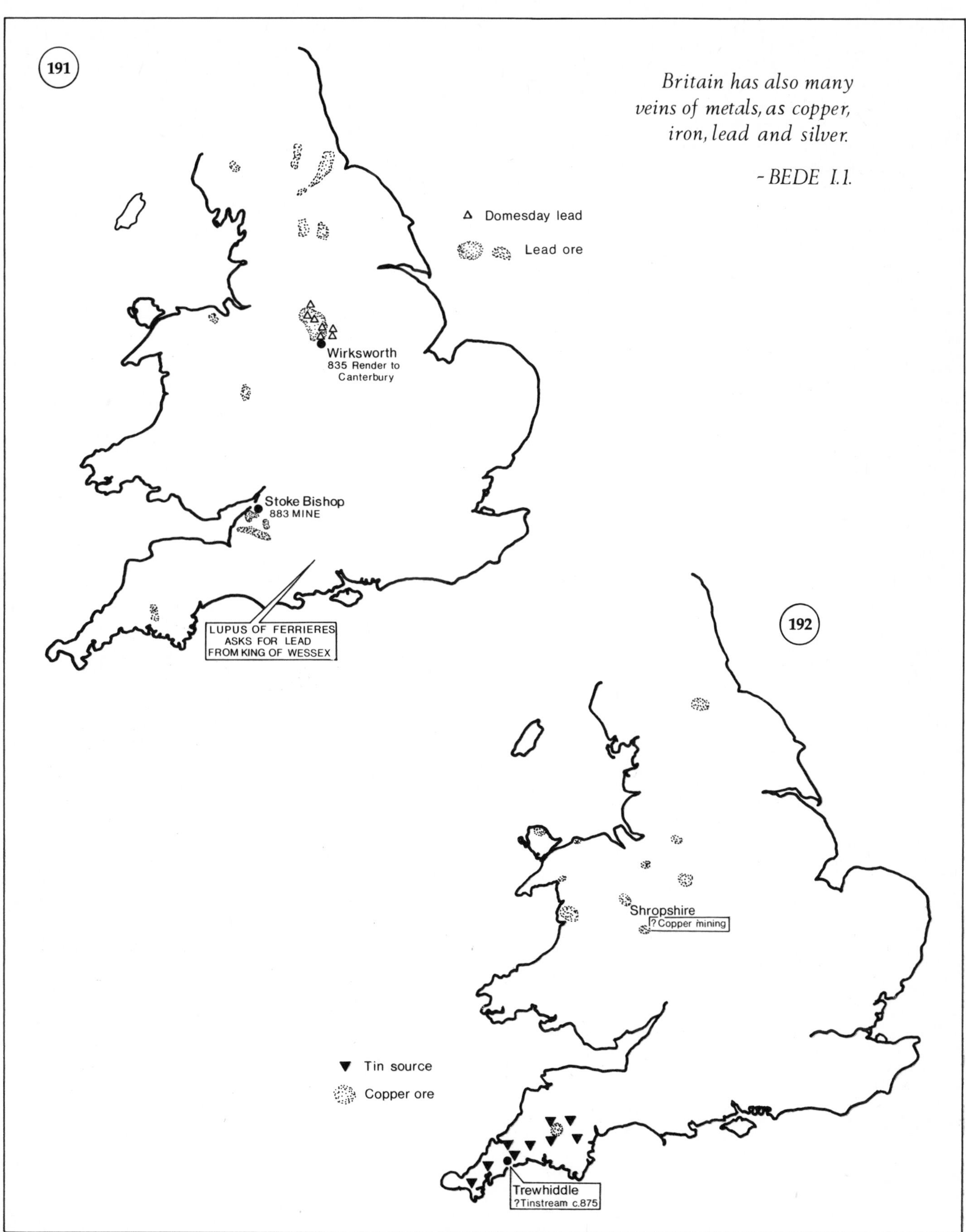
191
Britain has also many veins of metals, as copper, iron, lead and silver.
- BEDE I.1.
Domesday lead
Lead ore
Wirksworth
835 Render to Canterbury
Stoke Bishop
883 MINE
LUPUS OF FERRIERES ASKS FOR LEAD FROM KING OF WESSEX
192
Shropshire
? Copper mining
Tin source
Copper ore
Trewhiddle
?Tinstream c.875

191–192 Lead and other metals

Agriculture (193–196)

This atlas unfortunately includes very little information on the subject of agriculture: 'it is one of the real scandals of Anglo-Saxon archaeology that we still know less about the context and practices of the Anglo-Saxon "village" than we do about the Iron Age farm and the Roman Villa' (Graham-Campbell 1977, 520). The medieval distribution of the open-field system is well known and many inferences have been drawn from it by earlier historians of the Anglo-Saxon period (map **193**). It may be that the system is early and is linked with the entry phase of Saxon settlement. When this problem is finally faced we shall expect the answer to throw light on the parallel problems of the open-field systems in France (map **194**). They appear to have some correlation in this area with the distribution of Germanic place names, indicating settlement as opposed to areas of hegemony in the Frankish entrance phase (map **195**).

Of the agricultural maps that can be drawn only the one of vineyards has been included as all the rest contain so little information as to be practically useless. The vineyard map (**196**) is of interest even if in fact it shows more information on climatic amelioration than on general agricultural practice.

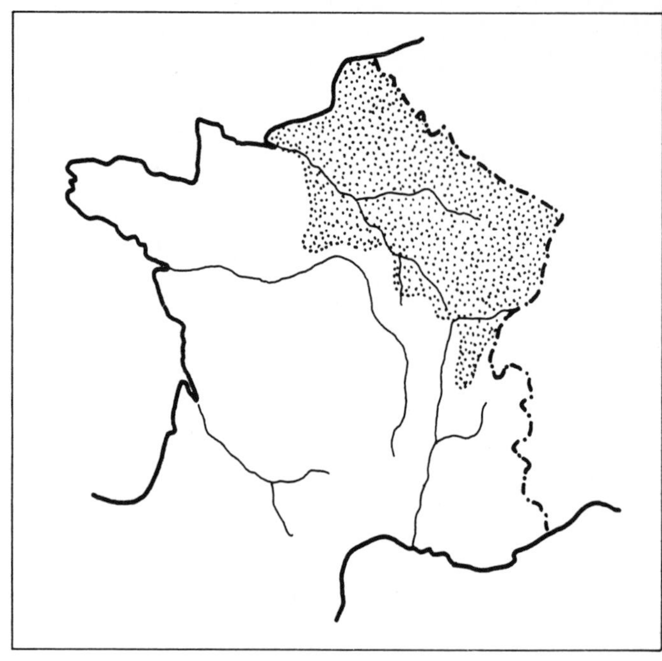

194 Open fields in France

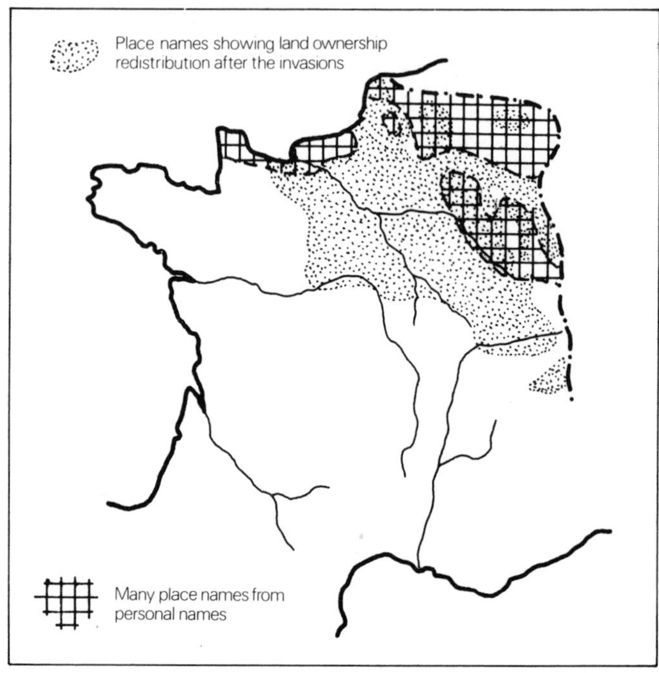

195 Germanic place names in France

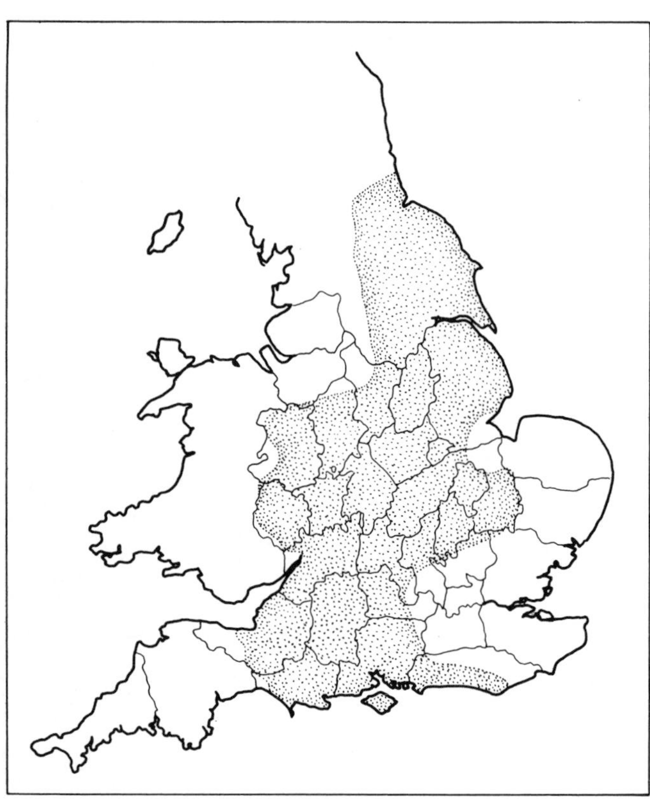

193 Medieval open fields in England

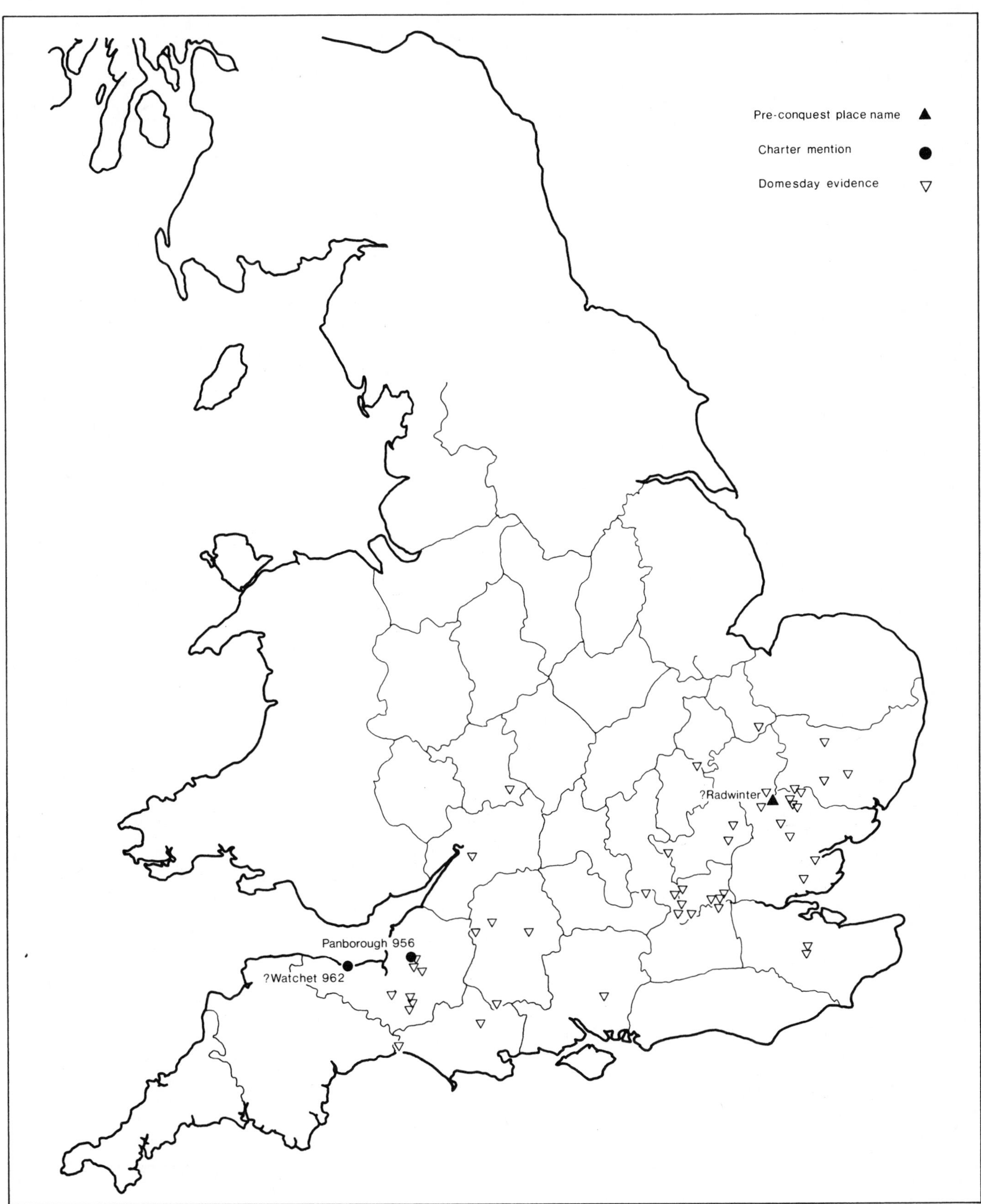

196 Vineyards

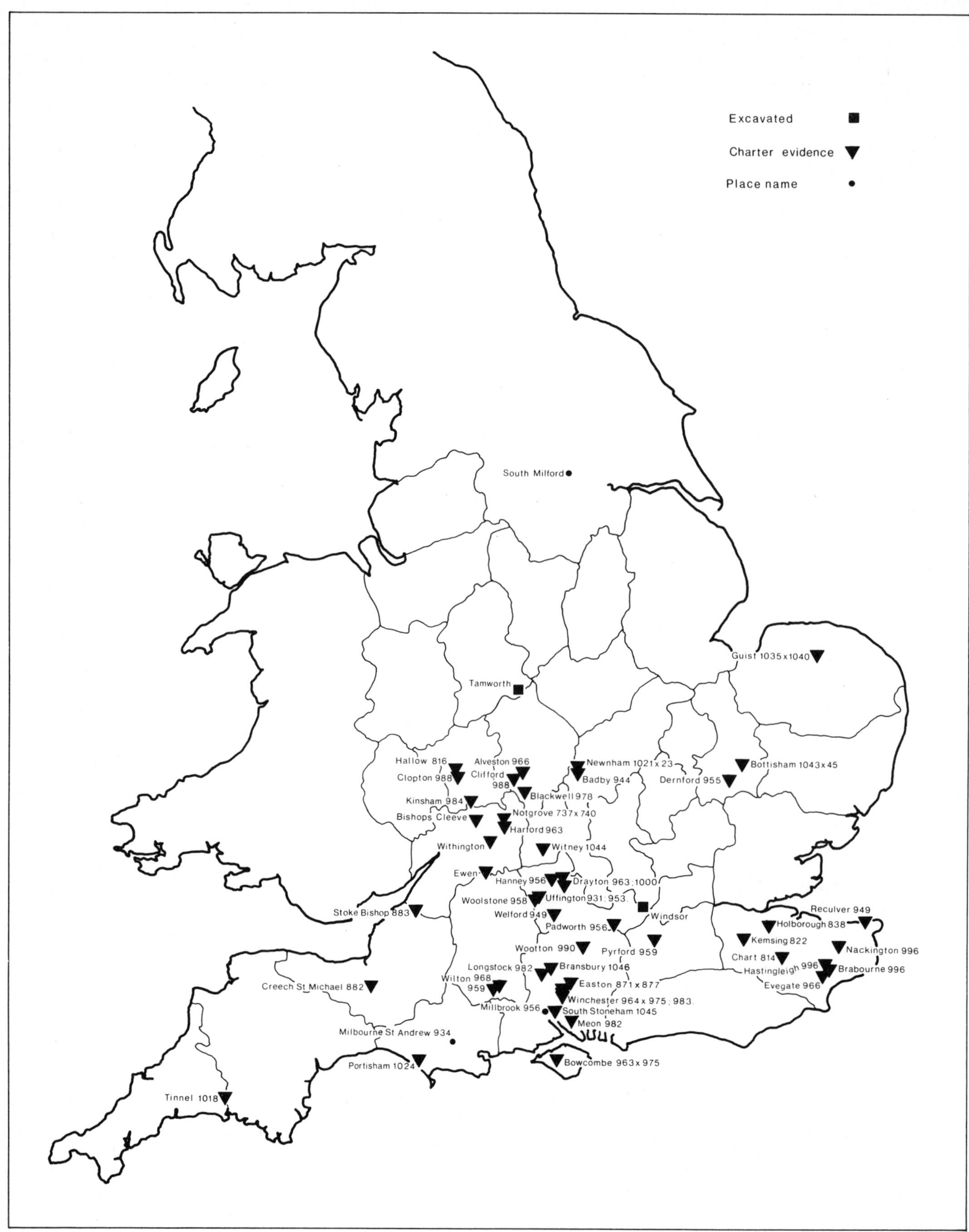
Excavated
Charter evidence
Place name
South Milford
Guist 1035 x 1040
Tamworth
Hallow 816
Clopton 988
Alveston 966
Clifford 988
Newnham 1021 x 23
Badby 944
Bottisham 1043 x 45
Dernford 955
Kinsham 984
Blackwell 978
Bishops Cleeve
Notgrove 737 x 740
Harford 963
Withington
Witney 1044
Ewen
Hanney 956
Drayton 963; 1000
Woolstone 958
Uffington 931; 953.
Windsor
Stoke Bishop 883
Welford 949
Padworth 956
Reculver 949
Holborough 838
Kemsing 822
Nackington 996
Wootton 990
Pyrford 959
Chart 814
Hastingleigh 996
Brabourne 996
Evegate 966
Longstock 982
Bransbury 1046
Wilton 968
959
Easton 871 x 877
Creech St Michael 882
Winchester 964 x 975; 983.
Millbrook 956
South Stoneham 1045
Meon 982
Milbourne St Andrew 934
Portisham 1024
Bowcombe 963 x 975
Tinnel 1018

197 Mills

Mills (197)

With the excavation of the Tamworth mill (Rahtz 1978) there has been more interest shown in this form of Anglo-Saxon technology. They are a common feature in charters from the ninth century and show that the vast numbers to be seen in the Domesday Survey were not a new feature. As it is not possible here to discuss all of the early place names, only three pre-Conquest examples are shown on map **197**.

A few mills had considerable engineering works attached to them to bring water from some distance, and all represent a mixture of skills and technologies, involving carpentry, millstones, metals and siting.

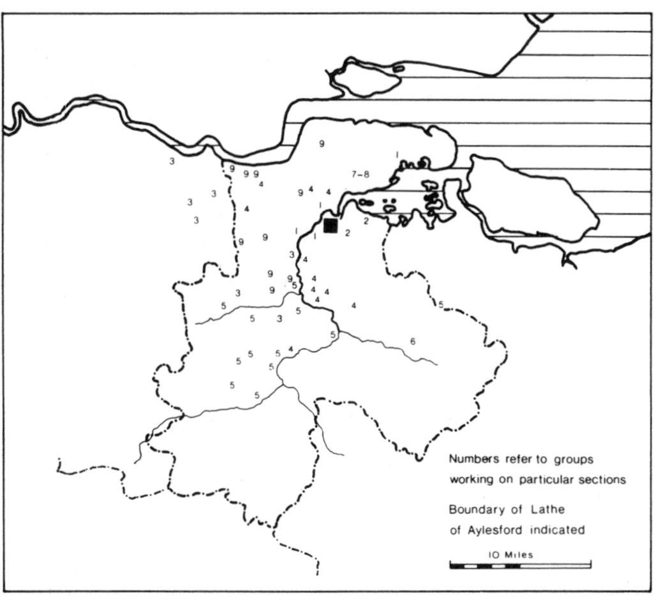

198 Estates owing work on Rochester Bridge ?973 × 988

Roads (198–199)

In a rare lapse, Stenton decided that the highway was unknown in Anglo-Saxon England. He was wrong. Long-distance thoroughfares were in use throughout the late Saxon period; some can be identified because they carry the name of their far-distant destination, as with the London Way; some use the same name throughout their length, as with the Foss; some are directly referred to, as with the road from Nottingham to York (map **199**).

That a system of 'king's highways' protected by royal prerogative existed in our period we should not doubt. Athelstan's journey with all his court from Winchester to Nottingham in eight days, the moving of Saint Aethelwold's body sixty miles in two days from where he died to his burial in Winchester (an example of the unexpected insights to be gained from such unlikely sources as the Life of Saint Aethelwold or the History of the Translation of Saint Aelfheah), Harold's dash from Yorkshire to Hastings, or the movement of lead from Wirksworth to Canterbury could hardly have been undertaken by people creeping apologetically along the margins of irate peasants' fields, or blundering through trackless woods. The insistence of the charters on bridgework points also to the royal interest in communications. Although these bridges had a defensive role in some cases, it is not possible that works of this complexity, widely scattered over the face of Anglo-Saxon England, connected two muddy lanes and were only part of a system of farm tracks. The bridges form part of a system of thoroughfares, for although the reference to the Royal Roads is strictly post-Conquest it refers to a period before 1066, and one at least of the roads (Watling Street) was called a 'royal street' in 940.

An example of the widespread responsibility for bridges throughout the countryside is provided by Rochester (map **198**) where a surviving document lists the obligations of various estates for work on the bridge, detailing the actual part of the structure concerned.

The bridges at London and Rochester were two of the great engineering feats of the age; there were similar bridges at Pont de l'Arche and at Paris and a greater and more famous example at Mainz. Einhard's **Life of Charlemagne**, chap 17, records:

The bridge over the Rhine at Mainz, which is five hundred feet long, this being the width of the river at that point. The bridge was burned down just one year before Charlemagne's death. He planned to rebuild it in stone instead of wood.

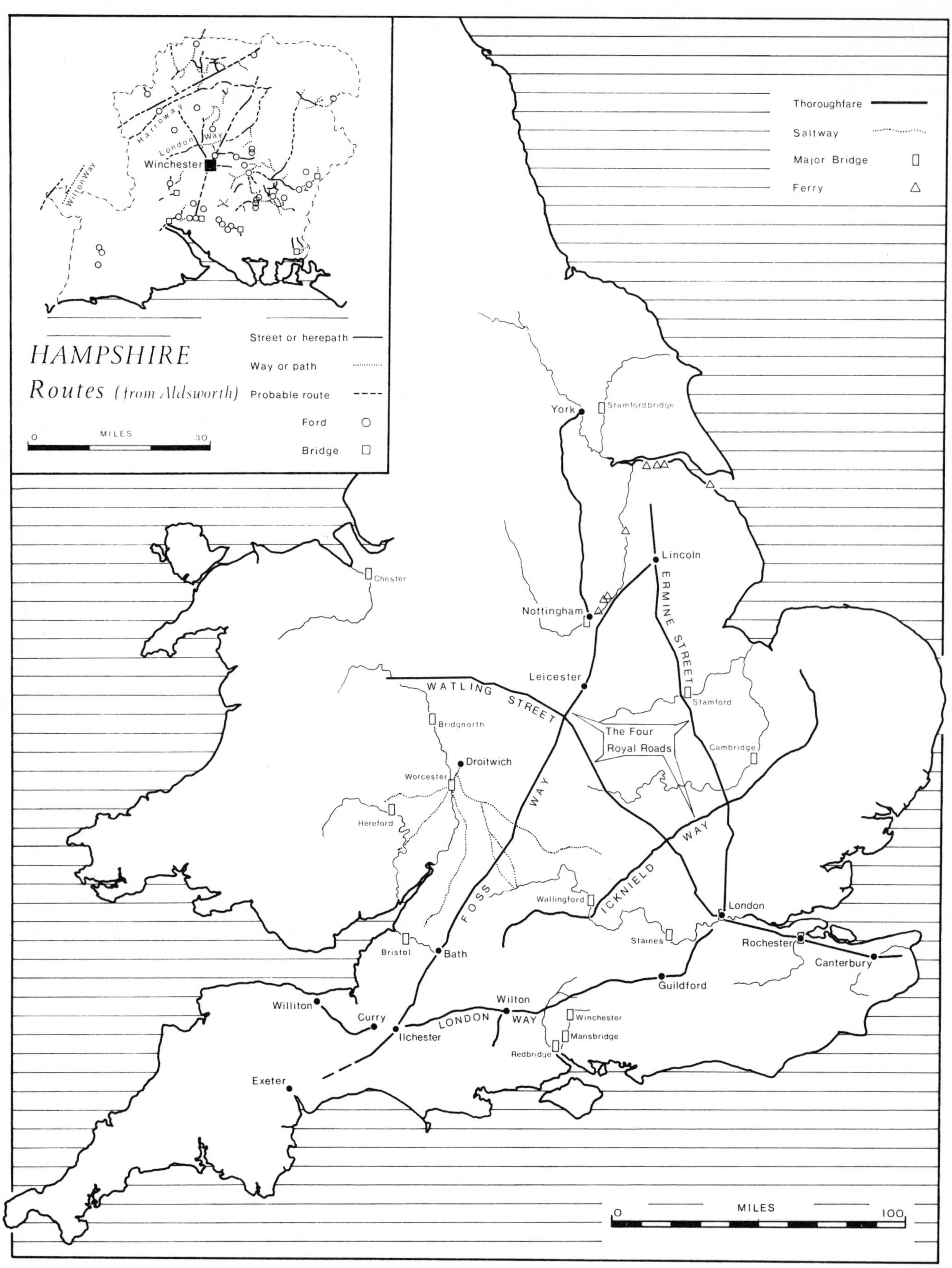

199 Major roads in Anglo-Saxon times with an inset of Hampshire routes (from Aldsworth)

Building Stone (200–202)

In a pioneering piece of research Professor Jope has identified the building stones in churches and memorials across southern Britain (map **200**). From this he has shown that the material came from four great quarry areas and was transported across considerable distances (Jope 1964). Half-ton quoins were moved over sixty miles, a fact which points to communications, organization and planning of a high degree. It should be realized from map **190** that there are other stone buildings using stone gathered from a variety of sources, but the idea that all Saxon stone structures, religious or secular, were cobbled together from old Roman buildings must be discarded.

The patterns of trade are affected by the political patterns of the time, and the early identifiable mica schist honestones from the Eidsborg in southern Norway travelled widely in the Danelaw and even farther afield (map **201**). It would appear that some may have travelled directly across either as ballast or as a part cargo, whilst some may have been traded via Rokleiv and Dorestadt. Whichever way they came they supplied a necessity, for every Saxon peasant carried with him a knife and, hanging on a string around his neck, his hone to sharpen it (Ellis 1969).

In the lava flows of the Eifel mountains there are quarries dating from all periods, from prehistoric to modern. The quality and ease of working of the stone from Mayen (usually known as Niedermendig after one of the villages in the area) has ensured its wide and continuous use (map **202**). The enclosed bubbles of air in the stone mean that as the millstones or querns made from the lava wear down the surfaces remain abrasive, while the bubbles also make the querns light. Querns from this material are to be found in Carolingian forts in Saxony and widely in the north-west of Europe in the period 700–850. They were carried as blanks to Dorestad and over to Hamwih (Saxon Southampton), and the worked querns are then found in such settings as the Tamworth watermill. These are probably the stones referred to in the correspondence between Offa and Charlemagne (Whitelock 1955, 781). They are an indicator of trade in basic commodities at an early period and have a strikingly similar distribution to the sceatta coinage.

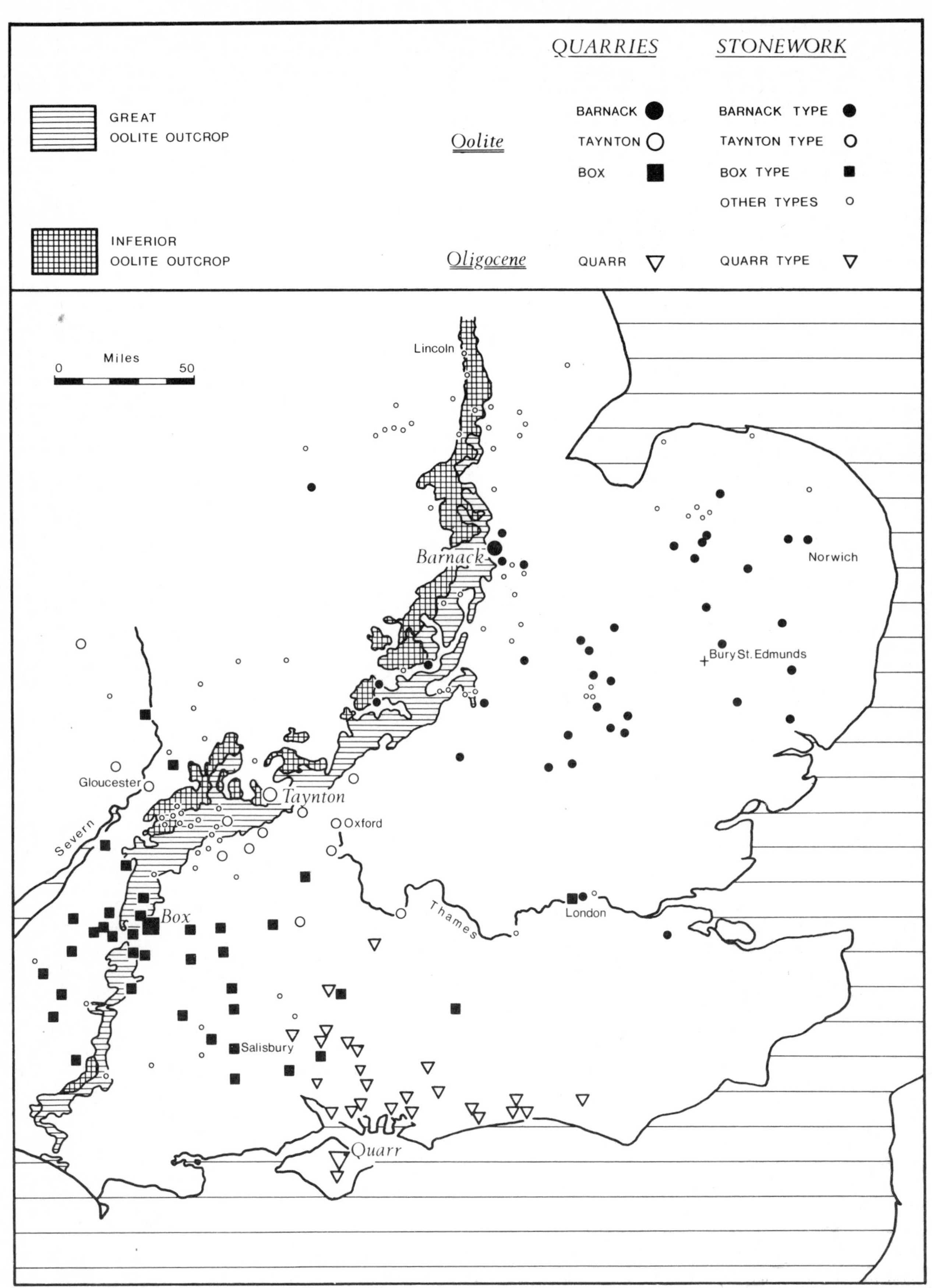

200 Fine building stone eighth to eleventh century (after Jope)

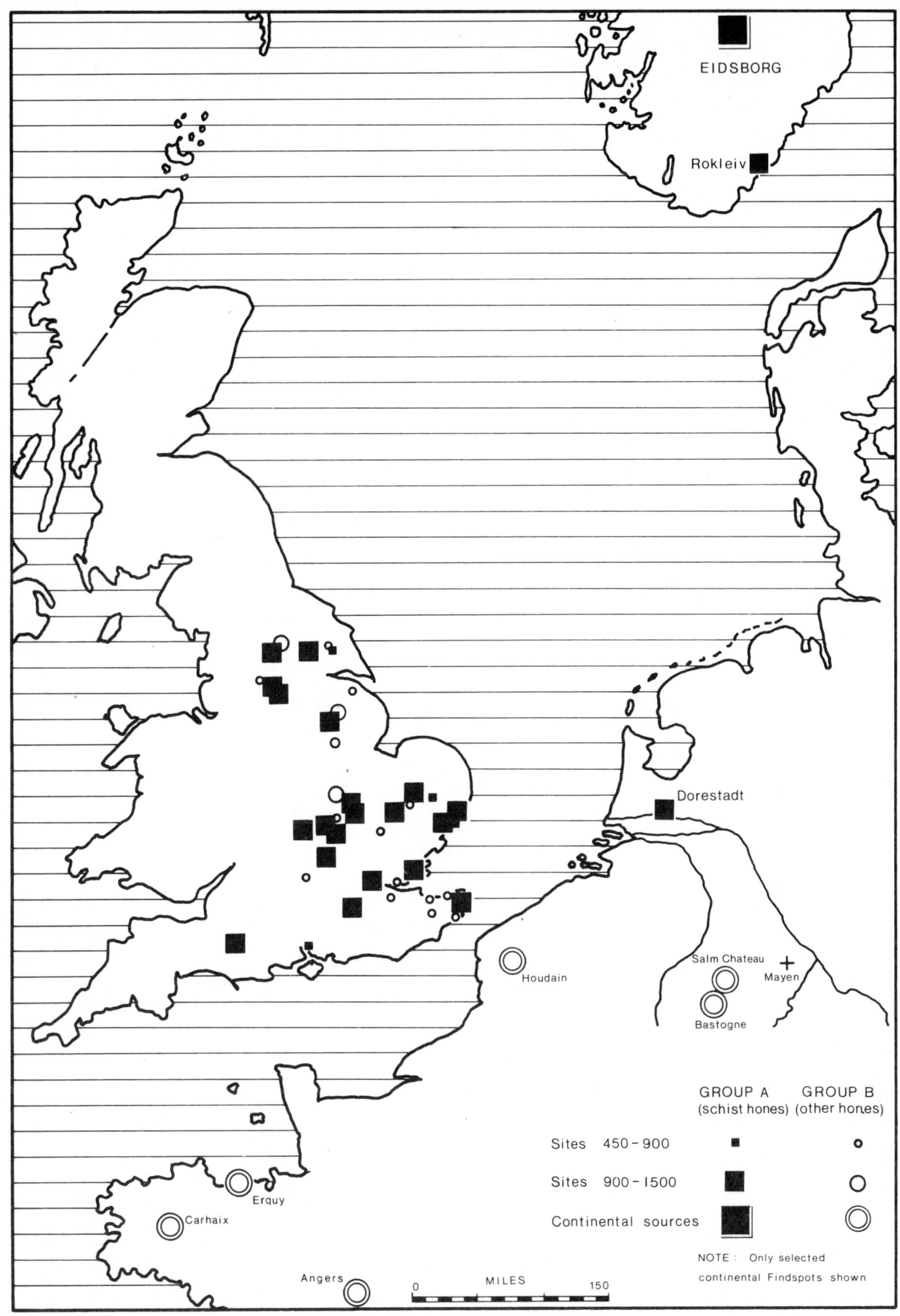
EIDSBORG
Rokleiv
Dorestadt
Salm Chateau
Mayen
Houdain
Bastogne
GROUP A
(schist hones)
GROUP B
(other hones)
Sites 450-900
Sites 900-1500
Continental sources
NOTE: Only selected continental Findspots shown
Erquy
Carhaix
Angers
0
MILES
150

201 Honestones

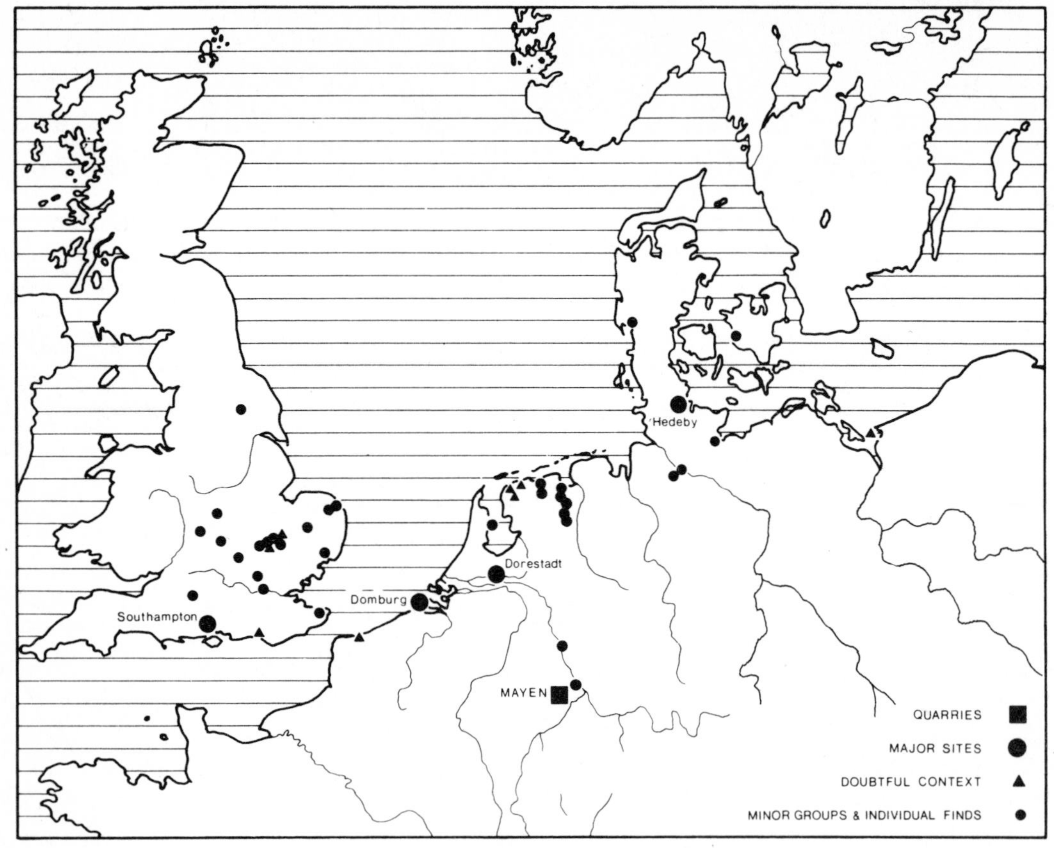

202 Niedermendig lava (after Parkhouse)

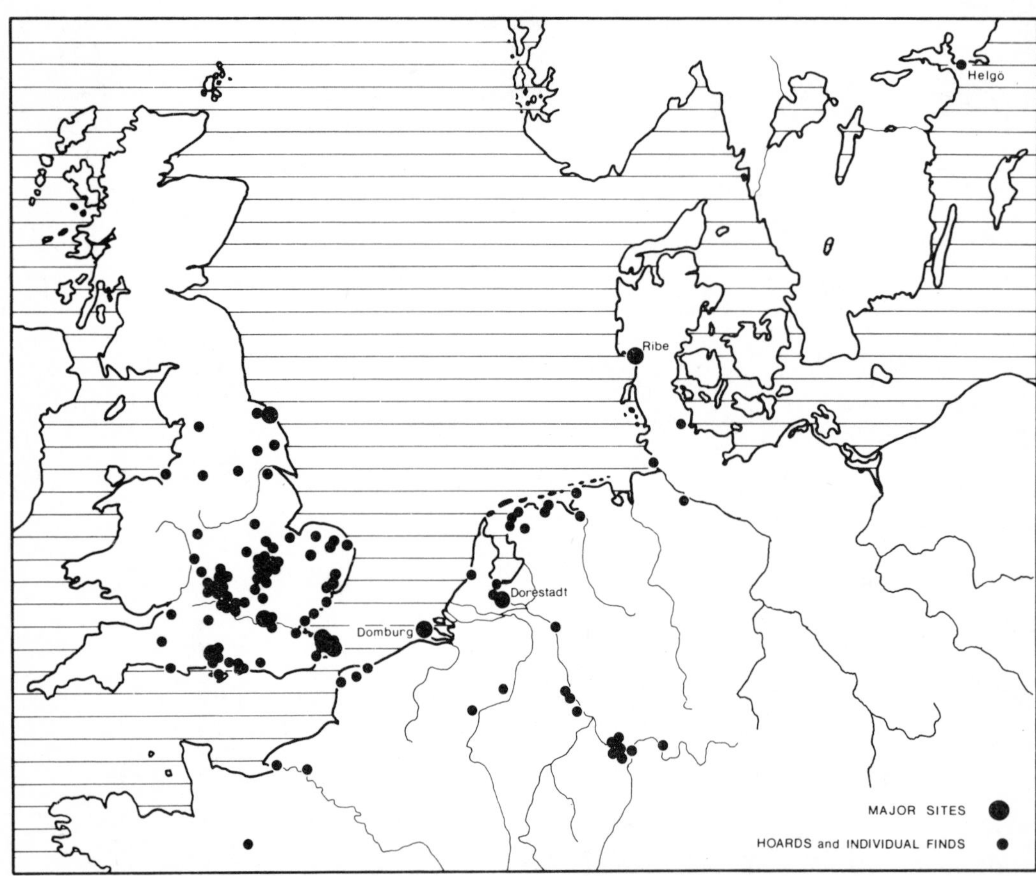

203 Distribution of finds of sceattas in England and on the Continent

Coins (203–207)

The small flan deniers of silver known by the antiquarian name of **sceattas** come in a wealth of designs mostly without any inscription. They date from around the 690s, when they replaced the **thrymsa**, until they were in turn replaced by the coinage of Offa and the Kentish kings, although there is a hiatus of uncertain length between the two coinages (map **203**). They were struck at a number of centres, in the same way as the contemporary Merovingian coinage (map **204**) and with little central control. The sceattas (regrettably, Dolley's suggestion that they should be known as proto-pennies has not been taken up) were struck at London, Canterbury, Rochester, York and Southampton and have the distinction of being found widely across northern Europe, particularly in large hoards in Frisia. One point which is often missed is that with the multiplicity of issues in Merovingian Gaul the anepigraphic issues of sceattas would be acceptable anywhere in Gaul. In fact the evidence of the hoards in France together with the distribution in the Rhineland shows that it would be helpful to regard the sceattas as the northern fringe of Merovingian coinage, mixing with it where the two coinages overlapped.

The distribution of the sceatta finds in England is very specific, and rather inexplicable (map **205**). The concentration around the east Kent coast is what one would expect when one takes into account the lively trade with Domburg, Dorestadt and the Rhineland, but there is a wider distribution along an axis from north Wiltshire to Norfolk, southern Mercia. There are also sceattas in southern Northumbria and on the south coast, but the southern Mercian concentration is striking. It may, as with the Niedermendig lava, reflect a trade for England to the Rhineland of Mercian woollen goods carried, in the main, by Frisian traders from London, Kent and Southampton.

The particular finds from a large number of Roman sites and from some Iron Age hillforts raise questions about the role of these sites as central places in the eighth century.

Following the reorganization of the Frankish coinage by Pippin III, 'Pepin le Bref', in 755 and the marking of that reorganization by a new coin, the denarius on a wider flan, the Saxons issued a new coinage. The penny was of similar type to the denarius and was first struck by the kings of Kent in small quantities. Offa followed c.780 with a penny series which is outstanding in both quality and design. It is noticeable that the distribution of finds of the coins of Offa follows that of the sceattas (map **206**). In the north the Northumbrians went their own way continuing the sceatta series with an increasingly debased coinage which soon became the base metal, fiduciary, issue the **stycas** which was out of step with the rest of European coinage and survived until the Danish invasions (map **207**).

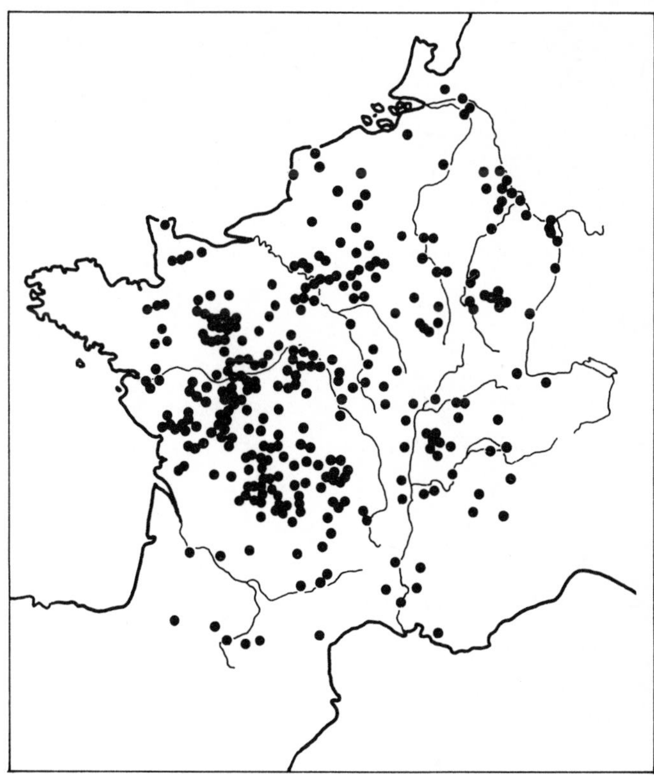

204 Merovingian mints

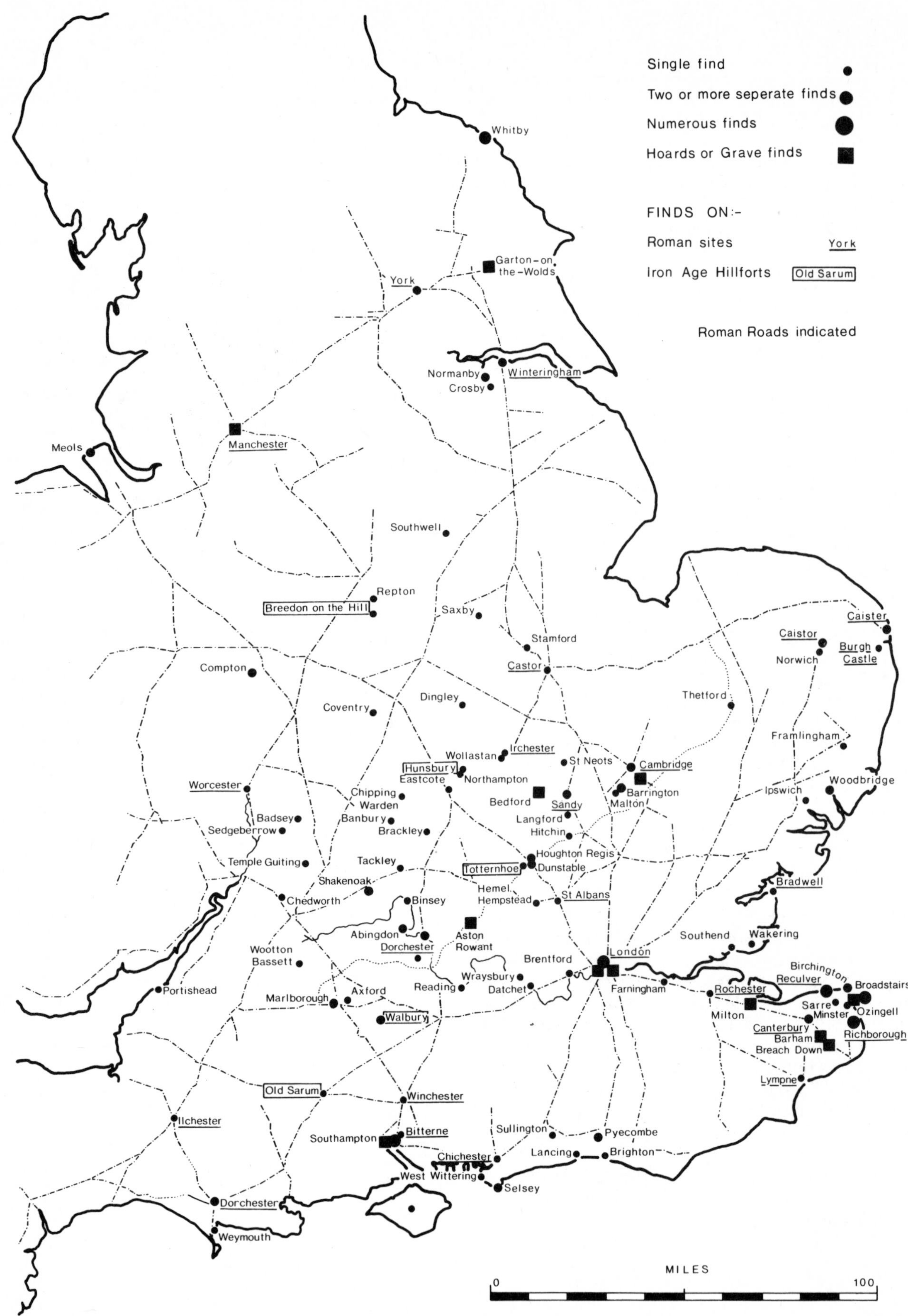
Single find
Two or more seperate finds
Numerous finds
Hoards or Grave finds
FINDS ON:-
Roman sites
York
Iron Age Hillforts
Old Sarum
Roman Roads indicated
Whitby
Garton-on the-Wolds
York
Normanby
Crosby
Winteringham
Manchester
Meols
Southwell
Repton
Breedon on the Hill
Saxby
Stamford
Castor
Caister
Caistor
Norwich
Burgh Castle
Compton
Dingley
Coventry
Thetford
Framlingham
Irchester
Wollaston
Hunsbury
Eastcote
Northampton
St Neots
Cambridge
Barrington
Malton
Woodbridge
Ipswich
Worcester
Chipping Warden
Banbury
Brackley
Bedford
Sandy
Langford
Hitchin
Badsey
Sedgeberrow
Temple Guiting
Tackley
Houghton Regis
Totternhoe
Dunstable
Bradwell
Shakenoak
Chedworth
Binsey
Hemel Hempstead
St Albans
Abingdon
Dorchester
Aston Rowant
Southend
Wakering
Wootton Bassett
Brentford
London
Wraysbury
Datchet
Reading
Farningham
Birchington
Reculver
Broadstairs
Rochester
Sarre
Minster
Ozingell
Milton
Portishead
Marlborough
Axford
Walbury
Canterbury
Barham
Breach Down
Richborough
Lympne
Old Sarum
Winchester
Ilchester
Southampton
Bitterne
Sullington
Pyecombe
Lancing
Brighton
Chichester
West Wittering
Selsey
Dorchester
Weymouth
MILES
0
100

205 Sceattas: insular findspots (after Metcalf)

206 Offa's coinage: findspots

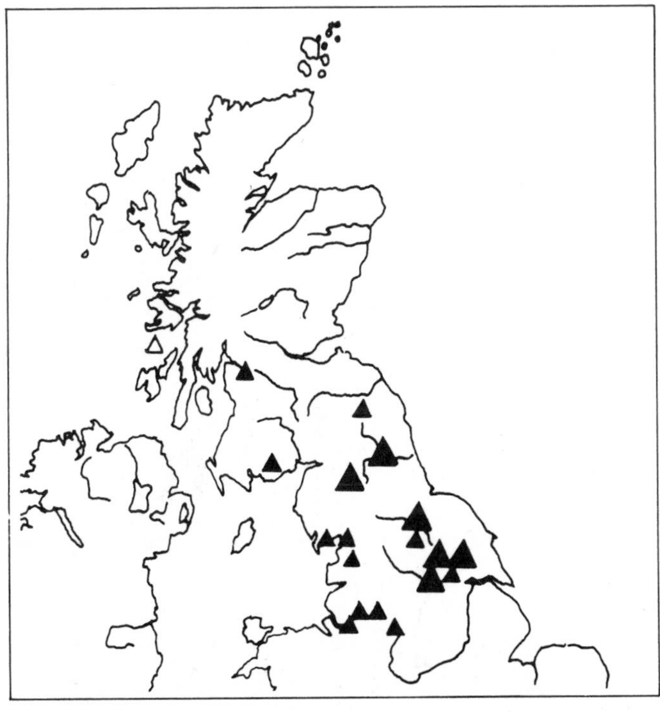

207 Stycas: distribution of hoards

The Mints of Carolingian Europe (208–211)

The rise of the towns of Anglo-Saxon England, their multiplication and their association with the expansion of minting, is also intimately linked with trade and town patterns in Northern France. It is useful as a control for our thinking about the English situation to consider the places with which the Saxons were trading on the other side of the Channel.

The number of mints in France and their concentrations are not matched in England until a century after the distribution in France charted on these maps (**208–211**). In the reign of Charles the Bald, a time of intense Viking attack and of civil war, there seems to have been a considerable expansion of minting, and (one may speculate) also of urban activity (map **210**). It is of interest to note that the full citation of the place names on the coinage of Charles the Bald includes a designation of the status of the minting place and these can be used to show a typology of towns that was in use in the ninth century. This typology should have some validity when compared with those constructed by more recent scholars. It should be noted that, in common with Gildas and Bede (map **43**), the Franks were aware of the Roman origins of their towns and these towns have the title **civitates**, the **de novo** sites are carefully named with what appears to be some technical sophistication (map **211**). Unfortunately, although there is some Frankish influence on the Anglo-Saxon coinage, it is rare for English coins to carry these descriptions; some do appear on the coins, particularly those of Athelstan; London, Winchester, Bath, Canterbury, Chester, Chichester, Exeter, Gloucester, Leicester and Rochester are all **civitates**, a style which does not have here the specialised meaning of 'cathedral city' but means 'walled place of Roman origin'. Four mints are designated **urbs**: 'Darent'. Lewes, Southampton and Oxford; all are walled but none are Roman. This distinction in the use of the terms is obviously a real one as can be seen from Asser **'de civitatibus et urbibus renovandis et aliis, ubi nunquam ante fuerant, construendis'** (what of the cities and towns he restored, and others, which he built where none had been before?).

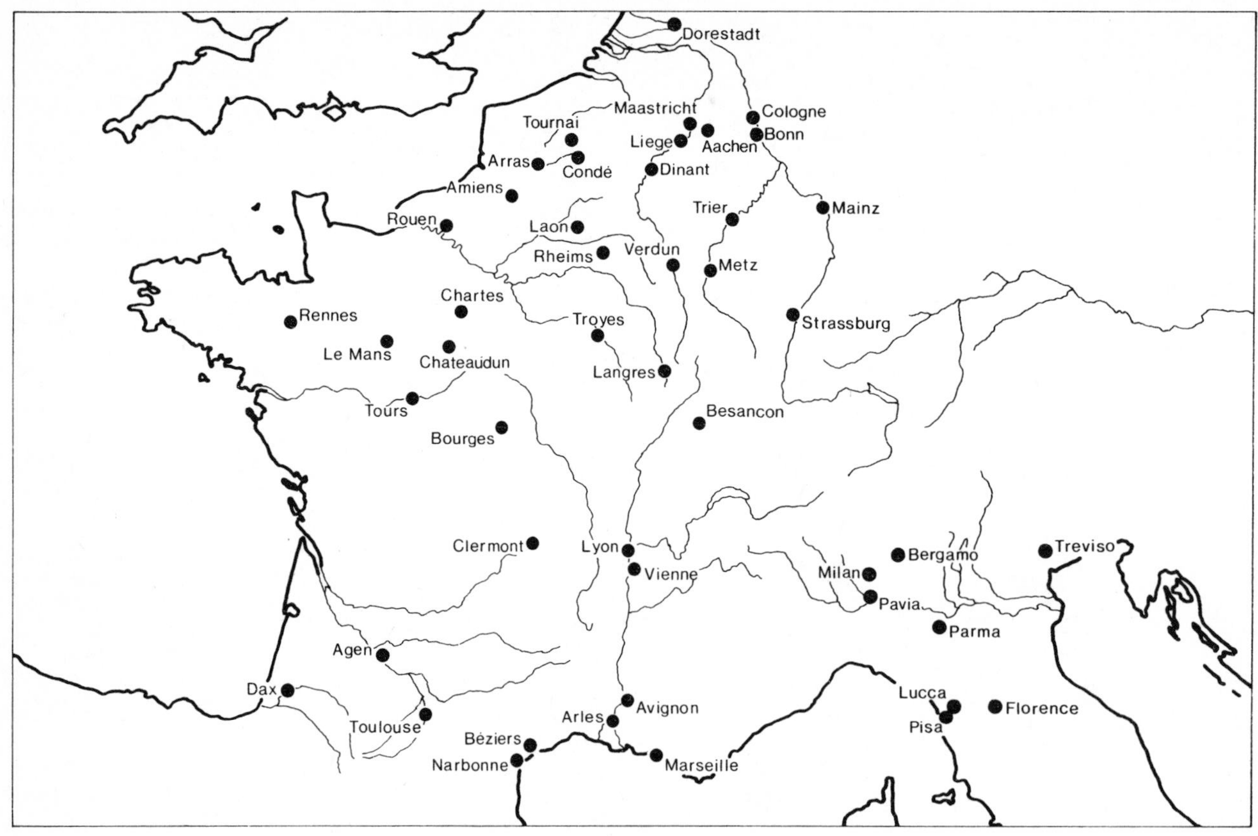

208 Mints of Charlemagne 768–814

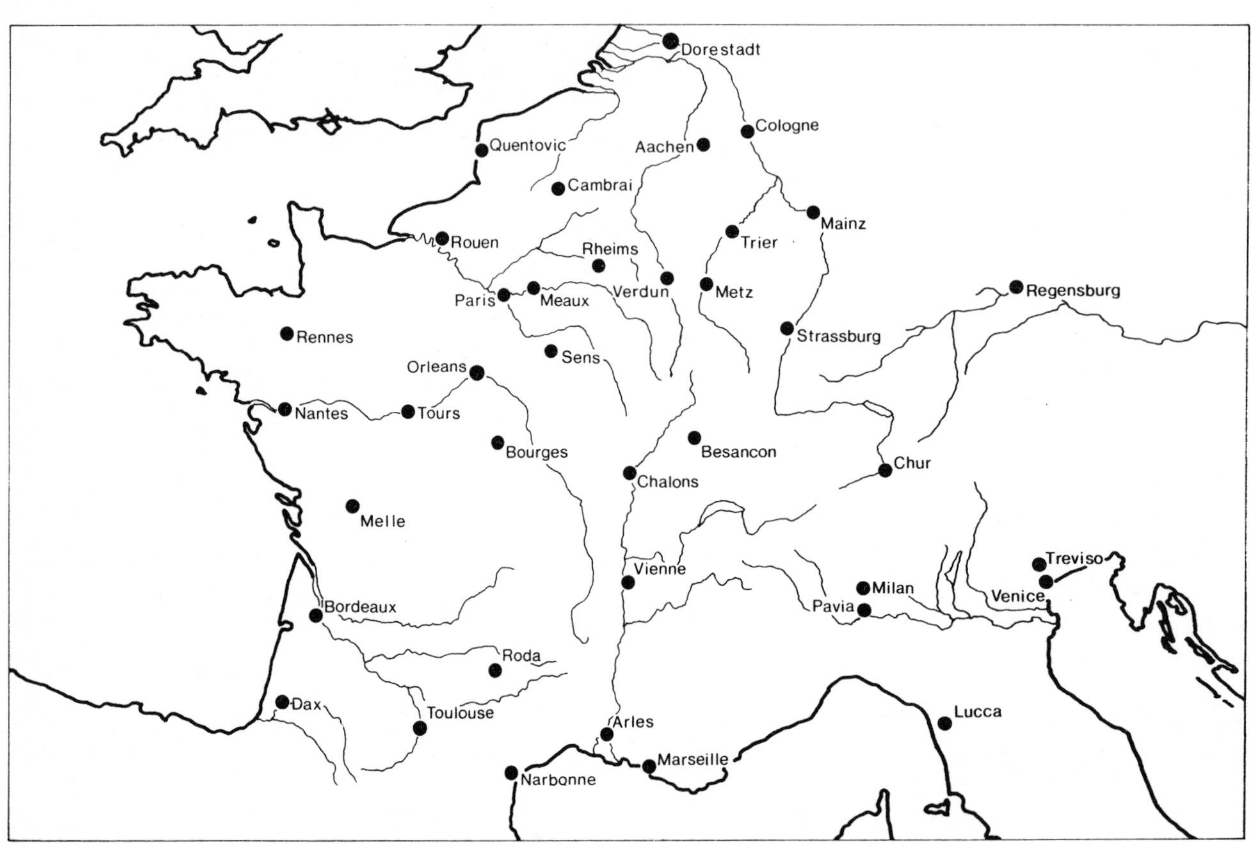

209 Mints of Louis the Pious 814–840

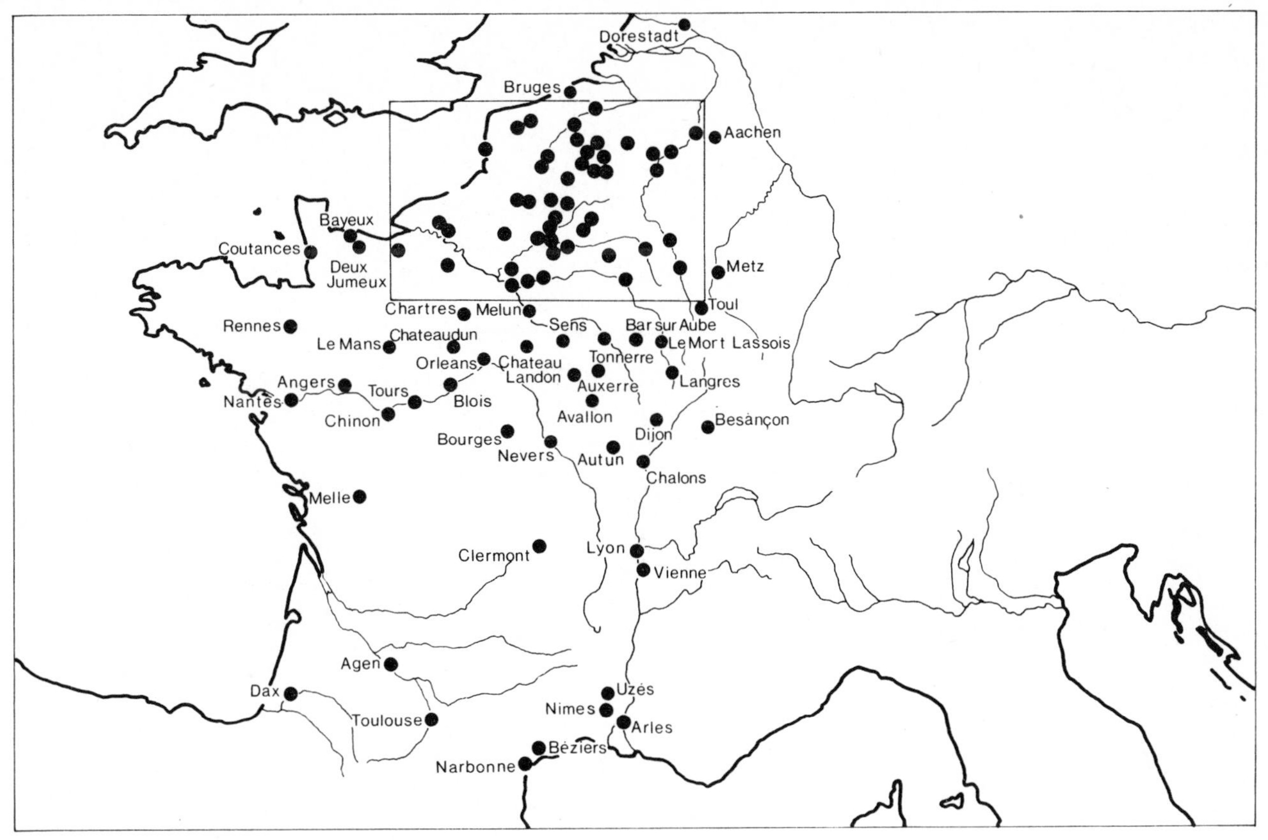

210 Mints of Charles the Bald 840–875

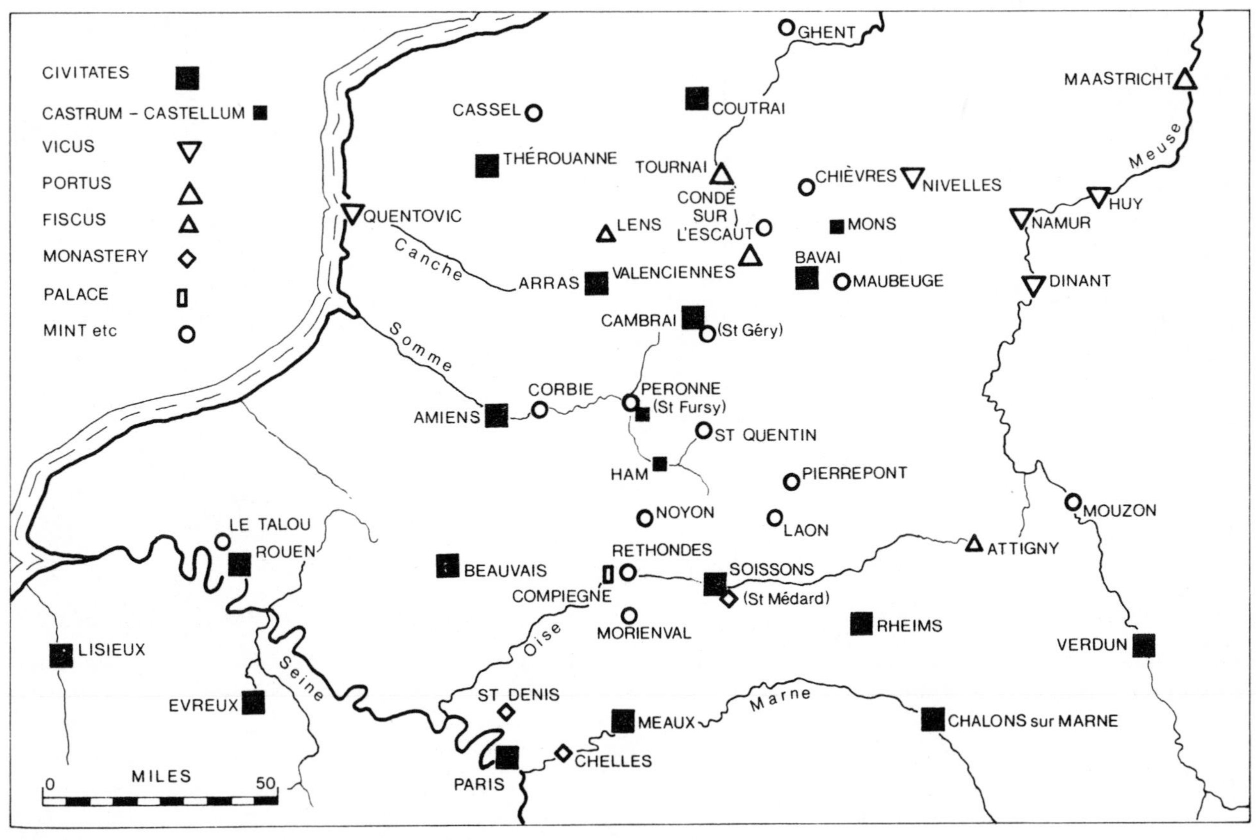

211 Northern area in the time of Charles the Bald

Mints in England (212–225)

The velocity of circulation of coinage in Anglo-Saxon England was remarkable (Metcalf 1978, 168), indicating a very brisk interchange of money, constant travel around the country and a national currency. It should not be thought that at this period the multiplicity of mints indicates purely localized coinages or localized areas of circulation. An example of this movement is the composition of the Pemberton's Parlour hoard from Chester (map **212**). This hoard was deposited c.979–80, which means that the earliest coins were no more than six years old. Yet the mints represented cover most of England, particularly the east Midlands. The farthest coin comes from Totnes in Devon.

The increase in mints during the period is charted by maps **213–221** (North 1963). On the later maps (**218–221**) only the new mints are named. Note that the visual effect of the maps can be deceptive as a small and intermittent mint can be seen alongside a major centre such as Lincoln. The exact location of these mints can be studied on the detailed town sheets (maps **226–234**). The maps are a little misleading in that many of the coins did not carry the name of the mint until the reform under Edgar in 973. Thus the mints of Edward the Elder (map **214**) reflect nothing except that two places are identified on the coins as mints. The later maps (**218–221**) reflect a pattern of surprising concentrations in the South and South-west whilst in the Midlands and the North one mint to a shire would seem to be general. The later reigns have the addition of minor mints reflecting the foundation of small, secondary, market centres.

A simple charting of the Anglo-Saxon mints does not enable us to make sensible judgements about these mints. It is possible to rank the mints and the method used here has been to count the number of known moneyers (**222–223**). This has been preferred to equating the number of surviving coins or recognized dies with the output of the mint, both for the sake of simplicity and to eliminate some of the factors of chance survival, it being felt that a moneyer's coin is more likely to survive than a coin from a particular die. This obviated some of the problems arising from the overrepresentation in the survivals of the mints of eastern England. The percentages have been worked out for each reign after 973 and then the average taken from the total reigns, thus making the whole calculation as insensitive as possible (for another, and probably superior approach see Metcalf 1978).

The chart (**223**) makes some interesting points but the map (**222**) gives a visual impression of the mints in their setting. It is clear that there is a ranking which would seem to reflect the role of the various mints: thus there are the great national mints at London, Lincoln and York; what would appear to be provincial centres at Exeter, Winchester, Stamford and Chester; shire centres such as Shrewsbury and Oxford; down to the minor mints and secondary market centres at such sites as Steyning and Frome. The map does issue a useful **caveat** against treating these places as being too much alike.

The greatest achievement of Anglo-Saxon studies since the war has been the clarity and order that has been brought to the study of the coinage, in particular by Professor Michael Dolley. Coins now rank as one of the major sources of insights into the administrative and organizational abilities of the Anglo-Saxon state. It is difficult for many scholars to break out of their particular field or for the general student to acquire the expertise of a specialism, and in fairness it is often true that certain areas of research do not assist the general student, for the rim forms of pots may not seem too relevant to the layman nor will the glories of diplomatic or scriptoria reveal themselves easily to all. But the numismatist has a great deal to offer in practically all fields and the evidence of the coin is so central to the mainstream of research into pre-Conquest England that the effort should be made. Suffice to say here that the management of the coinage and through it the general direction of the economy was so advanced in the last century of the Anglo-Saxon state that we must wonder at the sophistication of the directing personnel. The coinage was changed every six (later three) years, the old issue being demonetized, thus allowing a wealth tax to be taken; the weights could then be adjusted, either up or down, with effects on the rate of exchange and thus on exports and imports; mints were set up and standards controlled all over the kingdom. These and many other aspects of the coinage command attention.

The charts in **224** and **225** show which mints were striking coins at a particular time. Since they are based on obsolescent evidence (North 1963), they are but an interim statement to give some idea of the issues struck at each mint and the first appearance of that mint. It should be noted that when a mint struck for someone other than the named king (i.e. as a Viking mint) it is not included on these charts.

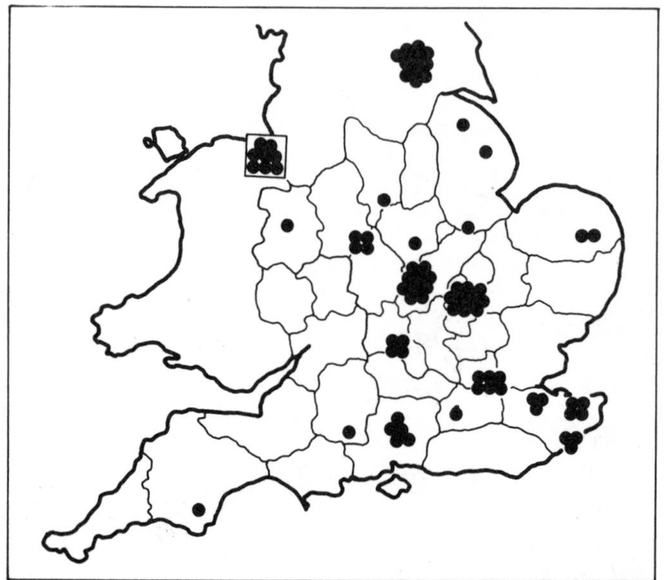

212 Mints of origin of coins in the Pemberton's Parlour hoard, Chester

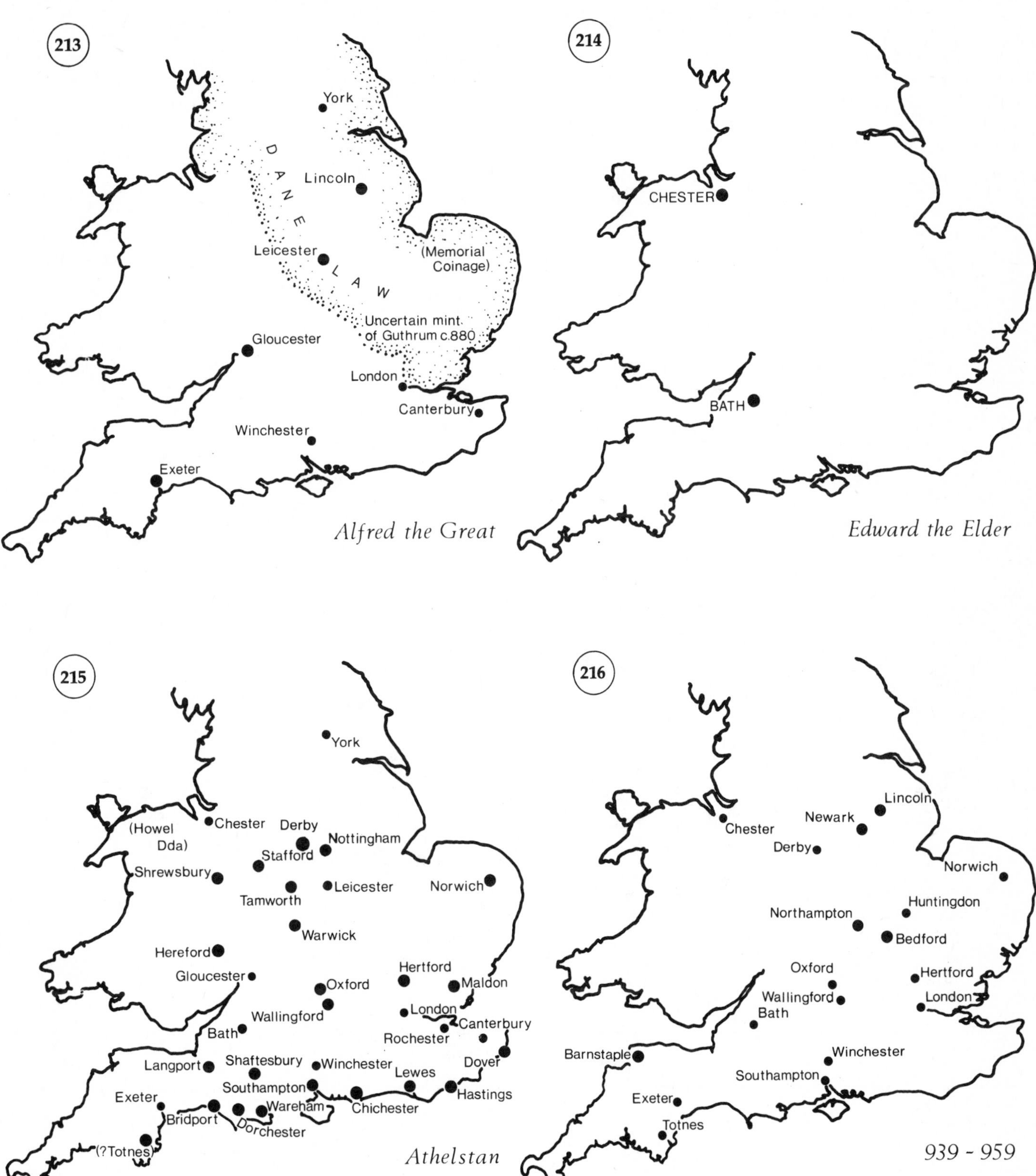

213–216 Mints 871–959. The large dot shows new mints; the smaller dot existing mints

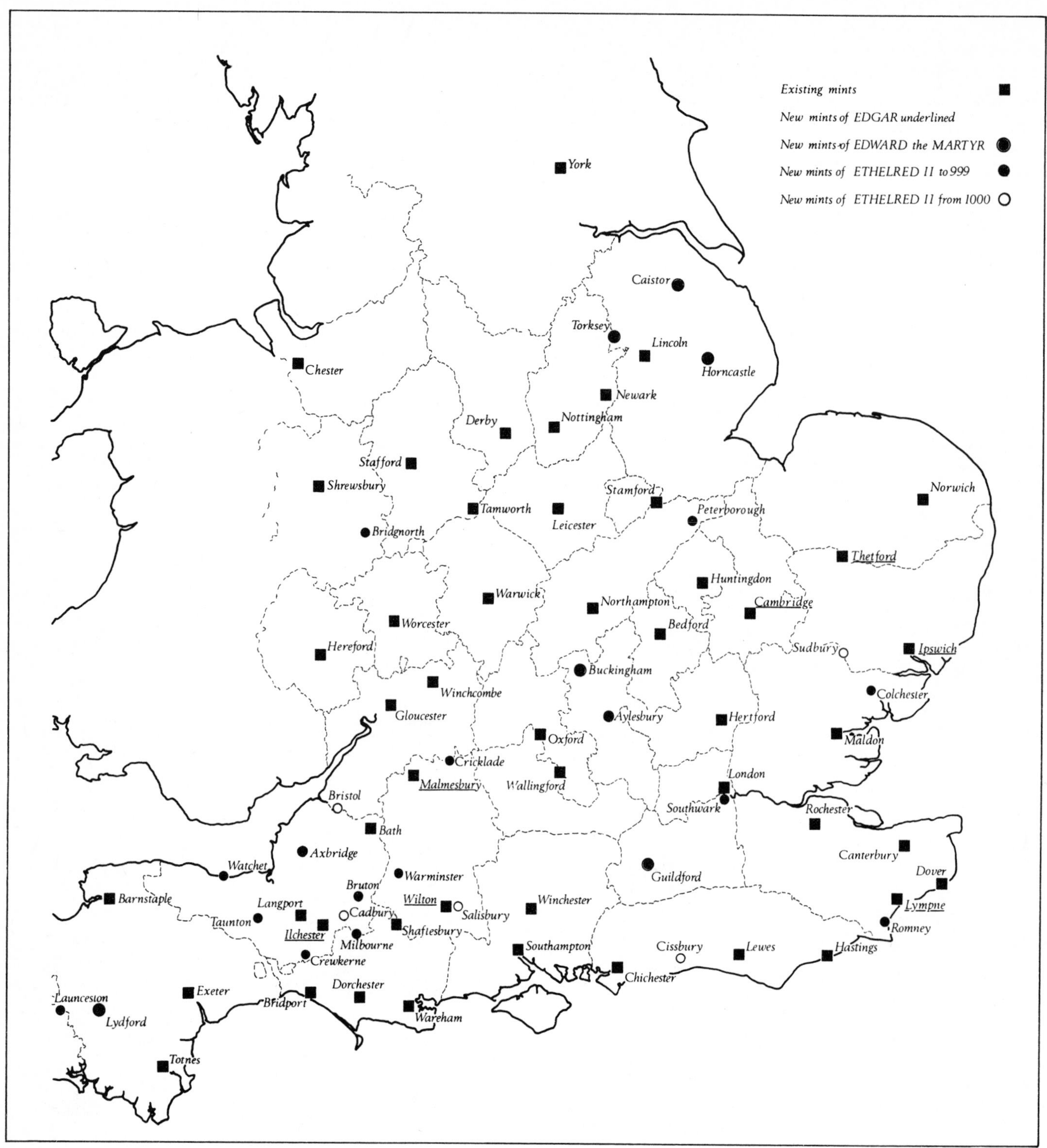

217 Mints 957–1016

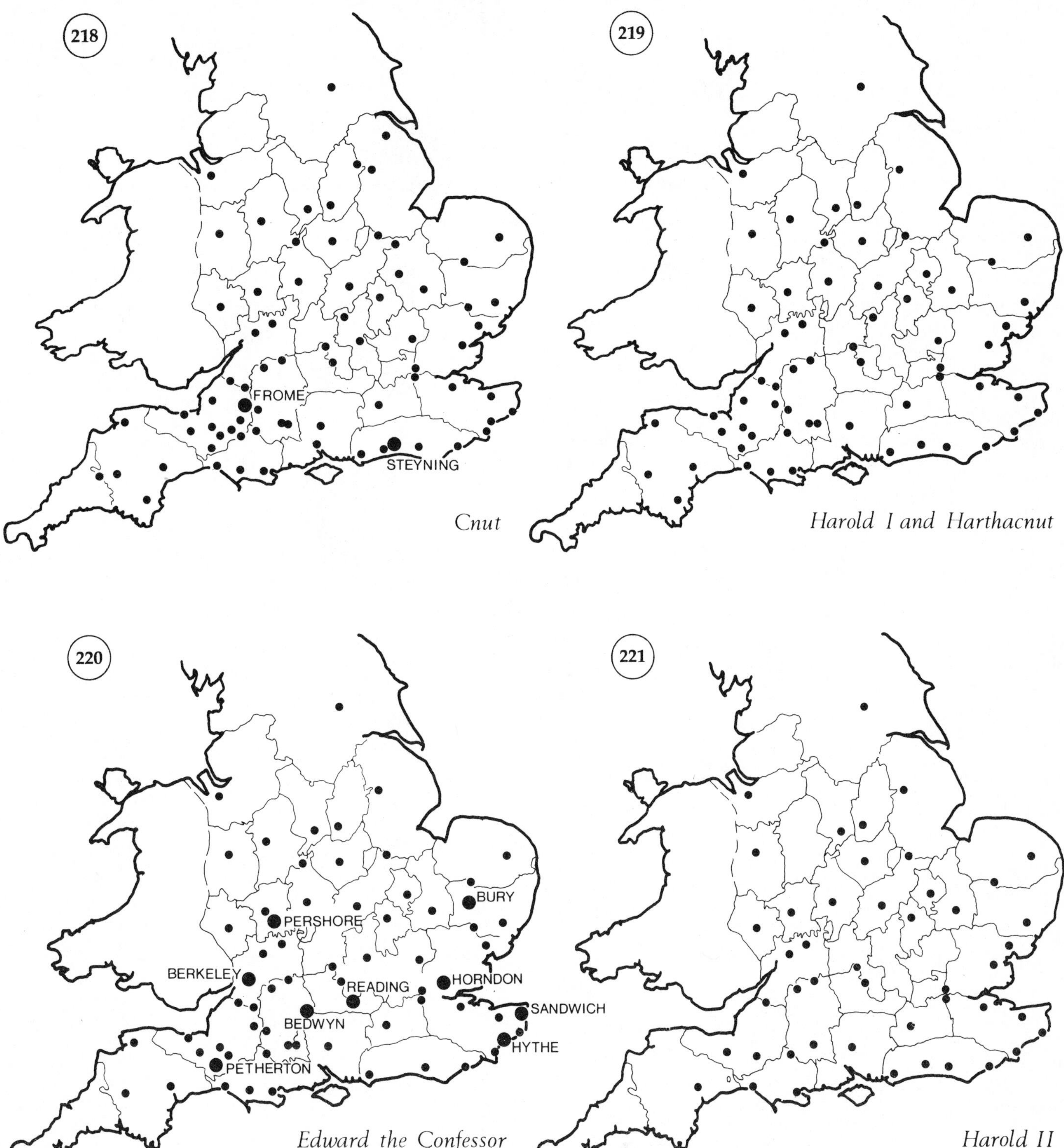

218–221 Mints 1016–1066. The large dot shows new mints; the smaller dot existing mints

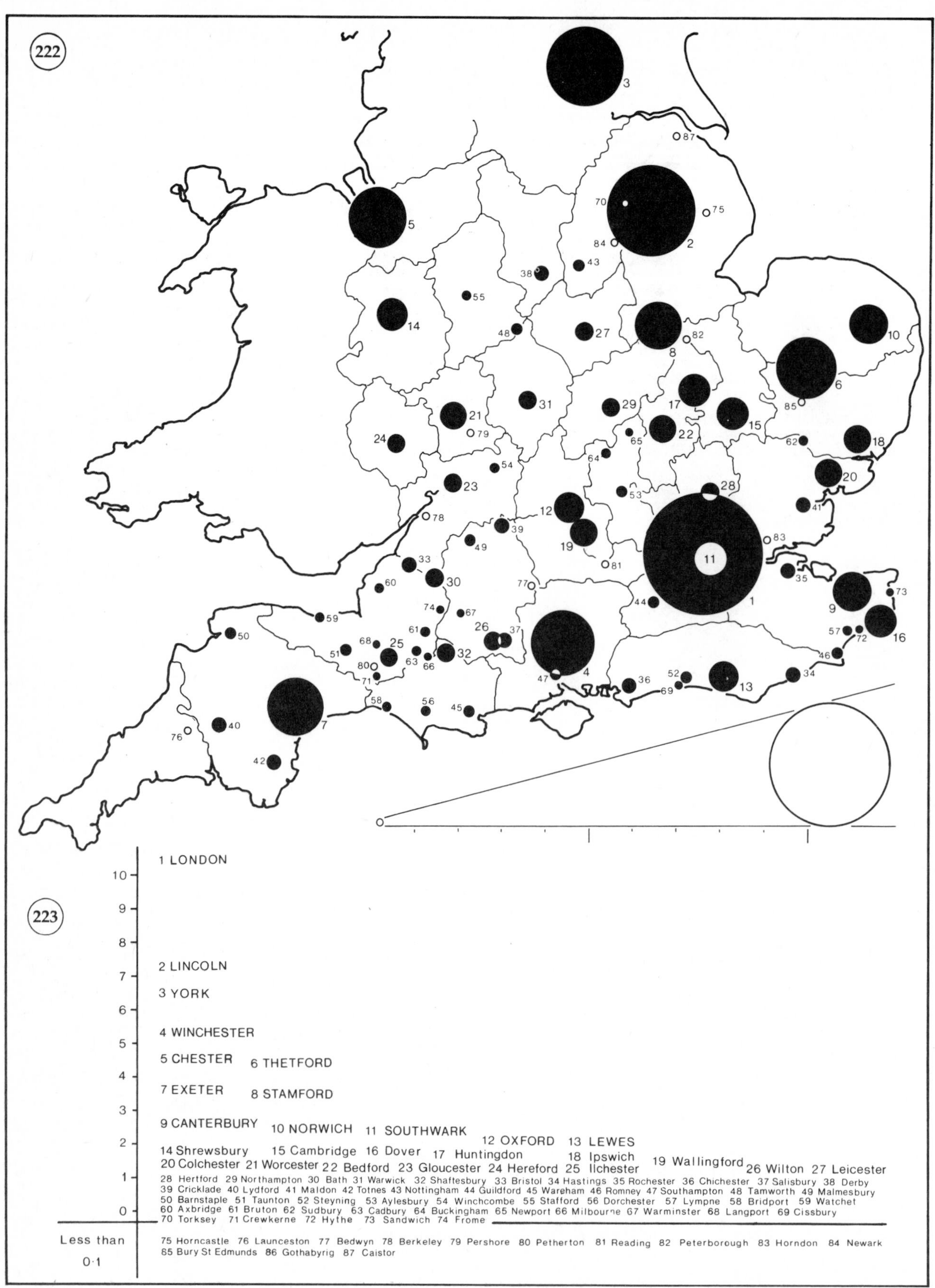
222
223
1 LONDON
2 LINCOLN
3 YORK
4 WINCHESTER
5 CHESTER 6 THETFORD
7 EXETER 8 STAMFORD
9 CANTERBURY 10 NORWICH 11 SOUTHWARK
12 OXFORD 13 LEWES
14 Shrewsbury 15 Cambridge 16 Dover 17 Huntingdon 18 Ipswich
19 Wallingford
20 Colchester 21 Worcester 22 Bedford 23 Gloucester 24 Hereford 25 Ilchester 26 Wilton 27 Leicester
28 Hertford 29 Northampton 30 Bath 31 Warwick 32 Shaftesbury 33 Bristol 34 Hastings 35 Rochester 36 Chichester 37 Salisbury 38 Derby
39 Cricklade 40 Lydford 41 Maldon 42 Totnes 43 Nottingham 44 Guildford 45 Wareham 46 Romney 47 Southampton 48 Tamworth 49 Malmesbury
50 Barnstaple 51 Taunton 52 Steyning 53 Aylesbury 54 Winchcombe 55 Stafford 56 Dorchester 57 Lympne 58 Bridport 59 Watchet
60 Axbridge 61 Bruton 62 Sudbury 63 Cadbury 64 Buckingham 65 Newport 66 Milbourne 67 Warminster 68 Langport 69 Cissbury
70 Torksey 71 Crewkerne 72 Hythe 73 Sandwich 74 Frome
Less than 0·1
75 Horncastle 76 Launceston 77 Bedwyn 78 Berkeley 79 Pershore 80 Petherton 81 Reading 82 Peterborough 83 Horndon 84 Newark
85 Bury St Edmunds 86 Gothabyrig 87 Caistor

222–223 The ranking of mints expressed as a percentage of total known moneyers

Mint	Alfred	Edward the Elder	Athelstan	Edmund	Eadred	Eadwig	Edgar: Pre-reform	Edgar: Reform 973	Edward the Martyr 975	Ethelred the Second: 1st Small cross 978	1st Hand 979	2nd Hand 985	CRUX 991	Intermediate Small cross 997	Long cross 997	Helmet 1003	AGNUS DEI 1009	Last Small cross 1009	Cnut: Quatrefoil 1017	Pointed Helmet 1023	Short cross 1029	Jewel cross 1035	Harold I: Jewel cross 1035	Fleur de Lys 1038	Harthacnut: Jewel cross 1035	Arms & Sceptre 1040	Edward the Confessor: PACX 1042	Radiate Small cross 1044	Trefoil Quadrilateral 1046	Short cross 1048	Expanding cross 1050	Pointed Helmet 1053	Sovereign Eagles 1056	Hammer cross 1059	Facing Small cross 1062	Pyramids 1065	Harold II 1066
AXBRIDGE																																					
Aylesbury																																					
BARNSTAPLE																																					
Bath																																					
BEDFORD																																					
Bedwyn																																					
BERKELEY																																					
Bridgnorth																																					
BRIDPORT																																					
Bristol																																					
BRUTON																																					
Buckingham																																					
BURY ST EDMUNDS																																					
Cadbury																																					
CAISTOR																																					
Cambridge																																					
CANTERBURY																																					
Chester																																					
CHICHESTER																																					
Cissbury																																					
COLCHESTER																																					
Crewkerne																																					
CRICKLADE																																					
Derby																																					
DORCHESTER																																					
Dover																																					
EXETER																																					
Frome																																					
GLOUCESTER																																					
Guildford																																					
HASTINGS																																					
Hereford																																					
HERTFORD																																					
Horncastle																																					
HORNDON																																					
Huntingdon																																					
HYTHE																																					
Ilchester																																					
IPSWICH																																					
Langport																																					
LAUNCESTON																																					
Leicester																																					
LEWES																																					
Lincoln																																					
LONDON																																					
Lydford																																					
LYMPNE																																					
Maldon																																					
MALMESBURY																																					
Milbourne Port																																					
NEWARK																																					

224 Mints striking 871–1066: part I

Mint	Alfred	Edward the Elder	Athelstan	Edmund	Eadred	Eadwig	Edgar		Edward the Martyr	Ethelred the Second									Cnut				Harold I		Harthacnut		Edward the Confessor										Harold II
							Pre-reform	Reform 973	976	1st Small cross 978	1st Hand 979	2nd Hand 985	CRUX 991	Intermediate Small Cross 997	Long Cross 997	Helmet 1003	AGNUS DEI 1009	Last Small Cross 1009	Quatrefoil 1017	Pointed Helmet 1023	Short Cross 1029	Jewel Cross 1035	Jewel Cross 1035	Fleur de Lys 1038	Jewel Cross 1035	Arms & Sceptre 1040	PACX 1042	Radiate Small Cross 1044	Trefoil Quadrilateral 1046	Short Cross 1048	Expanding Cross 1050	Pointed Helmet 1053	Sovereign Eagles 1056	Hammer Cross 1059	Facing Small Cross 1062	Pyramids 1065	1066
NEWPORT	□	□	□	□	□	□	■	□	■	□	■	□	□	□	□	□	□	□	□	■	□	□	□	□	□	□	□	□	□	□	■	■	□	■	□	□	□
Northampton	□	□	□	□	□	■	■	■	■	■	■	■	■	□	■	■	■	■	■	■	■	□	■	■	□	■	■	■	■	■	■	■	■	■	■	■	■
NORWICH	□	□	■	■	■	□	□	■	■	■	■	■	■	□	■	■	□	■	■	■	■	■	■	■	□	■	■	■	■	■	■	■	■	■	■	■	■
Nottingham	□	□	■	□	□	□	□	□	□	□	■	■	■	□	□	■	■	□	■	■	■	□	■	■	□	■	■	■	■	■	■	■	□	□	■	□	■
OXFORD	□	□	■	□	■	■	■	■	■	□	■	■	■	■	■	■	□	■	■	■	■	□	■	■	■	■	■	■	■	■	■	■	■	■	■	■	■
Pershore	□	□	□	□	□	□	□	□	□	□	□	□	□	□	□	□	□	□	□	□	□	□	□	□	□	□	□	□	□	□	□	□	□	■	□	□	□
PETERBOROUGH	□	□	□	□	□	□	□	□	□	□	■	□	□	□	□	□	□	□	■	□	□	□	□	□	□	□	□	□	□	□	□	□	□	□	□	□	□
Petherton	□	□	□	□	□	□	□	□	□	□	□	□	□	□	□	□	□	□	□	□	□	□	□	□	□	□	□	■	■	□	□	□	□	□	□	□	□
READING	□	□	□	□	□	□	□	□	□	□	□	□	□	□	□	□	□	□	□	□	□	□	□	□	□	□	□	■	■	□	□	□	□	□	□	□	□
Rochester	□	□	■	□	□	□	□	■	■	□	■	■	■	□	■	■	□	■	■	■	■	□	■	■	■	□	■	■	■	□	□	■	■	■	■	□	■
ROMNEY	□	□	□	□	□	□	□	□	□	□	□	□	□	□	■	■	□	■	■	■	■	□	■	■	■	□	□	□	□	□	□	□	□	□	□	□	□
Salisbury	□	□	□	□	□	□	□	□	□	□	□	□	□	□	□	■	□	■	■	■	■	■	■	■	■	■	■	■	■	■	□	□	■	■	□	■	□
SANDWICH	□	□	□	□	□	□	□	□	□	□	□	□	□	□	□	□	□	□	□	□	□	□	□	□	□	□	■	■	■	■	□	■	■	□	■	□	□
Shaftesbury	□	□	■	□	□	□	□	■	□	□	■	■	■	□	■	■	□	■	■	■	■	■	■	■	■	■	■	■	□	■	■	■	■	■	□	■	■
SHREWSBURY	□	□	■	□	□	□	■	■	□	□	■	■	■	□	■	■	□	■	■	■	■	□	■	■	□	■	■	■	■	■	■	■	■	■	■	■	■
Southampton	□	□	■	□	□	■	■	■	□	■	■	■	■	□	■	□	□	■	■	□	□	□	□	□	□	□	□	□	□	□	□	□	□	□	□	□	□
SOUTHWARK	□	□	□	□	□	□	□	□	□	□	□	□	■	□	■	■	□	■	■	■	■	■	■	□	□	■	■	□	■	■	■	■	■	■	■	□	■
Stafford	□	□	■	□	□	□	□	■	□	□	□	□	■	□	■	■	■	□	■	■	■	□	□	■	□	□	□	□	□	□	■	□	□	■	□	■	□
STAMFORD	□	□	□	□	□	□	□	■	■	■	■	■	■	□	■	■	■	■	■	■	■	□	■	■	■	■	■	■	■	■	■	■	■	■	■	■	■
Steyning	□	□	□	□	□	□	□	□	□	□	□	□	□	□	□	□	□	□	□	■	■	□	□	■	■	□	■	■	■	■	■	■	■	■	■	■	■
SUDBURY	□	□	□	□	□	□	□	□	□	□	□	□	□	□	□	□	□	■	■	■	□	□	□	□	□	□	□	□	□	□	□	■	■	■	■	□	□
Tamworth	□	□	■	□	□	□	■	■	■	□	■	■	■	□	■	■	□	■	■	□	■	□	□	■	□	□	□	□	■	□	■	□	■	■	■	■	□
TAUNTON	□	□	□	□	□	□	□	□	□	□	□	□	□	□	■	□	□	■	□	□	■	□	□	□	■	■	■	□	■	■	□	□	■	■	□	□	■
Thetford	□	□	□	□	□	□	■	■	■	□	■	■	■	□	■	■	□	■	■	■	■	□	■	■	□	■	■	■	■	■	■	■	■	■	■	■	■
TORKSEY	□	□	□	□	□	□	□	□	■	■	■	■	□	□	□	□	□	■	■	□	□	□	□	□	□	□	□	□	□	□	□	□	□	□	□	□	□
Totnes	□	□	□	□	□	■	■	□	■	□	■	■	■	□	■	■	□	■	■	■	□	□	□	□	□	■	□	□	□	□	□	□	□	□	□	□	□
WALLINGFORD	□	□	■	□	□	■	■	□	□	□	■	■	■	□	■	■	□	■	■	■	■	■	■	■	■	■	□	■	■	■	■	■	■	■	■	■	■
Wareham	□	□	■	□	□	□	□	■	□	□	■	■	■	□	■	■	□	■	■	□	■	□	□	□	□	■	■	■	□	■	■	■	■	■	■	■	■
WARMINSTER	□	□	□	□	□	□	□	□	□	□	□	□	□	□	■	□	□	■	□	■	■	□	■	□	□	□	□	□	□	□	■	□	□	□	□	□	□
Warwick	□	□	■	□	□	□	□	□	■	□	■	□	■	□	■	■	□	■	■	■	■	□	■	■	■	■	■	■	■	■	■	■	■	■	□	■	■
WATCHET	□	□	□	□	□	□	□	□	□	□	■	■	■	□	■	■	□	■	■	■	■	□	■	■	■	□	■	■	□	■	□	■	□	□	□	□	□
Wilton	□	□	□	□	□	□	■	■	■	■	■	■	■	■	■	□	□	■	■	■	■	□	■	■	□	■	■	■	■	■	■	■	■	■	■	■	■
WINCHCOMBE	□	□	□	□	□	□	□	■	□	□	□	□	■	■	■	■	□	□	■	■	□	□	□	□	□	■	□	□	□	■	■	□	■	■	■	■	■
Winchester	■	□	■	□	□	■	■	■	■	□	■	■	■	□	■	■	□	■	■	■	■	□	■	■	■	■	■	■	■	■	■	■	■	■	■	■	■
WORCESTER	□	□	□	□	□	□	□	□	□	■	■	■	■	■	■	■	□	■	■	■	■	□	■	■	■	■	■	■	■	■	■	■	■	■	■	□	■
York	□	□	■	□	□	□	■	■	■	■	■	■	■	■	■	■	□	■	■	■	■	□	■	■	■	■	■	■	■	■	■	■	■	■	■	■	■
Selected Unidentified Mints																																					
DARENT	□	□	■	□	□	□	□	□	□	□	□	□	□	□	□	□	□	□	□	□	□	□	□	□	□	□	□	□	□	□	□	□	□	□	□	□	□
Dernt	□	□	□	□	□	□	□	□	□	□	□	□	□	□	□	□	□	□	□	□	□	□	□	□	□	□	□	□	□	□	□	■	□	■	□	□	□
DORB	□	□	□	□	■	□	□	□	□	□	□	□	□	□	□	□	□	□	□	□	□	□	□	□	□	□	□	□	□	□	□	□	□	□	□	□	□
Dornc	□	□	□	■	□	□	□	□	□	□	□	□	□	□	□	□	□	□	□	□	□	□	□	□	□	□	□	□	□	□	□	□	□	□	□	□	□
DYR	□	□	□	□	□	□	□	□	□	□	□	□	□	□	□	□	□	□	□	□	□	□	□	□	□	□	□	□	□	■	□	□	□	□	□	□	□
Eanburh	□	□	□	□	□	□	□	□	□	□	□	□	□	□	□	□	□	□	■	□	□	□	□	□	□	□	□	□	□	□	□	□	□	□	□	□	□
ERL	□	□	□	□	□	□	□	□	□	□	□	□	□	□	□	□	□	□	□	□	□	□	□	□	□	□	□	□	□	□	□	□	□	□	□	□	□
Gothaburh	□	□	□	□	□	□	□	□	□	□	□	□	□	□	■	■	□	■	■	□	□	□	■	■	□	■	□	□	□	□	□	□	□	□	□	□	□
-LUTHEY	□	□	□	□	□	□	□	□	□	□	■	□	□	□	□	□	□	□	□	□	□	□	□	□	□	□	□	□	□	□	□	□	□	□	□	□	□
Orsnaforda	■	□	□	□	□	□	□	□	□	□	□	□	□	□	□	□	□	□	□	□	□	□	□	□	□	□	□	□	□	□	□	□	□	□	□	□	□
ROISENG	■	□	□	□	□	□	□	□	□	□	□	□	□	□	□	□	□	□	□	□	□	□	□	□	□	□	□	□	□	□	□	□	□	□	□	□	□
Smrierl	□	□	■	□	□	□	□	□	□	□	□	□	□	□	□	□	□	□	□	□	□	□	□	□	□	□	□	□	□	□	□	□	□	□	□	□	□
WEARDBURH	□	□	■	□	□	□	□	□	□	□	□	□	□	□	□	□	□	□	□	□	□	□	□	□	□	□	□	□	□	□	□	□	□	□	□	□	□
Wicneh	□	□	□	□	□	□	□	□	□	□	□	□	□	□	□	□	□	□	□	□	□	□	□	□	□	□	□	□	□	□	□	□	□	□	□	□	■

225 Mints striking 871–1066: part II

Towns and their Distribution (226–234)

A great deal of effort has been put into the study of the Anglo-Saxon town in the past two decades and the subject has been revolutionized by the work of urban archaeologists such as Martin Biddle (recent work is conveniently reviewed in Biddle 1976). This atlas is not the place in which to publish detailed and comparative town plans. The area-by-area maps (**226–234**) show only the distribution of all places which have claims to be considered a town, a fort, a mint or a market in the period 700–1066.

The series attempts to show all the forts and towns of which we have evidence. A division is made between fort and town, and between the late market centres and the earlier foundations which have a larger defensive role. Mints are underlined but the function of market cannot really be shown satisfactorily due to the haphazard nature of the evidence.

The town evidence is set against a background map showing evidence thought to be relevant. For example, roads are included but are only Roman roads known to have been used in medieval times; doubtful cases are shown broken; shires are shown with their boundaries as chain dotted lines (taking Domesday shires as the base); and relief is indicated. The maps have also been used as an index series in that sites shown on general maps can be located more accurately on these sheets — places indicated by small white circles have no urban significance.

It would be wrong not to remind the reader that the complexities of the early medieval town, indeed its sophistication, have been established in the past few decades. The king founded forts or walled towns (both termed **burhs**) which were also made into mints or markets (**ports**) by the royal prerogative if he so wished. The towns had their own law, officers, administration, they were often planned and the regular street patterns consisted of streets regularly maintained. In at least one case, Winchester, a water system served all the lower town. The pattern of towns built up slowly from a number of places with some of the attributes of a town in 700, through the few additions that we know about during the eighth century, to a great range of foundations in the period 870–930, followed by the foundation of a set of secondary centres in the years before 1066.

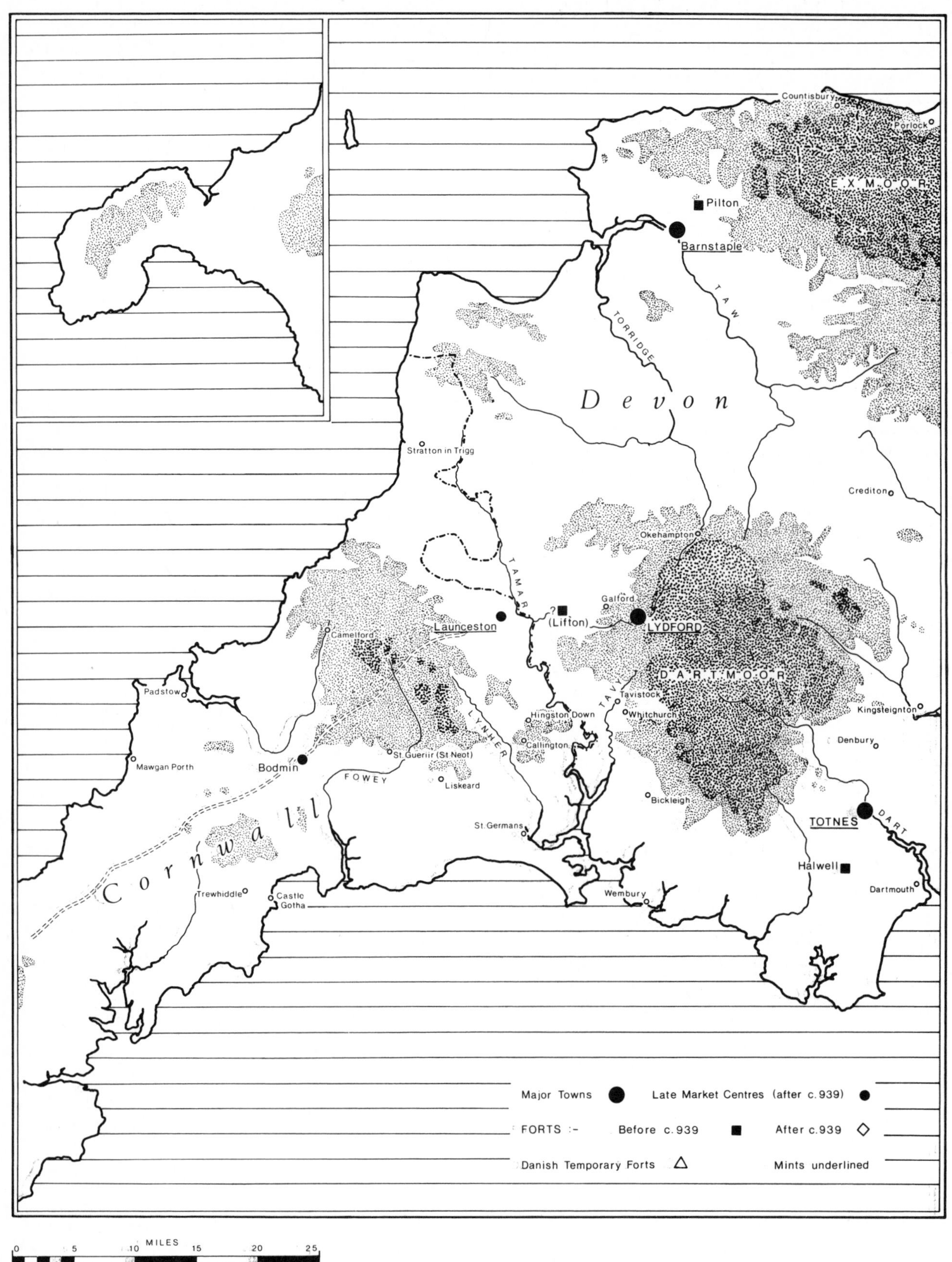

226 Towns in the south-west

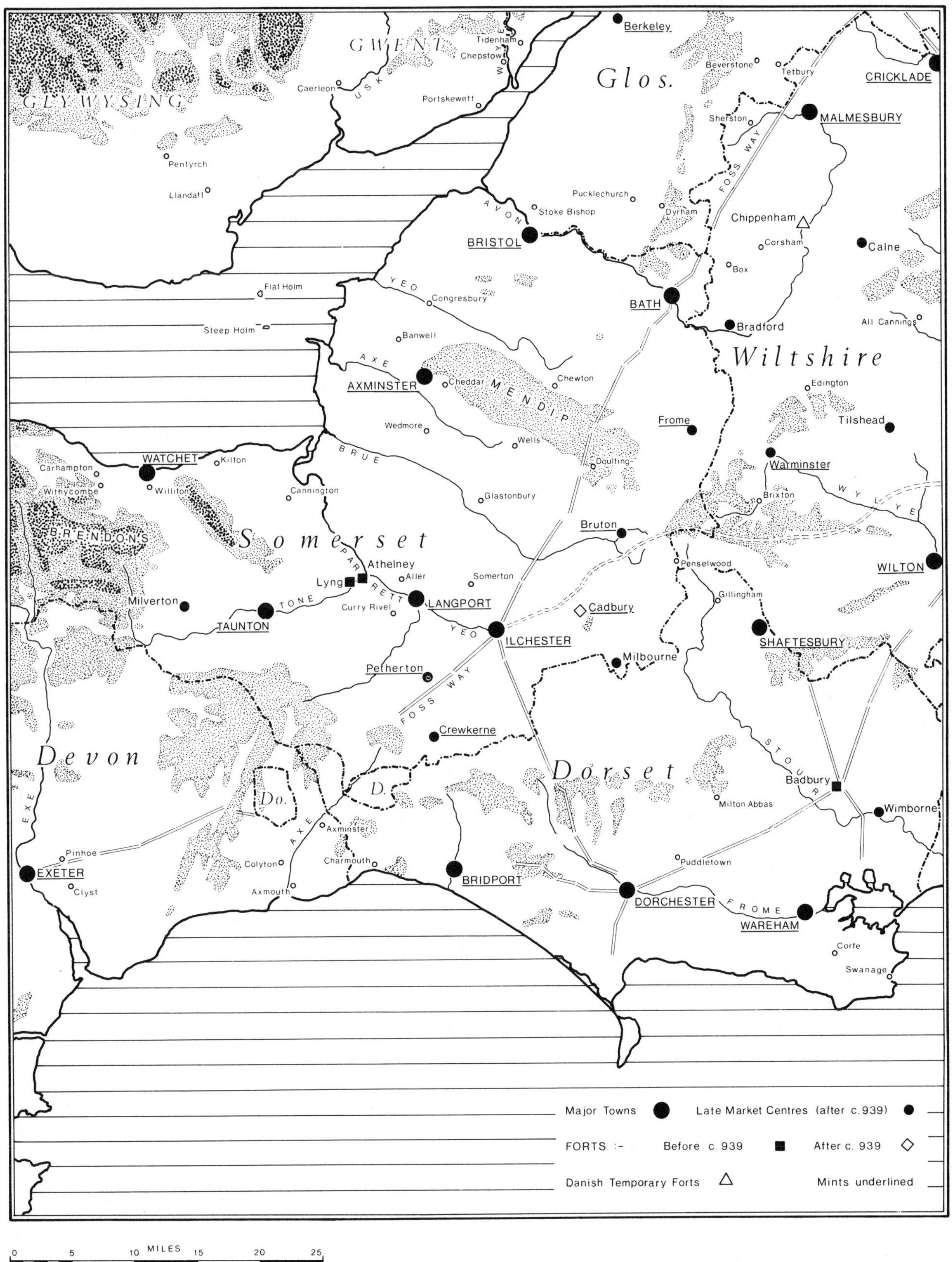

227 Towns in Somerset and Dorset

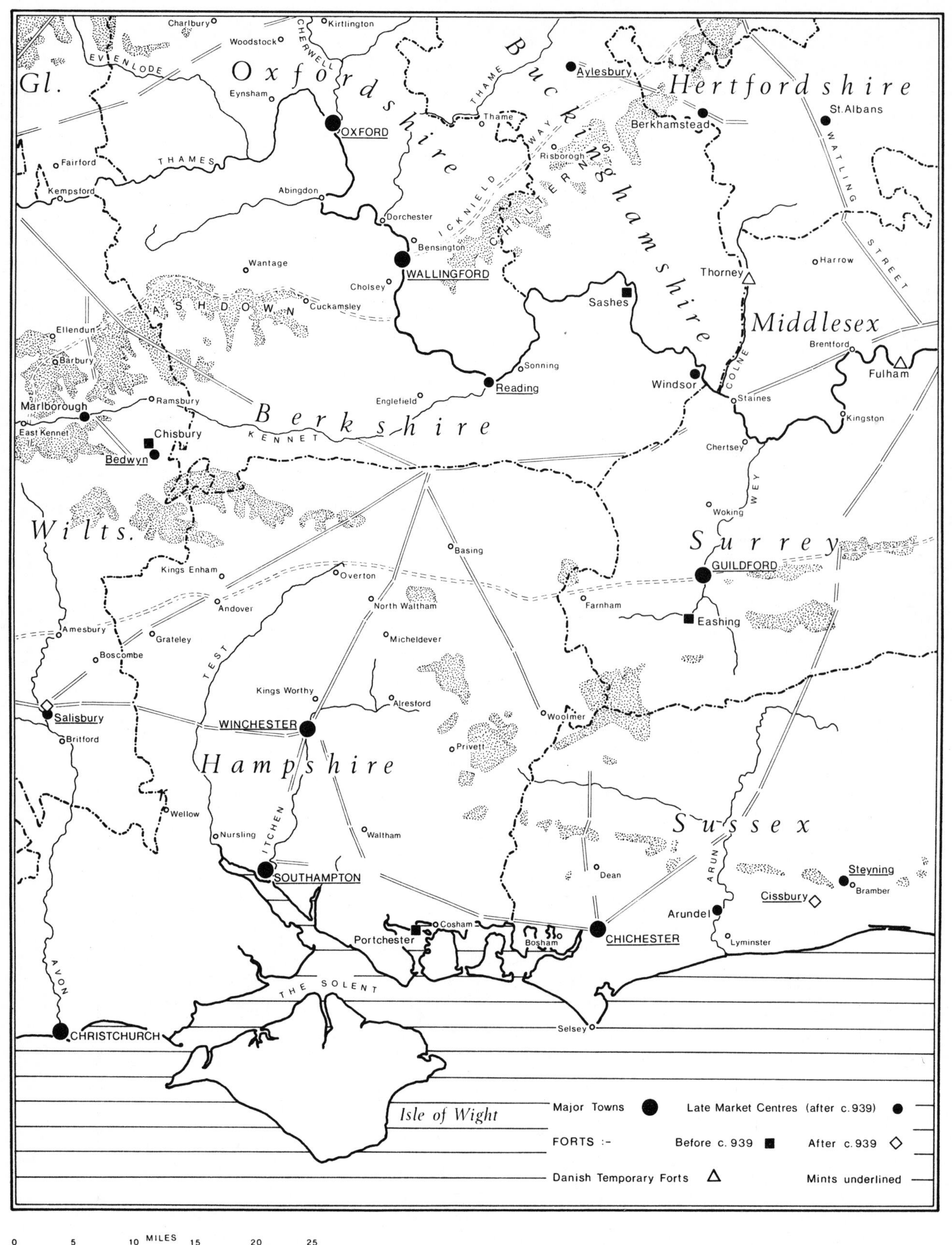

228 Towns in the south

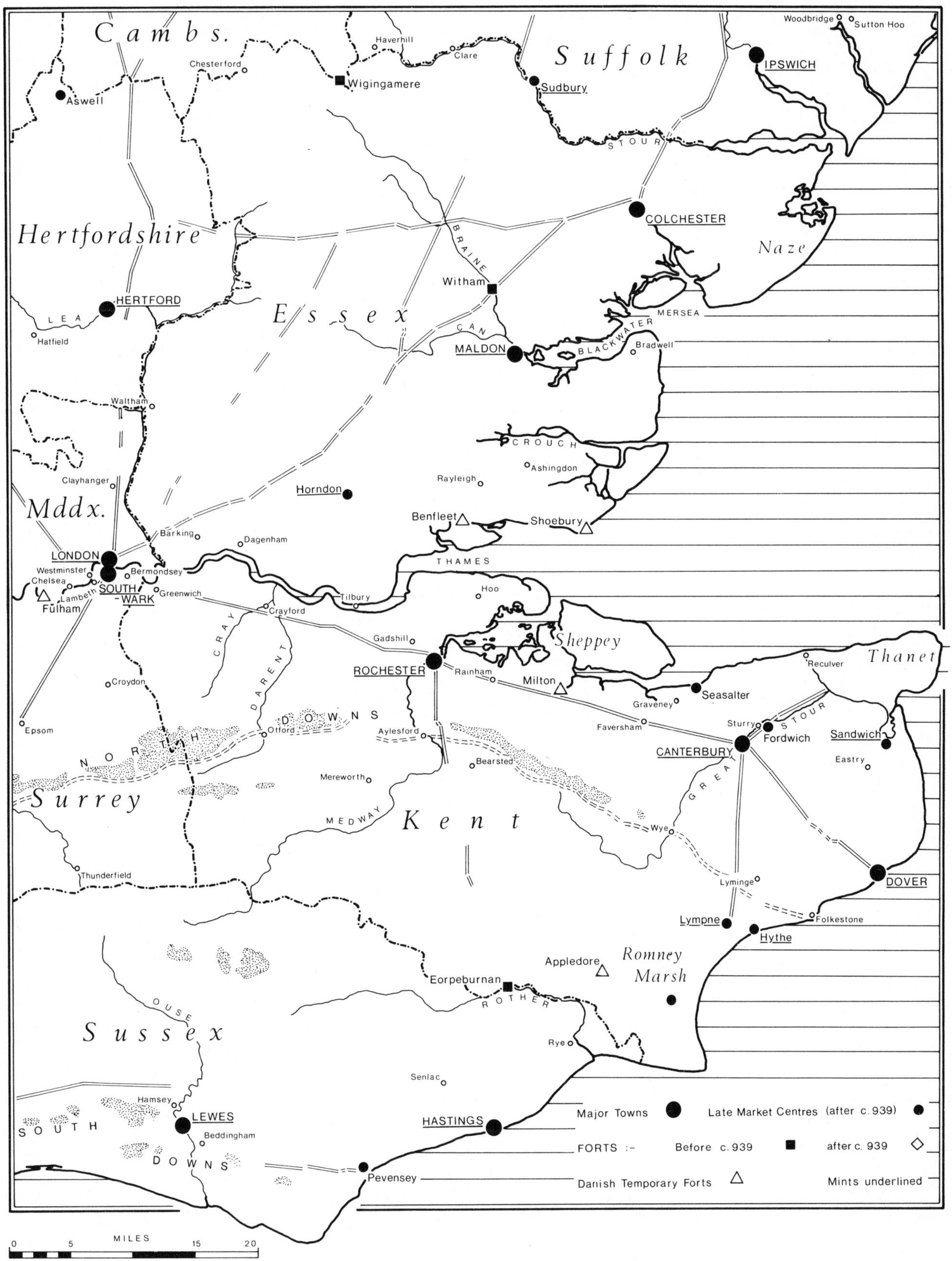

229 Towns in the south-east

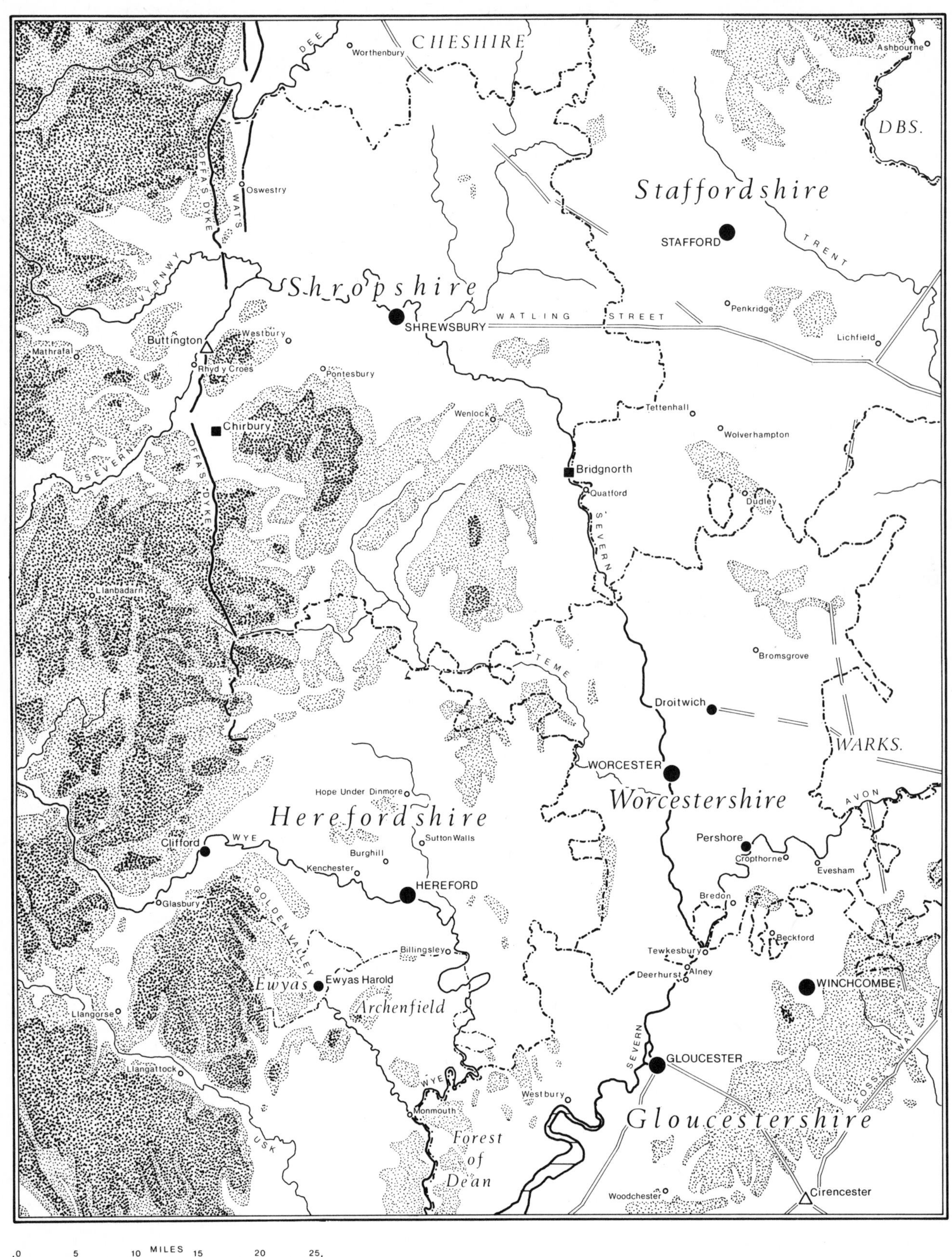

230 Towns in the west Midlands

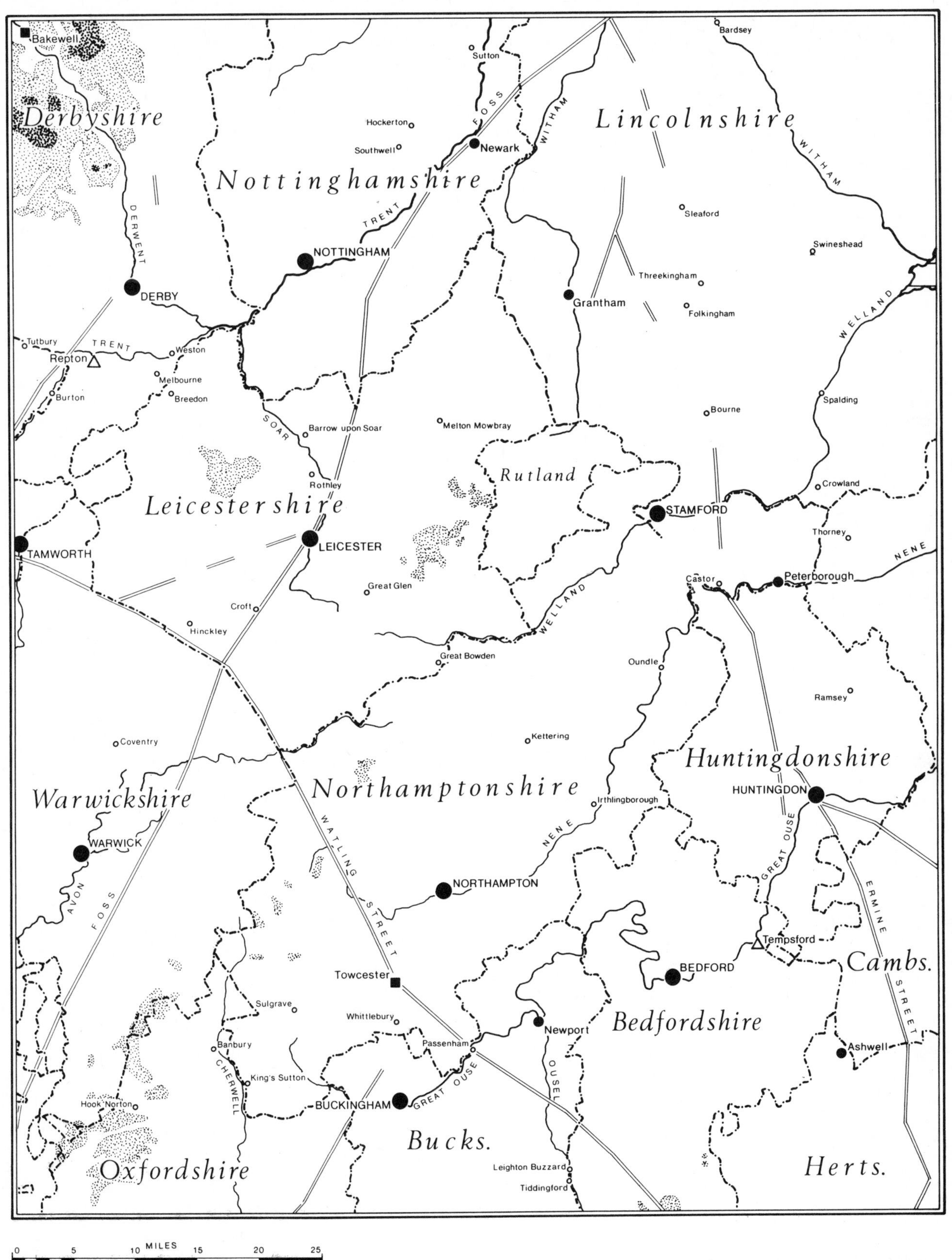

231 Towns in the east Midlands

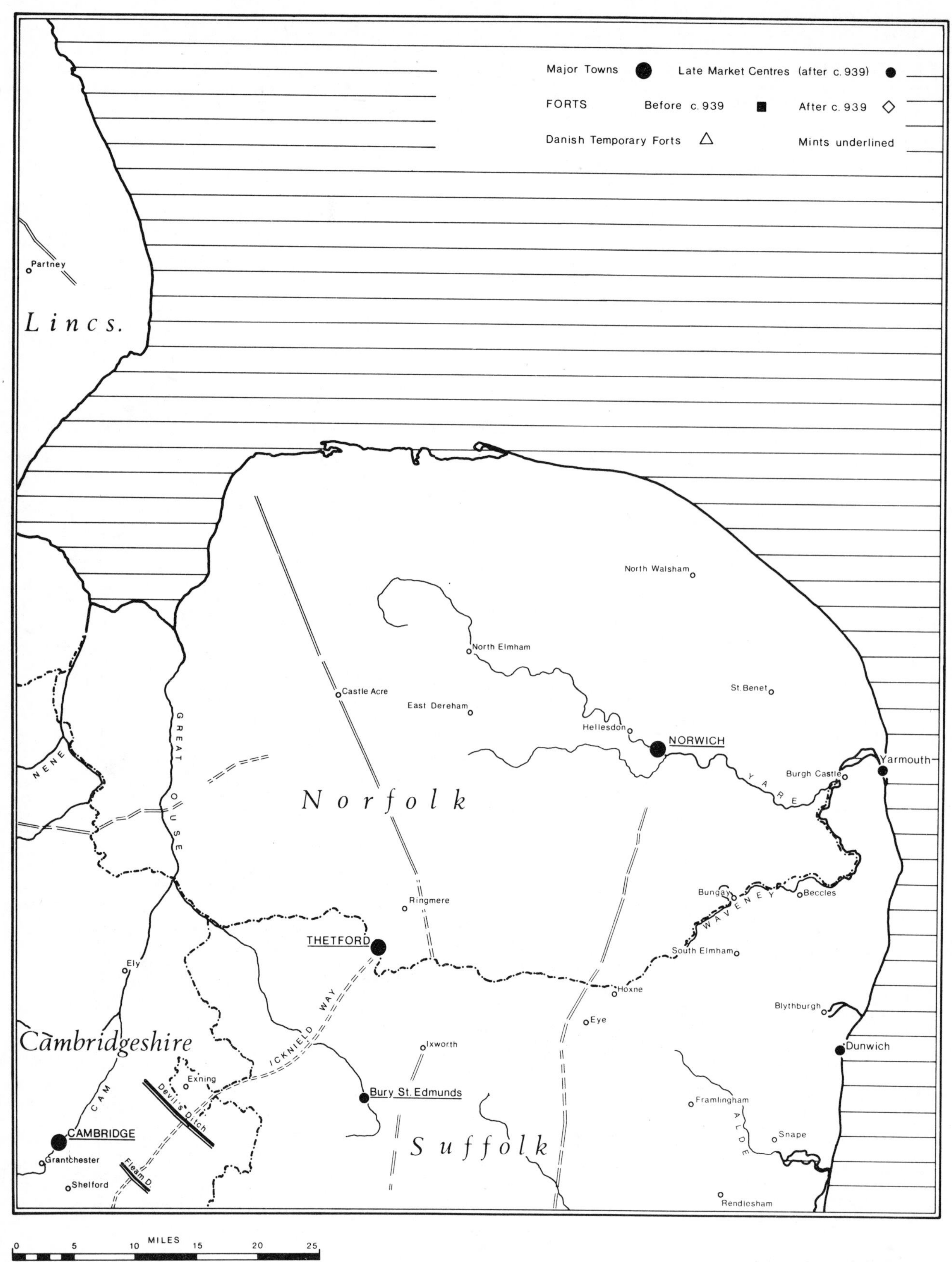

232 Towns in East Anglia

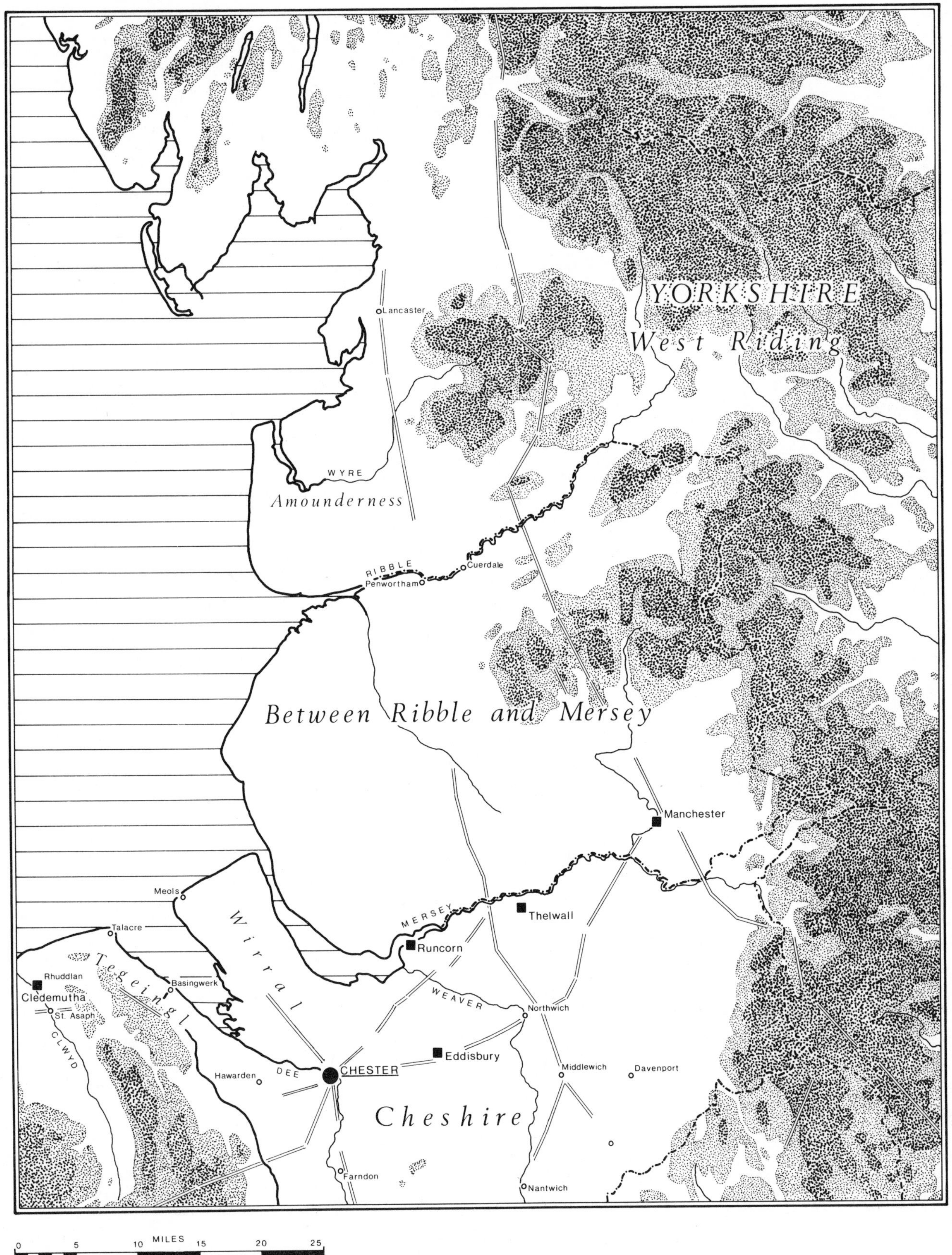

233 Towns in the north-west

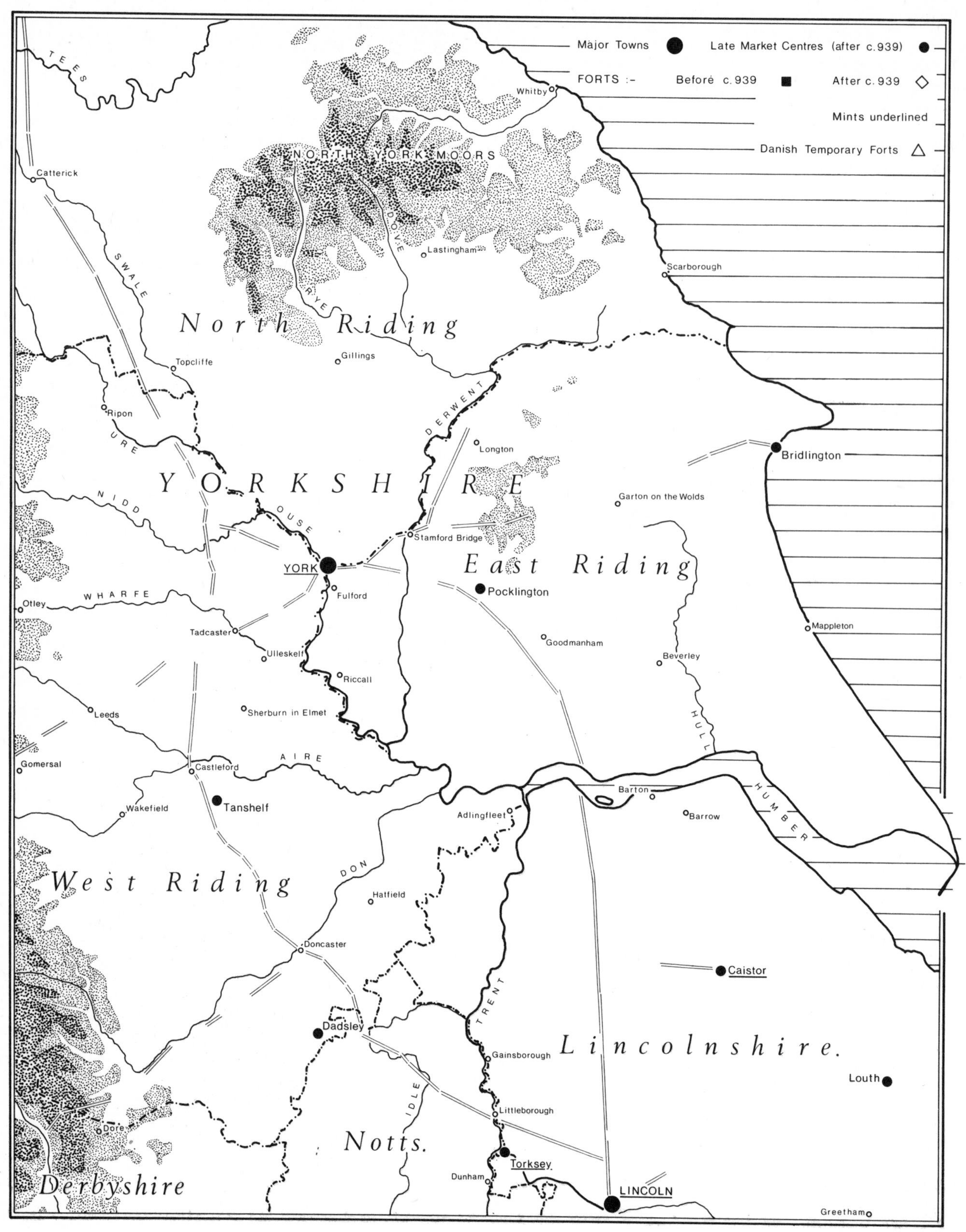

234 Towns in the north Midlands and Yorkshire

The Size of Towns and Forts (235–236)

In the central period (870–930), when the bulk of the **burhs** were founded, it should be clearly understood that the King founded forts or he founded towns — towns did not grow out of forts nor did they appear spontaneously. As this is an important fact I should explain briefly how we can be sure, and as the map series makes the distinction between fort and town that distinction should be justified. The walled area of a **burh** represents the plans and aspirations of its founder. It may fail, in which case the internal area will not be taken up by houses, streets, churches and markets. It may succeed beyond the founder's expectations, in which case it will form suburbs. In the known area of these **burh** foundations we have fossilized the policy of the Anglo-Saxon kings. If these areas are plotted (**235**) against date and we then mark in black those foundations that went on to become towns, we can see a clear pattern. The index of success used is whether the **burh** went on to achieve borough status in the Domesday Survey. If the diagram is simplified the pattern can be further emphasized (**236**).

It can now be seen that before the reign of Athelstan sites founded with less than 16 acres did not become towns, while those with over 21 acres were towns by 1066. The correlation is too great to avoid the conclusion that towns and forts were being founded as such. Some sites — Canterbury, York and London, for example — were towns before 850 but they are few in number, and we must realize that one of the grounds for choice of a site would be pre-existing settlements on that site, whether agricultural, religious or administrative. After the reign of Athelstan the pattern changes and we can see the emergence of centres where the defensive role was unimportant. Map **187** showed a series of secondary market centres burgeoning on royal holdings as the king attempted to increase revenue from his estates (see also Sawyer 1978, 61–2, and 73–4).

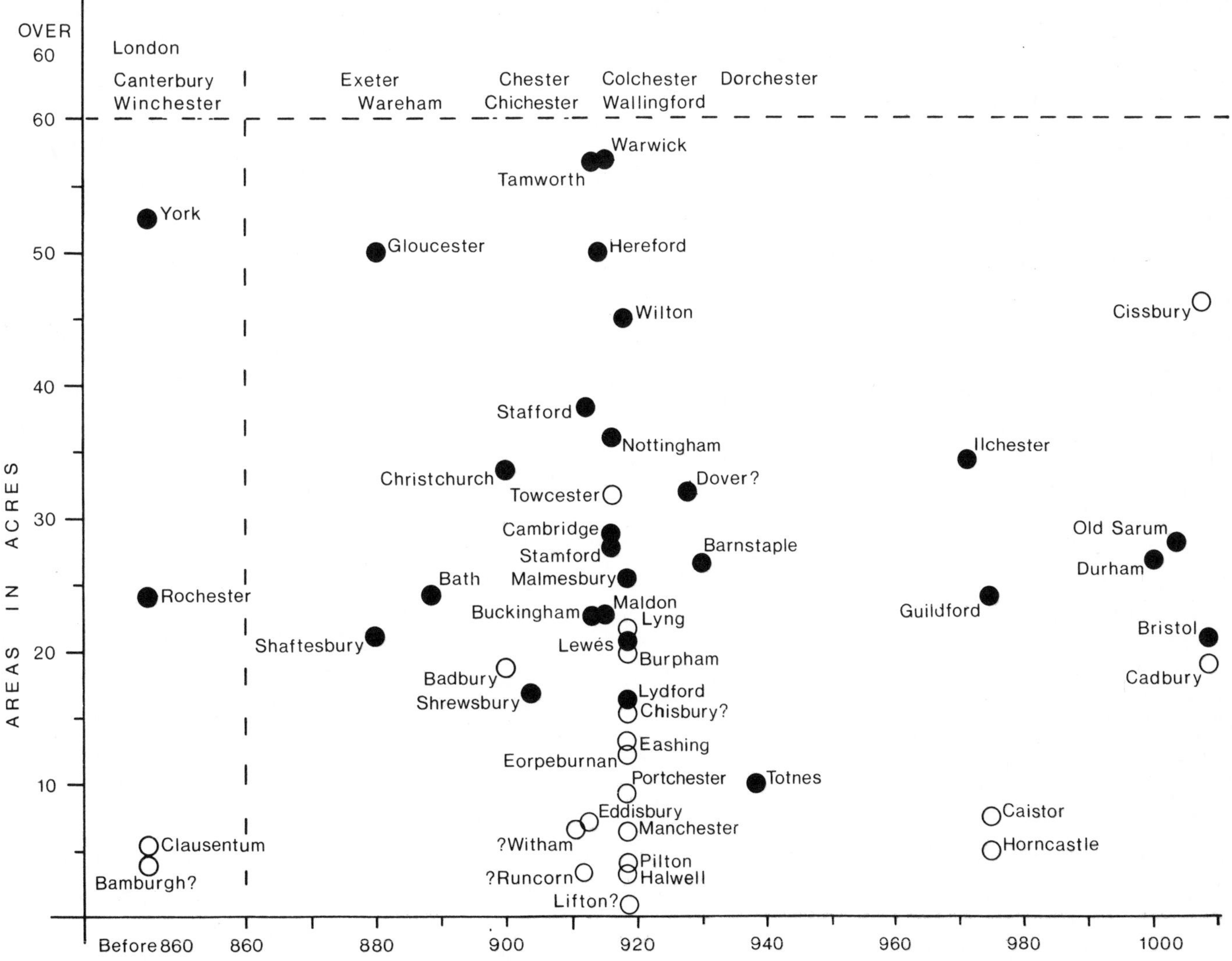

235 Areas of burhs. Those sites with an area of more than 60 acres are shown, correctly for date, across the top of the diagram

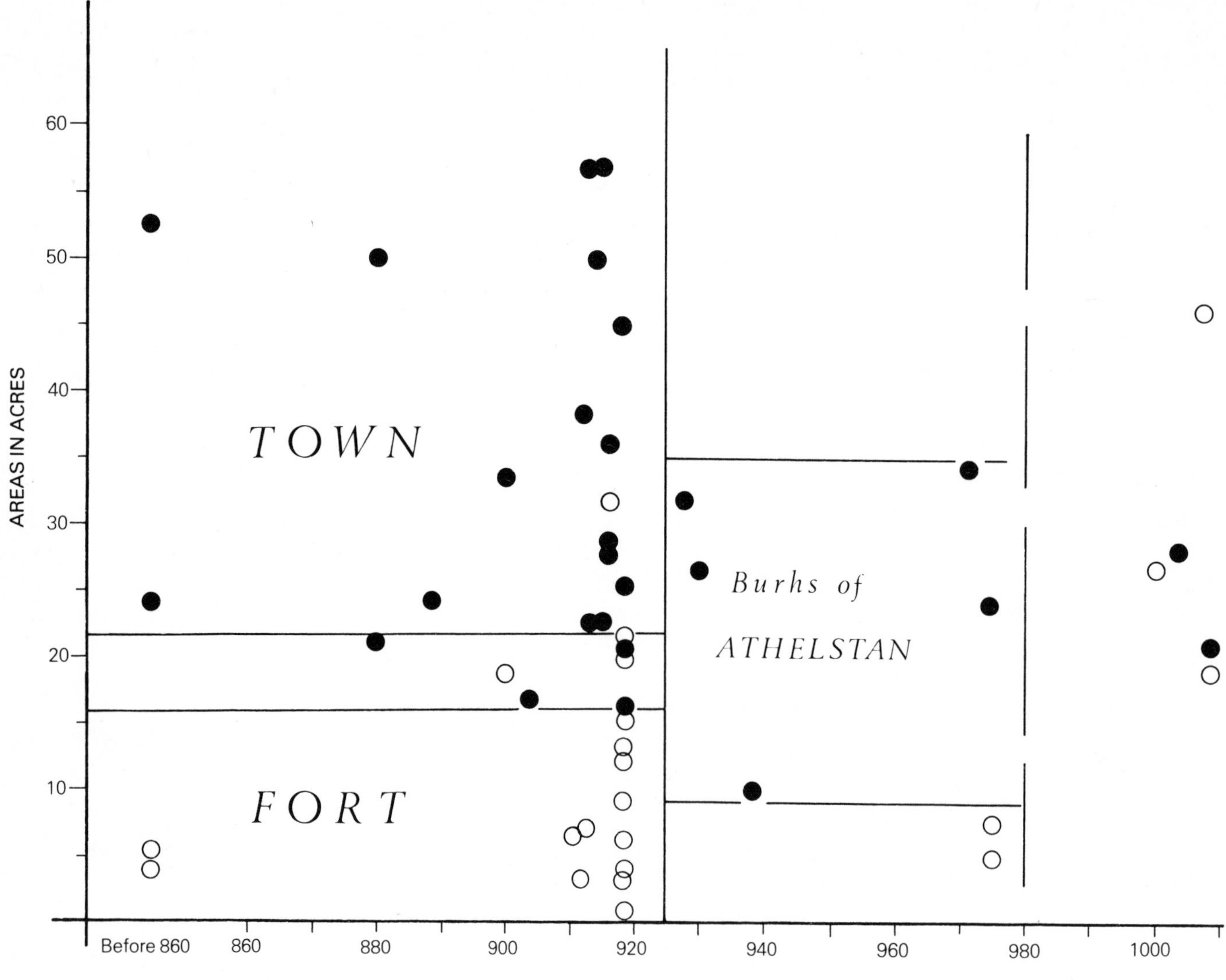

236 Areas of burhs: an abstraction

The Church

Introduction (237)

The Church was a great institution in Anglo-Saxon England with immense influence and a growing power. By the time this atlas takes note of it, paganism was for all major purposes dead, although it regained influence in the Danelaw for a while on a very minor scale.

The major advance of the period, and one not charted here, was the expansion of the parochial system, so that by 1066 most of England was organized into parishes. The other great concerns were the heroic efforts of the Anglo-Saxons to convert to the true faith the lands of their Continental ancestors and the monastic revival of the tenth century.

Before launching into the church history of the period 700–1066, or that part which is easily illustrated by maps, it may be as well to spare one background glance. The background and setting of the Roman mission of Augustine was such that it influenced the Anglo-Saxon Church, with its unique devotion to Rome and the Pope, throughout our period. A glance at map **237** will show two things: the vast numbers of bishoprics in the Mediterranean area (it should be noted that 'Archbishoprics' are an anachronism for the period: these were really 'Metropolitan Bishoprics'), all set by decree of the church fathers in cities not in villages; and the fact that Western Christendom would soon become a thin band across Europe once the Moors broke into Spain. All the churches of Spain and Africa would come into the hands of the Arabs and only North Italy, France and the British Isles were left to Rome. The Church in England was therefore an important part of the Catholic world. The borders of Christendom in the West were to rest in the early eighth century on the Rhine and the Pyrenees, the missions to Germany found it strategically necessary to broaden this narrow corridor between paganism and Islam.

The decree of the Church that no bishop should set up his seat in a village meant that Roman sites in England, perhaps long deserted, received a new lease of life with the arrival of Augustine's mission, and we must therefore treat with caution the choice of places on dogmatic grounds as evidence for continuing urban life in these centres.

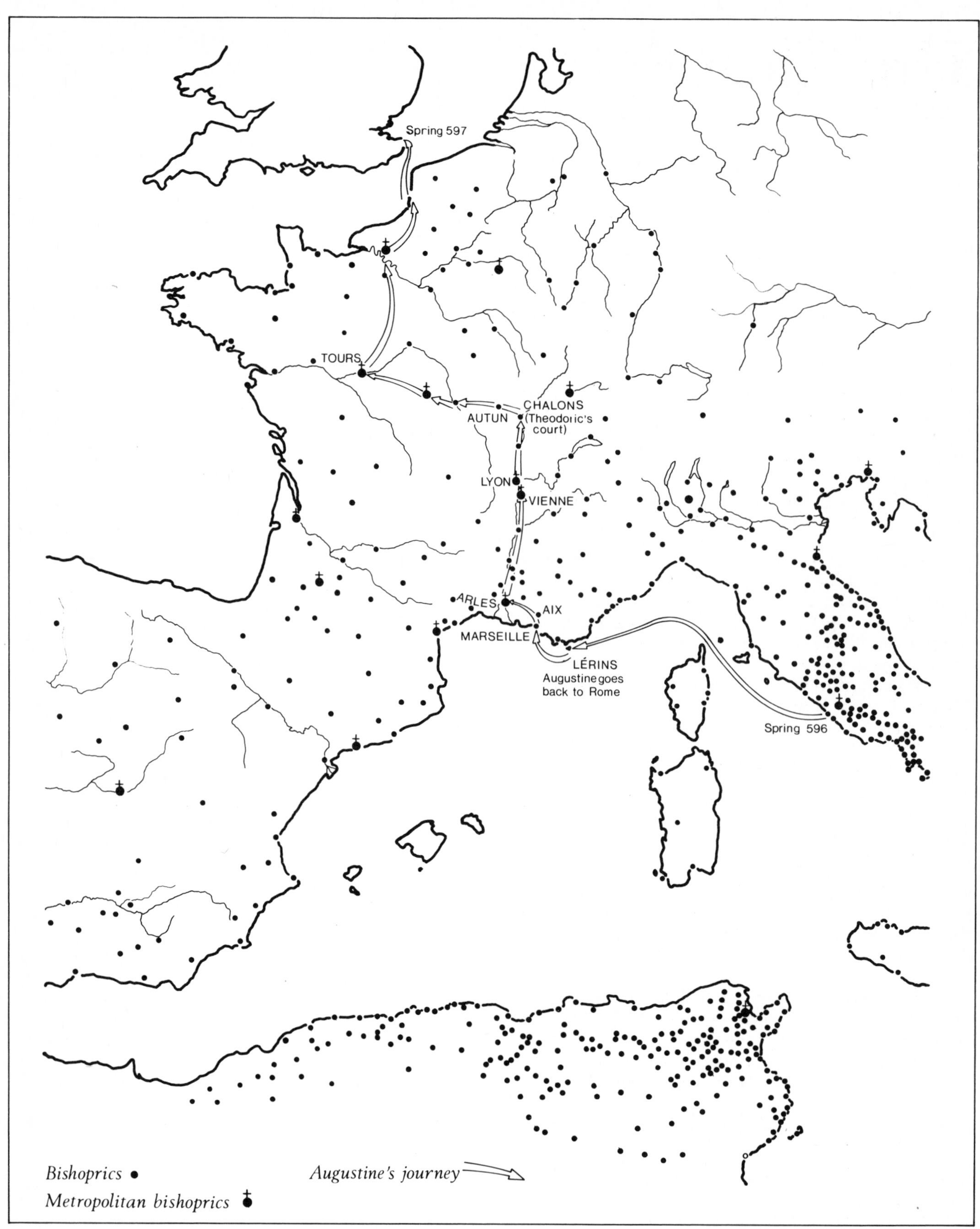

237 Western Christendom c.597

Dioceses (238–241)

The plan of Gregory to consecrate two metropolitans, one at London and one at York, each with twelve bishops under them, was never realized. It is doubtful whether the plan was made on the basis of accurate reports of the state of Britain at the time, or on some tome of late Roman geography in the Vatican library — whichever it was, neither was of much use. The twelfth suffragan of Canterbury was consecrated at Leicester in 737. York never obtained that number, nor did the southern metropolitan remove to London. There was provision for bishoprics for each of the various peoples and kingdoms, the Middle Angles, the West Saxons, the East Saxons and so on. In fact some sees were known by the folk name and not the seat: the Bishop of the Hwicce, was only later called the Bishop of Worcester.

The Mercian bishopric was split in 737 into Lichfield and Leicester, the West Saxon bishopric split into 'east and west of Selwood' (the sees of Winchester and Sherborne), and Selsey was founded to minister to the South Saxon Kingdom (map **238**). The situation then stayed constant, apart from one controversy over a new Archbishop for Mercia under Offa, until the Danish invasions.

The Danish invasions led apparently to a complete disruption of the North Midlands, East Anglian and Northumbrian church organization (map **239**). York continued in some form for most of the period, Lindsey, Hexham, Elmham and Dunwich disappeared completely, Leicester and Lindisfarne moved the site of the bishop's seat (map **240**). The body of St Cuthbert, the principal relic of Lindisfarne, was taken by the monks on their wanderings. The Lindisfarne community settled for many years at Chester-le-Street and finally moved to Durham. All this may be an oversimplification but the cessation of evidence for the area at this time must be significant.

After the Reconquest only Elmham was refounded, the Midlands and the north having to be content with the loss of two dioceses. York was left so impoverished that it was often linked to the wealthy bishopric of Worcester in an attempt to improve its finances.

In the area south of the Thames the West Saxon kings reorganized the bishoprics to give most shires a bishop of their own. The reorganization was completed by Athelstan founding a Cornish bishopric. There were problems, however, in finding a sufficient endowment and some amalgamations took place in the eleventh century (map **241**).

The boundaries of the sees are very conjectural before 900. The bounds of the dioceses of Worcester and Hereford appear to have expanded somewhat to the north in the period of the Danish invasions. The state of Northern and Eastern England in the late ninth century is badly documented. More detailed maps of the dioceses of Hereford, Worcester and East Saxons are to be found on maps **143** and **140**. The medieval boundaries of the dioceses are used on maps **250–258**.

Some of the changes affecting the dioceses can be followed more readily on the charts in **259–260**.

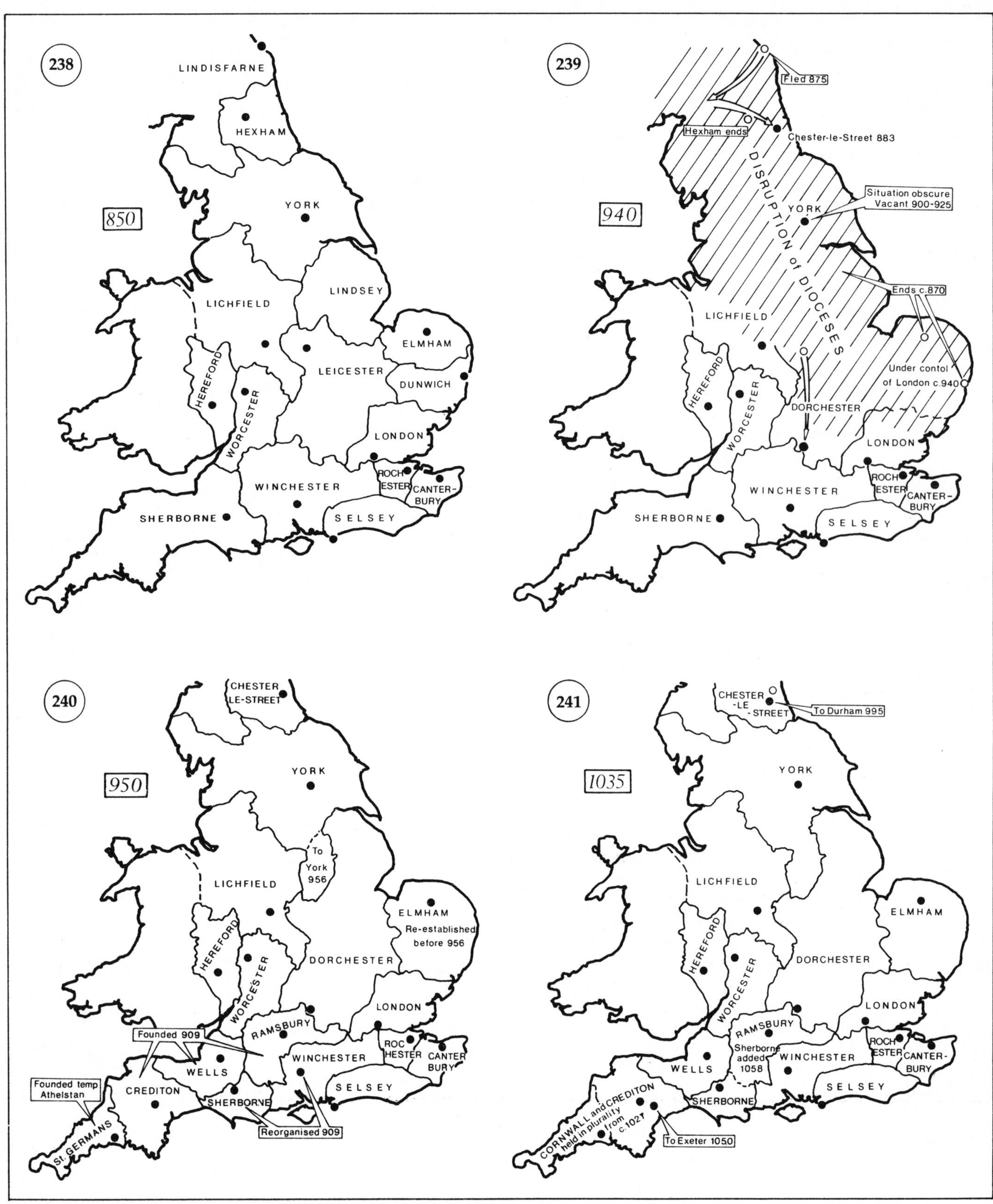

238–241 Dioceses 850–1035

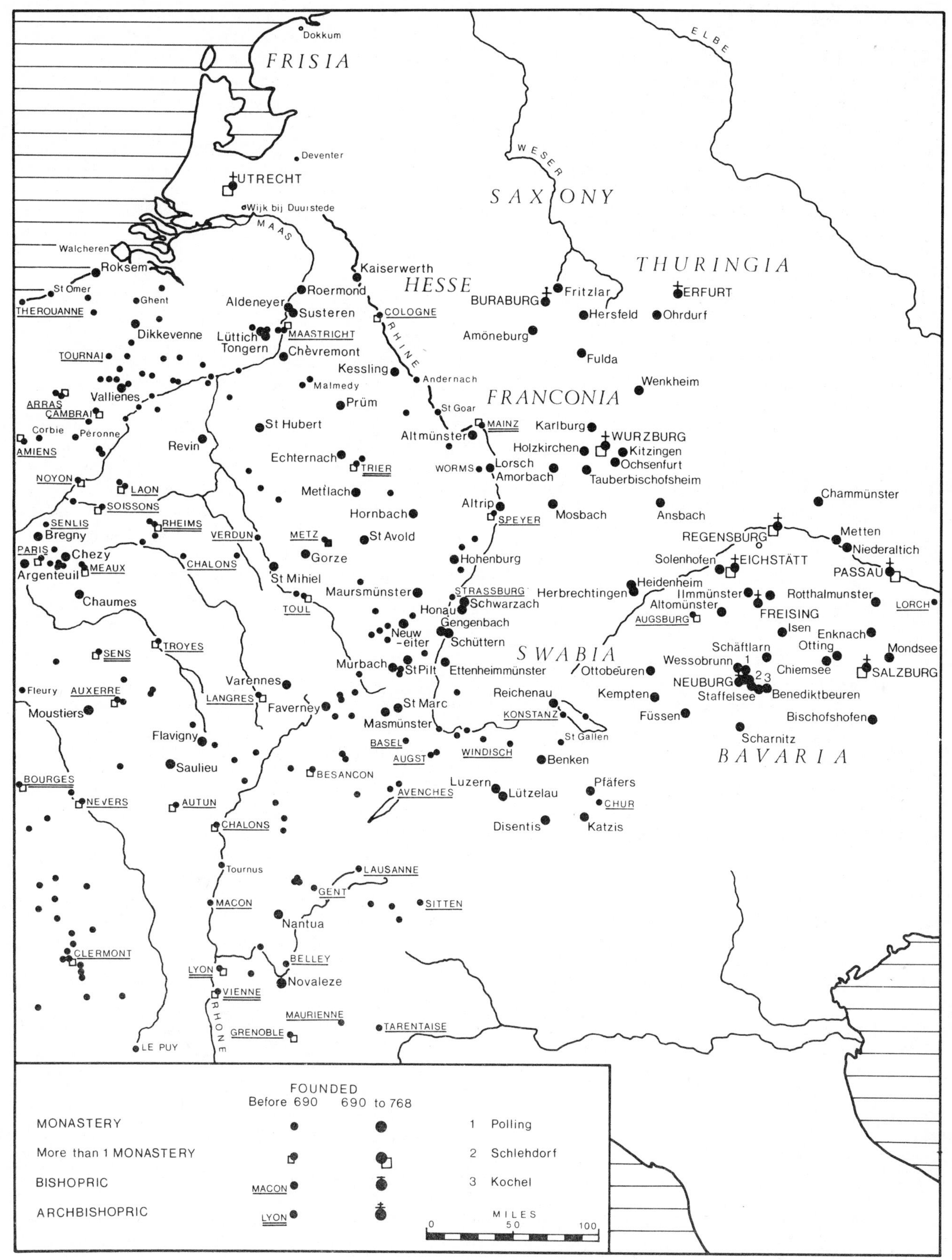

242 The Church in East Francia

Missionary Efforts (242)

The English Church's efforts to convert the heathen Germanic homelands started before the conversion of England was completed in Sussex. In 677 Wilfrid made some attempts to evangelize Frisia on his way to Rome. There was a succession of missionaries, Wihtberht, Willibrord, Boniface and Willehad, and their efforts are well documented in Stenton or more fully in Levison (1946). Map **242** is an attempt to place these successes in their Continental setting and to show that from the stagnation of the Merovingian Gallic Church to the completion of the mission the frontiers of Christendom had been pushed firmly forward from the line on which they rested for all of the seventh century to a new line by 768. By then the Church was firmly established in Bavaria and middle Germany. An impressive string of new bishoprics and monasteries supported this conversion and the stage was set for Charlemagne's attempts to move the missions still further. It should be noted that not all of the new foundations shown are either Anglo-Saxon influenced or Irish influenced.

Anglo-Saxons took part later in the conversion of the north, their most important contribution being in the early eleventh century in providing clergy for Norway.

The Monastic Revival (243–249)

The major ecclesiastic event of the tenth century was the reformation of monastic life (map **243**). History tends to be concentrated where the documentary evidence is thickest and the wealth of material on the saints of the reformation and their churches has meant that the subject is well covered. The standard works all have good accounts and Loyn (1962, 244) has charted the revival, with its houses and derivations; the matter is discussed in great and scholarly detail in Knowles (1963).

The Revival was necessary because of the decay of monastic life in the ninth century and not, as all the monastic chronicles reiterate, because of the Danish invasions. Many houses survived the period as secular colleges, establishments of canons which were very popular in the ninth and tenth century, and described in the charters as 'monasteries'. They were despised by the intolerant chroniclers of the reformed houses and have been little regarded since.

The Revival was only part of a much wider Revival of reformed monasticism in Western Europe in which Glastonbury can be seen as part of a chain from Cluny and Brogne to Ratisbon (map **244**). It is, of course, a great simplification, considering the interrelations within countries: for example, Fleury's influence was marked at Abingdon. The impact of the new monasteries and their ability to attract large benefactions in land should not be underestimated. The Revival had wide economic and political consequences.

A list exists (in several versions) of the relics of various saints and the places in which they rest in England. The date for the text as it now exists is c.1032; but it is clear from the layout and content of the surviving text that it is a conflation of an earlier, Mercian, text with a later, West Saxon, one. Map **245** shows all of the places mentioned, although some of the saints of Thorney and Winchester have had to be omitted through lack of space. The sites mentioned are those which were considered worthy of pilgrimage and as such they show a different aspect of popular religion, for Aelfric's **Lives of the Saints** shows that lengthy journeys were made around England in search of healing or blessing at the various sites, again an indication of the mobility of society. There are also some topographical observations within the text (Liebermann 1889; Rollason 1978).

All the monasteries of the Anglo-Saxon period known to me are shown on maps **250–258** below. The distributions change over the years and the houses are not contemporaneous. Map **246** gives the distribution of Benedictine monasteries and nunneries c.1060 (Godfrey 1962) and map **247** that of the Colleges of Secular Canons. It can be seen that the two tend to complement each other, although it would seem many colleges of secular canons still need to be added, e.g. St Frideswide's, Oxford. The secular canons are found mainly in the north-west Midlands and the North whilst the reformed houses are south of a line from Humber to Severn. This may also have some relevance to the attitudes taken against the Reform by various local magnates; certainly there seem to be provincial loyalties to various types of establishments.

The early Benedictine houses have been extensively studied (Knowles 1963) and it is instructive to examine the relative wealth of the monasteries. They are valued in Domesday and the results can be seen on map **248** and the chart in **249**. There were some very large landholders amongst them and the total approaches the value of the holdings of the king himself. Some of the holdings are of ancient foundation, resting on early benefactions of the kings and local magnates, for example, Glastonbury, Winchester and Canterbury; some belong to the great foundations of the Reform, and the efforts to raise funds for the benefices can be realized by the extent of the lands held in 1066; and some were only just coming into the first rank of landholders, for example, the seventh rank of Westminster must rely heavily on the benefactions of Edward the Confessor. These houses did not always receive 'fresh' benefactions and as a result of a change of policy of the royal house a monastery could be suddenly impoverished. Pershore, for example, must have been dramatically affected when its lands were appropriated elsewhere. The picture presented is only true of the mid-eleventh century although there are elements of an earlier picture.

The leading nunneries were Wilton and Shaftesbury, both rich from their royal associations in the tenth century. A confusing factor is the extent of the holdings of the bishops, and a similar map could have been drawn for these. Worcester was the richest but in many cases the ownership of lands was intermixed, as at Winchester, between the bishop and the monastic community living cheek by jowl with him.

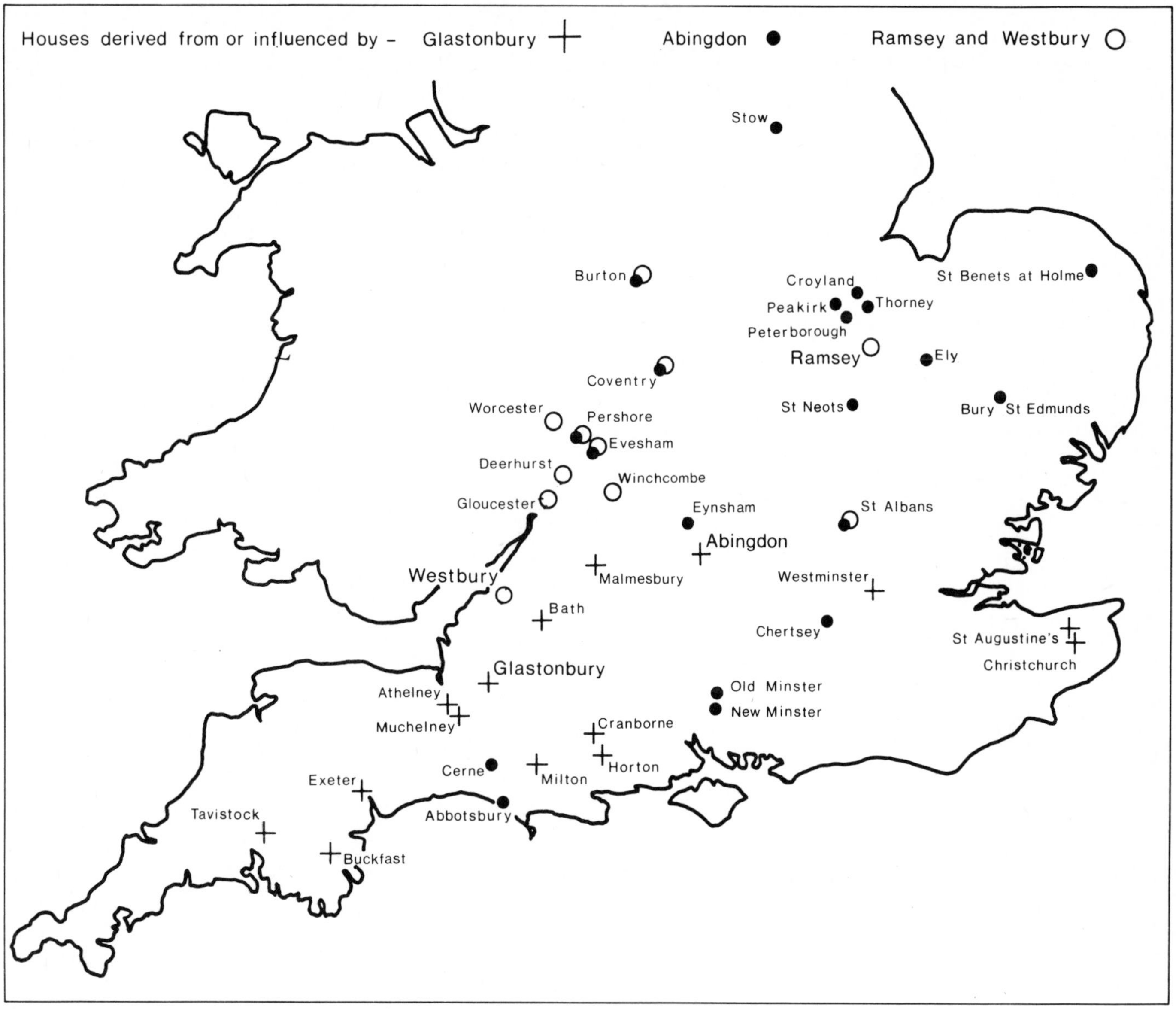

Houses derived from or influenced by – Glastonbury + Abingdon ● Ramsey and Westbury ○

Stow
Burton
Croyland
Peakirk
Thorney
Peterborough
St Benets at Holme
Ramsey
Ely
Coventry
St Neots
Bury St Edmunds
Worcester
Pershore
Evesham
Deerhurst
Winchcombe
Gloucester
Eynsham
St Albans
Abingdon
Westbury
Malmesbury
Westminster
Bath
Chertsey
St Augustine's
Christchurch
Glastonbury
Athelney
Muchelney
Old Minster
New Minster
Cranborne
Horton
Cerne
Milton
Exeter
Abbotsbury
Tavistock
Buckfast

243 The Monastic Revival in late Anglo-Saxon England (Loyn 1962)

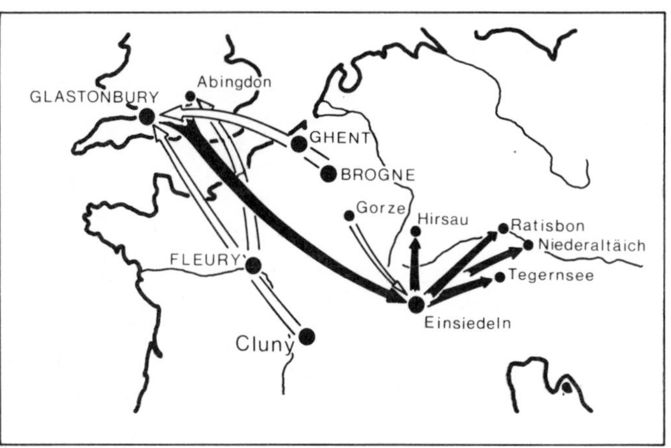

244 The interrelation of monastic rules in the tenth century

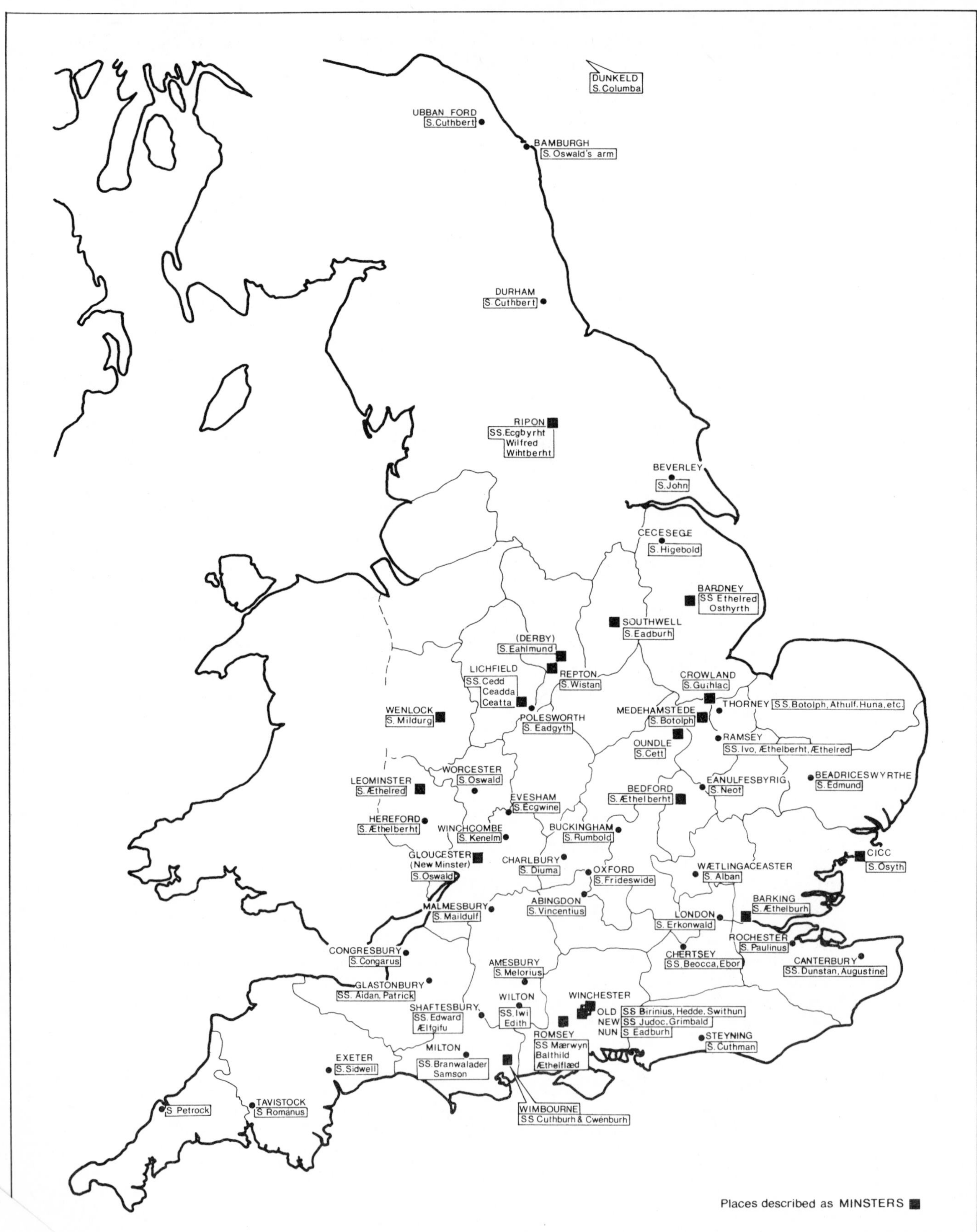

DUNKELD
S. Columba
UBBAN FORD
S. Cuthbert
BAMBURGH
S. Oswald's arm
DURHAM
S. Cuthbert
RIPON
SS. Ecgbyrht
Wilfred
Wihtberht
BEVERLEY
S. John
CECESEGE
S. Higebold
BARDNEY
SS. Ethelred
Osthyrth
SOUTHWELL
S. Eadburh
(DERBY)
S. Eahlmund
LICHFIELD
SS. Cedd
Ceadda
Ceatta
REPTON
S. Wistan
CROWLAND
S. Guthlac
THORNEY
SS. Botolph, Athulf, Huna, etc.
MEDEHAMSTEDE
S. Botolph
WENLOCK
S. Mildurg
POLESWORTH
S. Eadgyth
OUNDLE
S. Cett
RAMSEY
SS. Ivo, Æthelberht, Æthelred
WORCESTER
S. Oswald
LEOMINSTER
S. Æthelred
EANULFESBYRIG
S. Neot
BEADRICESWYRTHE
S. Edmund
BEDFORD
S. Æthelberht
EVESHAM
S. Ecgwine
HEREFORD
S. Æthelberht
WINCHCOMBE
S. Kenelm
BUCKINGHAM
S. Rumbold
GLOUCESTER
(New Minster)
S. Oswald
CHARLBURY
S. Diuma
OXFORD
S. Frideswide
WÆTLINGACEASTER
S. Alban
CICC
S. Osyth
ABINGDON
S. Vincentius
MALMESBURY
S. Maildulf
BARKING
S. Æthelburh
LONDON
S. Erkonwald
ROCHESTER
S. Paulinus
CONGRESBURY
S. Congarus
CHERTSEY
SS. Beocca, Ebor
CANTERBURY
SS. Dunstan, Augustine
AMESBURY
S. Melorius
GLASTONBURY
SS. Aidan, Patrick
WILTON
SS. Iwi
Edith
WINCHESTER
OLD SS Birinius, Hedde, Swithun
NEW SS Judoc, Grimbald
NUN S. Eadburh
SHAFTESBURY
SS. Edward
Ælfgifu
ROMSEY
SS Mærwyn
Balthild
Æthelflæd
STEYNING
S. Cuthman
MILTON
SS. Branwalader
Samson
EXETER
S. Sidwell
TAVISTOCK
S. Romanus
S. Petrock
WIMBOURNE
SS Cuthburh & Cwenburh
Places described as MINSTERS

245 The resting-places of the saints

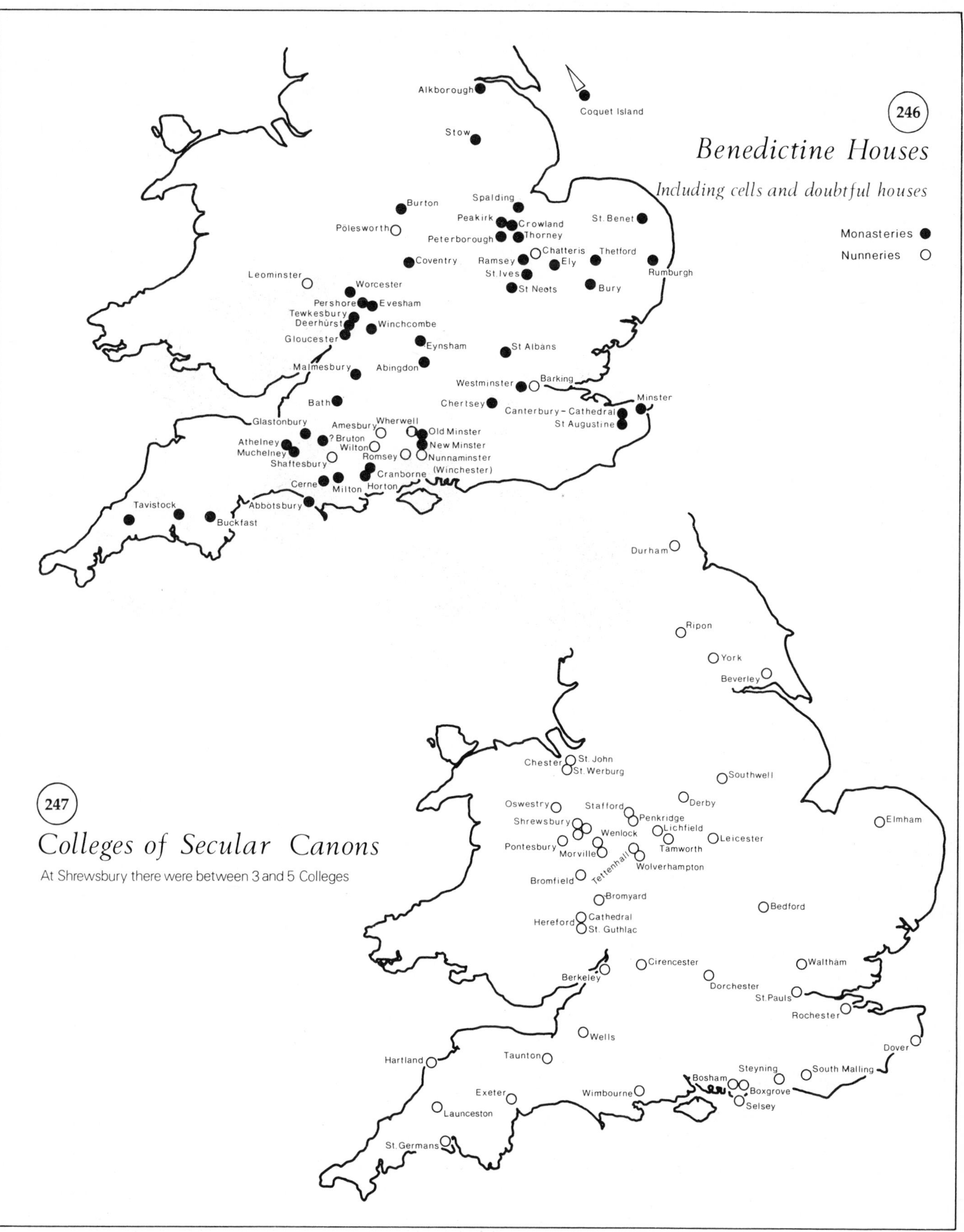

246
Benedictine Houses
Including cells and doubtful houses
Monasteries
Nunneries
Alkborough
Coquet Island
Stow
Spalding
Burton
Peakirk
Crowland
Thorney
Peterborough
St. Benet
Pōlesworth
Chatteris
Thetford
Coventry
Ramsey
Ely
Rumburgh
St. Ives
Leominster
Worcester
St Neots
Bury
Pershore
Evesham
Tewkesbury
Deerhurst
Winchcombe
Gloucester
Eynsham
St Albans
Malmesbury
Abingdon
Westminster
Barking
Bath
Chertsey
Minster
Canterbury - Cathedral
St Augustine
Glastonbury
Amesbury
Wherwell
Old Minster
? Bruton
Athelney
Wilton
New Minster
Muchelney
Romsey
Nunnaminster
Shaftesbury
(Winchester)
Cranborne
Cerne
Milton
Horton
Tavistock
Abbotsbury
Buckfast
Durham
Ripon
York
Beverley
Chester
St. John
St. Werburg
Southwell
247
Colleges of Secular Canons
At Shrewsbury there were between 3 and 5 Colleges
Oswestry
Stafford
Derby
Penkridge
Shrewsbury
Lichfield
Elmham
Wenlock
Leicester
Pontesbury
Morville
Tamworth
Tettenhall
Wolverhampton
Bromfield
Bromyard
Bedford
Hereford
Cathedral
St. Guthlac
Cirencester
Waltham
Berkeley
Dorchester
St. Pauls
Rochester
Wells
Dover
Hartland
Taunton
Steyning
South Malling
Bosham
Boxgrove
Exeter
Wimbourne
Selsey
Launceston
St. Germans

246–247 Benedictine houses and colleges of secular canons c. 1060 (after Godfrey 1962)

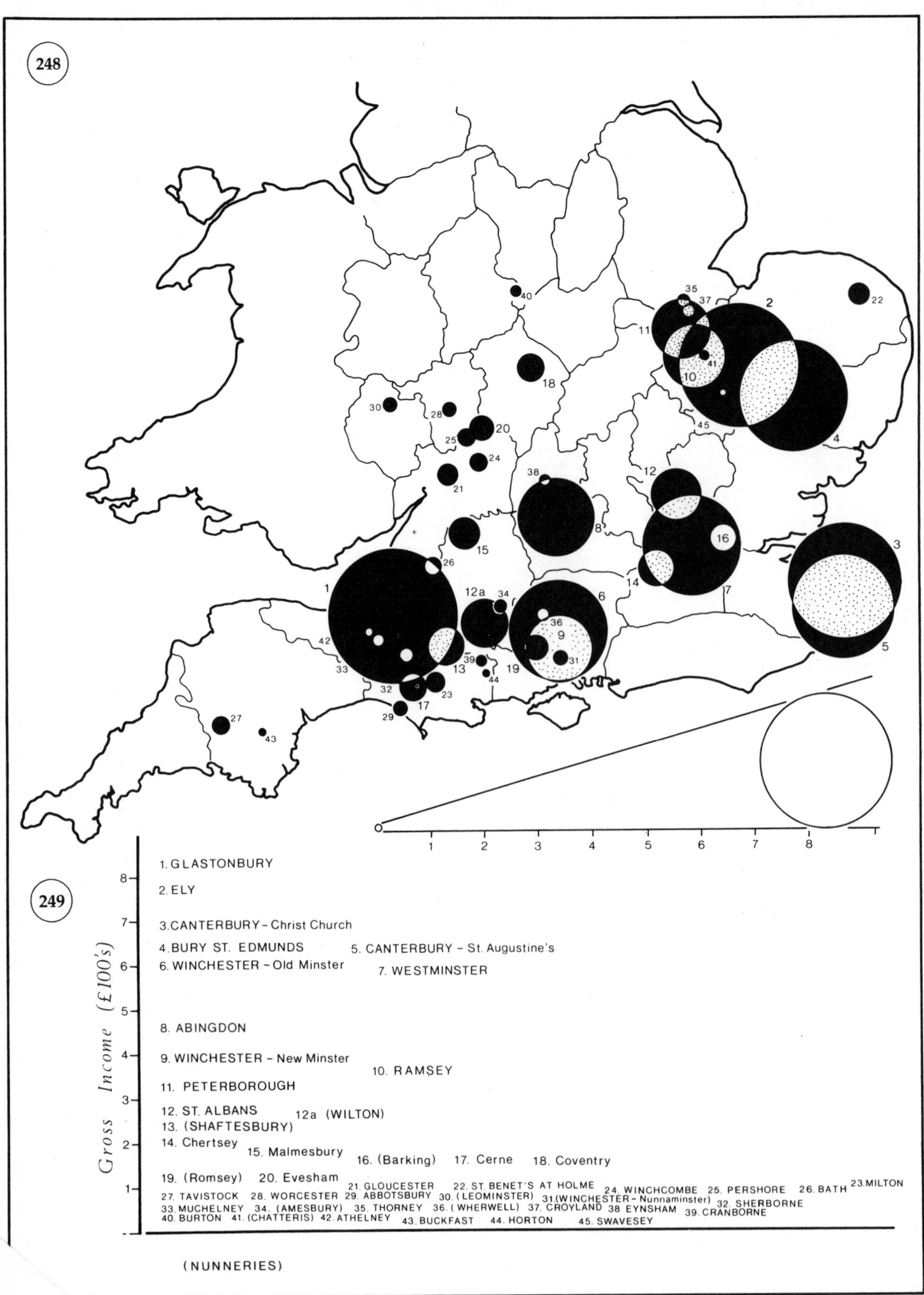
248
249
Gross Income (£100's)
1 2 3 4 5 6 7 8
1. GLASTONBURY
2. ELY
3. CANTERBURY - Christ Church
4. BURY ST. EDMUNDS
5. CANTERBURY - St. Augustine's
6. WINCHESTER - Old Minster
7. WESTMINSTER
8. ABINGDON
9. WINCHESTER - New Minster
10. RAMSEY
11. PETERBOROUGH
12. ST. ALBANS
12a (WILTON)
13. (SHAFTESBURY)
14. Chertsey
15. Malmesbury
16. (Barking)
17. Cerne
18. Coventry
19. (Romsey)
20. Evesham
21. GLOUCESTER
22. ST. BENET'S AT HOLME
23. MILTON
24. WINCHCOMBE
25. PERSHORE
26. BATH
27. TAVISTOCK
28. WORCESTER
29. ABBOTSBURY
30. (LEOMINSTER)
31. (WINCHESTER - Nunnaminster)
32. SHERBORNE
33. MUCHELNEY
34. (AMESBURY)
35. THORNEY
36. (WHERWELL)
37. CROYLAND
38. EYNSHAM
39. CRANBORNE
40. BURTON
41. (CHATTERIS)
42. ATHELNEY
43. BUCKFAST
44. HORTON
45. SWAVESEY
(NUNNERIES)

248–249 The Domesday valuation of monasteries and nunneries (£100s)

The Church and its Bishops (250–260)

Maps **250–258** are a palimpsest of the various periods and classes of information available to us. The diocesan boundaries are of the end of the Anglo-Saxon period, the monasteries are of all periods, as are bishop's seats. All churches which survive as architectural remains (Taylor and Taylor 1965) or as important archaeological remains have been included. The problem of the 'selected crosses and sculpture' is a major one; quite simply, there is no useful handlist available — even an interim one would be invaluable — as much of the work that has been done in the last few years has yet to be made more widely known. It is envisaged that these maps will need constant up-dating in view of the architectural, archaeological and monumental work now being carried out.

The chronologies in **259** and **260** enable one to establish contemporaneous bishops, but it is mainly intended to give some simplified view of the increase in dioceses to 870, the disruption of the Danish invasion period, the recovery, the increase in southern sees and their final amalgamation.

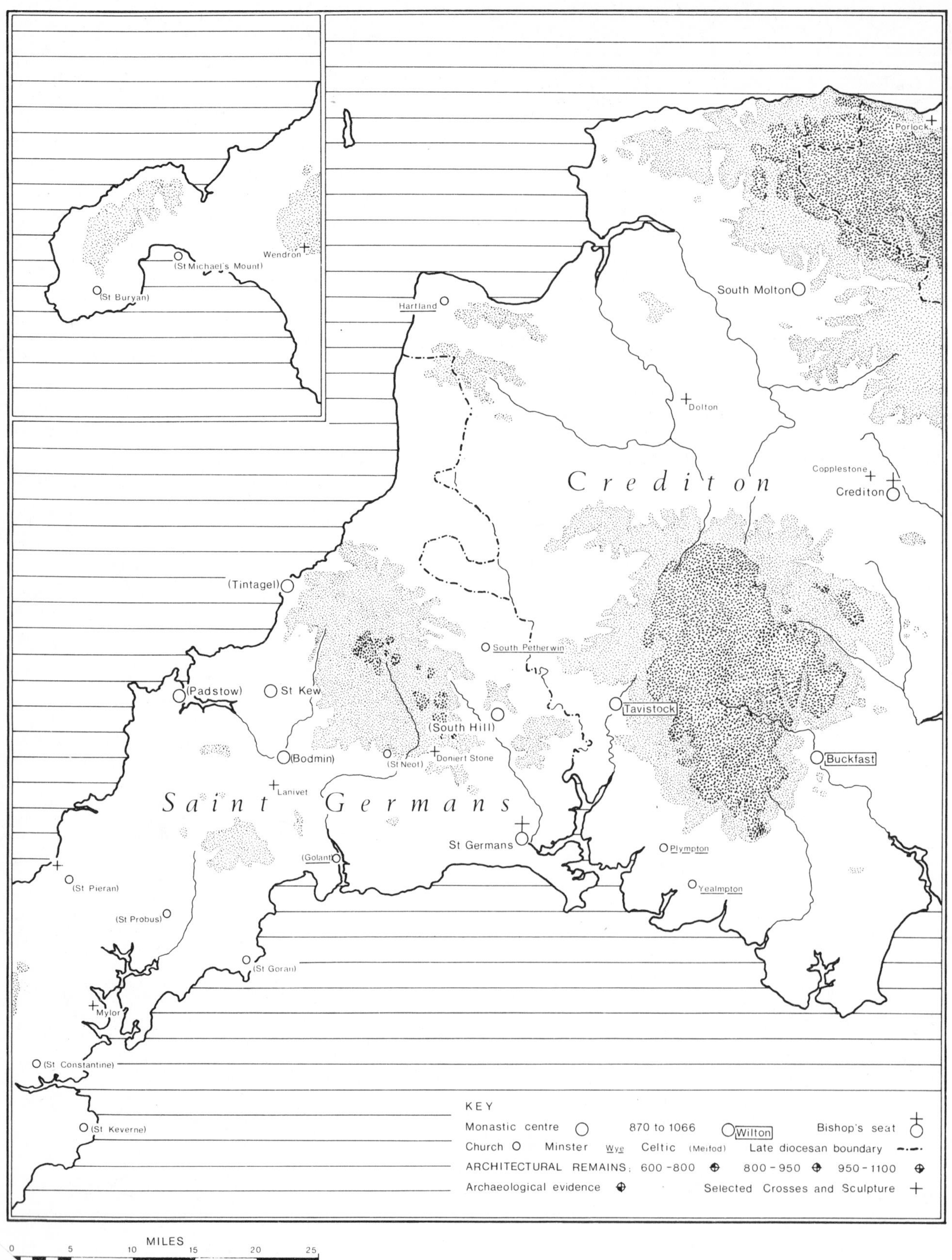
Porlock
Wendron
(St Michael's Mount)
(St Buryan)
South Molton
Hartland
Dolton
Copplestone
Crediton
Crediton
(Tintagel)
South Petherwin
(Padstow)
St Kew
Tavistock
(South Hill)
(Bodmin)
(St Neot)
Doniert Stone
Buckfast
Lanivet
Saint Germans
St Germans
(Golant)
Plympton
Yealmpton
(St Pieran)
(St Probus)
(St Goran)
Mylor
(St Constantine)
(St Keverne)
KEY
Monastic centre
870 to 1066
Wilton
Bishop's seat
Church
Minster
Wye
Celtic
(Meifod)
Late diocesan boundary
ARCHITECTURAL REMAINS; 600-800
800-950
950-1100
Archaeological evidence
Selected Crosses and Sculpture
MILES
0
5
10
15
20
25

250 The Church in the south-west

251 The Church in Somerset and Dorset

Hardwick
North Leigh
Minster Lovell
Eynsham
Aylesbury
Wheathampstead
Bibury
Headington
Haddenham
Northchurch
Waterperry
St Albans
Langford
Oxford
Dorchester on Thames
Inglesham
Abingdon
Dorchester
Faringdon
Cricklade
Highworth
Benson
Shrivenham
Kingsbury
Cholsey
Wantage
Cookham
Ashbury
Ramsbury
Streatley
Iver
White Waltham
Aldbourne
Sonning
Reading
Ramsbury
Wickham
Staines
Kingston
Avebury
Thatcham
Aldermaston
Chertsey
Alton Barnes
Bedwyn
Kintbury
Stratfield Mortimer
Cheam
Pewsey
Kingsclere
Woking
Stoke D'Abernon
Rushall
Hannington
Fetcham
Collingbourne Ducis
Steventon
Guildford
Netheravon
Whitchurch
Laverstoke
Farnham
Compton
Albury
Winchester
Quarley
Godalming
Wherwell
Barton Stacey
Amesbury
Thursley
Witley
Nether Wallop
Little Somborne
Headbourne Worthy
New Alresford
Kings Somborne
Tichborne
Britford
Winchester
Alderbury
Old Minster
Chilcomb
New Minster
Hinton Ampner
Mottisfont
Nunnaminster
Warnford
Chithurst
Woolbeding
Downton
Romsey
East Meon
Bolney
Corhampton
Selham
Breamore
Elsted
Stopham
Damerham
Nursling
South Stoneham
Waltham
Hardham
Hambledon
Redbridge
Singleton
Selsey
Stoughton
Botolphs
Boarhunt
Boxgrove
Arundel
Old Shoreham
Warblington
Chichester
Westhampnett
Titchfield
Fareham
Bosham
Poling
Sompting
Rumboldswhyke
Lyminster
Ferring
Nyetimber
West Wittering
Pagham
Christchurch
Selsey
Freshwater
Arreton
KEY
Monastic centre
870 to 1066
Wilton
Bishop's seat
Church
Minster Wye
Celtic (Meifod)
Late diocesan boundary
ARCHITECTURAL REMAINS
600-850
800 - 950
950 - 1100
Archaeological evidence
Selected Crosses and Sculpture
MILES
0
5
10
15
20
25

252 The Church in the south

Ablington
Meldreth
Pentlow
Long Melford
Hadstock
Ickleton
Stoke by Clare
Sudbury
Ashwell
Strethall
Wendens Ambo
?Domnoc
Reed
Little Bardfield
Earls Cölne
Westmill
Chickney
Walkern
Braughing
Great Tey
Colchester
Birchanger
Great Hallingbury
White Notley
Inworth
Little Hallingbury
Do.
West Mersea
Welwyn
Hertingfordbury
Boreham
Tollesbury
Springfield
Bradwell-on-Sea
Greensted
Waltham
Southminster
London
Kingsbury
Prittleswell
Upminster
Benfleet
Barking
Horndon
London
Westminster
Lambeth
Tilbury
Cliffe
Swanscombe
Northfleet
Minster
Wilmington
Darenth
Shorne
Reculver
Rochester
Lower Halstow
Orpington
Minster
Milton Regis
Lullingstone
Kingsdown
Wouldham
Newington
West Stourmouth
Cheam
Teynham
Stone
Faversham
Rochester
Canterbury
Wingham
Maidstone
St. Augustine
Canterbury
Eastry
Win.
Leeds
West Peckham
Charing
Kingston
Wye
Coldred
East Langdon
Whitfield
St Margarets at Cliffe
Willesborough
Lyminge
Paddlesworth
Dover
Aldington
Cheriton
Lympne
Folkestone
Worth
Bolney
Selsey
Wivelsfield
Lydd
Clayton
South Malling
Herstmonceux
Stanmer
Lewes
Beddingham
Arlington
Bexhill
Shoreham
Bishopstone
Jevington
MILES
0
5
10
15
20

253 The Church in the south-east

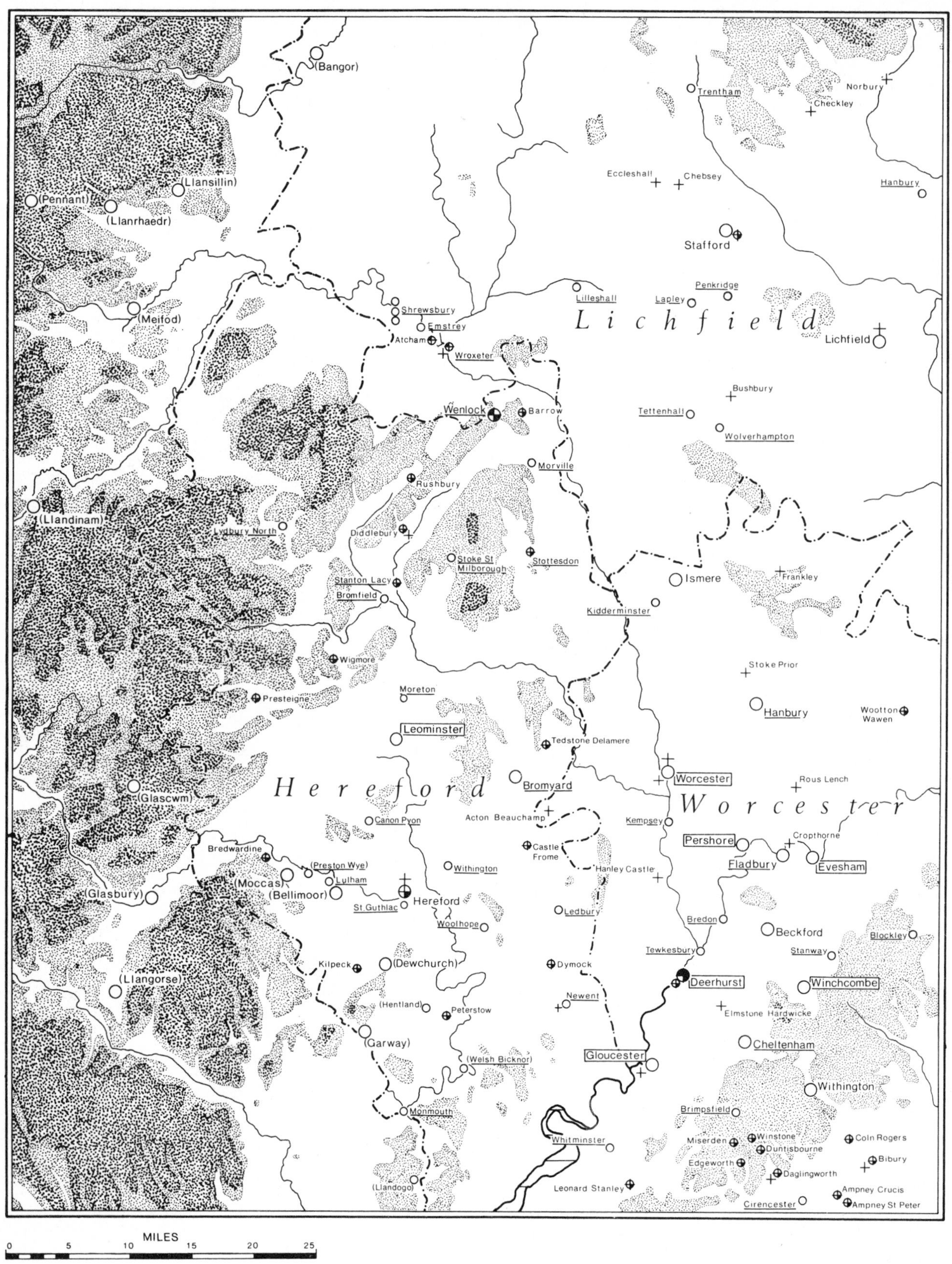

254 The Church in the west Midlands

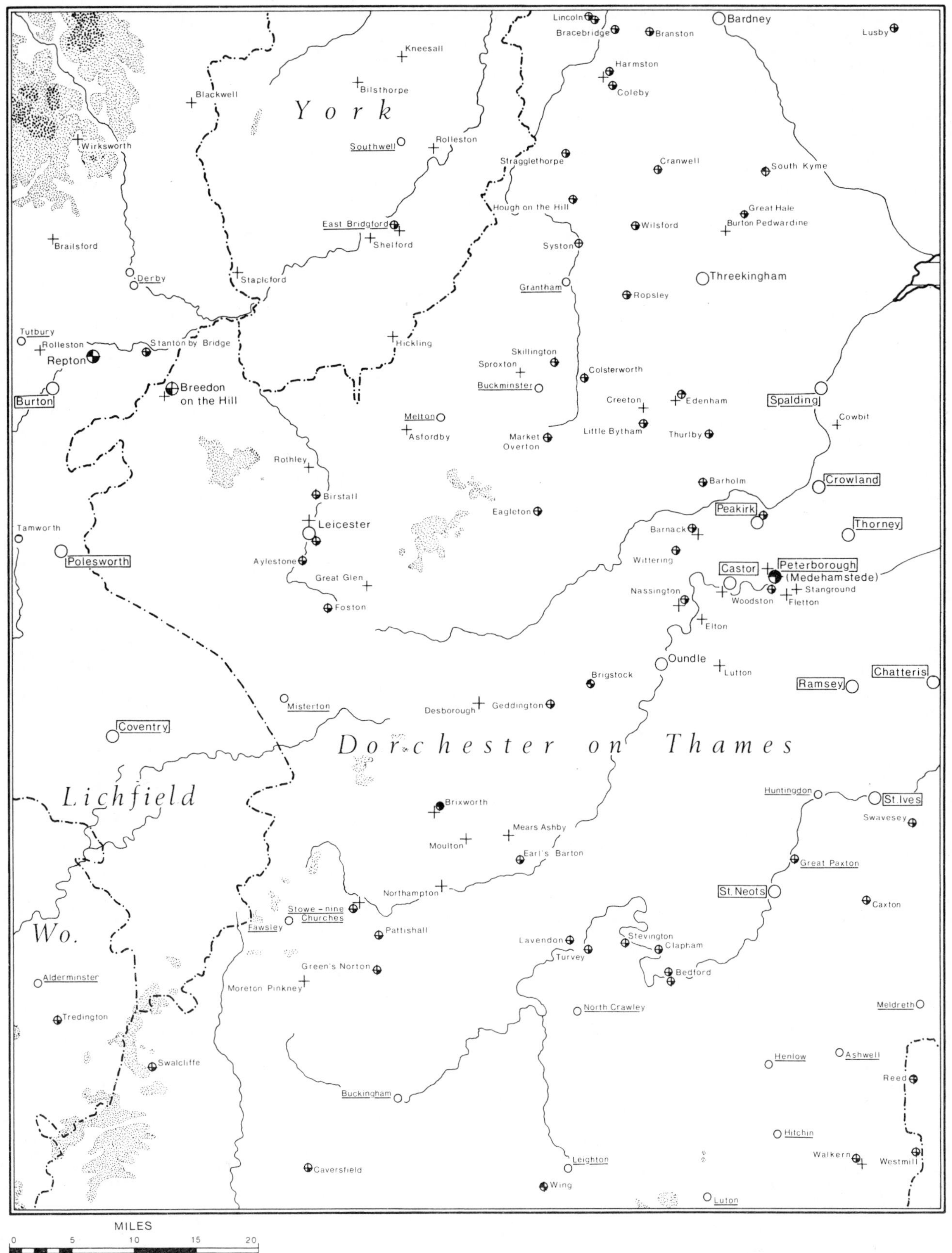

255 The Church in the east Midlands

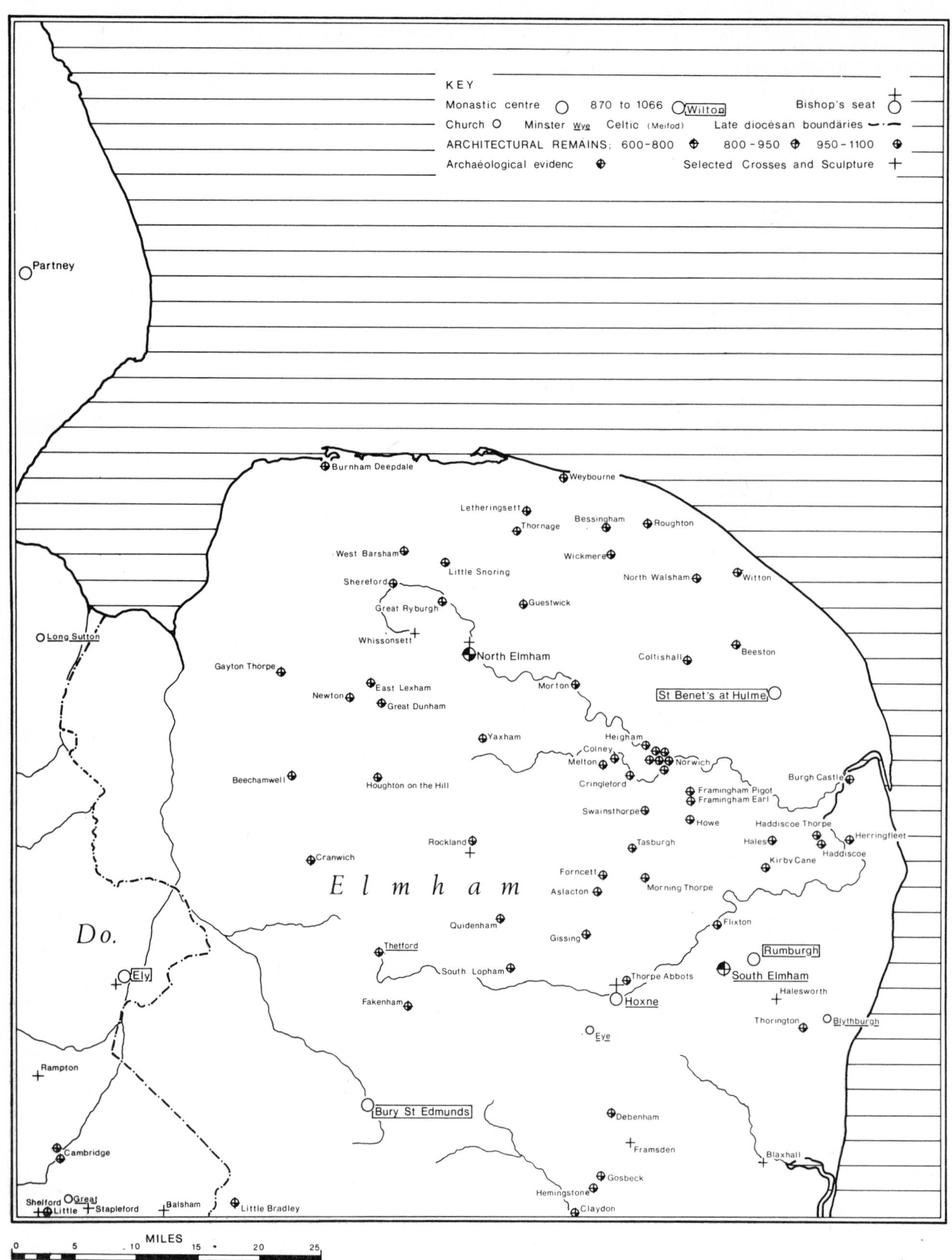
KEY
Monastic centre
870 to 1066
Wilton
Bishop's seat
Church
Minster Wye
Celtic (Meifod)
Late diocesan boundaries
ARCHITECTURAL REMAINS: 600-800
800-950
950-1100
Archaeological evidenc
Selected Crosses and Sculpture
Partney
Burnham Deepdale
Weybourne
Letheringsett
Thornage
Bessingham
Roughton
West Barsham
Little Snoring
Wickmere
North Walsham
Witton
Shereford
Great Ryburgh
Guestwick
Long Sutton
Whissonsett
North Elmham
Coltishall
Beeston
Gayton Thorpe
East Lexham
Newton
Great Dunham
Morton
St Benet's at Hulme
Yaxham
Heigham
Colney
Melton
Norwich
Beechamwell
Houghton on the Hill
Cringleford
Burgh Castle
Framingham Pigot
Framingham Earl
Swainsthorpe
Howe
Haddiscoe Thorpe
Herringfleet
Rockland
Tasburgh
Hales
Haddiscoe
Kirby Cane
Cranwich
Forncett
Morning Thorpe
Elmham
Aslacton
Flixton
Quidenham
Gissing
Do.
Thetford
Rumburgh
Ely
South Lopham
Thorpe Abbots
South Elmham
Halesworth
Fakenham
Hoxne
Thorington
Blythburgh
Eye
Rampton
Bury St Edmunds
Debenham
Framsden
Blaxhall
Cambridge
Gosbeck
Hemingstone
Shelford
Great
Little
Stapleford
Balsham
Little Bradley
Claydon
MILES
0
5
10
15
20
25

256 The Church in East Anglia

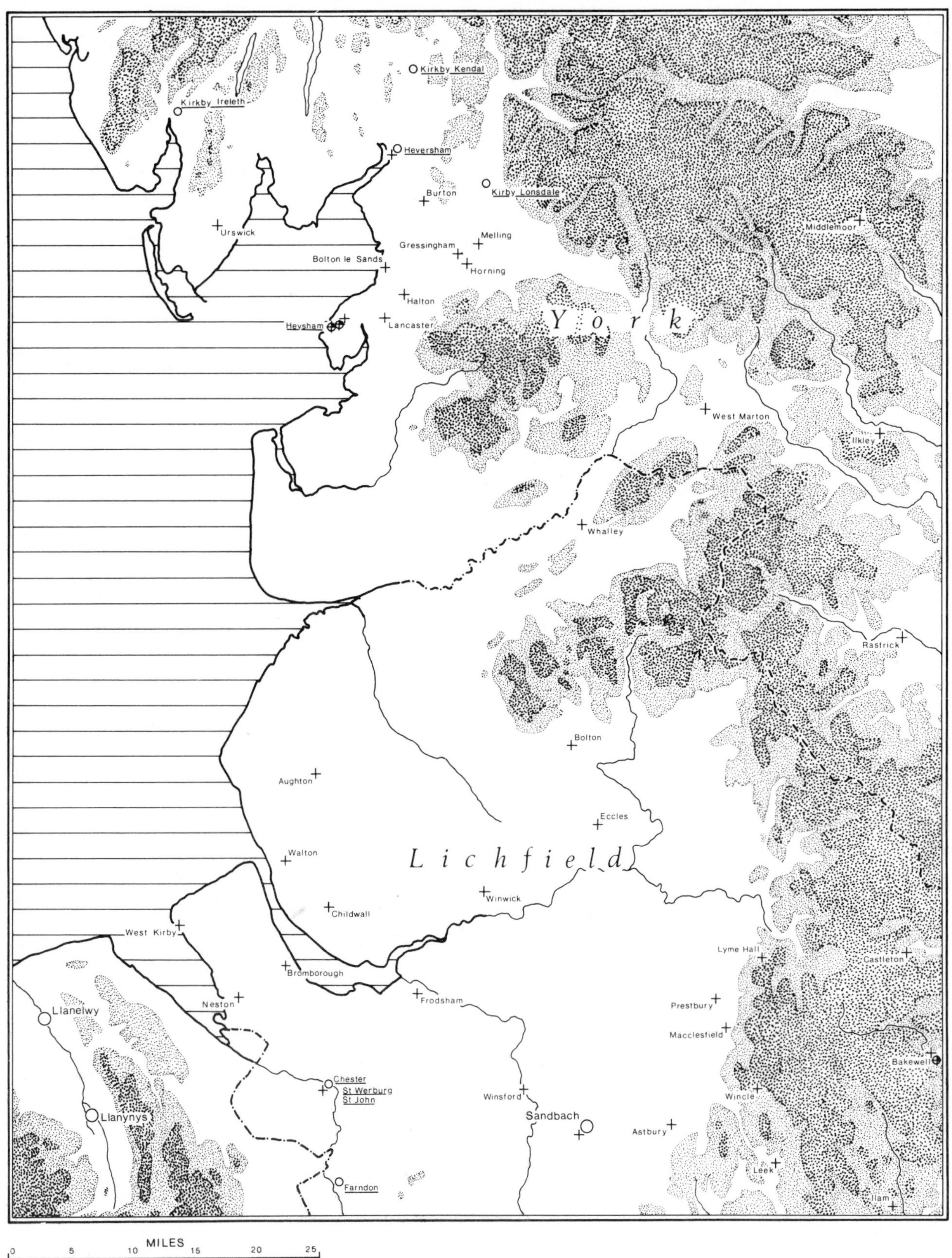

257 The Church in the north-east

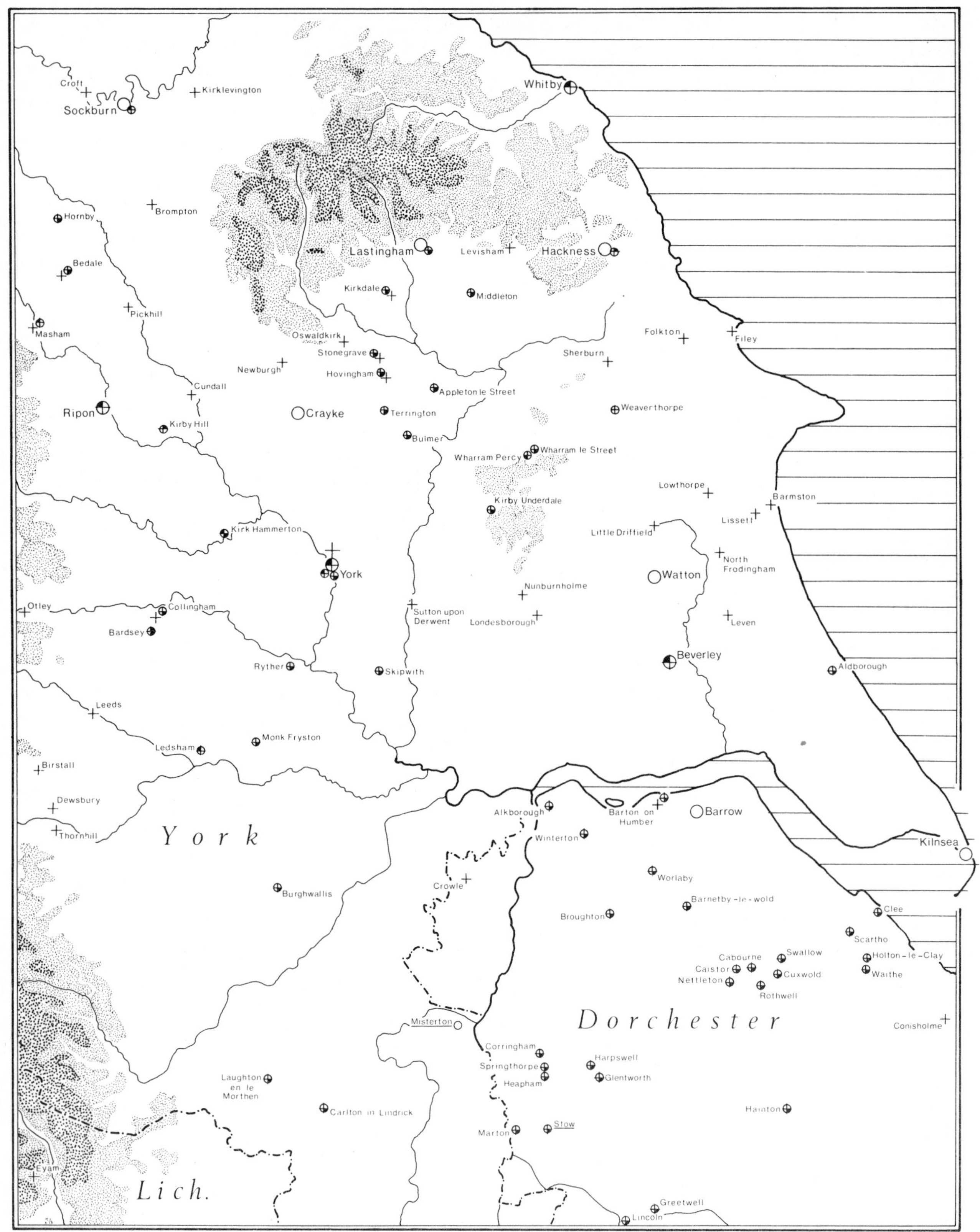

258 The Church in the north Midlands and Yorkshire

725 750 775 800 825 850 875

See	Bishops (in chronological order)
Canterbury	Beorhtwald; TATWINE; Nothelm; CUTHBEORHT; Breguwine; JAENBEORHT; Aethelheard; WULFRED; Feologild; Ceolnoth; Æthelred
Rochester	TOBIAS; Ealdwulf; DUNN; Eardwulf; DEORA; Waermund I; Beornmod; TATNOTH; Beadnoth; Waermund II; Cuthwulf
London	Wealdheri; Ingweald; Ecgwulf; Wigheah; Eadbeorht; Eadgar; Coenwealh; Eadbeald; Heathenbeorht; Osmund; Æthelnoth; Ceolbeorht; Deorwulf; Swithwulf; Heahstan
Winchester	DANIEL; Hunfrith; Cyneheard; Æthelheard; Ecgbeald; DUDD; Cynebeorht; Eahlmund; Wigthegn; Herefirth; Eadmund; EADHUN; Helmstan; SWITHUN; Eahlfrith; Tunbeorht; DENEWULF
Selsey	EOLLA; Sigga; Ealuberht; OSA; Gislhere; TOTA; Wihthun; Æthelwulf; Coenred; Gutheard
Sherborne	EALDHELM; Forthere; HEREWEALD; Æthelmod; DENEFRITH; Wigbeorht; EAHLSTAN; Heahmund; Æthelheah
Cornwall	Kentsec
Hereford	Tyrhtel; Torhthere; Wealhstod; Cuthbeort; PODDA; Ecca; Ceadda; Ealdbeort; ESNE; Ceolmund; UTEL; Wulfheard; BEONNA; Eadwulf; Cuthwulf; MUCEL; Deorlaf
Worcester	ECGWINE; Wilfrith I; MILDRED; Waermund; TILHERE; Heathured; DENEBEORHT; Heahbeorht; EAHLHUN; Waerfrith
Lichfield	HEADDA; EALDWINE; HWITA; Hemele; Cuthfrith; Beorhthun; HYGEBEORHT; Ealdwulf; Herewine; ÆTHELWEALD; Hunbeorht; Cynefrith; TUNBEORHT; Eadbeorht
Leicester	HEADDA; EALDWINE; Torhthelm; Eanbeorht; UNWONA; Wernbeorht; RETHUN; Ealdred; CEOBRED
Dunwich	Æscwulf; EARDRED; Ealdbeorht I; Eardwulf; Cuthwine; Ealdbeorht II; ECGLAF; Heardred; ÆLFHUN; Tidfrith; Waormund; WILRED; Æthelweald
Elmham	NOTHBEORHT; Heathulac; ÆTHELFRITH; Eanfrith; ÆTHELWULF; Eahlheard; SIBBA; Hunfrith; HUNBEORHT
Lindsey	EADGAR; Cynebeorht; ALWIG; Ealdwulf; Ceolwulf; Eadwulf; Beorhtred; Burgheard
York	BOSA; John; WILFRITH II; Ecgbeorht; ÆTHELBEORH; Eanbald I; Eanbald II; Wulfsige; Wigmund; WULFHERE
Lindisfarne	EADFRITH; Æthelweald; CYNEWULF; Hygebeald; ECGBEORH; Heathwred; Ecgred; Eanbeorht; EARDWULF
Hexham	JOHN; Wilfrith; ACCA; Frithubeorht; EAHLMUND; Tilbeorht; Aethelbeorht; Heardred; EANBEORHT; Tidfrith; EARDWULF
POPE	SERGIUS I; John VI; JOHN VII; Constantine; Gregory II; Gregory III; ZACHARIUS; Stephen II; PAUL I; Stephen III; HADRIAN I; LEO III; Stephen; PASCAL I; Eugenius; Valentinus; Gregory IV; Sergius II; LEO IV; Benedict III; Nicholas; Hadrian II; JOHN VIII

259 Bishops: chronology 700–880

See	Bishops (in chronological order, top to bottom)
Canterbury	Æthelræd; Plegmund; ATHELM; Wulfhelm; ODA; Ælfsige; Beorht-helm; DUNSTAN; Æthelgar; Sigeric; ÆLFRIC; ÆLFHEAH; LYFING; Æthelnoth; EADSIGE; Robert; STIGAND
Rochester	Swithwulf; Ceolmund; Cyneferth; BURGRIC; Beorht-sige; ÆLFSTAN; Godwine I; Godwine II; SIWARD
Selsey	Wighelm; Beorn-heah; Wulfhun; ALFRED; Beorthelm; Eadhelm; Æthelgar; ORD-BEORHT; Ælfmaer; Æthelric I; Grim-cytel; HECA; Æthelric II
Winchester	DENEWULF; FRITHE-STAN; Byrnstan; ÆLFHEAH I; Ælfsige I; BEORHT-HELM; Æthel-weald I; ÆLFHEAH II; Coenwulf; ÆTHEL-WOLD II; Ælfsige II; Ælfwine; STIGAND
Ramsbury	Athelstan; ODA; Ælfric I; OSWULF; Ælfstan; Wulfgar; SIGERIC; ÆLFRIC II; Beorht-wald; Ælfweald II; HEREMAN
Sherborne	WULFSIGE I; ASSER; Æthel-weard; Wærstan; Æthel-bald; Sigehelm; ALFRED; WULF-SIGE II; ÆLF-WEALD I; Æthelsige I; WULF-SIGE III; Æthelric; ÆTHEL-SIGE II; Beorhtwald; Ælfmaer; ÆLF-WEALD II
Wells	ATHELM; Wulfhelm I; ÆLFHEAH; Wulfhelm II; BEORHT-HELM; Cyne-weard; SIGEGAR; Ælfwine; Lyfing; Æthel-wine; BEORHT-WINE; Beorht-wig; DUDUC; Giso
Crediton	EADWULF; Æthelgar; ÆTHEL-WEALD; Sideman; ÆLFRIC; Ælfweald II; Ælfweald III; Eadnoth; Lyfing; (Exeter); LEOFRIC
St. Germans	Conan; DANIEL; Conan; Wulfsige; Ealdred; Æthel-red; BURH-WEALD
Dorchester	EAHLHEARD; Coenwulf; Wynsige; Oscytel; Leofwine; ÆTHELNOTH; Æscwig; Ælfhelm; Eadnoth I; ÆTHELRIC; Eadnoth II; ULF; Wulfwig
Lindsey	Alfred; Sige-frith
London	HEAHSTAN; WULFSIGE; Æthelweard; LEOFSTAN; Theo-dred; BEORHT-HELM; Dunstan; Ælfstan; WULF-STAN II; Ælfhun; ÆLFWIG; ÆLF-WEARD; Robert; William
Elmham	Æthel-weald; Eadwulf; ÆLFRIC I; Theodred I; Theodred II; Athel-stan; Ælfgar; Ælfwine; ÆLFRIC II; Ælfric III; Grimcytel; Stigand; Æthel-maer
Lichfield	Wulfred; Wig-mund; ÆLF-WINE; Wulfgar; CYNE-SIGE; Wynsige; ÆLF-HEAH; Godwine; Leofgar; Beorht-maer; Wulfsige; Leof-wine
Hereford	Deorlaf; Cyne-mund; EDGAR; Tidhelm; Wulfhelm; ÆLFRIC; ÆTHEL-WULF; Æthel-stan; Leofgar; Walter
Worcester	Wærfrith; ÆTHEL-HUN; Wilfrith II; Coenwald; DUNSTAN; OSWALD; EALDWULF; WULFSTAN II; Leofsige; Beorht-heah; Lyfing; EALDRED; Wulfstan II
York	Wulfhere; ÆTHEL-BALD; Hroth-weard; Wulfstan I; OSCYTEL; OSWALD; Edwald; EALDWULF; WULFSTAN II; ÆLFRIC PUTTOC; Æthelric; ÆLFRIC PUTTOC; Cynesige; EALDRED
Chester le-Str. / Durham	Cutheard; TILRED; Wigred; Uhtred; Seaxhelm; Ealdred; ÆLFSIGE; Durham: Ealdhun; Eadmund; Eadred; Æthelric; ÆTHEL-WINE
Pope	John; Martin II; Stephen; Formosus; JOHN; Benedict; SERGIUS III; JOHN X; Stephen; John XI; LEO VII; Stephen; Martin III; Agapetus II; JOHN XII; LEO VIII; JOHN XIII; Benedict; Benedict VII; JOHN XV; Gregory V; Silvester; JOHN XVIII; Sergius IV; Benedict VIII; JOHN XIX; Benedict IX; BRUNO; Victor II; Alex-ander II

Years: 900, 925, 950, 975, 1000, 1025, 1050

260 Bishops: chronology 880–1066

Bibliography

BARLOW, F. 1970: *Edward the Confessor*, London.

BIDDLE, M. 1976: 'Towns' in D. M. Wilson (ed.), *The Archaeology of Anglo-Saxon England*, London.

BRØNDSTED, J. 1965: *The Vikings*, London.

BROOKS, N. 1964: 'The unidentified forts of the Burghal hidage', *Med. Archaeol.* 74–90.

BRUCE-MITFORD, R. L. S. 1975: *The Sutton Hoo Ship Burial*, London.

CAMPBELL, J. 1979: in P. H. Sawyer, (ed.), *Names, Words and Graves*, Leeds.

COLGRAVE, B. 1956: *Felix of Crowland's Life of St Guthlac*, Cambridge.

DARBY, H. C. 1969: *The Domesday Geographies of England*, Cambridge.

DAVIES, W. 1978: *An Early Welsh Microcosm: Studies in the Llandaff Charters*, London.

DAVIES, W. and VIERCK, H. 1974: 'The contexts of tribal hidage: Social aggregate and settlement patterns', *Frühmitteralterliche Studien* 8.

DAVISON, B. K. 1972: 'The Burghal hidage fort of Eorpeburnan: a suggested identification', *Med. Archaeol.* 16, 123–7.

DOLLEY, R. H. M. 1966: *The Hiberno-Norse Coins in the British Museum*, London.

ELLIS, S. E. 1969: 'The petrography and provenance of Anglo-Saxon and Medieval English honestones, with notes on some other hones', *Bull. Brit. Museum (Natur. Hist.): Mineralogy* 2 (3), 133–87.

FAIRBRIDGE, R. W. 1966a: 'The changing level of the sea', *Scientific American* 202 (5).

FAIRBRIDGE, R. W. 1966b: 'Mean sea level changes, long term, eustatic and other', *Encyclopaedia of Oceanography*, New York.

FINBERG, H. P. R. 1961: *The Early Charters of the West Midlands*, Leicester.

FORD, W. J. 1976: 'Some settlement patterns in the central region of the Warwickshire Avon' in P. H. Sawyer (ed.), *Medieval Settlement, Continuity and Change*, London.

FOWLER, P. J. 1972: *Archaeology and the Landscape*, London.

FREEMAN, E. A. 1869–75: *The History of the Norman Conquest of England*, London.

GODFREY, J. 1962: *The Church in Anglo-Saxon England*, Cambridge.

GRAHAM-CAMPBELL, J. 1977: 'British antiquity – Western British, Irish and later Anglo-Saxon', *Archaeol. J.* 134.

HART, C. R. 1971: 'The tribal hidage', *TRHS* 5th series, 21.

HILL, D. H. 1969: 'The Burghal hidage – the establishment of a text', *Med. Archaeol.* 13.

HURST, J. G. 1976: 'The pottery' in D. M. Wilson (ed.), *The Archaeology of Anglo-Saxon England*, London.

JOPE, E. M. 1964: 'The Saxon building stone industry in southern and midland England', *Med. Archaeol.* 8.

KER, N. R. 1957: *Catalogue of Manuscripts containing Anglo-Saxon*, Oxford.

KNOWLES, D. 1963: *The Monastic Order in England*, Cambridge.

KNOWLES, D. 1965: *The Venerable Bede: The Ecclesiastical History of the English Nation*, London.

LAMB, H. H. 1978: *Climate, Present, Past and the Future*, London.

LEVISON, W. 1946: *England and the Continent in the Eighth Century*, Oxford.

LIBERMANN, F. 1889: *Die Heiligen Englands*, Hanover.

LOYN, H. R. 1962: *Anglo-Saxon England and the Norman Conquest*, London.

LOYN, H. R. 1971: 'Towns in late Anglo-Saxon England : the evidence and some possible lines of enquiry' in P. Clemoes and K. Hughes (eds.), *England before the Conquest*, Cambridge

LOYN, H. R. 1977: *The Vikings in Britain*, London.

McNEILL, P. and NICHOLSON, R. 1975: *An Historical Atlas of Scotland*, St Andrews.

METCALF, D. M. 1978: 'The ranking of boroughs: numismatic evidence from the reign of Ethelred II', in D. HILL (ed.), *Ethelred the Unready*, BAR 59.

NORTH, J. J. 1963: *English Hammered Coinage*, London.

ORDNANCE SURVEY, 1935: *Britain in the Dark Ages*, 1st edn, Chessington.

ORDNANCE SURVEY, 1966: *Britain in the Dark Ages*, 2nd edn, Chessington.

ORDNANCE SURVEY, 1973: *Britain before the Norman Conquest*, Southampton.

OXENSTIERNA, E. 1976: 'The Vikings' in B. M. Fagan, *Avenues to Antiquity*, San Francisco.

RAHTZ, P. and BULLOUGH, D. 1977: 'The parts of an Anglo-Saxon mill', *Anglo-Saxon England* 6.

ROBERTSON, A. J. 1939: *Anglo-Saxon Charters*, Cambridge.

ROLLASON, D. W. 1978: 'Lists of saints' resting-places in Anglo-Saxon England', *Anglo-Saxon England* 7, 61–94.

SAWYER, P. H. 1968: *Anglo-Saxon Charters*, London.

SAWYER, P. H. 1971: *The Age of the Vikings*, 2nd edn, London.

SAWYER, P. H. 1978: *From Roman Britain to Norman England*, London.

SKEAT, W. W. 1881: *Aelfric's Lives of Saints*, Oxford.

SMITH, A. H. 1965: *The Place-names of Gloucestershire*, Cambridge.

SMYTH, A. P. 1975: *Scandinavian York and Dublin*, Dublin.

SMYTH, A. P. 1977: *Scandinavian Kings in the British Isles 850–880*, Oxford.

STENTON, F. M. 1970: *Preparatory to Anglo-Saxon England*, Oxford.

STENTON, F. M. 1971: *Anglo-Saxon England*, 3rd edn, Oxford.

TAYLOR, H. M. and TAYLOR, J. 1965: *Anglo-Saxon Architecture*, Cambridge.

TYLECOTE, R. F. 1962: *Metallurgy in Archaeology*, London.

WHITELOCK, D. 1955: *English Historical Documents c. 500–1042*, London.

WHITELOCK, D. 1965: *The Anglo-Saxon Chronicles: A Revised Translation*, London.

WILLIAMSON, J. A. 1959: *The English Channel*, London.

WILSON, D. M. 1976: *The Archaeology of Anglo-Saxon England*, London.

WILSON, M. 1968: 'The Hwicce', *Trans. Worcs. Archaeol. Soc. 3rd Series* 2.

Index

This is an Index Locorum only, as befits an Atlas. Map numbers are used throughout. The English place names are placed within traditional counties rather than ephemeral local government units. These counties are identified by the English Placename Society abbreviations.

Aachen, Germany 49, 62, 208, 209, 210
Aarhus, Denmark 71
Abbotsbury, Do 243, 246, 249, 251
Abercorn, Scotland 41
Aberffraw, Wales 103
Abingdon, Brk 155, 158, 160, 163, 205, 228, 243, 244, 245, 246, 249, 252
Ablington, Ca 253
Aclea 46, 54
Acton Beauchamp, Wo 254
Adalvik, Iceland 74
Adlestrop, Gl 178
Adlingfleet, WRY 234
Agen, France 208, 210
Aggersborg, Denmark 71
Aghaboe, Ireland 47, 73
Ailech, Ireland 73
Aileen, Ireland 73
Airgialla, Ireland 103
Aix, France 237
Albury, Sr 252
Aldbourne, W 252
Aldborough, ERY 258
Alde River 232
Aldeneyer, Netherlands 242
Alderbury, W 252
Aldermaston, Brk 252
Alderminster, Wa 255
Alderton, Gl 178
Aldingbourne, Sx 148
Aldington, K 253
Alford, So 188
Algeciras, Spain 53
Aliscros Hundred, Wales 188
Alkborough, L 258, 246
All Cannings, W 227
Aller, So 22, 147
Alney, Gl 129, 230
Alpta Fjord, Iceland 74
Alresford, Ha 228
Altmünster, Germany 242
Altomünster, Germany 242
Alton, Ha 148
Alton Barnes, W 252
Alton Pancras, Do 166
Altrip, Germany 242
Alveston, Wa 197
Alvington, Gl 188
Amesbury, W 146, 148, 155, 159, 162, 228, 245, 246, 249, 252
Amiens, France 46, 47, 55, 63, 208, 211, 242
Amoneberg, Germany 242
Amorbach, Germany 242
Amounderness 233
Ampney Crucis, Gl 254
Ampney St Peter, Gl 254
Andernach, Germany 242
Andover, Ha 112, 159, 160, 162, 228
Andoversford, Gl 178
Andredesweald 23
Angers, France 46, 47, 54, 57, 201, 210
Anglesey 41, 46, 47, 103
Angmering, Sx 148
Anjou, France 46, 56
Annagassan, Ireland 46, 51, 73
Ansbach, Germany 242
Antonine Wall 41
Antrim, Ireland 73
Antum, Netherlands 66
Antwerp, Belgium 46, 50
Appledore, K 21, 229
Appleton le Street, NRY 258
Aquitaine, France 46, 49, 51, 54, 56
Archenfield, He 88, 143, 230
Ard Ladrainn, Ireland 73
Ardagh, Ireland 73
Ardbrachen, Ireland 47
Ardennes 47
Ardmore, Ireland 73
Ards, Ireland 46
Argailla, Ireland 73
Argenteuil, France 242
Arklow, Ireland 73
Arles, France 208, 209, 210, 237
Arlington, Sx 253
Armagh, Ireland 46, 47, 51, 54, 57, 73
Arosætna 136, 138
Arras, France 46, 47, 208, 211, 242
Arreton, Ha 148, 252
Arun River 228
Arundel, Sx 228, 252
Asfordby, Lei 255
Ashbourne, Db 230
Ashbury, Brk 252
Ashdown 47, 58, 228
Ashingdon, Ess 128, 163, 229
Ashton, Gl 178
Ashton, W 148
Ashwell, Hrt 229, 231, 253, 255
Aslacton, Nf 256
Aspatria, Cu 67
Astbury, Ch 257
Aston, Sa 142
Aston Blank, Gl 178
Aston Rowant, O 205
Atcham, Sa 254
Ath-Cliath, Ireland 47, 73
Ath-Cruthan, Ireland 47
Athelney, So 22, 147, 227, 243, 246, 249, 251
Athlone, Ireland 73
Attigny, France 211
Augsburg, Germany 242
Augst, Switzerland 242
Autun, France 210, 237, 242
Auxerre, France 210, 242
Avallon, France 210
Avebury, W 251, 252
Avenches, Switzerland 242
Avignon, France 208
Avon River, Do 189
Avon River, Gl 143
Avon River, Ha 228
Avon River, So 227
Avon River, Wa 178, 231
Avon River, Wo 230
Avonmouth, Gl 88
Avranchin 47
Axbridge, So 150, 152, 187, 217, 223, 224
Axe River, D 22, 227
Axe River, So 227
Axford, W 205
Axholme, Isle of 139
Axminster, D 146, 154, 227, 251
Axmouth, D 148, 227
Aylesbury, Bk 91, 217, 223, 224, 228, 252
Aylesford, K 128, 199
Aylestone, Lei 255

Badbury, Do 227, 235
Badby, Nth 197
Badsey, Wo 205
Bakewell, Db 97, 231, 257
Balsham, Ca 256
Bamburgh, Nb 41, 99, 111, 119, 235
Banbury, O 231
Bangor, Ch 41, 254
Bangor, Ireland 46, 73
Bann River, Ireland 73
Banwell, So 227, 251
Bar sur Aube, France 210
Barbury, W 228
Bardney, L 41, 84, 139, 145, 245, 255
Bardsey, L 231
Bardsey, WRY 258
Barham, K 205
Barholm, L 255
Barking, Ess 41, 140, 229, 245, 246, 249, 253
Barmston, ERY 258
Barnack, Nth 200, 255
Barnes, Sr 165
Barnetby le Wold, L 258
Barnstaple, D 216, 217, 223, 224, 226, 235
Barrington, Ca 205
Barrow, L 41, 139, 234, 258
Barrow, Sa 254
Barrow upon Soar, Lei 231
Barton, L 234, 258
Barton Stacey, Ha 252
Basel, Switzerland 242
Basing, Ha 58, 159, 228
Basingwerk, Wales 145, 233
Bassaleg, Wales 251
Bastogne, Luxemburg 201
Bath, So 15, 103, 123, 145, 149, 150, 152, 160, 162, 187, 199, 214, 215, 216, 217, 223, 224, 227, 235, 243, 246, 249, 251

Battle, Sx 20
Bavai, France 21
Bayeux, France 46, 55, 210
Beachley, Gl 133
Beaminster, Do 251
Bearsted, K 229
Beauvais, France 46, 47, 54, 62, 211
Beccles, Sf 232
Beckford, Gl 178, 230, 254
Beckley, Sx 148
Bedale, NRY 65, 258
Beddingham, Sx 148, 229, 253
Bedford 15, 47, 82, 89, 91, 121, 205, 216, 217, 220, 223, 224, 231, 245, 247, 255
Bedfordshire 82, 122, 126, 171, 173
Bedminster, So 251
Bedwyn, W 148, 187, 223, 224, 252
Beechamwell, Nf 256
Beeding, Sx 148
Beeston, Nf 256
Beggary Island, Ireland 46
Beja, Portugal 53
Belcham St Paul, Ess 165
Belfast Lough, Ireland 73
Belley, France 242
Bellimoor, He 254
Benediktbeuren, Germany 242
Benfleet, Ess 60, 63, 64, 229, 253
Benken, Switzerland 242
Bensington, O 70, 228
Bere Regis, Do 251
Bergamo, Italy 208
Bergen, Norway 71
Berkeley, Gl 143, 220, 223, 224, 227, 247, 251
Berkhampstead, Hrt 228
Berkshire 43, 120, 122, 159
Bernicia 41
Bernwood, Bk 91
Berrow River, Ireland 73
Besançon, France 208, 209, 210, 242
Bessin 47
Bessingham, Nf 256
Beverley, ERY 41, 99, 155, 234, 245, 247, 258
Beverstone, Gl 227, 251
Bexhill, Sx 253
Beziers, France 208, 210
Bibury, Gl 252, 254
Bickenhall, So 188
Bickleigh, D 226
Billingsley, He 132, 230
Bilmiga 136, 138
Bilsthorpe, Nt 255
Bingham, Nt 65
Binsey, O 205
Birchanger, Ess 253
Birchington, K 205
Birka, Sweden 71
Birr, Ireland 73
Birstall, Lei 255
Birstall, WRY 258
Bischofshofen, Austria 242
Bishop's Cleeve, Gl 178, 197
Bishopstone, Sx 253
Bitterne, Ha 205
Bitton, Gl 251
Blackwater River 107, 229
Blackwater, Ireland 73
Blackwell, Wa 197
Blaxhall, Sf 256
Blockley, Wo 178, 254
Blois, France 46, 54, 55, 210
Blythburgh, Sf 232, 256
Boarhunt, Ha 252
Bockhampton, Do 165
Bodmin, Co 226, 246, 250
Bolney, Sx 252, 253
Bolton le Sands, La 257
Bonn, Germany 47, 62, 208
Bordeaux, France 46, 52, 209, 253
Borg, Iceland 74
Borgar Fjord, Iceland 74
Bornholm, Denmark 71
Boscombe, Ha 228
Bosham, Sx 41, 228, 247, 252
Botolphs, Sx 252
Bottisham Ca 197
Bouin, France 46, 47, 49, 56
Boulogne, France 47, 49, 64
Bourges, France 46, 56, 57, 208, 209, 210, 242
Bourne, L 231
Bourton on the Water, Gl 178
Bowcombe, Ha 189, 197
Box, W 200, 227
Boxgrove, Sx 247, 252
Boxwell, Gl 251
Boyne River, Ireland 46, 73
Brabant 47
Brabourne, K 197
Bravebridge, L 255
Bradford on Avon, W 159, 187, 227, 251
Bradwell on Sea, Ess 41, 205, 229, 253
Brailsford, Db 255
Braine River 229
Bramber, Sx 228
Bransbury, Ha 197
Branscombe, D 148
Branston, L 255
Braughing, Hrt 253
Braydon, W 83
Breach Down, K 205
Breamore, Ha 252
Brecenamere, Wales 90
Brede River 20
Bredon, Wo 230, 254
Bredwardine, He 254
Breedon on the Hill, Lei 41, 142, 205, 231, 255
Brega, Ireland 47
Bregh, Ireland 46, 47
Bregny, France 242
Breida Fjord, Iceland 74
Breifne, Ireland 73
Bremhill, W 251
Brendons 227
Brentford, Middx 127, 128, 140, 145, 228
Bridgenorth, Sa 47, 61, 64, 86, 199, 217, 224, 230
Bridlington, ERY 234
Bridport, Do 150, 152, 215, 217, 223, 224, 227, 251
Brigham, Cu 67
Brighton, Sx 205
Brigstock, Nth 255
Brimpsfield, Gl 254
Bristol, Gl 15, 133, 199, 217, 223, 224, 227, 235
Bristol Channel 47
Britford, W 169, 228, 252
Brittany 46, 47, 101
Brixton, W 227
Brixworth, Nth 255
Broadstairs, K 205
Broadway, Wo 178
Broadwell, Gl 178
Brogne 244
Bromborough, Ch 257
Bromfield, Sa 247, 254
Bromley, K 165
Brompton, NRY 258
Bromsgrove, Wo 230
Bromyard, He 143, 247, 254
Broughton, L 258
Brue River 22, 227
Bruges, Belgium 210
Brunanburh 47, 100
Bruneswald 23
Bruton, So 187, 217, 223, 224, 227, 246
Bubbancombe, Do 166
Buckfast, D 243, 246, 249, 250
Buckingham 47, 82, 88, 150, 152, 155, 217, 223, 224, 231, 235, 245, 255
Buckinghamshire 82, 121, 122, 126
Buckminster, Lei 255
Bulmer, NRY 258
Bulverhythe, Sx 20
Bungay, Sf 232
Buraburg, Germany 242
Burcombe, W 251
Burford, O 145
Burgh Castle, Sf 41, 205, 232, 256
Burghill, He 230
Burghwallis, WRY 258
Burgundy 47
Burnham, So 148
Burnham Deepdale, Nf 256
Burpham, Sx 150, 152, 235
Burton, La 257
Burton on Trent, St 231, 243, 246, 249, 255
Burton Bradstock, Do 251
Burton Pedwardine, L 255
Bury St Edmunds, Sf 17, 200, 220, 223, 224, 232, 243, 245, 246, 249, 256
Buttington, Wales 60, 64, 230
Bytham, L 188

Cabourne, L 258
Cadbury, So 187, 217, 223, 224, 227, 235
Caddington, Bd 165
Cadiz, Spain 53
Caerleon, Wales 41, 132, 134, 227, 251
Caistor, L 139, 217, 223, 224, 234, 235, 258
Caistor, Nf 205
Caithness, Scotland 47, 99
Callington, Co 226
Calne, W 159, 161, 162, 187, 227, 251
Cam River 232
Cambois, Nb 67
Cambrai, France 209, 211, 242

Cambridge 15, 17, 47, 59, 94, 121, 199, 205, 217, 223, 224, 232, 235, 256
Cambridgeshire 122, 171, 173
Camelford, Co 226
Campodunum 41
Can River 229
Candover, Ha 148
Canford Magna, Do 251
Cannings Marsh, W 121
Cannington, So 148, 227
Canon Pyon, He 254
Canterbury, K 15, 19, 41, 46, 120, 122, 145, 146, 147, 162, 163, 199, 205, 215, 217, 223, 224, 229, 235, 238, 239, 240, 241, 245, 246, 249, 253, 259, 260
Cantwarena 136, 138
Carhaix, France 201
Carhampton, So 44, 50, 51, 148, 227, 251
Carlingford, Ireland 46, 47, 54, 73
Carlisle, Cu 41
Carlton in Lindrick, Nt 258
Cashel, Ireland 73
Cassel, France 211
Castle Acre, Nf 232
Castle Frome, He 254
Castleford, WRY 234
Castleton, Db 257
Castor, Nth 205, 231, 255
Catterick, NRY 41, 234
Caversfield, O 255
Caxton, Ca 255
Cecesege, L 245
Ceredigion, Wales 130
Cerne, Do 130, 189, 243, 246, 249, 251
Chalgrave, Bd 82
Chalons, France 209, 210, 237, 242
Chalons sur Marne, France 211
Chalons sur Saone, France 242
Chammünster, Germany 242
Charente, France 46, 56
Charlbury, O 228, 245
Charminster, Do 251
Charmouth, Do 227
Chart, K 197
Chartres, France 46, 47, 55, 56, 208, 210
Chateau Landon, France 210
Chateaudun, France 208, 210
Chatteris, Ca 17, 246, 249, 255
Chaumes, France 242
Cheam, Sr 252
Cheddar, So 22, 148, 156, 157, 160, 227, 251
Chedworth, Gl 205
Chelles, France 211
Chelsea, Mddx 70, 145, 147, 162, 229
Cheltenham, Gl 143, 178, 254
Chepstow, Wales 227
Cheriton, K 253
Chertsey, Sr 41, 243, 246, 249, 252, 253
Cherwell River 231
Cheshire 108, 134, 171, 173
Chester, Ch 15, 41, 47, 60, 64, 68, 84, 103, 115, 126, 134, 135, 160, 199, 214, 215, 216, 217, 223, 224, 233, 235, 247, 257
Chester le Street, Du 99, 239, 240, 241, 260
Chesterfield, Ess 229
Chevremont, Belgium 242
Chewton, So 148, 227, 251
Chezy, France 47, 63, 242
Chichester, Sx 61, 149, 150, 152, 205, 215, 217, 223, 224, 228, 235, 252
Chickney, Ess 253
Chiemsee, Germany 242
Chievres, Belgium 211
Chilcomb, Ha 252
Childs Wickham, Gl 178
Chilterns 120, 228
Chinon, France 210
Chippenham, W 47, 59, 145, 146, 147, 148, 154, 155, 158, 227
Chipping Camden, Gl 178
Chipping Norton, O 178
Chirbury, Sa 89, 178
Chisbury, W 149, 152, 228, 235
Chisledon, W 143
Chiswick, Mddx 165
Chithurst, Sx 252
Cholsey, Brk 119, 228, 252
Christchurch, Canterbury 159, 243
Christchurch, Ha 149, 150, 152, 235
Chur, Switzerland 209, 242
Ciltern (Forest) 23
Cilternsætna 136, 138
Cirencester, Gl 157, 162, 163, 230, 247, 254
Cissbury, Sx 217, 223, 224, 228, 235
Clacton, Ess 165
Clapham, Bd 255
Clapham, Sr 165
Clare, Sf 229
Claughton Hall, La 67
Clausentum (Southampton) Ha 149, 235
Claydon, Sf 256
Clayhanger, Middx 229
Clayton, Sx 253
Cledemutha, Wales 47, 98, 233
Clee, L 258
Clermont, France 208, 210, 242
Cliffe, K 253
Clifford, He 230
Clifford, Wa 197
Clifton Maybank, Do 166
Clogher, Ireland 73
Clonard, Ireland 46, 47, 73
Clondalkin, Ireland 73
Clones, Ireland 73
Clonfert, Ireland 47, 73
Clonmacnoise, Ireland 46, 47, 73
Clonmell, Ireland 47
Clontarf, Ireland 73
Clopton, Gl 178
Clopton, Wo 197
Cluny, France 46, 244
Clwyd River 233
Clyde River 41
Clyst, D 116, 227
Coblenz, Germany 62
Codanham, Ess 165
Codford St Peter, W 251
Colchester, Ess 15, 68, 93, 94, 155, 157, 223, 224, 229, 235, 253
Coldingham Scotland 41
Coldred, K 253
Coleby, L 255
Coleraine, Ireland 73
Colerne, W 251
Coleshill, Brk 145
Collingbourne Ducis, W 252
Collingham, WRY 258
Coln Rogers, Gl 254
Colne River 228
Colney, Nf 256
Cologne, Germany 46, 56, 62, 208, 209, 242
Colooney, Ireland 46
Colsterworth, L 255
Coltishall, Nf 256
Colworth, Sx 189
Colyton, D 156, 227, 251
Compiègne, France 211
Compton, Sr 205, 252
Connaille, Ireland 46, 73
Connacht, Ireland 46, 47, 73
Connemara, Ireland 46
Condé, France 47, 62, 63, 208
Condé sur L'Escaut, France 211
Cong, Ireland 73
Congresbury, So 227, 245, 251
Conisholme, L 258
Connor, Ireland 73
Conway River 70
Cookham, Brk 162, 252
Copford, Ess 165
Copplestone, D 250
Coquet Island, Nb 246
Corbie, France 211, 242
Corbridge, Nb 87, 95
Corby, Nth 188
Corfe, Do 161, 227
Corhampton, Ha 252
Cork, Ireland 46, 73
Cornwall 50, 59, 88, 147, 241
Corringham, L 258
Corsham, W 227
Cosham, Ha 125, 162, 228
Cotentin, France 47
Coutances, France 210
Coutrai, Belgium 47, 62, 211
Coventry, Wa 205, 231, 243, 246, 249, 255
Cowbit, L 255
Craeb Tulcha, Ireland 73
Cranbourne, Do 243, 246, 249, 251
Cranfield, Bd 188
Cranwell, L 255
Cranwich, Nf 256
Cray River 229
Crayford, K 229
Crayke, NRY 188, 258
Crediton, D 161, 226, 240, 241, 250, 260
Creech St Michael, So 197
Creeton, L 255
Crewkerne, So 148, 187, 217, 223, 224, 227, 251
Cricket, So 188
Cricklade, W 15, 83, 149, 150, 152, 187
Croft, Du 258
Crondall, Ha 148
Crowland (Croyland), L 17, 231, 243, 245, 246, 249, 255
Crowle, L 258
Croydon, Sr 145, 229
Cuckhamsley, Brk 119, 164, 228
Cuerdale, La 233
Cullompton, D 148, 251

Cumbria 103, 115
Cundall, WRY 258
Curry, So 199, 227
Cutsdean, Wo 178
Cuxwold, L 258
Cynibre 23

Dadsley, WRY 234
Dagenham, Ess 140, 229
Daglingworth, Gl 254
Dal Cais, Ireland 73
Dal Rista, Ireland 73
Dalar, Iceland 74
Dalby, Sweden 71
Dalriada, Scotland 46
Damarham, Ha 148, 159
Danelaw 47
Darent River 229
Darenth, K 253
Dart River 226
Dartmoor 226
Dartmouth, D 226
Datchet, Brk 205
Davenport, Ch 97, 233
Dawlish, D 189
Dax, France 208, 209, 210
Daylesford, Wo 178
Dean, Ha 23, 148
Dean, Sx 116, 147, 148, 228
Dean, Forest of 230
Debenham, Sf 256
Dee River 135, 230, 233
Deerhurst, Gl 143, 178, 230, 243, 246, 254
Deganwy, Wales 42
Deheubarth, Wales 131, 133
Deira 41
Deisi, Ireland 73
Denbury, D 226
Dengie, Ess 140
Derby 68, 91, 102, 123, 215, 216, 217, 223, 224, 231, 245, 247, 255
Dernford, Ca 197
Derry, Ireland 46, 73
Derwent River, Db 231
Derwent River, Yorkshire 41, 234
Desborough, Nth 255
Desmuma, Ireland 73
Deux Jumeux, France 210
Deventer, Netherlands 242
Devils Ditch 232
Devon 47, 159
Dewchurch, He 254
Dewsbury, WRY 258
Dewstan 41
Dibberford, Do 166
Diddlebury, Sa 254
Dijon, France 210
Dikkevenne, Belgium 242
Dinant, Belgium 208, 211
Dingley, Nth 205
Dinn Rig, Ireland 73
Ditchling, Sx 146
Dives, France 46
Dokkum, Netherlands 242
Dollar, Scotland 47
Dolton, D 250
Domburg, Netherlands 202, 203
Domnoc, Sf 253
Don River 234
Donaghmore, Ireland 47
Doncaster, WRY 234
Donemuthan 46
Doniert Stone, Co 250
Dorchester, Do 146, 155, 205, 215, 217, 223, 224, 227, 235
Dorchester on Thames, O 41, 70, 159, 205, 228, 239, 240, 241, 247, 260
Dore, Db 43, 102
Dore River 132
Dorestadt, Netherlands 46, 50, 52, 56, 201, 202, 203, 208, 209, 210
Dorset 125, 159
Doulton, So 227
Dover, K 215, 217, 223, 224, 229, 234, 235, 247, 253
Dowdeswell, Gl 178
Downpatrick, Ireland 47, 73
Downton, W 159, 252
Drangajokull, Iceland 74
Drangar, Iceland 74
Drayton, Brk 197
Drayton, Mddx 165
Droitwich, Wo 70, 189, 199, 230
Dromin, Ireland 46
Dromiskin, Ireland 46
Dromore, Ireland 73
Drumcliff, Ireland 73
Dublin, Ireland 46, 47, 51, 52, 54, 59, 73, 95, 103
Dudley, St 230
Duisburg, Germany 62, 63
Dulane, Ireland 47
Duleek, Ireland 47
Dumbarton, Scotland 41, 47, 56, 57
Dungeness 21
Dungiven, Ireland 73
Dunham, Nt 234
Dunkeld, Scotland 46, 47, 245
Dunmore, Ireland 47
Dunmow, Ess 165
Dunseverick, Ireland 47
Dunstable, Bd 205
Duntisbourne, Gl 254
Dunwich, Sf 41, 238, 259
Durrow, Ireland 73
Durham 119, 235, 245, 247, 260, 269
Dyfed, Wales 88, 103, 116, 130
Dykes 83
Dyle River 47, 64
Dymock, Gl 254
Dyrham, Gl 227

Eaglesfield, Cu 58, 67
Eagleton, Lei 255
Eamont, We 99, 155
Eardene 23
Earls Barton, Nth 255
Earls Colne, Ess 253
Eashing, Sr 148, 149, 150, 152, 228, 235
East Anglia 41, 46, 47, 60, 94, 122
East Bridgeford, Nt 255
East Dereham, Nf 232
East Engle 136, 138
East Firths, Iceland 74
East Grinstead, Sr 188
East Horn, Iceland 74
East Kennet, W 228
East Langdon, K 253
East Lexham, Nf 256
East Meon, Ha 252
East Pennard, So 251
East Saxons 41, 140
East Sexena 136, 138
East Willa 136, 138
East Wixna 136, 138
Eastcote, Wa 205
Easton, Ha 197
Eastry, K 19, 229, 253
Ebbsfleet, K 19
Echternach, Luxemburg 242
Edenham, L 255
Eddisbury, Ch 88, 233, 235
Edgeworth, Gl 254
Edington, W 47, 146, 148, 157, 160, 227
Eichstatt, Germany 242
Eidsborg, Norway 201
Einsiedeln, Germany 244
Elagh, Ireland 47
Ellendun, W 43, 228
Elmedesætna 136, 138
Elmet 23, 41
Elmham, Nf 238, 240, 241, 247, 259, 260
Elmstone Hardwick, Gl 254
Elsloo, Netherlands 47, 62
Elsted, Sx 252
Elton, Nth 255
Ely, Ca 17, 18, 41, 162, 232, 243, 246, 249, 256
Ely, Isle of 18
Emly, Ireland 73
Emstrey, Sa 254
En-Ema, Ireland 47
Englefield, Brk 228
Enknach, Austria 242
Eognacht, Ireland 73
Eorpeburnan, Sx 21, 149, 150, 152, 229, 235
Epsom, Sr 147, 229
Erfurt, Germany 242
Ermine Street 139, 231
Erquy, France 201
Eskilstuna, Sweden 71
Essex 47, 93, 120, 122
Ettenheimmünster, Germany 242
Evegate, K 197
Evenlode River 228
Everleigh, W 146
Evesham, Wo 230, 243, 245, 246, 249, 254
Evreux, France 46, 211
Ewen, W 197
Ewenny, Wales 251
Ewyas, He 143, 230
Ewyas Harold, He 230
Exe River 227
Exeter, D 15, 47, 59, 60, 99, 117, 149, 150, 152, 154, 155, 199, 213, 215, 216, 217, 223, 224, 227, 235, 241, 243, 245, 247, 251
Exminster, D 148, 251
Exmoor 226
Exning, Sf 232
Eyam, Db 258
Eye, Sf 232, 256

Eyja Fjord, Iceland 74
Eynsham, O 228, 243, 246, 249, 252
Eyrar, Iceland 74

Faerpinga 136, 138
Fairford, Gl 228
Fakenham, Sf 256
Falun, Sweden 71
Fareham, Ha 252
Faringdon, Brk 252
Farley, Ha 164
Farndon, Ch 154, 233, 257
Farndon, Nt 67
Farne Islands 41
Farnham, Sr 60, 228, 252
Farningham, K 205
Faroes 46, 78
Faverney, France 242
Faversham, K 146, 155, 189, 229, 253
Fawsley, Nth 255
Faxa Floi, Iceland 74
Felpham, Sx 148
Fennor, Ireland 46
Fens 9, 121
Feppingas 41
Ferns, Ireland 46, 73
Ferring, Sx 252
Fetcham, Sr 252
Filey, NRY 258
Finland 71
Five Boroughs 47
Fladbury, Wo 143, 254
Flanders 46
Flat Holm 227
Flatatunga, Iceland 74
Flavigny, France 242
Fleam Ditch 232
Fletton, Hu 255
Fleury, France 56, 242, 244
Flixton, Sf 256
Florence, Italy 208
Folkestone, K 109, 229, 253
Folkingham, L 231
Folkton, ERY 258
Forach 46
Fordrun, Scotland 99
Fordwich, K 19, 229
Forncett, Nf 256
Fortrenn, Scotland 46, 56
Fortriu, Scotland 46, 47
Foss Dyke 15, 139
Foss Way 139, 227, 230, 231
Foston, Lei 255
Fowey River 226
Framlingham, Sf 205, 232
Framlingham Earl, Nf 256
Framlingham Pigot, Nf 256
Framsden, Sf 256
Franconia 242
Frankley, Wo 254
Freising, Germany 242
Freshwater, Ha 252
Frisia 46, 47, 49, 52, 242
Fritzlar, Germany 242
Frodsham, Ch 257
Frome, So 155, 158, 187, 218, 223, 224, 227, 251
Frome River, Do 114, 125, 227
Frosta, Norway 71
Fulda, Germany 242
Fulford, ERY 234
Fulham, Middx 140, 165, 228, 229
Fussen, Germany 242
Fyn, Denmark 71
Fyrkat, Denmark

Gabran, Ireland 73
Gadshill, K 160, 229
Gainsborough, L 123, 124, 234
Galford, D 43, 226
Galicia, Spain 53
Galloway, Scotland 103
Garonne River 46, 56
Garton on the Wolds, ERY 205, 234
Garway, He 254
Gateshead, Du 41
Gayton Thorpe, Nf 256
Geddington, Nth 255
Gengenbach, Germany 242
Gent, France 242
Ghent, Belgium 46, 47, 49, 52, 54, 62, 211, 242, 244
Gifla 136, 138
Gillingham, Do 162, 227, 251
Gillings, NRY 41, 234
Gissing, Nf 256
Givoldi Fosse, France 46, 52
Glama, Iceland 74
Glamorgan, Wales 46, 49
Glasbury, Wales 230, 254
Glascwm, Wales 253
Glastonbury, So 22, 129, 145, 146, 156, 158, 159, 160, 227, 243, 244, 245, 246, 249, 251
Glaumbaer, Iceland 74
Glen, Lei 74
Glen Foichle, Ireland 46
Glen Mama, Ireland 73
Glen River 41
Glendalough, Ireland 46, 73
Glentworth, L 258
Gloucester 15, 47, 59, 70, 84, 88, 132, 133, 134, 143, 155, 160, 169, 178, 188, 200, 213, 215, 217, 223, 224, 230, 235, 243, 245, 246, 249
Gloucestershire 171, 173, 178
Glywysing, Wales 70, 227
Godalming, Sr 148, 252
Goddalir, Iceland 74
Gokstad, Norway 71
Golan, Co 250
Golden Valley, He 132
Gomersal, WRY 234
Gooderstone, Nf 67
Goodmanham, ERY 41, 234
Gorza, France 242, 244
Gosbeck, Sf 256
Gothenburg, Sweden 71
Gotland, Sweden 71
Granard, Ireland 73
Grantchester, Ca 41, 232
Grantham, L 231, 255
Grately, Ha 155, 228
Graveney, K 229
Great Bowden, Lei 231
Great Casterton, Ru 188
Great Dunham, Nf 256
Great Glen, Lei 231, 255
Great Hale, L 255
Great Hallingbury, Ess 253
Great Ouse River 82, 83, 231, 232
Great Ryburgh, Nf 256
Great Shelford, Ca 256
Great Stour River 229
Great Tey, Ess 253
Green's Norton, Nth 255
Greensted, Ess 253
Greenwich, K 122, 123, 124, 127, 229
Greetham, L 234
Greetwell, L 258
Grenoble, France 242
Gressingham, La 257
Gretton, Nth 188
Grimsey, Iceland 74
Guestwick, Nf 256
Guildford, Sr 15, 148, 199, 217, 223, 224, 228, 235, 252
Guist, Nf 197
Guiting, Gl 178
Guli, Norway 71
Gumby, Lei 145
Gwent, Wales 70, 130, 227
Gwenydd, Wales 47, 103, 130
Gyrwe 41

Hackness, NRY 41
Haddenham, Bk 252
Haddiscoe, Nf 256
Heddiscoe Thorpe, Nf 256
Hadleigh, Ess 165
Hadrian's Wall 41
Hadstock, Ess 253
Hainton, L 258
Hales, Nf 256
Halesworth, Sf 256
Halford, Wo 178
Hallow, Wo 197
Halton, La 257
Halwell, D 149, 150, 152, 226, 235
Ham, France 211
Hamble River 41
Hambledon, Ha 252
Hamburg, Germany 46, 52
Hampnett, Gl 178
Hampshire 114, 117, 120, 159, 164, 199
Hamsey, Sx 155, 229
Hanbury, Wo 143, 254
Hanley Castle, Wo 254
Hanney, Brk 197
Hannington, Ha 252
Hardham, Sx 252
Hardwick, Bk 252
Harford, Gl 145, 178, 197
Harmston, L 255
Harpswell, L 258
Harrow, Middx 228
Harroway 199
Hartland, D 148, 247, 250
Hartlepool, Du 41
Hastingleigh, K 197
Hastings, Sx 122, 150, 152, 215, 217, 223, 224, 229

Hatfield, Hrt 41, 229, 234
Haukadal, Iceland 74
Haverhill, Sf 229
Hawarden, Wales 233
Headbourne Worthy, Ha 252
Headington, O 162, 252
Heapham, L 258
Heathfeldland 136, 138
Heathfield 139
Heavenfield 41
Hebrides 46, 47
Hedeby, Germany 46, 71, 202
Heigham, Nf 256
Hekla, Iceland 74
Helgo, Sweden 71, 203
Hellesdon, Nf 232
Hemel Hempstead, Hrt 140, 205
Hemingstone, Sf 256
Hendrica 136, 138
Henlow, Bd 255
Hentland, He 254
Herefinna 136, 138
Hereford 15, 68, 70, 88, 99, 132, 134, 135, 143, 155, 199, 215, 217, 223, 224, 230, 235, 238, 239, 240, 241, 245, 247, 254, 259, 260
Herefordshire 134, 171, 173
Herringfleet, Sf 256
Hersfeld, Germany 242
Herstmonceux, Sx 253
Hertford 15, 41, 47, 68, 85, 86, 215, 216, 217, 223, 224, 229
Hertfordshire 122
Hertingfordbury, Hrt 253
Hesket, Cu 67
Hesse, Germany 242
Hessle, WRY 252
Heversham, La 257
Hewish, Do 166
Hexham, Nb 41, 238, 239, 259
Heysham, La 67, 257
Heytesbury, W 251
Hicca 136, 138
Hickling, Nt 255
Hidcote Boyce, Gl 178
Highclere, Ha 161
Highworth, W 252
Hinckley, Lei 231
Hingston Down, Co 43, 46, 50, 226
Hinton, Gl 178
Hinton Ampner, Ha 252
Hisau, Germany 244
Hitchin, Hrt 205, 255
Hjorleifshofdi, Iceland 74
Hlidrendi, Iceland 74
Hockerton, Nt 231
Hohenburg, Germany 242
Holar, Iceland 74
Holborough, K 197
Holcombe Rogus, D 166
Holland, Ess 165
Holme 47, 83
Holton le Clay, L 258
Holy River, Sweden 71
Holyhead, Wales 47
Holzkirchen, Germany 242
Hona, Germany 242
Hoo, K 145, 229
Hook Norton, O 47
Hope under Dinmore, He 230
Hordaland, Norway 71
Horn, Iceland 74
Hornbach, Germany 242
Hornby, NRY 258
Horncastle, L 139, 217, 224, 235
Horndon, Ess 220, 223, 224, 229, 253
Horning, La 257
Horsley, Gl 251
Horton, Do 243, 246, 249, 251
Houdain, France 201
Hough on the Hill, L 255
Houghton on the Hill, Nf 256
Houghton Regis, Bd 205
Hovingham, NRY 257
Howe, Nf 256
Howth, Ireland 46
Hoxne, Sf 46, 58, 232, 256
Hull River 234
Humber River 41, 102, 111, 123, 139, 234
Huna Floi, Iceland 74
Hunsbury, Nth 205
Huntingdon 17, 93, 216, 217, 223, 224, 231
Huntingdonshire 122, 126, 171, 173
Hurstbourne, Ha 148
Husavik, Iceland 74
Huy, Belgium 211
Hvita River, Iceland 74
Hwiccawudu 23
Hwicce 41, 141, 142
Hwinca 136, 138
Hythe, K 220, 223, 224, 229

Iceland 46, 47, 78
Icombe, Wo 178
Ickleton, Ca 253
Icknield Way 228, 232
Idle River 41, 234
Ilchester, So 15, 187, 199, 205, 217, 223, 224, 227, 235, 251
Ile de Groix, France 66
Ilkley, WRY 257
Ilminster, So 251
Ilmmünster, Germany 242
Imleach, Ireland 46
Ingleby, NRY 67
Inglesham, W 252
Ingolfshofdi, Iceland 74
Inworth, Ess 253
Inis Daimhle, Ireland 46
Inis Mochta, Ireland 47
Inis Patrick, Ireland 46
Inismurray, Ireland 46
Iona, Scotland 46, 47, 49
Ipswich, Sf 109, 121, 205, 217, 223, 224, 229
Irchester, Nth 205
Irthlingborough, Nth 145, 231
Isen, Germany 242
Islington, Mddx 165
Ismere, Wo 143, 254
Isore, Denmark 71
Itchen River 228
Iwerne Minster, Do 251
Iver, Bk 252
Ixworth, Sf 232
Jamtland, Sweden 71
Jarrow, Du 41
Jelling, Denmark 71
Jeufosse, France 46, 55
Jevington, Sx 253
Jokulsa River, Iceland 74
Jutland, Denmark 71

Kaiserwerth, Germany 242
Kalmar, Sweden 71
Karlburg, Germany 242
Katja, Iceland 74
Kattegat 71
Katzis, Switzerland 242
Kaupang, Norway 71
Kells, Ireland 47, 73
Kelston, So 251
Kemerton, Gl 178
Kempsey, Wo 254
Kempsford, Gl 228
Kempten, Germany 242
Kemsing, K 197
Kenchester, He 230
Kennet River 228
Kent 41, 46, 47, 93, 120, 122, 148, 159
Kerns, Ireland 47
Kessling, Germany 242
Kettering, Nth 231
Keynsham, So 251
Kidderminster, Wo 254
Kidjsberg, Iceland 74
Kildale 67
Kildare, Ireland 46, 47, 73
Killala, Ireland 73
Killaloe, Ireland 73
Killcullen, Ireland 47
Kilmacrenan, Ireland 73
Kilmersdon, So 251
Kilmore, Ireland 47, 73
Kilnsea, ERY 258
Kilpeck, He 254
Kilton, So 148, 227
Kings Enham, Ha 162, 228
Kings Somborne, Ha 252
Kings Sutton, Nth 231
Kingsbury, Middx 252
Kingsclere, Ha 159, 252
Kingsdown, K 253
Kingsteignton, D 226
Kingston upon Thames, Sr 146, 155, 157, 158, 160, 163, 228, 252, 253
Kinley, Gl 251
Kinsham, Wo 197
Kintbury, Brk 252
Kintyre, Scotland 46
Kirby Hill, WRY 258
Kirby Ireleth, La 257
Kirby Kane, Nf 256
Kirby Kendal, We 257
Kirby Lonsdale, La 257
Kirby Underdale, ERY 258
Kirk Hammerton, WRY 258
Kirkdale, NRY 258
Kirkjubaer, Iceland 74
Kirklevington, NRY 258
Kirtlington, O 161, 228
Kitzingen, Germany 242

Kjalarnes, Iceland 74
Kjol, Iceland 74
Kneeswell, Nt 255
Knook, W 251
Knowth, Ireland 47, 73
Kolding, Denmark 71

Ladby, Denmark 71
Lagarfljot, Iceland 74
Lagore, Ireland 47, 73
Laigin = Leinster
Laindon, Ess 165
Lambeth, Sr 168
Lambey Island, Ireland 46
Lambourn, Brk 148
Lancaster 233, 257
Lancing, Sx 205
Landeyjar, Iceland 74
Langaness, Iceland 74
Langford, Bd 205
Langford, O 252
Langres, France 208, 210, 242
Langport, So 150, 152, 187, 215, 217, 223, 224, 227
Lanivet, Co 250
Laon, France 62, 208, 211, 242
Larkstoke, Gl 178
Lastingham, NRY 41, 234, 258
Launceston, Co 217, 223, 224, 226, 247
Laughton on le Morthen, ERY 258
Lausanne, Switzerland 242
Lavendon, Bk 255
Laverstoke, Ha 252
Le Mans, France 46, 56, 57, 208, 210
Le Mont Lassois, France 210
Le Puy, France 242
Le Talou, France 211
Lea River 15, 47, 61, 64, 229
Lea River, Ireland 73
Leadon River 143
Leatherhead, Brk 164
Leckhamstead, Brk 164
Lechlade, Gl 178
Ledbury, He 254
Ledsham, WRY 258
Leeds K 253
Leeds, WRY 41, 234, 258
Leicester 87, 91, 95, 102, 123, 142, 145, 199, 213, 215, 217, 223, 224, 231, 238, 247, 255, 259
Leighlin, Ireland 47
Leighton Buzzard, Bk 231, 255
Leinster, Ireland 47, 103
Lens, France 211
Leominster, He 131, 132, 143, 245, 246, 249, 254
Leonard Stanley, Gl 254
Lerins, France 237
Letheringsett, Nf 256
Leven, ERY 258
Levisham, NRY 258
Lewes, Sx 150, 152, 215, 217, 223, 224, 229, 235, 253
Lexworthy, So 188
Lichfield, St 41, 70, 142, 145, 230, 238, 239, 240, 241, 245, 247, 259, 260
Liège, Belgium 47, 208
Liffey River, Ireland 73
Lifton, D 148, 149, 155, 226, 235
Lilleshall, Sa 254
Limen River 21
Limerick, Ireland 47, 52, 73
Limpley Stoke, W 251
Lincoln 15, 17, 41, 68, 123, 139, 200, 213, 216, 217, 223, 224, 234, 255, 258
Lincolnshire 126
Lindes farona 136, 138
Lindisfarne, Nb 41, 46, 49, 238, 259
Lindsey 41, 46, 111, 124, 139, 238, 259, 260
Linkoping, Sweden 71
Lisbon, Portugal 53
Lisieux, France 211
Liskeard, Co 226
Lismore, Ireland 47, 73
Lissett, ERY 258
Little Bardfield, Ess 253
Little Bradley, Sf 256
Little Bytham, L 255
Little Compton, Gl 178
Little Driffield, ERY 258
Little Hallingbury, Ess 253
Little Shelford, Ca 256
Little Snoring, Nf 256
Little Sombourne, Ha 252
Littleborough, L 41, 234
Littleborough, Nth 139
Littleport, Ca 18
Ljungby, Sweden 71
Llamain, Ireland 73
Llanbadarn, Wales 230
Llanbadarn Fawr, Wales 130
Llancarfan, Wales 251
Llandaff, Wales 227, 251
Llandinam, Wales 254
Llandoga, Wales 254
Llandough, Wales 251
Llanelwy, Wales 256
Llangattock, Wales 230
Llangorse, Wales 230, 254
Llanhaedr, Wales 254
Llansilin, Wales 254
Llanwit, Wales 251
Llanynys, Wales 257
Llyn, Wales 47
Loch Derg, Ireland 73
Loch Lein, Ireland 73
Loire River, France 47, 54, 55, 62
Londesborough, ERY 258
London 15, 41, 46, 47, 51, 54, 58, 68, 70, 110, 112, 120, 122, 123, 124, 126, 127, 128, 129, 140, 145, 147, 155, 156, 160, 162, 163, 169, 199, 200, 205, 213, 215, 216, 217, 223, 224, 229, 235, 238, 239, 240, 241, 245, 253, 259, 260
London Way 199
Long Ashton, So 251
Long Melford, Sf 253
Long Sutton, L 256
Longstock, Ha 197
Longton, ERY 234
Lorch, Austria 242
Lorrha, Ireland 46
Lorsch, Germany 242
Lothian, Scotland 103
Lough Candin, Ireland 46
Lough Corrib, Ireland 47, 73
Lough Cuan, Ireland 47
Lough Erne, Ireland 47, 73
Lough Febhail, Ireland 46
Lough Foyle, Ireland 73
Lough Neagh, Ireland 73
Lough Ree, Ireland 47
Louth, L 46, 73, 139, 234
Louth, Ireland 73
Louvain, Belgium 47, 63
Lower Halstow, K 253
Lowthorpe, ERY 258
Lucca, Italy 208, 209
Luimneach = Limerick 73
Lulham, He 254
Lullingstone, K 253
Lund, Sweden 71
Luneburg Heath, Germany 47, 62
Lusby, L 255
Lusca, Ireland 46
Lustleigh, D 148
Luton, Bd 87, 255
Luttich, Belgium 242
Lutton, Nth 255
Lutzelau, Switzerland 242
Luzern, Switzerland 242
Lydbury North, Sa 254
Lydd, K 253
Lydford, D 113, 149, 150, 152, 217, 223, 224, 226, 235
Lyme, D 189
Lyme Hall, Ch 257
Lyminge, K 188, 229, 253
Lyminster, Sx 148, 155, 228, 252
Lympne, K 47, 60, 64, 205, 217, 223, 224, 229, 253
Lyon, France 208, 210, 237, 242
Lyng, So 149, 150, 152, 227, 235

Maas River 242
Maastricht, Netherlands 208, 211, 242
Macclesfield, Ch 257
Machaway, Wales 133
Macon, France 242
Maes Rhosmeilion, Wales 83
Magnadair, Ireland 73
Magnis (Kenchester), He 143
Magonsætan 141
Maidstone, K 253
Mainz, Germany 208, 209, 242
Maldon, Ess 47, 86, 90, 93, 107, 109, 215, 217, 223, 224, 229, 235
Malmedy, Belgium 242
Malmesbury, W 41, 147, 149, 150, 152, 187, 217, 223, 224, 227, 235, 243, 246, 249, 251
Malton, Ca 205
Malung, Sweden 71
Man, Isle of 41, 115
Manchester, La 96, 205, 233
Mangarit, Ireland 46
Mansbridge, Ha 199
Mappleton, ERY 234
Market Overton, Lei 255
Marlborough, W 187, 205, 228
Marne River 46, 63
Marseilles, France 208, 209, 237

Marton, L 258
Masham, NRY 258
Masmunster, France 242
Mathrafal, Wales 230
Maubeuge, France 211
Maugersbury, Gl 178
Maurienne, France 242
Maursmunster, France 242
Mawgan Porth, Co 226
Mayen, Germany 201, 202
Mayo, Ireland 73
Mears Ashby, Nth 255
Meath, *see* Midhe, Ireland 46
Meaux, France 46, 56, 63, 209, 211, 242
Medway River 229
Meifod, Wales 254
Meirakkaslesta, Iceland 74
Melbourne, Db 231
Melbury Bubb, Do 251
Melbury Osmund, Do 251
Meldreth, Ca 253
Melksham, W 251
Melle, France 52, 209, 210
Melling, La 257
Melrose, Scotland 41
Melton, Nf 256
Melton Mowbray, Lei 231, 255
Melun, France 46, 56, 210
Menappes, Belgium 47
Mendip, So 227
Menevia, *see* St Davids
Meols, Ch 15, 205
Meon, Ha 148
Meonware 41
Mercia 41, 42, 46, 47, 100, 119, 147, 157
Mere, W 251
Mereworth, K 146, 229
Mersea, Ess 60, 61, 64, 229
Mersey River 233
Metlach, Luxemburg 242
Metten, Germany 242
Metz, France 208, 209, 210, 242
Meuse River 47
Micheldever, Ha 146, 228
Middle Angles 41
Middlesex 41, 122, 140
Middleton, NRY 258
Middlewich, Ch 189, 233
Midhe, *see* Meath, Ireland 47, 73
Milan, Italy 208, 209
Milbourne, D 148
Milbourne Port, So 187, 217, 223, 224, 227
Milbourne St Andrew, Do 197
Milfield, Nb 41
Millbrook, Ha 197
Milton, Do 243, 245, 246, 251
Milton, K 47, 60, 64, 155, 205, 229
Milton Abbas, Do 227
Milton Regis, K 253
Milverton, So 187
Minster, K 19, 205, 246, 253
Minster in Sheppey, K 253
Minster Lovell, O 252
Miserden, Gl 254
Misterton, Lei 255
Misterton, Nt 258
Mitton, Wo 178
Moccas, He 254
Moerheb 23
Mondsee, Austria 242
Monk Fryston, WRY 258
Monkwearmouth, Du 41, 46, 49
Monmouth, Wales 230, 254
Monmow River 132
Mons, Belgium 211
Montfaucon, France 47, 63
Moreton, He 254
Moreton in the Marsh, Gl 178
Moreton Pinkney, Nth 255
Morienval, France 211
Morning Thorpe, Nf 256
Morton, Nf 256
Morville, Sa 247, 254
Morganwg, Wales 130
Mosbach, Germany 242
Mosfell, Iceland 74
Mottisfont, Ha 252
Moulton, Nth 255
Moustiers, France 242
Mouzon, France 211
Muchelney, So 246, 249, 251
Mucking, Ess 188
Mumha, *see* Munster
Munster, Ireland 46, 47, 73
Murbach, France 242
Mydalls Jokull, Iceland 74
Mylor, Co 250
Myrar, Iceland 74
Myrcenes landes 136, 138
Myvatn, Iceland 74

Nackington, K 197
Nadder, W 146
Namur, Belgium 211
Nantes, France 46, 51, 54, 209, 210
Nantua, France 242
Nantwich, Ch 189, 233
Narbonne, France 208, 209, 210
Nas, Ireland 46, 73
Nassington, Nth 255
Navestock, Ess 165
Naze 229
Neasden, Mddx 165
Nene River 15, 17, 231, 232
Neston, Ch 257
Nether Wallop, Ha 252
Netheravon, W 252
Nettleton, L 258
Neuburg, Germany 242
Neuss, Germany 56
Neuweiter, France 242
Nevers, France 210, 242
New Alresford, Ha 252
New Minster, Winchester 159, 243, 245, 246
Newark, Nt 216, 217, 223, 224, 231
Newburgh, NRY 258
Newent, Gl 254
Newfoundland 78
Newington, K 253
Newnham, Nth 197
Newport, Bk 223, 225, 231
Newport, Wales 251
Newton, Nf 256
Nidaros, Norway 71
Nidd River 41, 234
Niebla, Spain 53
Niederaltlich, Germany 242, 244
Nieuport, Belgium 46
Nijmegen, Netherlands 62
Nimes, France 210
Nivelles, Belgium 211
Noirmoutier, France 46, 50, 52
Norden, Germany 63
Nordra River, Iceland 74
Nore River, Ireland 73
Normanby, L 205
Normandy, France 47, 115, 123
North Crawley, Bk 255
North Curry, So 251
North Downs 229
North Elmham, Nf 232, 256
North Frodingham, ERY 258
North Gyrwa 136, 138
North Leigh, O 252
North Mouth 19
North Petherton, So 251
North Walsham, Nf 232, 256
North Waltham, Ha 228
North York Moors 234
Northampton 15, 87, 91, 93, 102, 121, 205, 216, 217, 223, 225, 231, 255
Northamptonshire 122, 126, 171, 173
Northchurch, Hrt 252
Northey, Ess 107
Northfleet, K 253
Northwich, Ch 189, 233
Northumbria 41, 47, 58, 59, 60, 157
Norwich 15, 68, 118, 200, 205, 215, 216, 217, 223, 225, 232, 256
Notgrove, Gl 178, 197
Nottingham 15, 46, 47, 58, 67, 68, 95, 97, 99, 123, 145, 155, 160, 199, 215, 217, 223, 225, 231
Novaleze, France 242
Noxgaga 136, 138
Noyon, France 46, 47, 55, 211, 242
Nuits, Germany 46
Nunburnholme, ERY 258
Nunnaminster, Winchester 159, 245, 246
Nunney, So 251
Nursling, Ha 228, 252
Nyetimber, Sx 252

Oakley, Ha 146
Ochsenfurt, Germany 242
Oddi, Iceland 74
Odense, Denmark 71
Odstock, W 161
Offa's Dyke 135, 230
Offaly, Ireland 47
Offerthun, L 189
Ohrdurf, Germany 242
Ohtgaga 136, 138
Oise, River 47
Oissel, France 46, 55
Oland, Sweden 71
Old Minster, Winchester 158, 159, 243, 245, 246
Old Romney, K 21
Old Sarum, W 205, 235

Old Shoreham, Sx 252
Olfusa River, Iceland 74
Oppland, Sweden 71
Oraefa Jokull, Iceland 74
Orihuela, Spain 53
Orkney 46
Orleans, France 46, 54, 55, 56, 57, 209, 210
Ormond, Ireland 46
Ormside, La 67
Orpington, K 253
Orsett, Ess 163
Orwell River 128
Oseberg, Norway 71
Oslo, Norway 71
Osraige = Ossory, Ireland 73
Ossory, Ireland 47, 103
Oswaldkirk, NRY 258
Oswestry, Sa 41, 230, 247
Otford, K 128, 229
Otley, WRY 234, 258
Ottobeuren, Germany 242
Oundle, Nth 41, 231, 245, 255
Ouse River, Sx 15, 229
Ousel River 82, 231
Overton, Ha 228
Owless, Ireland 46
Oxara, Iceland 74
Oxford 15, 68, 120, 123, 125, 150, 152, 154, 162, 163, 167, 200, 215, 216, 217, 223, 225, 228, 245, 252
Oxfordshire 121, 122, 171, 173, 178
Ozingell, K 205

Paddlesworth, K 253
Padstow, Co 226, 249
Padworth, Brk 197
Pagham, Sx 252
Pamplona, Spain 53
Panborough, So 196
Pant River 41
Papey, Iceland 74
Papos, Iceland 74
Paris, France 46, 47, 52, 55, 56, 63, 209, 211, 242
Parma, Italy 208
Parrett River 22, 46, 52, 227
Partney, L 41, 139, 232, 256
Pas de Calais 46
Passau, Germany 242
Passenham, Bk 93, 231
Pattishall, Nth 255
Pavia, Italy 208, 209
Peaclond 23
Peakirk, Nth 243, 246, 255
Pecsætna 136, 138
Pegglesworth, Gl 178
Pencader, Wales 130
Penkridge, St 146, 160, 230, 247
Pennant, Wales 254
Penselwood, So 127, 227
Pentlow, Ess 253
Pentyrch, Wales 227
Penwortham, La 233
Perigueux, France 46, 52, 56
Peronne, France 211, 242
Pershore, Wo 143, 220, 223, 225, 230, 243, 246, 249, 254
Peterborough, Nth 17, 18, 41, 145, 217, 223, 225, 231, 243, 245, 246, 249, 255
Peterstow, He 254
Petherton, So 220, 223, 225, 227
Pevensey, Sx 20, 229
Pewsey, W 148, 252
Pfafers, Switzerland 242
Pickhill, NRY 258
Pierrepont, France 211
Pilton, D 149, 150, 152, 226, 235
Pinhoe, D 116, 226
Pinnock, Gl 178
Pisa, Italy 208
Pitminster, So 251
Pitres, France 66
Plaish, Sa 142
Plympton, D 250
Pocklington, ERY 234
Poitiers, France 46, 54, 56
Poitou, France 46, 57
Polesworth, St 245, 246, 255
Poling, Sx 252
Pont de l'Arche, France 46, 56
Pontesbury, Sa 230, 247
Ponts de Cé, France 56
Port Lairge, Ireland 73
Portchester, Ha 149, 150, 152, 228, 235
Portisham, Do 197
Portland, Do 46, 49
Portskewett, Wales 134, 227
Potterne, W 251
Powys, Wales 42, 130
Prestbury, Ch 257
Prestbury, Gl 178
Presteigne, He 254
Preston Wye, He 254
Prittleswell, Ess 253
Privett, Ha 228
Prum, Germany 47, 62, 242
Pucklechurch, Gl 156, 188, 227
Puddletown, Do 161, 227
Pwll Dyfech, Wales 130
Pyecombe, Sx 205
Pyrford, Sr 197

Quarley, Ha 252
Quarr, Ha 200
Quatford, Sa 230
Quentovic, France 46, 51, 209
Quidenham, Nf 256

Radwinter, Ess 196
Rainham, K 229
Raith Bile, Ireland 73
Rampside, La 67
Rampton, Ca 256
Ramsbury, W 228, 240, 241, 252, 260
Ramsey, Hu 17, 18, 231, 243, 245, 246, 249, 255
Raphoe, Ireland 73
Rastrick, WRY 257
Rathangen, Ireland 73
Rathmulcah, Ireland 73
Ratisbon, Germany 244
Rayleigh, Ess 229
Reading, Brk 47, 58, 67, 205, 220, 223, 225, 228, 252
Reculver, K 15, 19, 41, 49, 197, 205, 229, 253
Redbridge, Ha 41, 199, 252
Reed, Hrt 253, 255
Regensburg, Germany 209, 242
Reichenau, Germany 242
Rendelsham, Sf 41, 232
Rennes, France 208, 209, 210
Repton, Db 47, 59, 67, 142, 145, 205, 231, 245, 255
Rethondes, France 211
Revin, France 242
Reyda Fjord, Iceland 74
Reykjanes, Iceland 74
Reykjavik, Iceland 74
Rheims, France 47, 62, 63, 208, 209, 211, 242
Rhine 46
Rhone River 46, 242
Rhuddlan, Wales 133, 233
Rhyd y Groes, Wales 130, 230
Ribble River 233
Ribe, Denmark 71, 203
Riccall, ERY 234
Richborough, K 19, 41, 205
Ringmere, Nf 121, 232
Ringsted, Denmark 71
Ripon, WRY 41, 99, 234, 245, 247, 258
Risborough, Bk 70, 228
Rochester, K 41, 46, 47, 51, 63, 115, 162, 198, 199, 205, 215, 217, 223, 225, 229, 235, 238, 239, 240, 241, 245, 247, 253, 259, 260
Rockland, Nf 256
Roda, France 209
Roermond, Netherlands 242
Rokleiv, Norway 201
Roksem, Belgium 242
Rolleston, Nt 255
Rolleston, St 255
Rome 59, 147
Romney, K 217, 223, 225
Romney Marsh 46, 229
Romsey, Ha 245, 246, 249, 252
Ropsley, L 255
Roscommon, Ireland 46, 73
Roskilde, Denmark 71
Rother River 21, 229
Rotherfield, Sx 148
Rothley, Lei 231, 255
Rotthalmünster, Germany 242
Rothwell, L 258
Rouen, France 46, 47, 49, 51, 54, 63, 208, 209, 211
Roughton, Nf 256
Rous Lench, Wo 254
Rowberrow, So 251
Rumboldswyke, Sx 252
Rumburgh, Sf 246, 256
Runcorn, Ch 47, 89, 233, 235
Rushall, W 252
Rushbury, Sa 254
Rye, Sx 20, 21, 229
Rye River 234
Ryther, WRY 258

Saberton, Gl 178
Saffron Walden, Ess 67

St Albans, Hrt 41, 140, 205, 228, 243, 245, 246, 249, 252
St Asaph, Wales 233
St Augustine's, Canterbury 243, 246, 253
St Benet's at Holme, Nf 232, 243, 246, 249, 256
St Bertin, France 46, 47, 55
St Clair sur Epte, France 47
St Constantine, Co 250
St Davids, Wales 122
St Denis, France 211
St Eulalia, Spain 53
St Feron, France 46
St Florent, France 54
St Fursey, France 211
St Gallen, Switzerland 242
St Germans, Co 226, 240, 247, 250
St Gery, France 211
St Goar, Germany 242
St Goran, Co 250
St Gueriir, Co 147, 226
St Hilaire, France 46
St Hubert, Belgium 242
St Ives, Hu 17, 246, 255
St Keverne, Co 250
St Kew, Co 249
St Lo, France 47, 64
St Marc, France 242
St Margaret's at Cliffe, K 253
St Mary's, Wales 103
St Medard, France 211
St Mihiel, France 242
St Mullins, Ireland 73
St Neot, Co 226
St Neots, Hu 17, 205, 243, 245, 246, 255
St Omer, Belgium 46, 62, 242
St Osyth, Ess 165, 245
St Pauls, London 247
St Petroc, Co 108, 245
St Pieran, Co 249
St Pilt, France 242
St Probus, Co 250
St Quentin, France 47, 211
St Riquier, France 49
St Valéry, France 46
St Wandrille, France 52
Saintes, France 46, 52
Salisbury, W 117, 187, 200, 217, 223, 225, 228
Salm Chateau, Luxemburg 201
Salzburg, Austria 242
Sampton, K 189
Sandbach, Ch 257
Sandon, Hrt 165
Sandwich, K 19, 46, 52, 109, 119, 120, 123, 124, 125, 168, 169, 220, 223, 225, 229
Sandy, Bd 205
Santon Downham, Sf 67
Sarpsborg, Norway 71
Sarre, K 19, 205
Sashes, Brk 150, 152, 228
Saucourt, France 47, 62
Saulieu, France 242
Saxby, L 205
Saxony 46, 54, 56, 242
Scarborough, NRY 234
Scartho, L 258
Schaftlern, Germany 242
Scharnitz, Austria 242
Scheldt, River 46, 52, 54, 62
Schuttern, Germany 242
Schwarzach, Germany 242
Scirwudu 23
Seaborough, So 188
Sealwudu 23
Seasalter, K 229
Seckington, Wa 145
Sedgeberrow, Wo 205
Sedlescombe, K 20
Seine, River 46, 47
Selham, Sx 252
Selja, Norway 71
Selsey, Sx 41, 205, 228, 238, 239, 240, 241, 247, 252, 259, 260
Senlac, Sx 259
Senlis, France 242
Sens, France 209, 210, 242
Severn River 15, 135, 142, 143, 178, 200, 230
Seville, Spain 53
Shabh Ratha, Ireland 47
Shaknoak, O 188, 205
Shaftesbury, Do 150, 152, 159, 161, 163, 215, 217, 223, 225, 227, 235, 245, 246, 249, 251
Shalbourne, W 159
Shannon River, Ireland 47, 73
Shelford, Ca 232
Shelford, Nt 255
Sheppey, K 46, 54, 128, 229
Sherborne, Do 146, 166, 238, 239, 240, 241, 251, 259, 260
Sherburn, ERY 258
Sherburn in Elmet, WRY 234
Shereford, Nf 256
Sherington, Gl 127
Sherston, Gl 127, 227
Shelland 46
Shilton, O 178
Shipston on Stour, Wo 178
Shoebury, Ess 60, 229
Shopland, Ess 165
Shoreham, Sx 253
Shorne, K 253
Shrewsbury, Sa 15, 70, 134, 135, 215, 217, 223, 225, 230, 235, 247, 254
Shrivenham, Brk 252
Shropshire 126, 134, 162, 171, 173, 192
Sidbury, D 251
Sigtuna, Sweden 71
Silvas, Portugal 53
Singleton, Sx 252
Sitten, Switzerland 242
Sjaelland, Denmark 71
Skaga Fjord, Iceland 74
Skaggerak 71
Skalholt, Iceland 74
Skane, Sweden 71
Skara, Sweden 71
Skellig Michael, Ireland 46, 49, 73
Skillington, L 255
Skipwith, ERY 258
Skjalfandi, Iceland 74
Skogahverfi, Iceland 74
Skye 46
Slane, Ireland 46, 47
Slaney River, Ireland 73
Sleaford, L 231
Slesvig, Germany 71
Sligo, Ireland 46
Smaland, Sweden 71
Snaefellsness, Iceland 74
Snape, Sf 232
Soar River 231
Sockburn, Du 258
Sogne, Norway 71
Soissons, France 211, 242
Solent 41, 228
Somerford Keynes, W 251
Somerset 125, 159, 187
Somerset Levels 22
Somerton, So 42, 146, 158, 227
Somme River, France 46, 47, 52, 62
Sompting, Sx 252
Sondertalje, Sweden 71
Sonning, Brk 67, 228, 252
South Downs 229
South Elmham, Sf 232, 256
South Gyrwa 136, 138
South Hill, Co 250
South Kyme, L 255
South Lopham, Nf 256
South Malling, Sx 247, 253
South Milford, WRY 197
South Molton, D 250
South Petherton, So 187, 251
South Petherwin, Co 250
South Saxons 41
South Stoneham, Ha 197, 252
Southam, Gl 178
Southampton, Ha 46, 51, 112, 146, 150, 152, 154, 188, 202, 205, 215, 216, 217, 223, 225, 228
Southend, Ess 205
Southey Creek, Ess 107
Southminster, Ess 165, 253
Southwark, Sr 150, 152, 217, 223, 225, 229
Southwell, Nt 205, 231, 245, 247, 255
Spain 46, 51, 52
Spalda 136, 138
Spalding, L 17, 231, 246, 255
Speyer, Germany 242
Springfield, Ess 253
Springthorpe, L 258
Sproxton, Lei 255
Stad, Iceland 74
Staffelsee, Germany 242
Stafford 68, 87, 215, 217, 218, 223, 225, 230, 235, 247
Staffordshire 126, 171, 173, 186
Staines, Mddx 120, 199, 228, 252
Stamford, L 15, 17, 41, 47, 95, 123, 126, 188, 199, 205, 217, 223, 225, 231, 235
Stamfordbridge, ERY 199, 234
Stanground, Hu 255
Stanmer, Sx 253
Stanton by Bridge, Db 255
Stanton Lacy, Sa 254
Stanway, Gl 254
Stapleford, Ca 256
Stapleford, Nt 255

Stavanger, Norway 71
Stavelot, France 47
Steep Holme 88, 227
Stepney, Mddx 165
Steventon, Ha 252
Stevington, Bd 255
Steyning, Sx 146, 218, 223, 225, 228, 245, 247
Stiklestad, Norway 71
Stinsford, Do 251
Stogumber, So 251
Stoke Bishop, Gl 191, 197, 227
Stoke by Clare, Sf 253
Stoke D'Abernon, Sf 252
Stoke Orchard, Gl 178
Stoke Prior, Wo 254
Stoke St Milborough, Sa 254
Stone, K 253
Stonegrave, NRY 258
Stoneham, Ha 41
Stong, Iceland 74
Stopham, Sx 252
Stottesdon, Sa 254
Stoughton, Sx 252
Stow, L 188, 243, 258
Stow on the Wold, Gl 178
Stowe Nine Churches, Nth 255
Stoughton, Sx 252
Stour River, K 19, 63
Stour River, Do 227
Stour River, Sf 229
Stragglethorpe, L 255
Strangford Lough, Ireland 47, 73
Strassburg, France 208, 209
Strathclyde, France 46, 47, 95, 99, 100, 103
Stratton in Trigg, Co 148, 226
Stratton on the Fosse, Wa 178
Straum Fjord, Iceland 74
Streatley, Brk 252
Strethall, Ess 253
Sturminster, Do 148, 251
Sturry, K 229
Sudbury, Sf 15, 217, 223, 225, 229, 253
Suir River, Ireland 73
Sulgrave, Nth 231
Sullington, Sx 205
Surrey 41, 93, 122, 159, 186
Sussex 114, 120, 122, 159
Susteren, Netherlands 242
Suth Sexena 136, 138
Sutherland, Scotland 47
Sutton, Brk 168
Sutton, Gl 178
Sutton, He 145
Sutton, Nt 231
Sutton, Sr 148
Sutton, Sx 148
Sutton Hoo, Sf 229
Sutton upon Derwent, ERY 258
Sutton Walls, He 230
Swainsthorpe, Nf 256
Swalcliffe, O 255
Swale River 41, 234
Swallow, L 258
Swanage, Do 227
Swanscombe, K 253
Swavesey, Ca 249, 255
Swineshead, L 231
Syston, L 255

Tackley, O 205
Tadcaster, WRY 41, 234
Taghmore, Ireland 47
Talacre, Wales 67, 233
Tamar River 99, 226
Tame River 142
Tamworth, St 47, 68, 87, 102, 142, 145, 155, 197, 215, 223, 225, 231, 235, 247, 255
Tanshelf, WRY 158, 234
Tara, Ireland 73
Tarentaise, France 242
Tasburgh, Nf 256
Tauberbiscofsheim, Germany 242
Taunton, So 15, 187, 217, 223, 225, 227, 247, 251
Tavistock, D 113, 226, 243, 245, 246, 249, 250
Tavy River, D 226
Taynton, O 200
Tebworth, Bd 82
Tedstone Delamere, He 254
Tegeingl, Wales 233
Tegernsee, Germany 244
Teignton, D 116
Teme River 143, 230
Temple Guiting, Gl 205
Tempsford, Bd 91, 92, 121, 131
Terrington, NRY 258
Terryglass, Ireland 46
Test River, Ha 228
Tetbury, Gl 143, 227, 251
Tettenhall, St 47, 85, 230, 247
Tewkesbury, Gl 178, 230, 246, 254
Teynham, K 253
Thame River 228
Thames River 15, 41, 121, 140, 178, 200, 228
Thanet, Isle of 19, 41, 46, 54, 56, 108, 229
Thatcham, Brk 159, 252
Thelwall, Ch 96, 233
Thetford, Nf 17, 46, 58, 68, 118, 121, 205, 217, 223, 225, 232, 246, 256
Therouanne, France 46, 47, 52, 55, 211, 242
Thingvellir, Iceland 74
Thistel Fjord, Iceland 74
Thjorsa, Iceland 74
Thorington, Sf 256
Thornage, Nf 256
Thorney, Middx 60, 64, 228
Thorney, Nth 17, 231, 243, 245, 246, 249, 255
Thornhill, WRY 258
Thrandheim, Norway 71
Threekingham, L 231, 255
Thuin, France 62
Thundersfield, Sr 148, 155, 229
Thuringia, Germany 242
Thurlbury, L 255
Thursley, Sr 252
Tichbourne, Ha 252
Tidenham, Gl 131, 132, 227
Tiddingford, Bk 47, 82, 83, 231
Tilbury, Ess 41, 253
Tillingham, Ess 165
Tilshead, W 187, 227, 251
Tinnel, D 197
Tintagel, Co 250
Tintinhull, So 251
Tipperary, Ireland 46
Titchfield, Ha 252
Tiverton, D 148
Todenham, Gl 178
Tollesbury, Ess 253
Tolleshunt, Ess 165
Tomgraney, Ireland 73
Tomsætan 142
Tone River 227
Tongern, Belgium 242
Tonnerre, France 210
Tonsberg, Norway 71
Toot Hill, Ha 164
Torksey, L 47, 59, 217, 223, 225, 234
Torridge River 226
Totnes, D 15, 215, 216, 217, 223, 225, 226, 235
Tottenham, Mddx 165
Totternhoe, Bd 205
Toul, France 63, 210, 242
Toulouse, France 46, 56, 208, 209, 210
Tournai, Belgium 47, 208, 242
Tournos, France 242
Tours, France 46, 47, 49, 54, 55, 208, 209, 210, 237
Towcester, Nth 91, 93, 231, 235
Tredington, Wa 255
Trelleborg, Denmark 71
Trent River 15, 41, 123, 139, 142, 230, 231, 234
Treviso, Italy 208, 209
Trewhiddle, Co 192, 226
Trier, Germany 62, 208, 209, 242
Trigg, Co 148
Trill, Do 166
Troyes, France 63, 208, 242
Tuam, Ireland 73
Tulach, Ireland 73
Turlestane, He 188
Turvey, Bd 255
Tutbury, St 255
Tweed River 41
Twickenham, Mddx 140
Tyne River 41, 47, 59, 68
Tynemouth 46
Tyninghame, Scotland 102
Tyrconnell, Ireland 47

U Neill, Ireland 46
Ubbanford, Scotland 24
Uffington, Brk 197
Ui Bruin Ai, Ireland 73
Ui Maine, Ireland 73
Ui Neill, Ireland 73, 103
Uisnech, Ireland 73
Ulaid, Ireland 73, 103
Ulleskelf, WRY 234
Ulster, Ireland 46, 47
Unaloek, Iceland 74
Unecung-ga 136, 138
Up Cerne, Do 166
Upleadon, Gl 143
Upminster, Ess 253
Upper Swell, Gl 178

Uppland, Sweden 71
Uppsala, Sweden 71
Ure River 234
Urswick, La 257
Usk, Wales 132
Usk River 132, 227
Utrecht, Netherlands 46, 50, 55, 210, 242

Valence, France 46
Valenciennes, France 211
Valliènes, France 242
Valthjofstadir, Iceland 74
Vanern, Sweden 71
Vapnafjord, Iceland 74
Varennes, France 242
Vasteras, Sweden 71
Vatna Jokull, Iceland 74
Vatnas Fjord, Iceland 74
Vattern, Sweden 71
Vaxjo, Sweden 71
Venice, Italy 209
Verdun, France 63, 208, 209, 211, 242
Viborg, Denmark 71
Vienne, France 208, 209, 210, 237, 242
Vyrnwy River 230

Waithe, L 258
Wakefield, WRY 234
Wakering, Ess 205
Wakerley, Nth 188
Walbury, Brk 205
Walcheren, Netherlands 46, 242
Walkern, Hrt 253, 255
Wallers, France 64
Wallingford, Brk 119, 123, 149, 150, 152, 199, 215, 216, 217, 223, 225, 228, 235
Waltham, Ess 169, 229, 247, 253
Waltham, Ha 116, 228, 252
Walthamstow, Mddx 67
Wantage, Brk 147, 148, 159, 162, 228, 252
Wantsum Channel 19
Wantsum River 19
Warblington, Ha 252
Wardour, W 147
Wareham, Do 47, 59, 146, 149, 150, 152, 161, 215, 217, 223, 225, 235, 251
Warminster, W 154, 187, 217, 223, 225, 227, 251
Warnford, Ha 252
Warwick 15, 88, 150, 152, 215, 217, 223, 225, 231, 235
Warwickshire 126, 171, 173, 178
Wash 17, 139
Watchet, So 109, 113, 150, 152, 187, 196, 217, 223, 225, 227
Waterford, Ireland 46, 47, 73, 103
Waterperry, O 252
Watling Street 102, 123, 228, 230
Wat's Dyke 135, 230
Watton, ERY 41, 258
Waveney River 232
Weald 20
Wear River 41
Weaver River 233
Weaverthorpe, ERY 258
Wedmore, So 22, 147, 148, 227
Welland River 15, 17, 231
Wellesbourne 145
Welford, Brk 197
Wellow, Ha 148, 155, 228
Wells, So 22, 148, 155, 227, 228, 240, 241, 247, 251, 260
Welsh Bicknor, He 254
Welwyn, Hrt 253
Wembury, D 226
Wendens Ambo, Ess 253
Wenkheim, Germany 242
Wenlock, Sa 230, 245, 247, 254
Wensley, WRY 67
Weogorenaleag 23
Weser River, Germany 242
Wessex 43, 100, 119
Wessorunn, Germany 242
West Barsham, Nf 256
West Firths, Iceland 74
West Horn, Iceland 74
West Kirby, Ch 257
West Marton, La 257
West Mersea, Ess 253
West Peckham, K 253
West Runton, Nf 188
West Seaton, Cu 67
West Sexena 136, 138
West Stourmouth, K 253
West Willa 136, 138
West Wittering, Sx 205, 252
West Wixna 136, 138
Westbury, Gl 131, 143, 230, 243, 251
Westbury, Sa 230
Westbury, W 251
Western Settlement, Greenland 78
Westerna 136, 138
Westford, Norway 71
Westhampnett, Sx 252
Westmannaeyjar, Iceland 74
Westmill, Hrt 253, 255
Westminster, Mddx 167, 169, 229, 243, 246, 249, 253
Weston, Db 231
Weston on Avon, Gl 178
Weston sub Edge, Gl 178
Wexford, Ireland 46, 73, 103
Wey River 15, 228
Weybourne, Nf 256
Weymouth, Do 205
Whalley, La 257
Wharfe River, WRY 234
Wharram le Street, ERY 258
Wharram Percy, ERY 252, 258
Wheathampstead, Hrt 252
Wherwell, Ha 159, 160, 246, 249, 252
Whissonsett, Nf 256
Whitby, NRY 41, 205, 234, 258
Whitchurch, D 148, 226
Whitchurch, Do 251
Whitchurch, Ha 252
White Waltham, Brk 252
Whitestaunton, So 188
Whitfield, K 253
Whithorn, Scotland 41
Whitminster, Gl 254
Whittington, Gl 178
Whittlebury, Nth 155, 231
Whittlesea, Hu 18
Whittlesea Dyke 18
Whittlesea Mere 17, 18
Whitwell, Db 102
Wicanbeorg 54
Wickham, Brk 252
Wickham St Paul, Ess 165
Wicklow, Ireland 73
Wickmere, Nf 256
Widerigga 136, 138
Widford, Gl 178
Wight, Isle of 41, 120, 228
Wigingamere 47, 91, 92, 229
Wigmore, He 254
Wihtgara 136, 138
Wijk bij Duurstede, Netherlands 242
Wilhamstead, Bd 188
Willersley, Gl 178
Willesborough, K 253
Williton, So 199, 227
Wilmington, K 253
Wilsford, L 255
Wilton, So 251
Wilton, W 58, 117, 146, 150, 152, 154, 155, 159, 160, 169, 187, 197, 199, 217, 223, 225, 227, 235, 245, 246, 249, 251
Wilton Way 199
Wiltshire 117, 122, 125, 159, 171, 173, 187
Wimbourne, Do 146, 227, 245, 247, 251
Winchester, Ha 15, 41, 46, 55, 99, 119, 123, 146, 147, 148, 149, 150, 152, 154, 155, 157, 160, 162, 163, 168, 169, 197, 199, 205, 213, 215, 216, 217, 223, 225, 228, 235, 238, 239, 240, 241, 249, 252, 260
Winchcombe, Gl 143, 156, 178, 217, 223, 225, 230, 243, 245, 246, 249, 254
Windisch, Switzerland 242
Windsor, Brk 169, 197, 228
Wing, Bk 255
Wingham, K 253
Winsford, Ch 257
Winstone, Gl 254
Winterbourne Steepleton, Do 251
Winterbourne Stoke, W 251
Winteringham, L 205
Winterton, L 258
Wirksworth, Db 142, 191, 255
Wirral, Ch 83, 233
Witham, Ess 47, 229, 235
Witham River 15, 17, 139, 231
Withington, Gl 143, 178, 197, 254
Withington, He 254
Withycombe, So 227
Witley, Sr 252
Witney, O 197
Wittering, Nth 255
Witton, Nf 256
Wivelsfield, Sx 253
Wocen Sætna 136, 138
Woking, Sr 228, 252
Wollaston, Nth 205
Wolverhampton, St 230, 247
Woodbridge, Sf 205, 229
Woodchester, Gl 230
Woodstock, O 162, 228
Woodston, Hu 255
Woodyates, Ha 146
Wool, Do 165

Woolbeding, Sx 252
Woolhope, He 254
Woolmer, Ha 147, 160, 228
Woolstone, Brk 197
Wootton, Ha 197
Wootton Bassett, Gl 205
Wootton Wawen, Wa 254
Worcester 15, 132, 142, 143, 150, 152, 178, 199, 205, 217, 223, 225, 230, 238, 239, 240, 241, 243, 245, 249, 254, 259, 260
Worcestershire 34, 171, 173
Worlaby, L 258
Worms, Germany 242
Worth, Sx 253
Worthenbury, Ch 230
Wouldham, K 253
Wraysbury, Bk 205
Wrekin 52, 142
Wreocen 23
Wrocensetnan 142
Wroxeter, Sa 254
Wurzburg, Germany 242
Wychbold, Wo 145
Wychwood, O 143
Wye, K 146, 229, 253
Wye River 15, 99, 132, 143, 230
Wylye River 227
Wyre River 233

Yant River 41
Yare River 232
Yarmouth, Sf 232
Yaxham, Nf 256
Yaxley, Hu 18
Yealmpton, D 250
Yeavering, Nb 41
Yeo River, So 22, 227
Yeovil, So 148
Yetminster, Do 251
Yonne River 63
York 15, 41, 46, 57, 59, 68, 85, 96, 102, 126, 155, 188, 199, 205, 213, 215, 217, 223, 225, 234, 235, 238, 239, 240, 241, 247, 258, 259, 260
Yser River 46, 47
Yssel, Netherlands 57
Yssel River 46
Ystrad Towy, Wales 130